MINDING BORDERS
RESILIENT DIVISIONS IN LITERATURE,
THE BODY AND THE ACADEMY

LEGENDA

LEGENDA is the Modern Humanities Research Association's book imprint for new research in the Humanities. Founded in 1995 by Malcolm Bowie and others within the University of Oxford, Legenda has always been a collaborative publishing enterprise, directly governed by scholars. The Modern Humanities Research Association (MHRA) joined this collaboration in 1998, became half-owner in 2004, in partnership with Maney Publishing and then Routledge, and has since 2016 been sole owner. Titles range from medieval texts to contemporary cinema and form a widely comparative view of the modern humanities, including works on Arabic, Catalan, English, French, German, Greek, Italian, Portuguese, Russian, Spanish, and Yiddish literature. Editorial boards and committees of more than 60 leading academic specialists work in collaboration with bodies such as the Society for French Studies, the British Comparative Literature Association and the Association of Hispanists of Great Britain & Ireland.

The MHRA encourages and promotes advanced study and research in the field of the modern humanities, especially modern European languages and literature, including English, and also cinema. It aims to break down the barriers between scholars working in different disciplines and to maintain the unity of humanistic scholarship. The Association fulfils this purpose through the publication of journals, bibliographies, monographs, critical editions, and the MHRA Style Guide, and by making grants in support of research. Membership is open to all who work in the Humanities, whether independent or in a University post, and the participation of younger colleagues entering the field is especially welcomed.

ALSO PUBLISHED BY THE ASSOCIATION

Critical Texts
Tudor and Stuart Translations • *New Translations* • *European Translations*
MHRA Library of Medieval Welsh Literature

MHRA Bibliographies
Publications of the Modern Humanities Research Association

The Annual Bibliography of English Language & Literature
Austrian Studies
Modern Language Review
Portuguese Studies
The Slavonic and East European Review
Working Papers in the Humanities
The Yearbook of English Studies

www.mhra.org.uk
www.legendabooks.com

TRANSCRIPT

Transcript publishes books about all kinds of imagining across languages, media and cultures: translations and versions, inter-cultural and multi-lingual writing, illustrations and musical settings, adaptation for theatre, film, TV and new media, creative and critical responses. We are open to studies of any combination of languages and media, in any historical moments, and are keen to reach beyond Legenda's traditional focus on modern European languages to embrace anglophone and world cultures and the classics. We are interested in innovative critical approaches: we welcome not only the most rigorous scholarship and sharpest theory, but also modes of writing that stretch or cross the boundaries of those discourses.

Editorial Committee
Chair: Matthew Reynolds (Oxford)
Robin Kirkpatrick (Cambridge)
Laura Marcus (Oxford)
Patrick McGuinness (Oxford)
Ben Morgan (Oxford)
Mohamed-Salah Omri (Oxford)
Tanya Pollard (CUNY)
Yopie Prins (Michigan)

Advisory Board
Jason Gaiger (Oxford)
Alessandro Grilli (Pisa)
Marina Grishakova (Tartu)
Martyn Harry (Oxford)
Linda Hutcheon (Toronto)
Calin-Andrei Mihailescu (London, Ontario)
Wen-Chin Ouyang (SOAS)
Clive Scott (UEA)
Ali Smith
Marina Warner (Birkbeck)
Shane Weller (Kent)
Stefan Willer (Berlin)

Managing Editor
Dr Graham Nelson
41 Wellington Square, Oxford OX1 2JF, UK

www.legendabooks.com/series/transcript

TRANSCRIPT

1. *Adapting the Canon: Translation, Visualisation, Interpretation*, edited by Ann Lewis and Silke Arnold-de Simine
2. *Adapted Voices: Transpositions of Céline's Voyage au bout de la nuit and Queneau's Zazie dans le métro*, by Armelle Blin-Rolland
3. *Zola and the Art of Television: Adaptation, Recreation, Translation*, by Kate Griffiths
4. *Comparative Encounters between Artaud, Michaux and the Zhuangzi: Rationality, Cosmology and Ethics*, by Xiaofan Amy Li
5. *Minding Borders: Resilient Divisions in Literature, the Body and the Academy*, edited by Nicola Gardini, Adriana Jacobs, Ben Morgan, Mohamed-Salah Omri and Matthew Reynolds

Minding Borders

*Resilient Divisions in Literature,
the Body and the Academy*

EDITED BY
NICOLA GARDINI, ADRIANA X. JACOBS, BEN MORGAN,
MOHAMED-SALAH OMRI AND MATTHEW REYNOLDS

Transcript 5
Modern Humanities Research Association
2017

Published by Legenda
an imprint of the Modern Humanities Research Association
Salisbury House, Station Road, Cambridge CB1 2LA

ISBN 978-1-909662-63-6 (HB)
ISBN 978-1-78188-366-2 (PB)

First published 2017

All rights reserved. No part of this publication may be reproduced or disseminated or transmitted in any form or by any means, electronic, mechanical, photocopying, recording or otherwise, or stored in any retrieval system, or otherwise used in any manner whatsoever without written permission of the copyright owner, except in accordance with the provisions of the Copyright, Designs and Patents Act 1988, or under the terms of a licence permitting restricted copying issued in the UK by the Copyright Licensing Agency Ltd, Saffron House, 6–10 Kirby Street, London EC1N 8TS, England, or in the USA by the Copyright Clearance Center, 222 Rosewood Drive, Danvers MA 01923. Application for the written permission of the copyright owner to reproduce any part of this publication must be made by email to legenda@mhra.org.uk.

Disclaimer: Statements of fact and opinion contained in this book are those of the author and not of the editors or the Modern Humanities Research Association. The publisher makes no representation, express or implied, in respect of the accuracy of the material in this book and cannot accept any legal responsibility or liability for any errors or omissions that may be made.

Trademark notice: Product or corporate names may be trademarks or registered trademarks, and are used only for identification and explanation without intent to infringe.

© Modern Humanities Research Association 2017

Copy-Editor: Richard Correll

CONTENTS

	Acknowledgements	ix
	Notes on the Contributors	x
	Introduction	1
1	Old and New Borders: A Geographical Approach DAVIDE PAPOTTI	17
2	Uncharted Borders: Mixed Realities and Representations of the Californio Period Community and Culture of San Diego, California JEFFREY SWARTWOOD	25
3	Body and Empire: Space and Borders in Second-Century Greek-Roman Culture CATHERINE DARBO-PESCHANSKI	41
4	The Mediterranean Novel Defying Borders ADRIAN GRIMA	53
5	Infra-materiality and Opaque Drifting CAROLINE BERGVALL	67
6	Minding Orientalist Margins: Colonial Nomos and Jonathan Scott's Revision of *The Arabian Nights* CLAIRE GALLIEN	76
7	Image, Text, and Conflict: Willie Doherty's 'At the Border' ROSIE LAVAN	97
8	The Mother Tongue as Border ANNE ISABELLE FRANÇOIS	115
9	The Edge of Thought: Extended Cognition and the Border between Mind and World MICHAEL WHEELER	135
10	On Entanglings: Disciplines, Materiality and Distributed Cognition PETER GARRATT	150
11	Cross-Channel Literary Crossings and the Borders of Translatability CÉLINE SABIRON	169

12 A Conversation across Borders: Marcel Proust's *Le Temps retrouvé* and its Translation into Estonian 187
MADLI KÜTT

13 When Do Different Literatures Become Comparable? The Vague Borders of Comparability and Incomparability 201
XIAOFAN AMY LI

Index 218

ACKNOWLEDGEMENTS

This book emerges from Oxford University's interdisciplinary research programme Oxford Comparative Criticism and Translation (OCCT), and in particular from a conference, 'Minding Borders', held in October 2014. OCCT is funded by The Oxford Research Centre for the Humanities (TORCH), St Anne's College and the John Fell OUP Research Fund, and by generous benefactions from Maria Ferreras Willetts, Fiona Lindblom and Arabella van Niekerk. The editors would like to express their gratitude for this support.

Our thanks go also to Mariachiara Leteo for compiling the index.

Oxford, September 2017

NOTES ON THE CONTRIBUTORS

Caroline Bergvall is a writer and artist who works across media, art forms and languages. Her projects alternate between books, audio pieces, live performances, works on paper and installations. Bergvall's books include *Drift* (2014), *Meddle English: New and Selected Texts* (2011) and *Fig* (2005). Her project, Raga Dawn, a sunrise vocal performance, premiered in September 2016. Of French-Norwegian origins, she is based in London and Geneva and was recently a Mellon Fellow at the Grey Center for Art and Enquiry, University of Chicago (2016).

Catherine Darbo-Peschanski is a Research Director at the CNRS (National Centre for Scientific Research) in Paris. She is member of the LAS (Laboratory of Social Anthropology, CNRS/EHESS/Collège de France) as a researcher in the Historical Anthropology of Ancient Greece. Currently, she is Senior Researcher at the MFO (Maison Française d'Oxford), in charge of the Classical Studies programme. Among others books, she has edited *Constructions du temps dans le monde grec ancien* (CNRS-Éditions, 2000) and *L'Acte fou: analyses comparées d'un mode d'action et de présence* (Garnier, forthcoming), and is the author of *L'Historia: commencements Grecs* (Gallimard, 2007). She is currently working on a book titled *The Body and its Spaces in Greek and Roman Antiquity*.

Anne Isabelle François, who completed her PhD at the École Pratique des Hautes Études (Paris) and the University of Dresden, has been Senior Lecturer (maître de conférences) in comparative literature at Sorbonne Nouvelle University (Université Sorbonne Nouvelle — Paris 3, part of Université Sorbonne Paris Cité) since 2003. A specialist in European literatures of the twentieth and twenty-first centuries, she pursues her researches as a member of the Centre d'Études et de Recherches Comparatistes.

Claire Gallien lectures in the English Department at Paul Valéry Montpellier 3 University. She is member of the Institute for Research on the Renaissance, the Neoclassical Age and the Enlightenment (IRCL, UMR 5186, CNRS) and specializes in early modern and Enlightenment orientalism. Her first book, *L'Orient anglais* (Oxford, SVEC), was published in 2011; her research interests cover issues and texts related to early modern and Enlightenment orientalism, travel literature, neo-Orientalism, postcolonial, global and comparative literatures and studies (esp. Arab and Indian), as well as translation studies.

Nicola Gardini is Professor of Italian and Comparative Literature at the University of Oxford and a Fellow of Keble College. His main fields of interest are the Renaissance, modern poetry, translation, and comparative literature. His most recent monographs are: *Rinascimento* (Einaudi, 2010) and *Lacuna* (Einaudi, 2014). He is also the author of novels, poetry collections, memoirs, and literary translations from English, Latin, and ancient Greek. He is a contributor to the cultural pages of *Il Corriere della sera*, the *Domenicale* of the *Sole 24 ore*, and the *TLS*. His novel *Le parole perdute di Amelia Lynd* (Feltrinelli, 2012) has just been published in English by New Directions (translated by Michael Moore).

Peter Garratt is Lecturer in the Department of English Studies at Durham University. His interests include the Victorian novel, the writings of John Ruskin, and the cognitive and medical humanities. He is the author of *Victorian Empiricism* (Fairleigh Dickinson, 2010) and the editor of *The Cognitive Humanities: Embodied Mind in Literature and Culture* (Palgrave Macmillan, forthcoming).

Adrian Grima is Senior Lecturer at the University of Malta. He also teaches Maltese language and literature at INALCO, Paris. His research focuses on Maltese literature, the novelist Juann Mamo and representations of the Mediterranean. His most recent publication is *The Teacher, Literature and the Mediterranean*, co-edited with Simone Galea (Sense, 2014). Adrian Grima has also published four collections of poetry in Maltese.

Adriana X. Jacobs is Associate Professor of Modern Hebrew Literature at Oxford and Fellow of the Oxford Centre for Hebrew and Jewish Studies. She is also a co-convenor of the research programme Oxford Comparative Criticism and Translation. She has published widely on Hebrew and Israeli poetry. Her monograph *Strange Cocktail: Translation and the Making of Modern Hebrew Poetry* is forthcoming from the University of Michigan Press. Her translations of the American Hebrew poet Annabelle Farmelant appear in *Women's Hebrew Poetry on American Shores: Poems by Anne Kleiman and Annabelle Farmelant* (Wayne State, 2016).

Madli Kütt is an Estonian translator currently working on her dissertation *The Fictional Subject and Imaginative Views in Marcel Proust's 'À la recherche du temps perdu' and its Translation into Estonian*. Her research interests are centred on translation studies, particularly concentrating on possible worlds theory, mental imagery in the processes of writing and translation, and 'small literatures'.

Rosie Lavan is Assistant Professor in Irish Studies at Trinity College Dublin. She is currently working on a book about Seamus Heaney and the contexts of his writing life, based on the doctorate she completed at the University of Oxford in 2014. Her postdoctoral project examines representations of the city of Derry in poetry, drama, life-writing, journalism and photography.

Xiaofan Amy Li is Lecturer in Comparative Literature at the University of Kent. She examines twentieth-century and contemporary French literature and culture, using a comparative perspective that engages with the French imagination of China and Sino-French cultural exchanges. She is the author of *Comparative Encounters between Artaud, Michaux and the 'Zhuangzi': Rationality, Cosmology and Ethics* (Legenda, 2015).

Tom Martin is a British photographer/videographer, specializing in documenting humanitarian issues in Africa and Asia, undertaking commissions for charities, NGOs and donors including the EU and UN. His publications range from *The Economist* and *The Independent* to *Italian Vogue* and the *Lancet*. Exhibitions include solo shows in Westminster and Kigali. He is currently a lecturer at Lincoln University, specializing in still and moving image documentary methodology, recently developing participatory photo projects in Bangladesh and South Sudan.

Ben Morgan is Associate Professor of German at the University of Oxford and Fellow and Tutor at Worcester College. He is the Modern Languages Convenor for the interdisciplinary research programme Oxford Comparative Criticism and Translation (OCCT). Recent publications include *Walter Benjamins anthropologisches Denken* (Rombach, 2012), edited with Carolin Duttlinger and Anthony Phelan, and the monograph *On Becoming God: Late Medieval Mysticism and the Modern Western Self* (Fordham, 2013).

Mohamed-Salah Omri is Professor of Arabic and Comparative Literature at Oxford. He is a founding member of Oxford Comparative Criticism and Translation (OCCT), a member of the British Academy Advisory Panel on the Middle East and North Africa and of the network, Arab Revolutions and New Humanism. His publications include *Nationalism, Islam and World Literature* (Routledge, 2006), a special issue of *Comparative Critical Studies* (2007), 'A Revolution of Dignity and Poetry' (*Boundary*, 2012) and 'Towards a theory of confluency — *tarafud*' (2015).

Davide Papotti is Associate Professor in Geography at the University of Parma. He studied at the University of Parma (*Laurea in Materie Letterarie* in 1993), at the University of Virginia (Master of Arts in Italian literature in 1996), and at the University of Padua (PhD in Geography in 2002). He also teaches for the Boston College and University of California overseas programs in Italy. He is the author of *Geografie della scrittura: paesaggi letterari del medio Po* (La goliardica pavese, 1996) and, with Marco Aime, *L'altro e l'altrove: antropologia, geografia e turismo* (Einaudi, 2012).

Matthew Reynolds is Professor of English and Comparative Criticism at Oxford where he chairs the interdisciplinary research programme Oxford Comparative Criticism and Translation (OCCT). Recent publications include *The Poetry of Translation: From Chaucer & Petrarch to Homer & Logue* (Oxford, 2011), *Likenesses: Translation, Illustration, Interpretation* (Legenda, 2013), *Translation: A Very Short Introduction* (Oxford, 2016) and the novel *The World Was All before Them* (Bloomsbury, 2013).

Céline Sabiron is a lecturer in English literature at Lorraine University (Nancy, France) and a research fellow at Wolfson College, Oxford. Her monograph *Writing the Border: Walter Scott and the Wandering Paths* (Provence University Press, 2016) has just come out, and she is currently working on transcultural dynamics between England and France through the prism of translation in the eighteenth and nineteenth centuries.

Jeffrey Swartwood is Associate Professor at the École Polytechnique near Paris and a member of the research group CLIMAS. His teaching and research focus on American civilization — especially Southwest border studies. Favouring an interdisciplinary approach, his work examines social constructs within California culture and their representation in literature and film. He is author of *Contested Territories: Mixed Identity Constructs and Hybrid Culture in San Diego, California (1770–1920)* (Maison des sciences de l'homme d'Aquitaine, 2015).

Michael Wheeler is Professor of Philosophy at the University of Stirling. His primary research interests are in philosophy of science (especially cognitive science, psychology, biology and artificial intelligence) and philosophy of mind. He is particularly interested in developing ideas at the interface between the analytic and the continental philosophical traditions. His book, *Reconstructing the Cognitive World: The Next Step*, was published by MIT Press in 2005.

INTRODUCTION

*Nicola Gardini, Adriana X. Jacobs, Ben Morgan,
Mohamed-Salah Omri and Matthew Reynolds*

As we write (Spring 2016), borders are everywhere in the news. The starkest headlines refer to the Mediterranean migration crisis. Twenty thousand Syrian refugees are gathered at the border with Turkey. The Schengen agreement, which had allowed for the free movement of people between many countries within Europe, has been partially suspended, while the European Union is increasingly militarizing its external borders: the island of Lampedusa — to give just one instance — is seen as a zone of border construction. Statistics on migration paint a picture of increasing tragedy and overwhelming proportions. In the 1990s, 200,000 people landed on European shores, while in 2015 alone one million people made that journey, with several thousand dying in the crossing. But it is not only in Europe and the Mediterranean that borders are newly resurgent, and newly under pressure.

Throughout the world, despite the fall of the Berlin Wall, barriers, fences and more walls proliferate, enforcing old borders and creating new ones.[1] Infamous examples include the Israeli so-called 'separation barrier' in the West Bank, the US fence along the Mexican border, walls separating North and South Korea, the Indian wall around Bangladesh (2500 miles), Morocco's sand wall, and the latest, a Tunisian trench along the border with Libya (250 kilometres). New technology creates new kinds of border and new controversies about them. Google has paid minimal tax in the United Kingdom because it claims that the profits it makes from UK citizens are located beyond the borders of the UK. On the roads of many cities, cameras enforce congestion zones where some vehicles are free to enter and others not. The FBI could not get past the security control on an iPhone used by a suspect in a mass shooting and tried to force Apple to unlock the device, calling attention to borders where our civil liberties and right to privacy lie.[2]

As these examples show, borders are not only important but also complex. The Turkish authorities are feeding and protecting refugees who are not allowed into their national territory — so the borders of their responsibility and action extend beyond the borders of their State. The new restrictions on movement within Europe are not a matter of new fences and passport offices but rather of targeted spot-checks against international databases. The Google argument does not rely on blunt geographical location so much as on the complex interrelations between tax jurisdictions. In this volume, we start by registering the newly obvious sophistication of political borders; we then explore how a refreshed understanding of bordering practices might interact with our thinking about other borders: of body and mind, of media, of languages and of disciplines. Our guiding idea is that, in these other fields no less than in politics, borders are often not easy to locate, let alone to pass. In an academic climate which typically celebrates the 'crossing of borders' as an interdisciplinary ambition, this difficulty needs to be remembered and explored.

Of course this book is itself subject to bordering practices: the essays are attached to authorial names; quotations are in inverted commas; the text is justified and corrected according to the norms of standard British English. These borders are necessary for the text to be readable in an academic vein, so we have not sought to break them. But we have stretched them a little so as to make them available to be thought about. Caroline Bergvall's contribution, for example, is a hybrid work that engages the conventions of the academic essay while also departing from them. We have arranged the essays in a sequence that we hope will be illuminating, moving from (on the whole) more usual to less usual meanings of the word 'border', from (generally) more material to more abstract instances; but we have not corralled them into discrete sections since this would be at odds with our enterprise. Like the volume as a whole, the introduction represents the shared work of the editors as a collective, but it also bears different authorial stamps at different times, section 1 on the complexity of borders having been written by Nicola Gardini, section 2 on practices of transbordering by Mohamed-Salah Omri, section 3 on textual drift by Adriana X. Jacobs, section 4 on borders and identity by Ben Morgan, and section 5 on translation and comparison by Matthew Reynolds. Equally, while the structure of this introduction does, for the most part, shadow the contents page it also refers to essays from across the volume where that suits our argument, thereby establishing pathways between them.

1. The Complexity of Borders: Mobility, Invisibility, Relationships, and Dwelling

As Davide Papotti makes clear in his essay for this volume, borders are never a matter of simple lines on the ground (ancient mythologies — see below — or the establishment of state borders in the US appear to be rather exceptional cases).[3] This is especially true now that electronic surveillance enables powerful states to track individuals anywhere, now that national fingerprint databases are becoming the norm or that proposals to require asylum seekers to wear identifying wristbands not only have been considered but also controversially enforced.[4] These practices remind us that borders can be mobile, particular, unpredictable, porous, permeable, even untraceable, while at the same time ensuring that movement across borders is meticulously recorded.

If our examples of borders have so far emphasized the limits and limitations of national sovereignty, these issues do not exhaust the meaning of the term. The notion of 'border' is akin to, and can include, those of margin, edge, boundary, and frontier, and therefore calls for a highly comparative critical and eclectic approach, as Jeffrey Swartwood advocates in his essay in this volume. Borders also demarcate a no man's land, an unaffiliated and unregulated space. Moreover, every language has its own ways of conveying the processes of bordering. Italian, for example, expresses the English 'border' with two terms: 'confine' and 'frontiera'. The former is quintessentially geographical, the latter suggests a controlling bureaucratic system and alludes to prohibition and exclusion. Walter Benjamin, whose own work explored crossings between languages, between historical periods, between genres and aesthetic media, committed suicide after being denied the right to cross the 'frontiera' — rather than the 'confine' — between Spain and France, his suicide provoked by the sort of controlling bureaucracy his own intellectual work had endeavoured continually to resist. The English 'frontier' is something else again, not a fixed line, but a shifting, receding one. In his seminal book *The Frontier in American History* (1893), Frederick Jackson Turner wrote:

> The most significant thing about the American frontier is that it lies at the hither edge of free land. [...] At first, the frontier was the Atlantic coast. It was the frontier of Europe in a very real sense. Moving westward, the frontier became more and more American. As successive terminal moraines result from successive glaciations, so each frontier leaves its traces behind it, and when it becomes a settled area the region still partakes of the frontier characteristics. Thus the advance of the frontier has meant a steady movement away from the influence of Europe, a steady growth of independence on American lines.[5]

The Border as a frontier is that which divides, but it is also that which, by dividing, joins. A border-frontier is a space of exchange. It brings together conflicting elements but also keeps them in some sort of balance; it brings order to the relations that it encourages and imposes. Catherine Darbo-Peschanski, in her contribution to this volume, reconstructs the social practices through which borders are maintained and cultivated as areas of contact, using as her example the Roman empire of the second century, and drawing attention to the degree to which geographical and political borders were treated with same conceptual tools as bodily borders.

But if a border is also a space to be inhabited, what kind of dwelling does a border allow? Do we live on, within or beyond them? Can we occupy borders and forget distinctions, prohibitions, or invitations? Under what conditions may we cross and pass? Would it be conceivable to transcend borders altogether? However contrived, borders are also necessary. They help to make differences obvious (life/death, health/illness, wealth/poverty etc.), while of course not abolishing their problematic and complex interrelations, to catalogue experience, to map reality, to name things, to subdivide not just space, but also time; and to conceptualize linguistic fields, from morphology to syntax, as well as the foreignness of national tongues. Borders allow for multiple affiliations to place, language and history. The hyphen, in this respect, brings two identities together and leaves open the possibility of further relations.

Again, it is Roman culture that supplies examples of borders as objects of reverence. Indeed, the Romans believed so much in borders that they had a god of borders, Terminus, and dedicated a festival, the Terminalia, in his honour.[6] Ovid speaks of him in *Fasti* II, 23:

> Terminus himself, at the meeting of the bounds, is sprinkled with blood of a slaughtered lamb, and grumbles not when a sucking pig is given him. The simple neighbours meet and hold a feast, and sing thy praises, holy Terminus: thou dost set bounds to peoples and cities and vast kingdoms; without thee every field would be a root of wrangling. Thou courtest no favour, thus art bribed by no gold: the lands entrusted to thee thou dost guard in loyal good faith. [...] What happened when the new Capitol was being built? Why, the whole company of gods withdrew before Jupiter and made room for him; but Terminus, as the ancients relate, remained where he was found in the shrine, and shares the temple with great Jupiter. Even to this day there is a small hole in the roof of the temple, that he may see naught above him but the stars. From that time, Terminus, thou hast not been free to flit: abide in that station in which thou hast been placed. Yield not an inch to a neighbour, though he ask thee, lest thou shouldst seem to value man above Jupiter. And whether they beat thee with ploughshares or with rakes, cry out, 'This is thy land, and that is his'.[7]

On 23 February, landowners met at the boundary stone that marked the beginning of one field and the end of another. This is not unlike the traditional English practice of 'beating the bounds', that is, walking ceremonially around the borders of parish, usually once a year. Since parish borders were not usually marked on the ground, participants re-affirmed them by their physical presence, and mapped them anew in their minds.

But despite the reverence for borders, the very marker itself could become a point of contention. Who claims the stone and the space it occupies is a question that has provoked longstanding tensions along borders, even among the closest neighbours. Remus was killed for trespassing across the ditch that Romulus had set around the walls of the newly founded *Roma*. Diodorus Siculus's account emphasizes the vulnerability of borders and the nature of borders as conflict-charged spaces. Having been pushed aside by his brother Romulus, Remus complained that the ditch around the city was too narrow and therefore could hardly protect from any attack. Romulus, then, said that whoever dared to trespass over the ditch should die. Remus did keep on saying the ditch was too narrow and, in order to prove this, he himself jumped over it. One of the diggers, mindful of the king's order, lifted the spade and hit Remus on the head, killing him.[8] According to Livy, it was Romulus himself who slew his brother.[9] Ovid's *Fasti* make no reference to the fratricide, but show us that border-making is a most solemn ritual, involving humans and gods:

> Romulus was accorded the government of the city. A suitable day was chosen on which he should mark out the line of the walls with the plough. The festival of Pales was at hand; on that day the work began. A trench was dug down to the solid rock; fruits of the earth were thrown into the bottom of it, and with them earth fetched from the neighbouring soil. The trench was filled up with mould, and on top was set an altar, and a fire was duly lit on a new hearth. Then pressing on the plough-handle he drew a furrow to mark out the line of the walls: the yoke was borne by a white cow and snow-white steer. The king spoke thus: 'O Jupiter, and Father Mavors, and Mother Vesta, stand by me as I found the city! O take heed, all ye gods whom piety bids summon! Under your auspices my this my fabric rise! May it enjoy long life and dominion over

a conquered world! My East and West be subject unto it!' So he prayed. Jupiter vouchsafed omens by thunder on the left and lightning flashing in the leftward sky. Glad at the augury, the citizens laid the foundations. [10]

Cormac McCarthy's novel *The Crossing* emphasizes both the socially constructed aspects of borders and the possibility of their renegotiation, drawing parallels between political boundaries and the space of exchange between the human and the animal. Sixteen-year-old Billy takes on the epic task of bringing back to the Mexican mountains a she-wolf who was eating his cows in New Mexico. His journey is a collection of borders, including the international boundary between the United States and Mexico. His very relationship with the wolf is a sort of borderland, in which he appears to make himself quite comfortably at home. At one point, though, he is stopped by Mexican police and made to yield up the she-wolf:

> You think that this country is some country you can come here and do what you like.
> I never thought that. I never thought about the country one way or the other.
> Yes, said the hacendado.
> We was just passin through, the boy said. We wasnt botherin nobody. Queríamos pasar, no más.
> Pasar o traspasar?
> The boy turned and spat into the dirt. He could feel the wolf lean against his leg. He said that the tracks of the wolf had led out of Mexico. He said the wolf knew nothing of boundaries. The young don nodded as if in agreement but what he said was that whatever the wolf knew or did not know was irrelevant and that if the wolf had crossed that boundary it was perhaps so much the worse for the wolf but the boundary stood without regard.[11]

If McCarthy's wolf shows an animal obliviousness to human territoriality, even human subjects well aware of the fact of borders can find them hard to locate, even where the aim is in fact to elude them. A Greek man who lives in Philadelphia entered the US illegally from Canada in the early 1970s by climbing one of the very tall bridges over the Niagara River, one of the most dangerous geographical points at that border.[12] But why there, when the border between Canada and the US ran for hundreds of miles, many of which were completely unguarded? Because, the man said, this was the only place where he could be sure the US started. The very first surveyors of the 49th parallel (the Canadian–American border) experienced the kind of uncertainty that the novelist Wallace Stegner, who grew up as an American very near the 49th parallel, acknowledged when he wrote in *Wolf Willow* (1955) that he never knew what nationality he really was. Nevertheless, invisibility or uncertainty, as these examples show, does not make borders any less coercive. Borders are minded, often mined, and increasingly mindless of the futility of exclusion and separation in a world governed by exchange and traffic enhanced by borderless means of communication and exacerbated by violent social conflict and economic inequality.

2. Practices of Transbordering or Dido and her Progeny

In the nineteenth century, when Arabists and orientalists were busy 'receiving' Arabic and other 'Oriental' texts, translating, editing and rewriting them, Arabs were coming face to face with new knowledge in Europe and at home, in Cairo, Aleppo and Tunis. Comparing the attitudes of Arabists and Arabs towards each other's cultural production tells stories of border crossing and bordering which continue to find echoes today. In both cases, we witness what can be called border moments, instances of when we encounter cultural and aesthetic practices which are radically different from our own frame of reference. 'Confronting radical difference is a decisive moment in critical and creative work alike [...]. It opens possibilities for border crossing as well as bordering, which include rupture, rejection, indifference, conflict and communication or reconciliation.'[13] When the Arabist Jonathan Scott faced radical difference in the Arabic text of the *Thousand and One Nights*, Claire Gallien tells us in her contribution to the present volume, he set about 'reframing, selection and restructuring' of the material. He was struggling with the text but also working within a frame of mind that was accustomed to imposing order on cultural material that he judged to be unruly, even dangerous. But how was this behaviour any different from that of his counterpart, the Egyptian scholar Tahtawi, the Arab translator of Fénelon's *Les Aventures de Télémaque* (1699)?

In his translation, Tahtawi, who had been to France in the 1830s and wrote a seminal book about his trip, had to transfer a belief system which was not only alien to his Islamic ethos but also a risky, even perilous adventure.[14] For how was he to justify to readers who believed in one God the translation of the biography of a demi-god into the language of the Quran? We don't have a record of Tahtawi's marginalia, as we do for Scott, but Tahtawi left a revealing introduction to his work. His undertaking goes to the heart of comparative criticism, world literature and theories of translation. It institutes a confluency of sorts, a trans-border ethics as well as a poetics, further addressed below. Tahtawi rationalizes his adventure by advancing three arguments. He contends that what the Greeks call a demi-god is to Muslims the jinni that can enter into 'sexual' relations with humans. Secondly, Arabic is so vast a language that it resembles an ocean capable of accommodating linguistic rivers and streams. Thirdly, *Télémaque* has already crossed the borders of the local and the national, and therefore deserves 'our' attention if Arabs are to become in harmony with the world.

Other Arab translators steered clear of such risk and erected a wall to protect the community from 'corrupting' foreign influences — as do today's Salafi and purist cultural and political movements, not to mention numerous Western writers and practices since antiquity. A number of essays in this book argue that these cultural and translational negotiations find parallels and instructive reminders in the physical world. The Mediterranean holds a particular interest in this regard given the current news of the day, and it is the focus of essays by Adrian Grima and Caroline Bergvall. The figure of Dido offers both a way to think about the contemporary Mediterranean and a perspective from which to reflect on the movements and status of the so-called boat people who daily cross its borders.

In Virgil's version of Dido's story the integrity of the cultural geography of empire and its memory were at stake.[15] Since boundaries were uncertain at the geographical level, they needed to be drawn with uncompromising rigour in the cultural and ethnic spheres. Love was not going to change Aeneas's destiny. Dido threatened the purity of Roman blood (blood boundary continues to be a common trope in literature and a potent, indeed perilous one in life) and the integrity of the originating myth. She was neither to go North nor to marry Aeneas. The Southern shore is where she belonged — just like today's migrants from the Southern shore of the Mediterranean Sea. Rome's frontiers were not to be transgressed but in fact were to expand and dominate: 'To Romans I set no boundaries in space or time. I have granted them dominion and it has no end.'[16] (This recalls, but in a critical way, how Roman borders could be interpreted in light of Galen's geometry, as Darbo-Peschanski's essay explores.) The Mediterranean was *mare nostrum*, their sea. The origins of the transformation of what Grima calls a 'shared space' into a 'Eurocentric imaginary' may be found here. Grima traces patiently the roots of the imagined Mediterranean as a shared space, in which writers sought ways out of the ethnic and religious boundaries, from Gabriel Audisio and Albert Camus in the 1930s to novels from Malta, Algeria and France. His study of Malika Mokeddem's French novel *N'zid* (2001), Ġużè Bonnici's Maltese novel *Lejn ix-Xemx* [Towards the Sun] (1940), Jean-Claude Izzo's *Les Marins perdus* [The Lost Sailors] (1997), and Massimo Carlotto's *Cristiani di Allah* (2008) shows a long line of attempts to imagine the sea as a mixed space, but also as an escape from what might be called the ideological and social boundaries of the land. The figure of Ulysses is claimed by Audisio and Mokeddem as a symbol of freedom and belonging to the sea. Yet, Grima recognizes that 'The borders and boundaries suggested by the narratives of the nation or religion held their ground'.

Not unlike the story of Ulysses, Dido's myth was to become the locus of contested boundaries that marked the contest over the Mediterranean Sea.[17] Empires came and went, though; borders changed and so have myths, in an endless cycle of translations and rewritings. In the 1980s, the Tunisian novelist Fawzi Mellah would attempt to ante-date, ignore and challenge Virgil's version by translating from Phoenician allegedly newly discovered letters sent by the queen to her brother. But in Mellah's translation, the errant queen regains her native Phoenician name, Elissa/Elisha ('There will even be poets who will distort it so that it sounds quite ridiculous', *Dee Do*).[18] Elissa is now a founder, an origin in her own right, who redraws borders and dominates peoples and lands. We all remember the story of the cow hide which was shredded into small pieces to cover the hill of Birsa, and set the boundaries of Carthage, that Carthage from where Hannibal would, in turn, defy barriers in his Punic conquests to vanquish Rome.

In Mellah's story, Dido is a drifter at sea (like the refugees in Caroline Bergvall's essay), moving aimlessly after cutting ties with her origins and land of birth, Sidon.[19] She was what North African migrants would call a border burner (*harragua*). A term originally coined to mean those who burn their identity papers as they set off towards Europe across the Mediterranean, it has firmly gained the meaning of crossing 'illegally', so much so that the term has become a metaphor for this kind of passage. In 1997, the same Mellah (his name means sailor, incidentally), a journalist at the time, wandered across the Mediterranean disguised as border burner and recorded his experience in the book *Clandestin en Méditerranée*. Here, he meditates on instances of alienation and recognition — Sicily, in its topography and Arabic past, is like the home left behind on the Southern shore, but is also where difference begins: 'At Messina [...] is where the East really ends: the West begins [...]'.[20]

It is instructive to compare practices and forms of understanding with practices at border moments. Tahtawi understood that his language and culture were able to understand, and indeed would be enriched by, foreign cultures. For this reason, he gives room for streams to flow into his language and culture and support their survival and growth. I call this relationship *tarafud*. The term *tarafud* does not exist as such in Arabic but is a coinage that blends the Latinate 'confluence' in the sense of 'flowing with' and the Arabic *rafd*, which suggests support and generosity. *Tarafud* is a metaphor of trans-border practice that can account for the movement of texts, ideas, disciplines as well as people, across boundaries. It is a concept which describes the relationships that shape world literatures, steering them away from hierarchy, domination and one-dimensional traffic, while also encompassing ideas of giving and hospitality.[21] The rare English word 'confluency' can perhaps convey both meanings. Latin-based and Anglo-Saxon languages are thus represented alongside Arabic in a linguistic performance of border crossing.

The critical interpretation of Arabic literature in Western languages can itself be viewed as a border crossing between the critical language of the academic discipline, the Arabic language and Arabic critical practice. For example, the fiction of Tunisian writer Mahmud al-Masadi, who embeds his work in classical Arabic literature as well as Western modernist writing, performs border crossing. Such a text is therefore better interpreted through a critical apparatus which not only recognizes the text's constitutive *tarafud* but also attempts to perform it by bringing both critical traditions and their languages to bear on the interpretation. At the level of academic disciplines, Area Studies, with its emphasis on contextual and language training, and Comparative Criticism enter relations of mutual support, not those of competitive division of labour as is often the case. The term can, and indeed has been, used recently as equivalent to interdisciplinarity in academic practice; to describe social movements (e.g., in Tunisia, particularly culture, trade unionism and protest movements). Here, it can render a practice of minding — thinking — borders in which migration becomes a confluence of people where mutual benefit and interaction, as well as mutual support in both host and home nations, are evoked as means of an imagined world without walls.

3. Textual Drift, Mixed Borders

Crossing, migrating, and translating are among the many movements that shape the texts and materials that this volume includes and engages, but how do we reconcile the aesthetic potential of these mobilities with their real life social and political implications? The ways in which a poem or photograph can defy borders may open up rich channels for thinking about works of art, what they mean and where they are located in contemporary culture, but can we still speak in these terms when the topic turns to an overburdened inflatable boat of refugees adrift in open sea, moving — unclaimed — between invisible maritime borders? Or a national referendum that reveals a deeply contested understanding of the border in an age of transnational movement and interconnectedness?

In her 2009 essay, 'A Cat in the Throat: On Bilingual Occupants', the poet Caroline Bergvall calls our attention to the sites and spaces through which languages move, exchange, transform. She refers to these as 'a point of traffic'. 'Language circulates in this conduit of air', Bergvall writes; 'The act of writing becomes less permanent, more acutely in flux'.[22] These movements are central to Bergvall's *oeuvre*, including her most recent output *Drift* (2015), a work of mixed media — photographs, etchings, user manuals, poetry — that is both an excavation of language as well as a critique of the ongoing migrant crisis. In *Drift*, Bergvall explores and traces the movements of language, and particularly the English language, in historical time, as it crosses into spaces where it encounters other languages and where it changes and departs from itself. When the poem emerges, the feeling of being in the space of a fixed poetic text is fleeting: in that very space languages blend, letters migrate between pages, 'everything passes into everything', says one — one of many — of her speakers.[23] In this respect, as in many others that the present volume explores, the lines between scholar, poet, translator and critic also mix and blur, as borders do.

Claire Gallien's contribution 'Minding Orientalist Margins: Colonial Nomos and Jonathan Scott's Revision of *The Arabian Nights*' examines the notes that the nineteenth-century orientalist Jonathan Scott made to the Montague manuscript of *The Arabian Nights*. Scott had undertaken the task of comparing Antoine Galland's eighteenth-century French version, from which English translations of the *Nights* derived, with the Arabic Montague manuscript. He intended to undertake an extensive retranslation of the text from the original Arabic but ultimately concluded that Galland's version was a more or less reliable source for English translators. Nevertheless, as Gallien shows, Scott's marginal notes on the Montague manuscript indicate that Scott grappled with perceived inconsistencies in the Arabic and with the overall structure and meaning of the text itself. Attending to these textual borders confirms that Scott's 'praxis does not take place in a vacuum', but rather reveals how the European orientalist relates to the Eastern text and strives to conform, reframe and domesticate it according to a colonial nomos.[24] What Scott's notes reveal is that a retranslation of *The Arabian Nights* based on the original Arabic text was necessary, but the possibility for this translation does not move past the manuscript's margins.

In her contribution to this volume, 'Infra materiality and opaque drifting', which is based in part on the artist talk that she gave at our 'Minding Borders' conference, Bergvall brings questions of translation and linguistic migration to bear on the global refugee crisis, focusing in particular on the notorious 'Left-to-Die' boat case. On 27 March 2011, a boat carrying 72 migrants from Libya to Italy ran into trouble shortly after departure. The migrants were left to drift on open water for several days, without food or fresh water, as various nations debated to whom fell the responsibility for their care. Tom Martin's photographs, which Bergvall incorporates in her account, initially conjure this sea as an unbounded cosmic space which reveals how easily migrant fates are concealed in the dark space of the ocean, but as the series progresses, white pixels begin to constellate, taking the shape of the boat that now must be acknowledged. Martin's photographic images prompt us to apply the skills of literary close reading and analysis to the grainy, opaque images of a migrant boat adrift on the Mediterranean, turning our act of reading into a practice of contemporary witnessing. Later investigations have confirmed that, as the boat passed through invisible maritime borders, its movements were being traced and recorded.

In her essay on the Irish photographer Willie Doherty and his 1995 series 'At the Border', Rosie Lavan addresses the ways in which the politics and governance of borders usually do not accord with the daily experience of the border. In particular, Doherty's work, which combines text and image, creates a tension between theory, perception and engagement in his depictions of the Northern Ireland border. Doherty's 'photographs with text' challenge the ways in which the Northern Ireland border has been documented, reported and narrated, creating a relation of instability between image and text that reveals to the viewer what is already understood by those who live along this borderline, namely, how 'within the border, borders proliferate, tesserating the interfaces and defiles of power and subjection that hold the state in place'.[25] Indeed, as Lavan argues, the very title 'at the border' suggests a location, a fixed point in place, that the image itself blurs, obfuscates and erases.

In 'The Mother Tongue as Border', Anne Isabelle François also probes the tension between national borders and the increasingly transnational, hyphenated affiliations that shape twenty-first-century relations to place and language. She investigates, but also problematizes, the (linguistic) borders of the term 'mother tongue', arguing that the relation between language and origins is an 'obsession' of twentieth-century Western literature. Many of the authors that she discusses share a displaced relation to their 'mother tongue' that motivates a quest to recover it as a point of origin; indeed, a poetics of displacement shapes these very texts. But a number of these works also address the ways in which 'origin' itself is illusory, and how a fixation with origins runs the risk of imposing the very constraints and borders that necessitated the search in the first place. In order to avoid replacing one hegemonic order with another, many of these writers, as François shows, continue to privilege their hyphenated, multilingual identities, and reconstruct the 'mother tongue' as an extensive, border-less metaphor. Artists like Bergvall and Doherty mix and remix textual and visual material in ways that not only challenge any notions of fixed forms and genres, but also activate ways of reading that are translational, transhistoric and radically hybrid. Their work evinces a poetics of drift but does not lose sight (literally, in both cases) of the political implications of this aesthetic. As Bergvall explains further in her essay, 'a transhistoric practice [...] generates an actual friction between historic investigation and contemporary witnessing'.[26] Such a practice encourages relations between materials that at first glance appear disconnected, for instance, the Anglo-Saxon poem 'The Seafarer' and the 'Left-to-Die' case, arguing on behalf of 'a palpable connection [...] between investigating ancient drama at their sometimes horrific residues and piecing together current crimes from unyielding signs at the scene'.[27] Gallien's investigation of the Montague manuscript challenges the borders of its colonial reading and translation, reincorporating the notes left adrift on its margins, like the scattered dots in Martin's grainy images of the left-to-die boat. By retracing the process from original to translation, and by minding, and being mindful of, the border between the two, she bears witness to the ways in which the Arabic text is continuously silenced and restrained.

Calling attention to the way a camera lens can focus so close to a geographic border that it seems to disappear entirely or pulling back the pages of a book to see how far the body of the text extends are all, in effect, ways of thinking outside of the frame of our own cultural, linguistic, social and geographic affiliations. But they are also possible because of a blurring of disciplinary distinctions, and the rich traffic that results from it.

4. Borders and Identity

As well as problematizing political and geographical borders, and accepting the challenge to conventional divisions between the disciplines that this problematization often entails, two essays in this volume question the borders of identity by re-thinking what, in an older philosophical vocabulary, would be called the relation between subject and object, mind and world. One of the intellectual sources for the new approaches is Heidegger's *Being and Time* which hopes to capture the complexity of situated human activity with the hyphenated term: being-in-the-world. For Heidegger, human life can't properly be imagined independently of the niches, both ecological and cultural, in which it flourishes. Human consciousness comes to an awareness of itself and its environment through its embedded and embodied activities: our purposive engagement discloses the world we inhabit and, with this world, ourselves. For Heidegger, this means that human identity is not, as he sarcastically phrases it 'a spiritual Thing which subsequently gets misplaced "into" a space', but constitutively, or as he phrases it 'existentially' spatial: 'Not until we understand Being-in-the-world as an essential structure of Dasein can we have any insight into Dasein's *existential spatiality*'.[28]

To grasp human identity as arising through and out of situated, shared, embodied practices has implications for the way we understand borders. For Heidegger, the model of a punctual self that could strictly delimit its identity, and police the incursions of the world, is not only methodologically flawed, but also spiritually and culturally stifling, for it prevents human beings from understanding what it means to be human: thrown into a specific cultural context that shapes the terms of our unfolding lives, and left with the challenge of confronting and re-appropriating this inheritance. There is no non-situated viewpoint to which we might flee to get a better sense of the human project, only the unfolding situation in which we find ourselves.[29] Heidegger himself was not concerned with cultural exchange. However, his philosophy suggests the necessity of a dialogue based on an honest engagement with one's own situatedness: a predicament which will in most cases reveal itself to be historically overdetermined; a site of a hybrid inheritance, and the compromises that demands. At the same time, Heidegger's model of being-in-the-world raises questions about the agent of such engagements. Our identities are constituted through and by our engagements with the world, which is to say through and by our engagements with others and with the objects on which our practices are dependent.

Michael Wheeler's essay expands on this insight to explore the fluid boundary between the human mind and its environment. Wheeler elaborates Andy Clark's and David Chalmers's idea of the 'extended mind' to argue that, re-grounded in shared meaningful activity, borders between mind and body are re-negotiable cultural achievements — moments of hard-won stability in the on-going process. If the borders of the mind are so labile, it remains open how we would answer the question: 'Who is doing the thinking?' An answer would need to include a thick description of the whole ecology: the different people, the tools, the context, the occasion. Lurking within the Heideggerian reconception of our being-in-the-world is the potential for a relational politics. Peter Garratt explicitly addresses the surprising parallels between cognitive approaches informed by Heidegger, such as those of Mike Wheeler or Andy Clark, and critics writing from ecological, feminist or new materialist perspectives. What all share is a questioning of familiar conceptual borders, and a commitment to embracing the disciplinary challenges that arise when the human subject can no longer be considered to be unproblematically removed from his or her world. Garratt shows how, in many disciplines, the trope of the border is being replaced with the metaphor of 'entanglement', which attempts to capture more complex forms of interaction than those that a simple dividing line might suggest. In the process, conceptions of human agency are reassessed, with philosophers like Andy Clark arguing that intentional action can be scaffolded by an enabling environment, whilst other thinkers, writing in a New Materialist vein, are concerned by the ways in which an argument such as Clark's reduces the environment to human concerns, allowing the human to spill dangerously and anthropocentrically into the surrounding world. Once again, we see how both challenging and preserving borders can be important conceptual resources. Garratt adds that literary texts have a special role in reflecting on these issues, insofar as they engage with complex, historically rooted practices, and grapple with the moral and philosophical problems that the enmeshment of a human life with others and with its environment inevitably produces.

5. Translation and Comparison

There are similar problems to those we have discussed so far with the common Western view of translation which sees it as transferring a text or a meaning from one language to another, crossing a border between languages as decisively as a flight from Helsinki to Moscow crosses a border between States. Derrida famously took issue with this view in his 1985 essay 'Des tours de Babel'. Since the word 'Babel' appears in English, French and many other languages, he argued, how can it be said to 'belong' to any one of them? It follows that we cannot 'déterminer rigoureusement l'unité et l'identité d'une langue, la forme décidable de ses limites' [determine rigorously the unity and identity of a language, the decidable form of its limits].[30] Languages are not distinct entities between which translation can jump. They do not have a clear border separating the words that are citizens of one from the words that are citizens of another.

Derrida might equally have pointed to the many words that are shared between languages with only slight variations of spelling and pronunciation. Look at how much overlap there is between French and English in the phrases just quoted: determine/*déterminer*, rigorously/*rigoureusement*, unity/*unité*, identity/*identité*, language/*langue*, form/*forme*, decidable/*décidable*, limits/*limites*. In the Chinese scriptworld, the written characters that spread across languages such as Chinese, Japanese and Korean have a somewhat similar effect. It is the State apparatus of dictionaries, grammar books and education that regulates such overlaps, patrolling and defining, deciding that 'form' is the correct Standard English spelling and 'forme' the correct Standard French one. But the actual usage of individual people varies widely and often does not obey the prescriptions of the language authorities. There is a continuum of complex variations happening both within languages and across them, with the markers of identity being complex and fluid. Styles and registers are cross-hatched by dialectal and idiomatic variation. The word 'forme' might easily appear — by typo, mis-spelling or for literary effect — in a text that is otherwise Standard English, as might the word 'form' in a text that is otherwise Standard French. A writer might choose to use the word 'langue' in an English essay, confident that readers will understand its Saussurean definition, and thereby announcing membership of a particular sort of English community, one which mostly uses the English language but has an awareness of French theory. Speakers of the many dialectal varieties of English, of Multicultural London English, or of the multitudinous global kinds of English or creoles involving English, present more complex performances of identity.

So translation is not the simple crossing of a simple border, but rather a practice that inhabits a landscape rather like that described by Jeffrey Swartwood in his essay for this volume, a realm of 'uncharted borders' and 'mixed realities and representations'. One stark example is Robert Browning's 1877 translation of Aeschylus's *Agamemnon* which subjects its English vocabulary to the influence of Greek verbal compounding and syntax. 'I know of nightly star-groups the assemblage', proclaims the watchman at the beginning, in phrasing which shows the influence of the Greek which lies behind it: 'ἄστρων κάτοιδα νυκτέρων ὁμήγυριν'.[31] John Dryden's 1697 translation of Virgil's *Aeneid* does not sound as strange as Browning's *Agamemnon*, but the influence of Latin on its phrasing is clear from the opening words: 'Arms, and the man I sing' ('Arma virumque cano').[32] And here is the beginning of W. G. Sebald's 2001 novel *Austerlitz*, translated by Anthea Bell:

> In the second half of the 1960s I travelled repeatedly from England to Belgium, partly for study purposes, partly for other reasons which were never entirely clear to me, staying sometimes for just one or two days, sometimes for several weeks.

> [In der zweiten Hälfte der sechziger Jahre bin ich, teilweise zu Studienzwecken, teilweise aus anderen, mir selber nicht recht erfindlichen Gründen, von England aus wiederholt nach Belgien gefahren, manchmal bloß für ein, zwei Tage, manchmal für mehrere Wochen.][33]

The English of this passage has been shaped by its encounter with Sebald's German.

Where do these pieces of writing sit in relation to the varied borders that divide and traverse languages? The language of the Sebald-Bell *Austerlitz* cannot be categorized as 'foreign' or even 'Germanic'; but it does have a particular stylistic identity which has roots in Sebald's German (which is itself particular) as well as English. Even Browning's *Agamemnon* resists the label 'foreign' (or 'foreignizing', in the terminology of translation studies): syntactic inversion and surprising compounds are long-established elements of the tradition of English verse. The identity of this translation arises from a complex intermingling of Aeschylean language (itself a very distinctive kind of Greek) with an English which is not simply 'English' but rather a particular variety: Browningesque, poetical, Victorian, etc. Translation inhabits a border country where identities blend and clash.

The two essays on translation in this volume explore similar instances in more detail. Céline Sabiron, in 'Cross-Channel Literary Crossings and the Borders of Translatability', shows that novels by Sir Walter Scott such as *Waverley* (1814) and *Rob Roy* (1817) complicate the borders between languages by mingling English and Scots. This posed a particular challenge to their French translator, Auguste Jean-Baptiste Defauconpret: he downplayed the texts' linguistic complexity when he brought them into French, but they still had a hybrid fascination which made them immensely popular in France and throughout Europe. Madli Kütt, in 'A Conversation across Borders: Marcel Proust's *Le Temps retrouvé* and its Translation into Estonian' investigates the processes by which Proust shows thoughts emerging into consciousness and objects into perception. Again the linguistic complexity of this is lost in the Estonian translation by Tõnu Õnnepalu; but Estonian has other resources for blurring boundaries, not least because of the idea that Estonia is itself a border country. The translation can therefore 'open perspectives that Proust could not achieve on his own'.

Like translation, the discipline of comparative literature is often seen, to borrow a chapter title from Gayatri Chakravorty Spivak's book *Death of a Discipline* (2003), as a matter of 'Crossing Borders'. But here too, just as with translation, we need to keep in mind that the borders are complex and fuzzy, and that we create new ones by the ways in which we work. This is the topic of the last essay in this volume, Xiaofan Amy Li's 'When Do Different Literatures Become Comparable? The Vague Borders of Comparability and Incomparability'. Li considers how far terms from comparative philosophy can apply to comparative literature, and in doing so throws new light on the variety of ways in which 'comparison' can be understood.

Implicit in Li's essay, as in many of the contributions to this volume, is a recognition of the structuring power of our work as scholars and critics. Each of us is located, embedded in institutions, with habits and assumptions, inevitably interacting with the world from a point of view. If we are comparatists or translators then our work will involve the crossing of something that has been constructed as a border: that is part of the definition of translation and comparative literature. Yet, as we have seen, borders, and border-countries, and the process of traversing them are always difficult to describe. If we adopt a model of 'crossing borders' then we paradoxically contribute to simplifying and solidifying the idea of the border by envisaging it as something that can straightforwardly be got past: we downplay the overlaps and cross-hatchings which this introduction has outlined, and which will be further explored by the essays that follow. On the other hand, if we think of ourselves (in terms that go back to Homi Bhabha's *The Location of Culture*) as intellectually 'hybrid' or 'interstitial' we risk losing sight of the new borders that our work inevitably constructs, as it concentrates on some texts rather than others, and asks this question rather than that. Creating them by crossing them, destroying them only to rebuild them elsewhere, academics can't do without borders. What we can do is recognize and be mindful of the complexity of the bordering practices we are engaged in.

Notes to the Introduction

1. On walls see Claude Quétel, *Murs: une autre histoire des hommes* (Paris: Perrin, 2013).
2. <http://www.theguardian.com/world/2016/feb/05/syrian-refugee-numbers-continue-to-build-on-turkish-border>; <http://www.theguardian.com/world/2016/jan/25/refugee-crisis-schengen-area-scheme-brink-amsterdam-talks>; <http://www.theguardian.com/politics/2014/sep/29/what-is-google-tax-george-osborne>; <http://www.theguardian.com/technology/2016/feb/25/apple-fbi-iphone-encryption-request-response> [all accessed 27 February 2016].
3. See Mark Stein, *How the States Got their Shapes* (New York: Harper, 2008) and *How the States Got their Shapes: The People behind the Borderlines* (Washington, DC: Smithsonian Books, 2011).
4. Diane Taylor and Chris Johnston, 'Asylum seeker wristband policy to be dropped', *The Guardian* (25 January 2016), <http://www.theguardian.com/uk-news/2016/jan/25/government-to-be-challenged-in-commons-over-refugee-wristbands> [accessed 27 February 2016].
5. Frederick Jackson Turner, *The Frontier in American History* (New York: Barnes & Noble, 2009), pp. 2–3.
6. Thomas Oles, *Walls: Enclosure and Ethics in the Modern Landscape* (Chicago, IL: University of Chicago Press, 2015), p. 53.
7. Ovid, *Fasti*, trans. by James G. Frazer, 2nd edn (Cambridge: Harvard University Press/ Loeb Classical Library, 1996), p. 105.
8. Diodorus Siculus, *Library of History* VIII, 6, 1–3.
9. Livy, *History of Rome* I, vi, 3.
10. Ovid, *Fasti* IV, 818–36, trans. by James G. Frazer, pp. 249–51.
11. Cormac McCarthy, *The Crossing* (London: Picador, 1994), pp. 122–23.

12. Personal communication to one of the editors.
13. Matthew Reynolds, Mohamed-Salah Omri and Ben Morgan, 'Guest Editors' Introduction', *Comparative Critical Studies*, 12.2 (2015), 147–59 (p. 152).
14. Translation done between 1851 and 1854 and published in Cairo in 1867. al-Tahtawi, Rifa'a Rafi', *The position of stars in the adventures of Talimak* (in Arabic) (Cairo: 2002).
15. Virgil, *Aeneid*, trans. by Charles J. Bilson (New York: Dover Books, 1995).
16. *Aeneid*, trans. by Bilson, p. 36.
17. 'Sidonian Dido', in *Innovations of Antiquity*, ed. by Ralph Hexter and Daniel Selden (London: Routledge, 1993), pp. 332–90.
18. Fawzi Mellah, *Elissa*, trans. by Howard Curtis (London: Quartet Books, 1990), p. 160.
19. The famous speech attributed to the Berber leader, Tariq Ibn Ziyad, who conquered Spain in the eighth century, to his troops after reportedly burning their boats, 'the sea is behind you, and the enemy is in front of you'.
20. Fawzi Mellah, *Clandestin en méditerranée* (Tunis: CERES, 200), p. 59 (our translation).
21. See Mohamed-Salah Omri, 'Towards a Theory of *tarafud*: The Poetics and Ethics of Comparison' (in Arabic) in *The Comparative Lesson and the Dialogue of Literature* (Tunis: Bayt al-Hikma, 2015), pp. 13–52.
22. Caroline Bergvall, 'A Cat in the Throat: On Bilingual Occupants', *Jacket*, 37 (2009) <http://jacketmagazine.com/37/bergvall-cat-throat.shtml>.
23. Caroline Bergvall, *Drift* (Brooklyn, NY: Nightboat Books, 2014), p. 59.
24. See Claire Gallien's contribution in this volume.
25. Quoted in Rosie Lavan's contribution in this volume.
26. See Caroline Bergvall's contribution in this volume.
27. Ibid.
28. Martin Heidegger, *Being and Time*, trans. by John Macquarrie and Edward Robinson (Oxford: Blackwell, 1962), p. 83 (=SuZ 56 §12). Further references will be given parenthetically in the text following the convention of giving the page numbers in the standard German edition published by Niemeyer, pages number for which are given in the margins of the Blackwell edition: SuZ p. 56.
29. Heidegger, *Being and Time*, SuZ pp. 299–300.
30. Jacques Derrida, 'Des Tours des Babel', trans. by Joseph F. Graham, in *Difference in Translation*, ed. by Joseph F. Graham (Ithaca, NY: Cornell University Press, 1985), pp. 217, 173.
31. Robert Browning, *The Agamemnon of Aeschylus* (London: Smith, Elder, 1877), p. 1; Aeschylus, with an English translation by Herbert Weir Smyth, 2 vols (Cambridge, MA: Harvard University Press, 1926), <http://www.perseus.tufts.edu/hopper/text?doc=Perseus:text:1999.01.0003> [accessed 8 February 2016].
32. John Dryden, *Virgil's Aeneis*, 1. 1. Quoted from *The Works of John Dryden*, ed. by E. N. Hooker, H. T. Swedenberg, Jr., et al., 20 vols (Berkeley and London: University of California Press, 1956–2000), vol. v: Virgil, *Aeneid*, 1. 1.
33. W. G. Sebald, *Austerlitz*, trans. by Anthea Bell (London: Penguin, 2011), p. 1; W. G. Sebald, *Austerlitz* (Frankfurt: Fischer Taschenbuch, 2003), p. 9.

CHAPTER 1

Old and New Borders: A Geographical Approach

Davide Papotti

The geographical discourse of modernity had the concept of 'border' among its cornerstones.[1] The close association between the form of the modern nation-state and the political definition of its borders (which found visual expression through cartographic representation in maps) brought this concept to a high level of visibility and popularity. The consolidation of the geopolitical model of the nation-state generated a widespread interest among scholars in the definition of the concept of border, in the classification of its forms and aspects, and in the study of the conflicts that could arise around borders. As the British geographer W. Gordon East states in his classic work *The Geography behind History*, 'at all stages of its history a state has more or less known limits where it impinges on territories outside its jurisdiction and control. These borderlands form its frontier, and within them a boundary line may or may not be defined. In the frontier zone are usually concentrated a large part of the defensive forces and strongholds of the state, for the purpose of the frontier is to create a strong frame within which the state may exercise its functions and its citizens may live in security.'[2]

During the twentieth century geographical studies enriched the variety of approaches adopted in the study of the concept. Behind this growing complexity around the concept of 'border' lies the planning perspective on borders that disappeared because of historical events (such as the fall of the Berlin Wall and the consequent reunification of both the two German states and the city of Berlin) or because of the adoption of new international agreements (as in the case of the Schengen Agreement in 1985 that started the process of transformation of border functions among the signatory States).[3] The emphasis gradually shifted from the study of the operative functionality of the border to the broader perspective of analysis of the processes of territorialization that take place around and because of borders. The study of the function of borders in these processes of transformation brought a new attention to the concept of 'border regions'[4] and of 'border landscapes'.[5] Finally, one can also speak of a 'cultural turn' in the study of borders, meaning the advent of the study of the perception of borders among communities and individuals.[6] The concept of border, while maintaining a solid geopolitical origin, has been stretched towards new dimensions and meanings in recent decades, with a large component of metaphorical uses of the concept applied in different fields and contexts.[7]

This essay offers a brief re-reading of the notion of 'border' developed within geographical studies in the light of the new uses and tensions created by its contemporary enlarged uses. My first section will be devoted to the definition of the term; defining the key terms of a discourse is especially important in an interdisciplinary perspective. In the same section, I will address the typological classification of borders. Analysing how many kinds of borders exist and how geographers have classified them is a useful exercise for understanding tensions between the theoretical definition of the border and its appearances in complex geopolitical contexts around the world. In the second section, I will provide a few examples of the new questions that animate border studies in an attempt to grasp the dynamic nature of the border in contemporary 'fluid society'.[8] In doing so, I will also provide an overview of the institutional outcomes of the new research field of 'border studies', which reframes the study of borders in an interdisciplinary perspective.

Defining and Classifying Borders

What exactly is a border? As W. Gordon East states: 'The distinction in nomenclature between the frontier as a zone and the boundary as a line is essential to any clear discussion of the limits of state territories. The frontier in this sense appears at all periods of history, but the boundary, which has to be surveyed, drawn on maps, and perhaps also demarcated on the ground, is a relatively recent innovation'.[9] The identification of the border with a 'line' is rooted in the common geographical imagery. Many literary works rely on this dimension: a simple line that is traced on a territory to demarcate two separate parts.[10] Technically speaking, 'A boundary between states is actually a vertical plane that cuts through the rocks below (called the subsoil in legal papers when countries argue about it) and the airspace above. Only where this vertical plane intersects the Earth's surface (on land or at sea) does it form the line we see on a map.'[11]

Geography, with its specific emphasis on the territorial dimension, therefore has a fundamental place in border studies. As the Italian geographer Gianfranco Bussoletti states: 'Borders are geographical phenomena; they are therefore exceptionally meaningful and problematic spatial facts, since they are the expression of an "exclusive occupation" by a human group of a given territory. They sign the limits between different identities.'[12]

Traditionally, geography identified five functions for borders:[13] legal and juridical, fiscal, military, customs-related, and, last but not least, ideological. This brief overview of the different functions that a border can show, according to the layer of identity to which one refers, reinforces the idea of the complexity of this concept. The existence of the border is both material (the military function, for instance, is related to the presence of visible barriers and obstacles that regulate flows through borders) and immaterial (the border plays a strong role in shaping the imagery about the territorial control expressed by a State — the ideological function — and limits the spatial competence of fiscal and juridical powers).

Furthermore, the profile of a border is affected by the rituals that govern its 'rites of passage' (the 'customs' function which enters social imagery through the sometimes long, tiring and frustrating processes that are necessary for an individual to pass a border). The operative existence of a border is the result of a continuous exchange between its legal definition and its functional 'management' on the ground. In this perspective, as the Italian geographer Umberto Toschi states in his handbook of political geography published during the Second World War, 'the "perfect" border is a geographical abstraction'.[14] The 'absolute' border does not exist in reality, but it nevertheless projects its influence as a model.

The nature of the border lies in its function of separation. It establishes a 'here' and a 'there', it draws a line between two entities that, if not differentiated beforehand, become so when the border is imposed. Thus in geopolitical discourse the border can be seen as an artificial intervention aimed at separating. The Italian geographer Luciano Buzzetti, for instance, explains that the border can be an 'unnatural division of united entities, inadequate to adapt to social, economic, and cultural changes; thus it opposes the local interests that seek this unity, sacrificing them to the higher needs of the State'.[15]

In order to understand the meanings associated with the concept of 'border', it is necessary to investigate how geographers have classified the different typologies of borders that can be observed on the ground. A primary distinction can be made according to the environment in which a border lies. Thus we can speak of 'land borders' (which delimit the territory over which a political organism has full jurisdiction and full sovereignty) and 'maritime borders', which do not imply direct contact among different States, but rather multiple graduated contacts among the opposite land areas (territorial waters, exclusive economic zones, median line principle).[16]

Beyond this preliminary distinction between terrestrial and maritime borders, there are other criteria that support different typologies. A key adjective in the history of borders has been the word 'natural', to suggest the ancestral nature of some territorial borders. The rhetoric of the 'natural border' relies on the insinuation that there are some borders, which are, so to speak, already 'there', offered by nature, unquestionable and objective in their function of separation. When a border coincides with physical geographical features (such as rivers, watersheds, mountain ranges), it is often referred to as a 'natural' border. The human need to identify a line of discontinuity in a landscape interacts with the presence of a natural obstacle, blurring together the difficulty in crossing a certain stretch of land and the demarcation of a discontinuity in the identity of the territory: eventually they combine. When this physical base is lacking, one speaks instead of 'geometrical borders', which are based on the geographical coordinates system (longitude, latitude). These borders are the result of geopolitical negotiations: they are superimposed by human decisions. Examples of this kind of 'artificial' border are the border between the USA and Canada (based on the 49th parallel North), the border between Egypt and Libya (based on the 25th meridian East), and the border between North and South Korea (still today a highly militarized one, based on the 38th parallel North). This dialectic between supposedly 'natural' borders and 'geometrical' ones suggests that some borders are inherently more acceptable and justifiable than others. In fact, every border is a fully human creation.

It is also important to understand the ways in which a border is created and legitimized in political and social discourse. Since borders are such artificial entities it is crucial to understand how political discourses create their legitimacy. Geographers identify four stages in the creation of a border:

> *definition*: 'a process that involves the creation of a legal document, a sort of treaty, in which concrete elements of the landscape are described (or, in case of a geometrical border, the precise longitude or latitude is given)'
>
> *delimitation*: 'a process that involves the representation of a border on a cartographic basis'
>
> *demarcation*: 'a process that involves the configuration of the border on the ground, with steel poles, concrete pillars, fences, walls or other visible elements'.[17]

A border therefore has its roots in a verbal description which acquires legal value through the mutual recognition of it by political powers. After this discursive legitimation, cartography determines a higher degree of recognition, tracing a precise line on a surface. Many borders do not go on to the final stage of demarcation: for instance, the borders between counties, parishes, districts and administrative regions are often invisible to people crossing them. It is in fact comparatively rare for a border to find its ultimate legitimacy through obvious visibility, created by material elements positioned on the ground.

Besides this morphological distinction, there is also a 'genetic' classification which was defined by the American geographer Richard Hartshorne (1899–1992).[18] In this, the different types of border are identified through the relationship between the formation of the border and the process of settlement. Hartshorne identifies four different kinds of borders: antecedent boundaries, subsequent ones, superimposed boundaries, and relict boundaries. The antecedent border is defined and delimited before the consolidation of the human settlement. The subsequent border consolidates the evolution of a cultural landscape, usually following a long process of adaptation and modification. The superimposed border represents the result of a forced act, a decision taken in the isolated space of a governmental office. A relict border, finally, is a border whose traces remain in the landscape, though it is no longer active on the ground. The concept of 'de-functionalization' of borders[19] suggests the loss of a border's operative function, gradually disintegrated by the everyday practices of space.

New Perspectives on Border Studies

The fact that a border has a 'life-cycle', which comprises a birth, a growth, a maturity, and, sometimes, a death, poses the question of the longevity of borders through human history. How and when do borders survive? This issue brings into focus the multi-scale dimension of borders. Even though they are traditionally associated with the State dimension, borders can be present at different institutional and operative scales: municipal, provincial, and regional borders show the complexity and the gradual nature of the political partitions of territory. A transscalar approach is thus necessary in studying borders, observing the complexity of the different levels at which a border is operative.

Given the fact that borders separate different entities, it is important to consider whether they are able to grasp the complexity of social and collective identities. Do borders represent and express cultural differences (languages, ethnicities, religions)? Or do they just mirror consolidated political identities? It is of course impossible to draw a precise line between these spheres of meaning, because political decisions about territorial management are often based on linguistic, ethnic, religious and cultural differences, as they are perceived and commonly recognized in social discourse.

Borders are central elements in territorial organization and management (and therefore in the practice of territorial policies). In this perspective, instead of being seen as simple lines defining a perimeter that separates entities, they can be thought of as places of potential encounters. Artistic and literary portraits on and around borders have been at the centre of scholarly attention because the cultural re-interpretation of borders sheds new interpretative light on their functions and roles. Examples include the work by Louise Amoore and Alexandra Hall[20] on artistic interventions relating to the concept of 'border security' and the collective work on transits, margins, and borders in literature edited by Indiveri, Bonito and Novello.[21] The symbolic nature of borders is efficiently summarized by Gian Primo Cella: 'Exactly because the simplest way to define identities is recognizing by oppositions, borders, which need only one sign that can be transformed into a symbol, become indispensable in the construction of identities'.[22]

Postcolonial theory emphasizes the discursive nature of borders which are functional in asserting power. As Bjorn Sletto states: 'Boundary-making assumes a particularly significant role as an arbiter of relations of power. I am speaking here not of the instrumentality of boundary-making, i.e. boundary-making as a material tool of nation-building and territoriality. Instead, I propose to examine the discursive processes that accompany, challenge, and legitimize the (re)productions of the often contradictory lines that traverse post-colonial landscapes'.[23] In this view, borders are read as a cultural project emanating from power centres: 'From a Gramscian perspective, boundary-making can be understood as a cultural project implicated in the reproduction of spatial inequalities based on class and ethnicity, and also serving the state's attempts to maintain territorial control. Boundary-making is an example of the state's attempt to achieve "hegemony" through both cultural elements as well as economic power; i.e., internal state boundaries may be secured through "political domination" or culture, but they are always attempts to keep people in their place'.[24] This reading is tragically actual in the contemporary international context, where migratory processes, in several geopolitical contexts (the Mediterranean area, the US–Mexican border, the Middle East) are severely stressing the traditional form of international borders. The rhetoric of globalization adopted by many politicians and scholars speaks of a 'borderless' world; but, in fact, borders are simply re-adjusting to new globalized conditions, delocalizing their functions to inner complex boundaries and multiplying themselves under new forms.[25] The increased mobility of people on an international level, together with the complex processes of globalization that affected the international economy and politics,[26] gave the illusion of a world that was progressively dismissing its international boundaries. As the recent political crisis and civil war in Syria is showing at this very moment (February 2016), the growing flows of refugees and migrants do still meet borders, and even contribute to the growth of new forms of demarcation and boundary control (as in the case of the fenced barriers of barbed wire created in Hungary, Slovenia, Slovakia, and Croatia). At the same time, forms of bureaucratic control of the citizenship and of the right to move across international borders have been 'delocalized' in transport hubs such as airports, harbours and railways station, disseminating across the territory the traditional functions of borders.

The new theoretical dimensions for the study of borders and the new broadness of the interests in this topic are institutionally mirrored by the consolidation of a new interdisciplinary field of study called 'border studies'. This interdisciplinary framework brings together different disciplinary approaches from anthropology, sociology, geography, political sciences, history and juridical studies, among many others[27]. At the international level, one can also make reference to the Association for Borderlands Studies (ABS),[28] born in 1976 and currently based at the Karelian Institute of the University of Eastern Finland (which has published the *Journal of Borderlands Studies* since 1986),[29] the Association of European Border Regions, founded in 1971 under the auspices of the International Conference on Regional Planning,[30] the Border Crossing Network based in the Balkans and founded in 2003,[31] the Border Poetics/Border Culture Research Group based at the Arctic University of Norway.[32] Last, among the academic journals, one can mention the recently created *International Journal of Migration and Border Studies* published since 2014 by Inderscience, whose editor in chief is Professor France Houle of the Université de Montréal, in Canada.[33] What these examples tell us is that the concept of 'border' has undergone a profound critical analysis, following the tensions that characterize the contemporary existence and management of international borders. The revision of the traditional theory of borders has resulted in the creation of a dynamic 'critical border theory'.[34]

From this perspective, borders are at the same time 'old' and 'new'. They are old because they have been at the centre of the Western geopolitical discourse for centuries; because sometimes they have been there on the ground for a similar stretch of time (to mention just one example, among the oldest borders in Europe are the borders of Switzerland, which have recently been at the centre of processes of re-functionalization following the 1999 decision of the Swiss federal state to join the European Union's Schengen area of free circulation of people); and because they are associated with traditional and well-established practices of border-crossing regulations. On the other hand, they are new because they are facing new challenges of permeability, they are being asked to renew their practices of security and control, and they are being called upon to adapt to radical changes in the forms of human mobility. As Silvia Salvatici states, 'the historical depth in the construction of borders, the intertwining between their territorial profile and the level of identities and belongings, the different meanings attributed to borders by various political and local subjects: all of these are common acquisitions, that constitute the theoretical frame for new researches'.[35]

Notes to Chapter 1

1. Paul Guichonnet and Claude Raffestin, *Géographie des frontières* (Paris: PUF, 1974).
2. William Gordon East, *The Geography behind History* (London: Nelson, 1965), p. 98.
3. Henk Van Houtum, 'An Overview of European Geographical Research on Borders and Border Regions', *Journal of Borderlands Studies*, 15 (2000), 57–83; William Walters, 'Europe's Borders', in *Sage Handbook of European Studies*, ed. by Chris Rumford (London: Sage, 2009), pp. 485–505.
4. Guichonnet and Raffestin, *Géographie des frontières*.
5. *The Geography of Border Landscapes*, ed. by Dennis Rumley and Julian V. Minghi (London and New York: Routledge, 1991); Elena Dell'Agnese, 'Nuove geo-grafie dei paesaggi di confine', *Memoria e Ricerca*, 45 (2014), 51–65.
6. Alison Blunt, 'Cultural Geographies of Migration: Mobility, Transnationality and Diaspora', *Progress in Human Geography*, 31 (2007), 684–94.
7. *Borderscaping: Imagination and Practices of Border Making*, ed. by Chiara Brambilla, Jussi Laine, James W. Scott and Gianluca Bocchi (Farnham: Ashgate, 2015).
8. Zygmunt Bauman, *Liquid Modernity* (Cambridge: Polity, 2000).
9. East, *The Geography behind History*, p. 98.
10. Just to mention one example, the radio drama by the Italian writer Carlo Emilio Gadda (1893–1973) *Háry János* is set along a border line.
11. Harm De Blij and Alexander B. Murphy, *Human Geography: Culture, Society and Space*, 4th edn (Hoboken, NJ: Wiley, 1993), pp. 482–83.
12. Gianfranco Bussoletti, 'Confine', in *Le parole chiave della geografia*, ed. by Gino De Vecchis and Cosimo Palagiano (Rome: Carocci, 2003), pp. 161–64 (p. 161). The English translations of texts originally in Italian are mine.
13. Guichonnet and Raffestin, *Géographie des frontières*.
14. Umberto Toschi, *Appunti di geografia politica* (Bari: Macri, 1940).
15. Luciano Buzzetti, 'Il confine come problema geografico', in *Atti del Convegno di Studi in onore di Giorgio Valussi, Trieste 6–7 febbraio 1992*, ed. by Gianfranco Battisti and Pio Nodari (Trieste: Università degli Studi di Trieste — Dipartimento di Scienze Geografiche e Storiche, 1996), pp. 35–54 (p. 36).
16. Jerome D. Fellmann, Arthur Getis, Judith Getis et al., *Human Geography: Landscapes of Human Activities* (Boston, MA; and London: McGraw-Hill Higher Education, 2007), pp. 427–30, 440.
17. De Blij and Murphy, *Human Geography*, pp. 485–86. On the process of formation of borders see also Claude Raffestin, 'Confini e limiti', in *Europa: vecchi confini e nuove frontiere* ed. by Elena Dell'Agnese and Enrico Squarcina (Torino: UTET, 2005), pp. 9–17.
18. De Blij and Murphy, *Human Geography*, p. 486.
19. As defined by Gianfranco Lizza, Gianfranco, 'Funzione e defunzionalizzazione dei confini', in *Atti del Convegno di Studi in onore di Giorgio Valussi, Trieste 6–7 febbraio 1992*, ed. by Gianfranco Battisti and Pio Nodari (Trieste: Università degli Studi di Trieste — Dipartimento di Scienze Geografiche e Storiche, 1996), pp. 79–86.
20. Louise Amoore and Alexandra Hall, 'Border Theatre: On the Arts of Security and Resistance', *Cultural Geographies*, 17 (2010), 299–319.
21. *Finisterrae: scritture dal confine*, ed. by Magda Indiveri, Vito M. Bonito and Neil Novello (Rome: Carocci, 2007). On the concept of 'border' in literature see also *Frontiere Confini Limiti*, ed. by Marina Guglielmi and Mauro Pala (Rome: Armando, 2011) and Toni Veneri, 'Limites du lieu et barrières de l'espace', *Between*, 1 (2011) <http://ojs.unica.it/index.php/between>.
22. Gian Primo Cella, *Tracciare confini: realtà e metafore della distinzione* (Bologna: il Mulino, 2006), p. 17.

23. Bjorn Sletto, '"Indigenous people don't have boundaries": Reborderings, Fire Management, and Productions of Authenticities in Indigenous Landscapes', *Cultural Geographies*, 16 (2009), 253–77 (p. 255).
24. Ibid., p. 257.
25. David Newman, 'The Lines that Continue to Separate Us: Borders in our "Borderless" World', *Progress in Human Geography*, 30 (2006), 143–61; Anssi Paasi, 'Border Studies Re-animated: Going beyond the Relational/Territorial Divide', *Environment and Planning A*, 44 (2012), 2303–09.
26. For a geographical reading of globalization see Warwick E. Murray, *Geographies of Globalization* (London: Routledge, 2006).
27. Some examples of institutional centres in academia devoted to this field of study can be useful to exemplify the proliferation at the international level of this renewed interest for borders. Among many, one can mention the Centre for International Borders Research at Queens' University Belfast (Northern Ireland), the Centre for Cross Border Studies based in Armagh (Northern Ireland) and Dublin (Ireland), the International Boundary Research Unit (IBRU) — Centre for Borders Research at Durham University (United Kingdom), the Nijmegen Centre for Border Research at Radboud University Nijmegen (The Netherlands), the Centre for Regional and Transboundary Studies (CRTS) based at the University of Volgograd (Russia), the Border Studies Program at Earlham College in Richmond (Indiana, USA), Center for Border Studies at the Université de la Grande Région/Universität der Grossregion (part of a network of Universities based in Germany, France, Luxembourg and Belgium), and the Department of Border Region Studies at the University of Southern Denmark.
28. <http://absborderlands.org/> [accessed 22 January 2016].
29. < http://absborderlands.org/journal-of-borderlands-studies> [accessed 22 January 2016].
30. <http://www.aebr.eu/en/index.php> [accessed 25 January 2016].
31. <http://www.border-crossings.eu/> [accessed 31 January 2016]. The Association organizes a Summer School based in Konitsa, in Greece.
32. <https://en.uit.no/forskning/forskningsgrupper/gruppe?p_document_id=344750> [accessed 15 January 2016].
33. <http://www.inderscience.com/jhome.php?jcode=ijmbs> [accessed 9 January 2016]. This list does not of course pretend to be exhaustive, but rather to suggest the dissemination around the world of centres and programs for the study of borders. The growing attention and the importance of the interdisciplinary and transnational dimension in border studies (Blunt) have generated many recent publications, among them the publications of the EU Borderscapes program (Seventh Framework Programme of the European research Area — The European Commission: *EU Borderscapes State of the Debate Report I*, ed. by Vladimir Kolosov, 2012 <www.euborderscapes.eu>; Vladimir Kolosov and James W. Scott, *Selected Conceptual Issues in Border Studies*, EU Borderscapes Working Paper n. 4, 2013, <www.euborderscapes.eu>); *Borders, Regions, and People*, ed. by Martin Van del Welde and Henk van Houtom (London: Pion, 2000); Anssi Paasi, 'Political Boundaries', in *International Encyclopaedia of Human Geography*, ed. by Rob Kitchin et al. (Oxford: Elsevier, 2009), vol. VIII, pp. 217–27; Anssi Paasi, 'Borders and Border Crossings', in *A New Companion to Cultural Geography*, ed. by Nuala Johnson, Richard Schein and Jamie Winders (London: Wiley-Blackwell, 2013), pp. 478–93; Anssi Paasi, 'Borders', in *The Ashgate Research Companion to Critical Geopolitics*, ed. by Klaus Dodds, Merje Kuus and Joanne Sharp (London: Ashgate, 2013), pp. 213–29.
34. For 'an agenda for critical border studies' see Noel Parker, Nick Vaughan-Williams et al., 'Lines in the Sand? Towards an Agenda for Critical Border Studies', *Geopolitics*, 14 (2009), 582–87; for a review of the need to 'rethink the border in border studies' see Corey Johnson, Reece Jones, Anssi Paasi, Louise Amoore, Alison Mountz, Mark Salter and Chris Rumford, 'Interventions on Rethinking "the Border" in Border Studies', *Political Geography*, 30 (2011), 61–69.
35. Silvia Salvatici, 'Introduzione', in *Confini: costruzioni, attraversamenti, rappresentazioni*, ed. by Silvia Salvatici (Soveria Mannelli, Calabria: Rubbettino, 2005), pp. 7–21 (pp. 7–8).

CHAPTER 2

❖

Uncharted Borders

Mixed Realities and Representations of the Californio Period Community and Culture of San Diego, California

Jeffrey Swartwood

This chapter addresses the evolution of the unique regional culture to be found in the extreme Southwest of the United States borderlands in the San Diego area of southern California. It will present several aspects of the borders and border crossings — whether physical, cultural, or notional — that abound in this space. These multiple borders will be examined in terms of their imposition upon the perception and representation of regional history and culture as well as, periodically, their distinct omission from the public memory narrative. This text is organized around two principal themes, borders imposed and borders ignored, as they appear through the historical record and through academic study in traditional disciplines including literary and historical studies. While such an analysis could be extended to multiple cultural markers, the primary areas of focus in this work will surround spatial constructions — notably architecture — and literary representations of the nineteenth century. In treating each of these, questions of how borders shape regional culture will be addressed alongside those of how borders shape the representation and study of regional culture. In doing so, the lines binding cultural construction with cultural representation, blurred as they may be, may be better brought to light. This construction implies accepting a balance between an examination of the historical record and of its study, a balancing act which I hope will be successful in revealing connections that are perhaps sometimes obscured by disciplinary specialization and subsequent division.

One of the intriguing aspects of border studies, or perhaps more accurately in this case, borderland studies, along the US–Mexican border is that this border is one of those spaces which appears to belong to a broader, nearly global culture. The reason for this almost certainly lies in the proliferation of popularized representations: in the headlines concerning immigration, political restructuring, or the drug cartels; in contemporary literature such as Cormac McCarthy's *Blood Meridian* or his *Western Trilogy*; or in the cinema, from the escape route offered to John Wayne in

John Ford's 1939 *Stagecoach* to the binational *Mariachi Trilogy* (1999–2003) as well as the ominous implications in Orson Welles's *Touch of Evil* (1958) and mainstream yet regional comedy in the form of Cheech Marin's *Born in East LA* (1987). Along with CNN reports, fictional characters such as Zorro continue to feed the myths and realities whose profusion allows the reader, or the viewer, the impression that this border is familiar and accounted for in the mainstream cultural constructs of American, or even Western, culture.

In the dominant representations, the North–South dichotomy prevails in largely colonial terms: conquered and conqueror, rich versus poor, organization versus chaos, high culture versus low culture, or clinical versus affective. In the most simplistic representations, the border is a line of confrontation between any combination of these elements in nationalistic terms. In others, the contact zone implied by this confrontation becomes the focus, with increasing shades of grey including multiple code-switching and hybrid cultural constructions. The representation of these plural realities and perspectives can likewise be qualified through a multitude of disciplines: from Bolton's frontier histories to the cultural studies work of Mario Barrera, from Carmen Tafolia's bilingual literary constructions to the canonical American literary study of Richard Henry Dana's *Two Years before The Mast*.[1] Providing significant insight into the realities of the borderlands, each of the authors and disciplines evoked here contribute to understanding the nearly impossibly broad subject of US–Mexican border studies.

And yet, the very scale of this border, at nearly 3200 kilometres (1933 miles),[2] and the lengthy history involved in the settlement of the lands now touched by it, cannot but provide grounds for a more intimate rendering. The local dynamics and actors, varying considerably from one area to the next and over the course of several centuries, lead to variations that are invariably compromised in the narration of a simplified, homogenized tale of the border. In this text, my goal is to address the notion of borders as it can be applied to the historical evolution of the specific regional culture of San Diego, California. In order to do so, a multi- or rather a trans-disciplinary approach will be adopted; one that allows both the presentation and analysis of multiple aspects of the multiple borders which have been erected, imposed or omitted in the construction of this regional culture. Both contemporary and historical elements will be examined, in an effort to probe the impact of borders on this local culture and the ensuing legacy of the San Diego Californios. This positioning, outside of the restrictions of established disciplinary confines, allows the exploration of several types of borders, and in doing so perhaps poses more questions than responses. The intent, however, is not an exhaustive study but rather an introduction to the possibilities that may be opened when crossing over boundaries frequently imposed upon the analysis.

One of the most obvious features of contemporary Southern California is the US–Mexican border that separates the cities of San Diego, California, and Tijuana, Baja California.[3] What is sometimes forgotten in this oppositional representation is that this border was imposed only quite recently, with the signing of the Treaty of Guadalupe Hidalgo in 1848, and was rendered physically significant only in the early twentieth century with the expansion of a customs house first built at San Ysidro in 1874.[4] The idea of an actual physical barrier with the intention to seriously limit movement comes only much later in the historical record, with an effective fence appearing in the urban centre of San Ysidro only in the second half of the twentieth century. Prior to this time, it should be noted that 'the border', as *this* border is frequently termed locally, simply did not exist. Under successive Spanish and Mexican administrations,[5] the northern territorial border was situated far to the north, and there was an administrative and commercial continuity between the two Californias — Alta and Baja, north and south — in the region that became San Diego County.

What is interesting in this scenario is that upon its creation, the border existed, for all practical purposes, as a notion long before it did so in a physically tangible sense. In terms of local culture, the relative isolation of San Diego from both Mexican and American politics and populations meant that cross-border family ties, commercial exchange and land holdings were prevalent until the late nineteenth century. This changed only with the beginning of massive immigration from the Eastern United States, alongside the establishment of a border settlement that encouraged Mexican immigration to the corresponding area in Mexico, creating a demographic majority with no local ties to the respective 'other' side of the international boundary. In terms of the local 'Californio' culture, the border here does not result from the culmination of a clash or conflict between two cultures, but rather two nation-states. Thus, again in local terms, that cultural clash occurs only subsequently to the imposition of the border with its divisional implications. The progressive imposition of a border, both notional and physical, appears to have greatly influenced the evolution of local culture as well as the interpretation of its manifestations and representations. While examples can be found across multiple disciplinary areas, in the interest of developing a trans-disciplinary analysis we will focus on the telling examples of architecture and literature.

If we accept, in accordance with the views of Jacques Derrida or Baydar Gülsüm,[6] that architecture provides a significant form of cultural expression — both in terms of projection and in terms of reception — then the example of local hybrid forms proves to be quite interesting. Significant examples can be found in the study of three local buildings, sharing significant aesthetic characteristics, constructed between the mid-1830s and the mid-1850s, placing them in the transitional period between Mexican and United States' governance.[7] The three structures we will consider are the Spanish Mission San Diego de Alcala, the Rancho Guajome, and the Old Spanish Lighthouse. Superficially, each of these three buildings appears to share certain dominant characteristics: adobe construction with a white plaster finish coat, red tile roofs in the Spanish or Mediterranean tradition, and local brickwork. Placed side by side, the buildings appear to present a rather homogeneous architectural ensemble. And yet, important differences exist both in the structures themselves and in their representation in regional culture. A broad approach to regional historical and literary studies leads to the questioning of this homogeneous vision.

Chronologically, the Mission building is the oldest, having evolved from a structure begun in the late eighteenth century, during Spanish colonial rule. In a brief timeline, the mission compound peaked in terms of historical architectural development in the mid-1830s, prior to falling into disuse and ruin in the mid-nineteenth century, and was subsequently restored in the second half of that same century. This mission is referred to as a Spanish monument by writers such as Richard Henry Dana[8] and Helen Hunt Jackson,[9] as well as by historians such as William Smythe, author of the earliest canonical work of San Diego history.[10] The Rancho Guajome, built in 1853 by a Hispano-American couple,[11] is a large ranch complex north of urban San Diego, near contemporary Oceanside. This picturesque building has been interpreted as the quintessential rancho, defined as the 'finest existent example in the United States of the traditional Spanish-Mexican one story adobe hacienda' as cited in the literature of the State Park department that governs the site.[12] The 'Old Spanish Lighthouse' was built in 1855, subsequent to the United States' annexation of the area and the perception of the harbour as a necessary hub for international commerce and to facilitate the increasing presence of the US Navy. Thus even a cursory glance reveals historical disparity in the buildings, a disparity which becomes amplified upon closer examination.

Within the scope of this analysis, our principal interest lies in the way in which each of these buildings has been represented in relation to the US–Mexican border, as well as to other borders, as we hope to establish. Beginning with the mission, it is striking to note that despite the chronology it is systematically referred to as a pinnacle of Spanish, rather than Mexican, achievement. While it is true that the deepest roots of the structure lie rather in the eighteenth century than the nineteenth, the building such as it evolved was made possible only by the tallow and hide trade that blossomed beginning in the 1820s with the encouragement of international trade under Mexican rule. In the representation of the structure as Spanish, one must question why the implications of the international border and the period of Mexican governance are omitted in favour of a Spanish association.

The role of cultural and national associations becomes more intriguing when the two other structures are also considered. The dynamic of Mexican referential omission is shared with the Old Spanish Lighthouse, which despite the almost immediate adoption of its appellation after construction in 1855, was clearly neither historically Spanish nor old at the time. Further, despite a superficial resemblance evoked by red tiles and white plaster, in terms of function and construction, the building is the direct result of Anglo-American priorities that share no discernible association with the Spanish colonial policy of semi-isolation for the settlement.

The Rancho Guajome, on the other hand, despite its being contemporary to the lighthouse, is heralded as a key work of Mexican rancho culture even though it was built several years after annexation, in 1853, and by the Couts-Bandini family — from Southern Anglo as well as Hispanic origins. Not only was it built after the signing of the Guadalupe Hidalgo treaty, and thus chronologically situated in the American period of domination, but the structure also reveals elements that are clearly hybrid, revelatory of the mixed origins of the couple.

Fig. 2.1. Rancho Guajome. Image from the author's collection, 2013.

In Fig. 1, elements that are of particular interest to our analysis are apparent, including the extensively framed windows and clapboard siding. In their discussion of the rancho in architectural terms, Iris Engstrand and Thomas Scharf present an excellent synthesis of such architectural details 'incorporated from an American colonial tradition that included a finished fireplace, milled doors and windows of American sash design, continuous house-board sheds and a south orientation to protect from cold winter winds'.[13] More general structural elements that deviate from the local style of adobe constructions include the use of wooden framework into which the adobe blocks are fitted, as well as the organization of living space into a central hall flanked by rooms, a feature common to Southern American architecture.[14] That the builders willingly crossed boundaries concerning cultural architectural standards appears clear; the manner in which these crossings is represented, however, provides a more complicated field of analysis.

In light of these divergent depictions, the question becomes how to understand the differences in representing an architecture that is still largely coherent in the local setting and which appears to present a continuation of the development of a local style that had already long favoured the incorporation of outside elements.[15] Why then, are the structures not simply referred to as 'Californio' architecture? A first line of investigation is in accordance with the temporal sphere. In the first two cases, the buildings were either built, or first studied, in the early American period just subsequent to the US–Mexican War. When the lighthouse was built, the local architectural style was superficially adopted, but the nominal recognition of a recently defeated enemy, whose former citizens were undergoing massive land dispossession at the state level, would have been unacceptable in a socio-political sense. In the construction of a new identity for Anglo-American California, it thus appears to have been advantageous to replace the Mexican nomenclature — or even Californio, as a culture potentially too closely associated with Mexico — with the Spanish designation. This construct allows a Hispanic recognition that is conveniently removed in geographic terms by thousands of miles and in chronological terms by some thirty years.

While this explanation appears to correspond to the case of the lighthouse, it does not concur with the designation of the Rancho Guajome as 'Mexican'. The question may then be asked as to why in certain cases there is an appeal to the Spanish culture and in others to that of Mexican Californian culture when describing contemporary constructions. A partial response lies in the respective projection of certain cultural attributes upon the Spanish and Mexican periods. In need of a common regional identity in order to consolidate the multitude of immigrants from various regions and nations that began arriving in the 1850s, civic leaders quickly realized that sensitivity to a fictionalized and romanticized version of the Spanish colonial past could be an effective tool. Elevated to high culture status in the areas of architecture and religion, the Spanish Dons could be praised from a distance that no contemporary border issue transgressed. In a sense, ignoring both temporal and physical borders in this case allowed a greater unification of the regional population: acknowledging the Hispanic contribution and valorizing its affective characteristics while avoiding the issue of regional territorial annexation from Mexico and the increasingly second-class status of citizens of Mexican heritage. In an urban centre in which the Hispanic Californio population still represented a significant demographic and social force, this abstraction of the border thus allows a coherent and functional, though largely fictionalized, construction to flourish.

Providing an interesting counter-example, the contemporary case of the Rancho Guajome appears to disproportionately valorize the Mexican cultural presence. How exactly does a hybrid American-period rancho built by a mixed-heritage couple (Couts being of Anglo-American extraction and Isabella Bandini-Couts being of Peruvian-Mexican origins)[16] become, via its representation, Mexican? Several reasons appear to account for this variation. The first of these is that the ranch is physically removed from the urban centre, some thirty miles north in an area that remained rural well into the twentieth century. It thus remained largely outside the scope of the main currents of urban civic development. In fact, the ranch came into greater fame only after Helen Hunt Jackson's 1884 novel *Ramona* used it as a setting in which it is indirectly placed, with great literary licence, in Mexican California. The importance of this novel cannot be overstated in the development of the California culture, giving rise to successive waves of Ramona-based tourism which lasted well into the early 1920s. Thus there was an economic imperative associated with the imposition of borders — both chronological and national — upon a structure that was in reality a local hybrid construct. In this case, the Mexican assignation of Rancho Guajome appears to have been facilitated by several factors: that the ranch was popularized only after San Diego developed a civic identity which was no longer directly threatened by the association with Mexico, that the ranch site was isolated enough to pose no real threat to the establishment of a new identity paradigm, by the fact that ranching remained a low-culture domain that did not threaten Anglo-American cultural domination in the region, and by an increasing simplification of the historical past into national factions as the respective national identities of both the United States and Mexico progressively became more consolidated and distinct.

Thus, through the filter of the border which was increasingly formalized and codified, a confrontational approach is increasingly favoured: if it's not 'Anglo' then it must be 'Mexican'. As the outward appearance of the rancho buildings cannot be easily associated with the dominant period trends in mainstream American architecture, it is therefore relegated to the 'other' side of the border. By virtue of a binomial border-based paradigm imposed on the reading of local culture, in spite of the known historic dates and architectural details, the structure is thus transformed into a 'Mexican' architectural artefact just as other period buildings were transformed into 'Spanish' structures. This process of national assignation, of imposing border-related identity constructions onto the regional culture appears to have accelerated as the nineteenth century progressed into the twentieth.

The lasting impact of such an assignation is difficult to assess quantitatively, but an anecdote may provide some insight to the important implications surrounding complex questions of identity and origins. On my most recent visit to the Rancho,[17] I watched as a teacher guided a group of school-age children through the site. At one moment, she paused to reflect on how 'All of this was Mexican, was ours before the Americans came. This is what we lost...' This simple statement can find several levels of interpretation. Of course, on the one hand, this statement is not incorrect: the Rancho Guajome represents the continuation of a strong local culture that underwent great change following the United States' regional annexation. However, this culture under Mexican rule had not yet produced such an architectural or cultural object.[18] That only became possible with the funds from cattle sales to the gold fields that boomed following US annexation, and with the contributions of Cave Couts in terms of culturally influenced design and technology. The structure can definitely be qualified as Californio, but cannot in any accurate way be considered as distinctly Mexican. And yet the affiliation of the speaker, in spite of the fact that she was addressing her audience in English, is clear. She was apparently identifying with a Mexican heritage when using the terms 'ours' and 'we'.

While the process through which both the Mexican and the American national identities grew stronger and better defined throughout the nineteenth and twentieth centuries is complicated and largely outside the scope of this work, the following elements can be highlighted. The War of 1846–48 with its American victory provided not only a new international border, but a relative sense of conqueror and conquered, in which US citizens clearly felt dominant. In the wake of the Mexican Revolution of 1910 to 1927, the Mexican sense of national loss from the 1846–48 conflict was then used as a unifying factor in the creation of a more homogenized national identity from the Mexican point of view, in this case as victims of northern aggression. As immigration to the San Diego border region rose in the late nineteenth and throughout the twentieth century, this developed sense of national loss appears to have been increasing applied to the border region. By the late twentieth century, the polarized view appears to be accordingly divisive, as the loss of the border region is amplified with the perception of its relative worth, via the extensive development that has taken place. Rather than concerning the sparsely populated, semi-autonomous desert region described by Dale Salomon[19] in his biography of Pío Pico — the last Mexican governor of California — the loss of San Diego could be perceived through the filter of more recent demographic and material development.[20] Again, from a base in historical architecture, in order to adequately assess both the object of study and its representations, we are drawn into a cycle of ever-broadening border crossings including identity constructions, relative national histories, and literary representations, just to name a few.

To take this analysis a final step further, one could question the hybrid identity of 'Spanish-Mexican hacienda' that is the current referential term for the Rancho Guajome in the State Park Service documentation. Crossing yet another historical and temporal border, this construction appears to create an agglomeration of Spanish and Mexican heritage, while nomenclaturally removing the Anglo-American connection, though the latter is historically indisputable. This point is of particular interest as it affirms that the borders placed on cultural production and identification are profoundly fluid in nature. Perhaps, as the nature of the Hispanic community in Southern California evolves, a broader definition of local Hispanic culture is deemed more inclusive. Perhaps the border that is projected between the Anglo and Hispanic periods is considered more important than that between the two Hispanic periods of governance. The divisions between cultural history and history are here apparent and divergent.

In each of these cases, both in accordance with and sometimes in spite of the historical record, borders — in multiple senses — are manipulated in order to correspond not to a historical reality but to a perceived social reality. Once in place, these new 'realities' become rooted in canonical local and national culture and are rarely questioned. These constructed representations find themselves subsequently cited as examples, not only in the popular discourse, but in academic texts as well. The elevation of Spanish as opposed to Mexican culture, conveniently appropriated by civic leaders in the 1950s, is subsequently found in William Smythe's *History of San Diego*, a text that continues to serve as a reference for non-specialized historians. Similarly, the appropriation of Mexican lands, which is a tragically real historical event, can be found described in various social histories as being exemplified by the loss of the 'Mexican' Rancho Guajome to the Anglo-Americans — a scenario that is both chronologically and culturally impossible.

If the imposition of an international border on regional culture can be examined through the physical manifestations of architectural production, it is no less apparent in the comparative examination of regional literary constructions. Long considered valuable historical references, the re-examination of literary works provides a complementary if sometimes controversial source of analysis for the reaching impact of borders on the historic Californio community. A brief introduction to the notion of borders in the literary space allows us to complement the analysis of the physical space, as well as to reveal the constant interaction between these two spheres. Several significant works of nineteenth-century regional literature exist, including Richard Henry Dana's *Two Years before the Mast*, Helen Hunt Jackson's *Ramona* and William Heath Davis's *Seventy Five Years in California*.[21] Perhaps the most telling of these works in the context of this analysis is that of Dana — as his *Two Years before the Mast* has become one of the canonical pillars of nineteenth-century American literary studies — noted as both a travel narrative and coming of age tale. This autobiographical work recounts the author's two years working along the California coast during the peak years of the tallow and hide trade and offers detailed descriptions of the cultural and physical spaces in which he moved in period San Diego.

What is of interest in the context of an analysis of crossing borders, however, is not only its depictions of San Diego at the height of its Mexican period development, but also the complexity of the work in identity, linguistic and political terms. Dana's work contains a small but significant quantity of Spanish words and phrases, and a larger implied relationship with the Hispanic Californio culture that largely defined San Diego society in the 1830s.[22] The author discusses at some length his immersion in, and profound love for, the culture of Mexican California and yet the work is systematically categorized in literary study programs as an example of nineteenth-century Anglophone, American literature. Traditional literary studies have downplayed the Spanish language content and homogenized its complex cultural narratives in accordance with a national or nationalist cultural discourse, but if the work were to be re-examined from a linguistic or socio-identity studies positioning, the results might place this work on both a cultural and an identitarian boundary line rather than squarely on one side or another of the border. Rather than accepting the affective associations that the author has with the Spanish language and Hispanic culture, the canonical interpretation reduces them to exotic by-lines in the larger travel narrative. In a reversal of this position, one might suggest that the travel narrative is the by-line to the more important questions of personal discovery and identity construction. This positioning crosses not only disciplinary but also national borders by placing the emphasis on the individual narration. While the dominant language of narration is certainly English and while Dana certainly brings many of his New England biases to the page, one can question whether the work is exclusively that of an Anglophone Yankee, or whether more subtle linguistic and national identities are being revealed in the work. One can also question, in light of the work's widespread distribution and influence, whether the imposition of the national and cultural border has a role in this interpretation. Such a line of analysis can be drawn in parallel to the reassessment of the architectural identity of the Rancho Guajome in which the dominant interpretation of the work, aligned with an oppositional national construction, is questioned in a local context.

Three aspects of Dana's use of Spanish language are worth analysing. The first of these is that he uses Spanish in his narrative, both explicitly and implicitly. The second is that the use of Spanish evolves in the work. And the third, which is perhaps key in the analysis of how borders are imposed upon the representation of this work in the literary canon, the language use represented in Dana's interactions in Mexican California reverses in the printed narrative what was the linguistic reality of the original, oral situational context of his voyage. In a Spanish-dominant society Dana was obliged, as he states in his text, to conform to the dominant linguistic structure within the limits of his capacities. In his subsequent representation of this interaction, however, the dynamics of code-switching are completely reversed.

That Spanish is present in the narrative is indisputable. In Chapter 16, for example, Dana uses Spanish language terms both to evoke the exotic and to describe elements that simply did not exist in his native English cultural context. These range from the 'pulperías', or general stores, where he shops to the 'gente de razón' with whom the better classes associate.[23] While superficially, the inclusion of Spanish appears to reinforce the 'otherness' of his Hispanic counterparts, a more complex linguistic identity may be identified if one considers the extent of Spanish used or evoked. In using two languages, Dana appears as both a participant in and a critical observer of this culture, whose narrative language itself appears to be torn between these roles. While he expresses a tremendous admiration for certain aspects of Hispanic Californian culture, he also renders explicit that the region's inhabitants are of a somewhat inferior constitution when compared to those of his native Northeast.

While a full analysis of the author's language use is beyond the scope of this investigation, it is notable that, in the earlier stages of the work, the author stresses the occurrence of Spanish conversation either through the use of italicized Spanish words or by the explicit mention that Spanish is being used. This usage occurs in a context in which the author also refers to the Californios he encounters as 'lazy fellows' who respond all too frequently to his queries with a shrug of the shoulders and a 'Quién sabe?'[24] Yet, this usage, which could be dismissed as simple exoticism, is not without particular interest: firstly, because it reveals that the author was in fact conversant in Spanish and had thus already crossed a certain linguistic and cultural frontier and, secondly, because his linguistic identity appears to evolve throughout the narrative. While the episodes revealing this change are few in number, they are significant. By the time that Richard Henry Dana meets Don Juan Bandini — a San Diegan returning from Mexico — in 1836, he not only fails to draw attention to a language distinction through the use of italics as a visual marker, but he also describes both the person and language of Juan Bandini in almost glowing terms. The following phrase is indicative of this passage.

> He had a slight and elegant figure, moved gracefully, danced and waltzed beautifully, spoke good Castilian, with a pleasant and refined voice and accent and had, throughout, the bearing of a man of good birth and figure.[25]

Several aspects of this short description bear mention. First of all, the person of Juan Bandini is described in positive terms, including an allusion to high-cultural characteristics such as waltzing. Then, through a combination of allusions to a Spanish past and language, he is elevated above the derogatory perception of Mexicans that many in the United States shared in the mid-nineteenth century. And finally, in a linguistic element which might easily go unnoticed, the author feels himself comfortable enough with his own Spanish skills to assess those of his interlocutor. This last point perhaps indicates that, beyond a simple liking taken to a single person met in his voyages, the author was undergoing a cultural and linguistic transformation himself — viewing Californios with a diminished national and linguistic filter as opposed to that presented only a year before upon his arrival in California.

The transmission of this change upon the printed page consists of at least two principal factors involving borders, both dependent upon the dominant socio-linguistic patterns of Dana's native region. Upon the author's return to a largely mono-lingual Northeast, Dana reverts to an almost mono-lingual identity within a collectively English-dominant cultural context.[26] This change, a sort of self-imposed linguistic border, is reinforced by the author's desire to publish his manuscript in the context of a national culture which, though far from monolingual, was both English-dominant and only just coming into substantial contact with the Hispanic Southwest.[27] Dana, as well as his publisher, must have been concerned with the issue of the readership's acceptance of foreign language elements and non-standard cultural identifications. Therefore, the audience's reaction to the text — both as it existed and as it was planned for in the publication phase — must be taken into account in our analysis. This narrative modification, imposing borders upon language use in accordance with what Myriam Suchet refers to as a *seuil de lisibilité* or 'readability threshold'.[28] Simply put, in order to meet the expectations of his intended audience, Dana had to balance the linguistic realities of his time in California with those, even if only assumed, of his public. He apparently does so by limiting the quantity of Spanish used, and by clearly identifying it by the use of italics. Within this construct, a reader largely unfamiliar with the Spanish language automatically experiences the perception of Spanish speakers as a linguistic and, by extension, national 'other' each time italics appear on the printed page. This construction is reinforced by the conveniently provided, non-italicized English translations which allow the reader to remain in a largely monolingual zone. Again, what appears in this process of transmission is the imposition of borders or at the very least their enhancement in comparison to the reality that the author apparently experienced while in San Diego.

A thorough investigation of the writing and editing process of *Two Years before the Mast* would require not only a literary analysis of the text itself, but a historical analysis of the period publishing industry as well as cultural studies and sociological insights into the real and imagined demographics, educational profile, linguistic characteristics, expectations and purchasing trends of Richard Henry Dana's target audience, all within the socio-historical context. Such an endeavour, while requiring consequential resources and expandable to include other works,[29] could offer a greater opportunity for understanding the complex representation of cultural interaction which are currently potentially oversimplified. One could plausibly question whether such an exploration is justified. In the specific context of San Diego studies, it is arguable that it is. In a region whose population has expanded remarkably in the past century, and whose growth is overwhelmingly based on immigration, the manner in which local culture was and is perceived by those immigrants prior to their arrival cannot but have affected their expectations and behaviours upon arrival. Understanding how this process affects the cultural landscape of San Diego, the seventh largest city in the United States, and the broader American culture at large, may be worth such an effort.

The brief presentation of just a few elements in the representations of Californio culture serves as an entry point to the subject of the multiplicity of borders in the study of this region. If the literary and architectural cultural representations produced over just a few decades inspire new, transdisciplinary analysis, the scope of material to be examined anew and with what methodology to proceed remains to be established. While the dominant border — that between the United States and Mexico — is prevalent in each of these examples, it is certainly not the only boundary. And even this element is not treated in a consistent manner, varying between disciplines as well as over temporal and physical space. Mechanisms of imposition of the notional and physical border appear to colour the representations of this culture, as do mechanisms of omission, which vary in response to the perceived needs of multiple levels of cultural generation and consumption.

When addressing the issues that arise in the study of identity in San Diego, one partial explanation for the multiple, and often conflicting, use of borders, can be found in the sheer size of the subject at hand. Over two centuries of post-colonial interaction, involving three periods of national domination leading not only to the seventh largest urban area in the United States but also the most crossed international border in the world have led to the congruence of multiple realities. Such a large city and clash of cultures cannot be overly simplified in a satisfactory manner. San Diego studies comprise both border and borderland studies, rendering both continuing Californio heritage and multiple imported, or locally fabricated, identities and cultural characteristics. Just as the national boundaries have proved flexible, those related to projected identity, individual or collective, also reveal patterns of flux. What appears to remain constant, however, is the relative use of the various borders, through inclusion or exclusion in a dominant discourse, as identifiers and tools within a given paradigm.

Within the wider subject of analysis, the borders between disciples of study are also often tangible, almost as much so as the physical barriers that are imposed between nations. And these divisions have great implications in terms of methodologies, sources, and interpretations, but also in terms of acceptance of extra-disciplinary analysis. This rift pertains to specific studies, for example the divergence of literary analysis of Richard Henry Dana, Jr.'s work, from that which would be found in a linguistic or sociological examination of the same pages. Whereas the former retains the now canonical view of Spanish in the text as a mere form of exotic evocation, the latter would certainly see evidence of both a level of personal bilingualism and of a hybridization of language evocative of exchange and more complex identity constructions on both the personal and community levels.

Similarly the use of physical references in cultural analysis could take into greater consideration specific historical realities, often themselves under constant re-evaluation as new documentary or analytical evidence comes to light. Current re-evaluation of the role of African-American pioneers such as Nate Harrison through extensive archaeological study of his homestead site is an example of a way in which new material may challenge longstanding views of local history.[30] At what point does the physical reality of a site rich in artefacts depicting a relatively high material standard of living and complex trade associations with neighbouring communities intersect with that of an isolated and economically excluded settler of minority origins? Another physical area is that of architecture, in which the dismissal of Cliff May's Hispanic revival style as a simple parody of a long-vanished Californio cultural production may be questioned in light of the architect's own Californio roots and personal history. The issues at stake are complex and partially contextually inspired in a region whose demographic and cultural evolution continues at a rapid pace. Is the voice and vision of a regional architect less influential than that of a critic issuing from a more dominant Anglo-American cultural construct? And by what objective criteria can a structure such as the Rancho Guajome with its hybrid conception and construction be considered an authentic cultural product whereas later works professing a similar cross-cultural conception be critically reduced to caricature? Knowing that neither architectural example technically dates from the Mexican or even the broader historical Hispanic period of domination, their assessment and appropriation appear to be part of an identity construction narrative that actively plays on inclusion and exclusion. In a period of demographic transition, does the Rancho Guajome as symbol of Mexican loss also become a symbol of Mexican reappropriation, despite the relative incongruence of such a term with the realities of the structure? These examples, along with those developed earlier in this chapter, show the extent of the influence of both disciplinary and national boundaries on the very conception of cultural production and study.

Without constant cross-referencing, the dominant discourses in differing fields using different methodologies and references risk becoming increasingly divergent and potentially inaccurate. Determining the local Californio legacy in this context becomes a daunting task indeed whose scale, despite a reduced physical setting, is vast. Despite the challenges, however, the willingness to undertake this collective analysis appears to be growing in correlation to Mario Barrera's vision of reassessment or the concept of a necessary transdisciplinary complexification of California studies developed by Terry Jones and Kathryn Klar.[31] Crossing the borders that are made apparent in comparative border studies, or at least adopting a new awareness of their existence and roles, is a journey that allows a greater convergence of the multiple, sometimes conflicting or competing, realities that appear through academic and broader cultural representations.

Notes to Chapter 2

1. Richard Henry Dana, Jr., *Two Years before the Mast* (New York: Signet, 1964).
2. According to the US Census, which takes its information from the following: U.S.–Canada lengths: International Boundary Commission, 2003; U.S.–Mexico lengths: U.S. Geological Survey; and The National Atlas of the United States, 1976, Borders, <http://nationalatlas.gov/articles/mapping/a_general.html>.
3. The Spanish name of the Mexican state Baja California implies another interesting border: that between Alta California, now become the State of California in the United States and Baja California. Despite the international boundary, the maintenance of the terms Baja or 'lower' implies continuity with its correspondent to the north, thus transgressing this frontier.
4. The boundary itself was marked by a stele erected in 1851 following an official survey of the line imposed by the Treaty of Guadalupe Hidalgo; see Charles Hughes, 'La Monjonera and the Markings of California's U.S.–Mexican Boundary Line, 1849–1851', *The Journal of San Diego History*, 51.3 (2005), 126–47. The slow growth of the official passage point between the two nations is described in greater detail by the department of Chicano Studies of San Diego State University in their Mexican and Chicano History: See San Diego State University Department of Chicano Studies, Chapter 6.6.
5. Spanish settlement in San Diego started in the year 1769 and continued to 1821, when the Mexican state officially raised its flag at the presidio during a ceremony that does not appear to have generated much local interest (see William E. Smythe, *History of San Diego: An Account of the Rise and Progress of the Pioneer Settlement on the Pacific Coast of the United States*, vol. 1 (San Diego: History Co., 1908), p. 114). Mexican governance continued de facto until the United States' military occupation in 1846 and annexation in 1848.
6. Jacques Derrida clearly states his view of architecture as an 'art of representation' in cultural terms — see interview with Jacques Derrida, 'Architecture Where The Desire May Live', in *Rethinking Architecture: A Reader in Cultural Theory*, ed. by Neil Leach (London and New York, Routledge, 1997), pp. 317–23 (p. 319). Baydar Gülsüm discusses the cultural importance of architectural symbols in a post-colonial cultural identifier in his article 'The Cultural Burden of Architecture', *The Journal of Architecture*, 57.4 (2004), 19–27.
7. While the Treaty of Guadalupe Hidalgo was signed in 1848 after the two-year Mexican-American War, it is important to note that transitions — whether governmental or cultural — were not immediate affairs. Just as the development of a Mexican national identity subsequent to independence from Spain in 1821 took time, so did the domination of Anglo-American culture.
8. Dana, pp. 110, 112.
9. Helen Hunt Jackson, *Ramona* (New York: Avon, 1970), pp. 223–23.
10. Smythe, *History of San Diego*, pp. 71–76. Smythe describes various aspects of the Mission's past throughout both the Mexican and Spanish periods, but reserves his positive assessment for the years under Spanish control.
11. Cave J. Couts and Isabella Bandini were of Anglo-American and Peruvian-Mexican heritage, respectively. Couts immigrated to California as part of his military service and quickly integrated the local Californio community, marrying with Isabella in 1851.
12. United States Department of the Interior, National Parks Service, National Survey of Historic Sites and Buildings, 'Statements of Significance', 9 February 1967.
13. Ingrid Engstrand and Thomas Scharf, 'Rancho Guajome: An Architectural Legacy Preserved', *The Journal of San Diego History*, 20.1 (Winter 1974), p. 260. Online at <http://www.sandiegohistory.org/journal/1974/january/guajome/>.
14. Carole Rifkind describes this regional association in her *Field Guide to American Architecture*. See Carole Rifkind, *A Field Guide to American Architecture* (New York: Plume, 2004), pp. 3–4.
15. A broader history of hybrid architecture is outside the scope of this work, but it appears clear that from the earliest phases of private architectural development, influences from outside of the Spanish colonial realm are to be found. Examples include construction details in the Casa de Bandini and the Casa de Estudillo in Old Town, San Diego. For a synthesis of the role of

hybrid architecture in the San Diego landscape, see Jeffrey Swartwood, *Contested Territories: Mixed Identity Constructs and Hybrid Culture in San Diego, California (1770–1920)* (Pessac: Maison de Sciences de l'Homme d'Aquitaine, 2014), pp. 171–75.
16. Juan Bandini was a Peruvian immigrant to Mexican San Diego who quickly established himself among the local, Californio elite. His case is of interest in that, participating in maritime commerce and other commercial activities, he favoured annexation. After the 1850s, however, his initial view was increasingly questioned.
17. Visit in April 2012.
18. This is especially true considering that the rancho, as it currently exists, reveals signs of an extensive renovation in the 1920s that included many elements not originally included in the buildings — including wooden siding and a large wooden sewing room in an early twentieth-century Anglo-American style.
19. Carlos Salomon, *Pío Pico: The Last Governor of Mexican California* (Norman: University of Oklahoma Press, 2010. The author provides not only an insightful view of the life of Pío Pico, but also a substantial development of the context particular to California within the broader scope of Mexican national development and United States expansion.
20. Salomon, pp. 22–44, pp. 68–92.
21. William Heath Davis, *Seventy-Five Years in California* (San Francisco: John Howell, 1967). The author offers an interesting point of view, that of a doubly nationalized Californio — immigrating to Mexican California in 1831 and adopting Mexican citizenship, prior to reassuming US citizenship following annexation in 1848. His sympathy for the Mexican and Californio cultures are made quite clear.
22. Another San Diego community that Dana devoted a great deal of consideration to was that of the Hawaiians, who were present in great numbers. While often left out of modern studies of the local culture, the Sandwich Islanders were present in significant numbers in mid-nineteenth-century San Diego and played a role in the complex dynamics of development (Dana, *Two Years*, pp. 135, 137–43).
23. Dana, *Two Years*, pp. 110, 112.
24. '*Quién sabe*' can be literally translated as 'who knows'. Dana, *Two Years*, pp. 111, 115
25. Ibid., p. 223.
26. An interesting comparison could be made with the writing in Dana's journal, which has unfortunately not survived. As such, one must be contented at present with the author's assertion that 'nothing is given there that I did not strictly believe to be true'; see Richard Henry Dana, *An Autobiographical Sketch (1815–1842)* (Hamden, CT: Shoe String Press, 1842), p. 65.
27. The 1830s witnessed, notably, the increase of Anglo immigration into Texas and the subsequent revolution and independence of that State. This was part of a greater collective and individual westward and southern expansionist movement that continued throughout the mid-nineteenth century.
28. Miriam Suchet, *Textes hétérolingues et textes traduits: de 'la langue' aux figures de l'énonciation. Pour une littérature comparée différentielle* (Montréal: Université Concordia, 2010). In her thesis, the author describes the conditions necessary for reception as well as their effects upon transmission in a narrative.
29. Two other texts mentioned in this work, Helen Hunt Jackson's *Ramona* and William Heath Davis's *Seventy Five Years in California*, alongside such regional classics as Maria Amparo Ruiz de Burton's *The Squatter and the Don* are each susceptible to analysis along the lines established here. Each narrative provides not only a representation of the San Diego Californio culture as it developed, but also insight into how that culture was perceived and how this perception subsequently influenced later development, especially in regards to how local culture is influenced by the imposition of the international border.
30. See excavation notes from Dr Seth Mallios regarding the ongoing excavations at the Harrison homestead site. Seth Mallios, et al., *Archaeological Excavations at the Nate Harrison Site in San Diego, California: Archaeological Field Report* (San Diego, CA: San Diego State University, 2005).
31. Mario Barrera encourages the constant re-evaluation of historical notions, especially in regards to cultural and historical constructs on the border. Mario Barrera, *Race and Class in the Southwest:*

A Theory of Inequity (Notre Dame, IN: University of Notre Dame Press, 1979), pp. 3–4. See also Michael J. Morratto and Joseph L. Chartkoff, 'Archaeological Progress since 1984', in *California Prehistory: Colonization, Culture and Complexity*, ed. by Terry L. Jones and Kathryn A. Klar (Lanham, MD: AltaMira Press, 2010), pp. 1–9.

CHAPTER 3

Body and Empire: Space and Borders in Second-Century Greek-Roman Culture

Catherine Darbo-Peschanski

During the reign of the Antonine and Severan dynasties, from Hadrian (117–138) in the second century AD to Caracalla (198–218) in the third, the Roman Empire is at its widest. It extends from North Africa to Mesopotamia (modern-day Iraq, Kuwait, the northern section of Syria, parts of South-eastern Turkey and South-western Iran); from Britannia (modern-day Great Britain) to Egypt; from the Atlantic coast to the Danube, reaching a surface area around 5 million square kilometres. One of the most prominent ancient physicians, Galen (129–216 AD), was living in that time.

This paper aims to show how the organizational principles of the body/soul entity in the works of Galen, on the one hand, and the geographical, historical and political organizational principles that preceded him but remained significant in his time, on the other hand, partake in the same 'discourse' of time and space distribution.[1] I refer here to the meaning Michel Foucault gives the term 'discourse'. In Foucault's *Archaeology of Knowledge*,[2] a 'discourse', and the 'statements' (*énoncés*) of which the 'discourse' comprises, no longer have a linguistic sense. Rather, they name the rules that render meaningful every expression, just as much discursive as practical. In this respect, a 'statement', and even more so a 'discourse', cannot be found directly and explicitly in any particular discursive or practical expressions.

From Foucault follows an important implication: with regard to Galen's conceptions of the human body, on the one hand, and the socio-political organization of Roman Empire's borders, on the other, it is important to note that these two components do not serve as a metaphor for the other. Rather, they participate in the same 'discourse', along with many others 'statements' that would be interesting to list and analyse elsewhere, but exceed the scope of my examination.

I suggest that we are dealing with a 'discourse' which could be termed *discourse of assimilation by contact*. According to this relationship, the borders, whatever they are and whatever field they belong to, refer to dynamic rather than static and steady divisions. It is the contact between two elements, as determined by their limit, that proves dynamic and transformative. Thus the outline of something just needs to touch something else for the two original elements to transform themselves into parts of an ever more inclusive whole. Therefore, the inside parts of the whole tend to exhaust the space outside; this extension goes as far as there is nothing left to join or just nothing at all, in other words, emptiness.

I. The Geometric Paradigm

In Galen's time, the body/soul, geographical and political spaces, as well as historical time, are seen as geometric or as geometrically featured.

Galen's geometric bodily parts

In Galen's view, a living body is a solid. It has a surface: the skin, sometimes considered as an *ultimate* surface, *eschatê epiphaneia* — namely the surface which directly encounters the outside — and is bounded by an outline, *perigraphê*. This solid also includes parts, and the criterion for being a part consists not only of having a proper outline but also of being connected (*synaptein*) to another neighbouring part at one or several points. Conversely, the criterion for being 'one' or 'single' (*hen*) is to have no contact point at all with another body:

> Just as every animal is said to be one (*hen*) because, having a certain individual circumscription (*perigraphên idian echon*), it is manifestly not joined to (*synaptein*) another animal at any point, so also its parts, the eye, nose, tongue or encephalon, are said each to be one, because each clearly has circumscription of its own. But if it were not joined to the neighbouring parts at some point, but were altogether separate, then it would not be a part at all, but simply one. Therefore, all bodies that do not have their own circumscription at every point and are not everywhere joined to others are called parts. And if this is true, animals will have many parts, some large, some small and some also not divisible at all into another form. The usefulness of all of them is related to the soul.[3]

Not surprisingly, in that geometrical conception, each part has a *geometrical* figure (*schêma*). The stomach, for instance, is both rounded (*peripherês*) and elongated (*promêkês*). Its roundness is explained in these terms:

> Among the *geometrical* figures and with an equivalent perimeter (*isên tên perimetron*), the circle (*ho kyklos*) is the less vulnerable (*dyspathestaton*) and, among the solids, the sphere has the largest capacity for storage.[4]

So Nature's foresight has provided the body with the most useful instruments and their usefulness refers to their specific function in a body, which looks like a place, isolated when seen as a whole from the outside, and divided into more or less connected parts inside.

By contrast, in Western contemporary physiology, the human living body originates in the multiplication and functional differentiation of cells that are the common basis of every tissue, organ and system of organs. The contemporary view of the internal interconnectedness of all material parts contrasts with the mosaic of connected individual pieces of which the Galean body is made.

Between geometry and topography

Geometry, of both planes and solids, was perfectly developed in Galen's time and he was likely aware of it, particularly the Euclidean tradition that still provides his basic definitions.[5] Interestingly, Euclid's *Elements* and Galen's discourse on the parts resort to some common vocabulary. However, it is important to underscore that Euclid's mathematical treatise defines figures and solids in ambiguous terms, as both geometrical and topographical.

A *surface* (*epiphaneia*) is that which has length and breadth only (I. def. 4).

The *edges* (*perata*) of a surface are lines (I. def. 5).

A *boundary* (*horos*) is that which is an extremity of anything (I. def. 13).

A *figure* (*schêma*) is that which is contained (*periechomenon*) by any boundary or boundaries (I. def. 14)

A *circle* is a plane figure contained (*periechomenon*) by one line such that all the straight lines falling upon it from one point among those lying within the figure equal one another.

A *solid* (*stereon*) is that which has length, breadth, and depth (IX. def.1)

A face of a solid is a surface (*epiphaneia*) (IX. Def. 2)

When a semicircle with fixed diameter is carried round and restored again to the same position from which it began to be moved, the figure so comprehended is a *sphere* (*sphaira*) (IX. 14).

The *axis of the sphere* is the straight line which remains fixed and about which the semicircle is turned (IX. Def. 15).[6]

Indeed, Bernard Vitrac,[7] a French editor and commentator of the *Elements*, in his writing on the aforementioned *horos* ('boundary'), reminds us that, according to Proclus, the word goes back to the time when estate boundaries were set up again and therefore means a specific kind of limit, one that refers to areas. In the same way, modern commentators stress the vagueness of words such as 'limit' (*peras*) and 'encompassed in' (*periechomenos*): they make Euclid's definitions mathematically 'nebulous' but nevertheless introduce topographical overtones to geometrical definitions[8].

Scholars like Bernard Vitrac and David Joyce also note that in Euclidian and post-Euclidean geometry, the concept of 'figure' (*schêma*) applies both to plane figures and to solids (e.g., the circle and the sphere[9]), and that 'in order to be a figure (*schêma*) a region must be bounded, that is, held by a boundary'[10]. On this point, Euclidean geometry differs from plane modern geometry in that the latter does not include the notion of a boundary in the definition of what contains a figure, while modern topology continues to use this word only in relation to solids.[11]

Moreover, the Euclidean principle 'nowhere does a non-connected figure occur' fits with Galen's idea of each part of the body as connected to another in some point of its perimeter.[12] Actually disconnected figures (*schêmata*) occur only in modern topology.[13] As Joyce says in the following topological example:

> Given a circle and a line that does not intersect that plane, when that circle is rotated around the line in space, a solid results called a torus. The intersection of that torus with the original plane is the figure that consists of the original circle and another on the other side of the line. Considered as a single figure it is disconnected. In the *Elements* it would be called two figures.[14]

According to Euclid and probably Galen as well, a plane and a space can be geometrically featured through the same notion of figure which relates to that of a territorial boundary and, just like geometrical figures and solids (*schêmata*), parts in a body (*schemata* also) are never disconnected.

Geographical space

Second century geography divides the world space in the same way: the inhabited area as a whole and its individual parts. When it deals with particular regions (*chôrai*), it takes the name of chorography. Furthermore, it surrounds inhabited land with deserts, unknown areas, or the ocean. At the same time, as Galen does for the body, Claudius Ptolemy (90–168 AD) renews geography by applying his mathematical knowledge.[15] Actually he sets up a system of coordinates of each place, spanned all over his inhabited world maps. He also summarizes his predecessors' works and clearly partakes in their global representation. In the first lines of his *Geography*, he writes:

> World geography is an imitation (*mimêsis*) through drawing of the entire occupied part of the world together with things that are, broadly speaking, connected (*synaptein*) with it. It differs from regional geography in that regional geography cuts particular places out and sets them out apart and by themselves, registering together (*synapographomenê*) practically everything down to the least things therein (for example, harbours, towns, districts, branches of principal rivers, and so on) while the essence of the world geography is to show the known world as a single (*hen*) and continuous (*synechês*) entity, its nature and how it is situated [taking account] only of the things that are in contact with it in its broader general outlines (*perigraphai*) (such as gulfs, great cities, the more notable peoples and rivers, the more noteworthy things of each kind.[16]

Undoubtedly Ptolemy is just drawing (*graphein*) the inhabited world and one could rise the objection that, by dividing geography into world geography and chorography, he is proposing either a holistic or a partial point of view for the one drawing. In fact, his drawing claims to be an imitation (*mimêsis*), meaning a realistic representation of the world (following its usage in Greek and Roman antiquity, at least from Plato to Philostratus).

In the physical world, the inhabited area seems to be the same as Galen's body (or conversely): firstly, it looks 'single' or 'one' (*hen*); secondly, connected (*synaptein*) parts occupy its inside space, making it *synechês*, namely making parts join one another in a kind of *continuum*; finally, perimeters (*perigraphai*) surround it (here the plural refers to several outlines that enclose it from one end to the other). On the outside stretch deserts, then the ocean as the ultimate and unsurpassable limit, surrounding the earth.

As Ptolemy says in Book VII of his *Geography*, in the East, in the West, in the North and in the South alike stretch 'unknown' regions, that is regions about which nobody can know anything, because they belong to torrid or glacial areas that nobody can inhabit or visit. In the West and in the North, beyond the unknown regions, the ocean occupies space.

Such a representation comes from a long-standing tradition. In the first century AD, Strabo, for instance, made the world an actual island:

> Perception and experience alike inform us, that the earth we inhabit is an island: since wherever men have approached the termination of the land, the sea, which we designate ocean, has been met with: and reason assures us of the similarity of those places which our senses have not been permitted to survey. For in the east the land occupied by the Indians, and in the west by the Iberians and Maurusians, is wholly encompassed [by water], and so is the greater part on the south and north. And as to what remains as yet unexplored by us, because navigators, sailing from opposite points, have not hitherto fallen in with each other, it is not much, as any one may see who will compare the distances between those places with which we are already acquainted. Nor is it likely that the Atlantic Ocean is divided into two seas by narrow isthmuses so placed as to prevent circumnavigation: how much more probable that it is confluent and uninterrupted! Those who have returned from an attempt to circumnavigate the earth, do not say they have been prevented from continuing their voyage by any opposing continent, for the sea remained perfectly open, but through want of resolution, and the scarcity of provision.[17]

Moreover, the way he pictures the world in regions calls for geometrical description. When Strabo criticizes Eratosthenes, a previous geographer of the third century BC, for cutting territories into portions rather than defining them by rivers, mountains, sea, and, where possible, by nations, he does not deny that territories have 'a natural outline and are distinguished by a regular form', and he states:

> a simple and general description may be said always to answer the purpose. In regard to size, it is sufficient to state the greatest length and breadth; for example, that the habitable earth is 70,000 stadia long, and that its breadth is scarcely half its length. And as to form, to compare a country to any geometrical or other well-known figure, for example, Sicily to a triangle, Spain to an ox-hide, or the Peloponnesus to a plane-leaf. The larger the territory to be divided is, the more general also ought its divisions to be.[18]

Finally, whether he acts as a geographer or as a chorographer, Strabo pictures the world inside the outline of the ocean as composed of contiguous regions (*synaptontes*, *synecheis*) that he crosses over, either in reality, on a map or through geometrical deduction.

Two centuries before, and for the first time, the historian Polybius, relying on the Aristotelian opposition between the general and the particular (*katholou/kath' hekastou*), divides historical events into those arising in some particular regions of the world and those interweaving *almost* all of its parts. He says 'almost' because he still grants that Rome, which has carried out the interweaving through its conquests, may expand even further.[19] For now it is enough to notice that Polybius mingles geographical spaces with historical events to show the emergence of a single (*hen*) historical movement in an almost single world, the parts of which now become interconnected:

> For what gives my work its peculiar quality, and what is most remarkable in the present age, is this. Fortune has guided almost all the affairs (*schedon hapanta ta tês oikoumenês pragmata*) of the world <u>in one direction</u> (*pros hen ekline meros*) and has forced them to incline towards <u>one and the same end</u> (*kai panta neuein enagkase pros hena kai to auton*); a historian should likewise bring before his readers <u>under one synoptical view</u> (*hupò mian synopsin*) the operations by which she has accomplished her general purpose. [...] As it is, I observe that while several modern writers deal with particular wars (*tous kata meros polemous*) and certain matters connected with them, no one, as far as I am aware, has even attempted to inquire critically when and whence the general and comprehensive scheme of events (*tên de katholou kai sullêbdên oikonomian*) originated and how it is led up to the end.[20]

Now, not surprisingly, these three authors picture the object of their research as a body. In Ptolemy's view, chorography is a partial *mimesis*, like the drawing of just one part of a head in a portrait, whereas world geography is a general *mimesis*, the drawing of the whole. In its ultimate role, chorography holds the key to describing just one part of the above mentioned whole as if one represented just the ear or the eye alone. But cartography is the viewing of the whole, the analogy being that it is concerned with showing the whole head.[21]

Strabo, for his part, wants the world to be *dissected limb by limb*, in resemblance to natural and regular shapes of the bodily parts, but Polybius asserts that making regional history without taking into account the whole globalized world is like stripping a body of life by dissecting it:

> There, however, are some instances in which one may justly accuse Eratosthenes, Strabo says. There is a difference in dissecting *limb by limb*, or merely cutting off *portions* [indiscriminately], (for in the former you may only separate parts having a natural outline, and distinguished by a regular form; this the poet alludes to in the expression, 'Cutting them limb from limb' (*Odyssey* ix. 291; *Iliad* xxiv. 409) whereas in regard to the latter this is not the case,) and we may adopt with propriety either one or other of these plans according to the time and necessity. So in Geography, if you enter into every detail, you may sometimes be compelled to divide your territories into *portions*, so to speak, but it is a more preferable way to separate them into limbs, than into such chance pieces; for thus only you can define accurately particular *points and boundaries*, a thing so necessary to the geographer.[22]

As for Polybius, he states:

> It has always seemed to me that men, who are persuaded that they get a competent view of universal from episodical history, are very like persons who should see the limbs of some body, which had once been living and beautiful, scattered and remote; and should imagine that to be quite as good as actually beholding the activity and beauty of the living creature itself. But if some one could there and then reconstruct the animal once more, in the perfection of its beauty and the charm of its vitality, and could display it to the same people, they

would beyond doubt confess that they had been far from conceiving the truth, and had been little better than dreamers. For indeed some idea of a whole may be got from a part, but an accurate knowledge and clear comprehension cannot. Wherefore we must conclude that episodical history contributes exceedingly little to the familiar knowledge and secure grasp of universal history. While it is only by the combination and comparison of the separate parts of the whole, — by observing their likeness and their difference, — that a man can attain his object: can obtain a view at once clear and complete; and thus secure both the profit and the delight of History.[23]

II. The Roman Empire

The whole and the parts

Following these remarks about bodily, geographical and historical space, a last point in our preliminary approach to the 'discourse' of assimilation by contact, regards the administrative and political organization of the Roman Empire roughly since Augustus, that is, the first century BC down to our period (the second century AD) and beyond.

All Roman Emperors, at least up to the second century AD, claimed to extend the territory of the empire as far as the ultimate borders. Indeed, the idea of extending the Roman imperium 'to the ends of the earth' (*ultimos terrarum fines*) and the ideology of an empire without limits (*imperium sine fine*) became common in the second century BC, while being the standard characteristic of the ideal emperor.[24] The aim was to fully cover the inhabited world surface. There were, of course, pauses in the process.[25] A 'grand map'[26] was worked out through a systematic world cartography. C. W. Whittaker convincingly holds that maps, starting from Agrippa's, 'connected to the project initiated by Caesar and completed by Augustus, whereby distinguished geographers were sent out to bring back their findings from various parts of the world'.[27] 'But according to *Cosmographia* of Julius Honorius,' C. W. Whittaker continues, 'these scholars apparently occupied themselves with collecting not cosmic projections but *local topographic details*'.[28] In other words, in those partial itineraries, the aim of indicating key towns and distance between places, and stressing upon the relation between centre and periphery with a propagandistic purpose, were prevalent. That fact seems to indicate that the aim of expansion does not primary impel the cartography work. Neither cosmographic maps, where the inhabited land is surrounded by deserts and the ocean, nor local itineraries seem to have included survey maps to help expansion. Moreover, cartographic and chorographic sources do not include any provisional frontiers for military plans to change at any time.

In general maps the territory appears divided into joined provinces, the number of which grew through new conquests. Such maps helped to know the Empire in greater detail but also to enhance control over peoples.[29] Imperial and senatorial powers function as centres of the system, just like, in Galen's idea, nature functions as the artificer (*demiurgos*) of the form and disposition in the self-reproducing process of body and soul, and just like the soul benefits from the activities of the various parts of the body, surrounded by the ultimate surface of the skin.[30]

In the period under investigation, bodily as well as geographical, historical, administrative, and political spaces turn out to be, on the one hand, limited by an ultimate perimeter, that interrupts contact with anything else (the empty or unreachable stretches outside) and, on the other, saturated with interconnected geometrical parts.

Dynamism

This model is not as static as it may first appear. Let us come back to Galen.

Galen's conception of the bodily organization *logically* entails movement. In theory, indeed, any single body would only need one contact with another one *to become* a part. Of course, an individual human body does not actually lose its closure when it joins another. In that case, the whole of humanity would be destined to gradually become only one single enormous body. But this relativistic principle proves essential if one considers more closely the relationship with the outside from the inside of the body.

Nature has provided human beings with three main and closely linked faculties (*dynameis*), as causes of genesis, growth and nutrition of the body: the alteration faculty (*alloiôtikê dynamis*), the attraction faculty (*helktikê dynamis*), and the excretion faculty (*ekkritikê dynamis*). As for nutrition, Galen often recalls the principle according to which every part of the body is able *to attract* the juices that the stomach provides by cooking the ingested food, *to convert* some of them into its own flesh and *to get rid* of the others as superfluous.[31] Such is the functioning of nutrition and excretion that, as well as respiration in another way, needs the body to be open to the outside. In this context, Galen is also ready to agree with the Hippocratic thesis according to which the skin's ultimate surface may also allow access to the inside of the body. Thus, if the stomach can pull out the superfluous by vomiting, it is not surprising that: 'something should be transferred from the extreme skin surface and so reach the intestine and the stomach'.[32] But, in the event of some kind of stress, such as excessive cold, the skin gives access to the hurting agent. As a consequence, it disrupts the regular nutrition-excretion functioning of the parts:

> It is therefore neither unlikely nor impossible that, when the part adjoining the skin becomes suddenly oppressed by an unwonted cold, it should at once be weakened and should find that the juice previously deposited beside it without discomfort had now become more of a burden than a source of nutrition and should therefore strive to put it away. Finally, seeing that the passage outwards was shut off by the condensation, it would turn to the remaining exit and would thus forcibly expel all the wasted matter at once into the adjacent part; this would be the same to the part following it; and the process would not cease until the transference finally terminated at the inner ends of the vein (that is, I add, the juice returns towards its original source).[33]

Then the body can neither extend itself by annexing new parts nor, conversely, keep its parts behind the skin border. So Galen laments this impossible self-sufficiency (*autarkeia*) of the body.[34]

Yet, the problem is resolved by resorting to the meaning that *autarkeia* acquired earlier in the Hippocatic corpus: 'balance'. From this alternative perspective, the inside parts continually need to adapt the qualities that diet and exercise provide to those of the outside environment.[35] Thanks to this continuous adjustment to the world beyond its perimeter, the body can somehow purge the environment of its radical otherness and thereby gradually communicate with it, at least inasmuch as climate and natural resources allow, namely as far as the human body does not meet the deserts and the ocean, where nobody can survive.

The theoretical dynamism, in Galen's view, of the relation between the parts and the whole, turns out to be an actual dynamism, when it concerns the expansion of the Roman Empire. It is generally acknowledged today that the borders of the Roman Empire were provisional zones of cultural and economic exchanges rather than defensive lines and limits of identity.[36] Though marked by fortified lines such as Hadrian's Wall, the borders of the Empire favoured contacts that could turn the outside territories into parts of the inside Empire. In the past, historians who considered borders as fixed and defensive linear frontiers misunderstood the meaning of the Latin word for border: *limes*. This word means both a border and a 'path towards', expressing mobility of a provisional situation rather than a permanent demarcation.

War created the first contact, but the integration process did not merely entail the subjection of peoples. Generally new Roman territories became provinces or sometimes vassal states stretching beyond the borders of the provinces themselves. During the Severan dynasty, the number of provinces grew to forty. At first, the central political power imposed borders irrespective of ethno-cultural identities. Later, though, borders could be moved on the basis of newly emerging needs or because a great city asked for new divisions. Also, the administrative system of the provinces evolved over time, which also determined changes in territorial partitions.

Finally, and above all, integration contact relied on the inclusive character of Roman citizenship which was extended to all inhabitants of the Empire in 212 AD. It did not remove local citizenships, but enabled individuals to get more rights and greater prestige, in competition with the local elite.

At least from a theoretical perspective, the Roman Empire appears to be a huge mechanism of integration through contact. Whenever it was making contact with outside peoples, it changed them into parts of its own structure, involving them in its living process. When describing a similar process in the human body, Galen brings up the notion of *sympatheia*, namely the capacity of tuning oneself to bad things as well as to good things. In the same way Roman contacts with other peoples did not mean assimilation but cultural exchange.

Such are some features of the organization of the bodily, geographical, historical, administrative and political space in the second century AD. In this sketch, I have suggested that they are ruled by a 'discourse' according to which, dynamically, contact between two entities transform them into parts of an extensive whole, the borders of which are emptiness, the ultimate limits of the earth.

Notes to Chapter 3

1. On the relationship between the body and soul in Galen, see Armelle Debru, *Le Corps respirant: la pensée physiologique chez Galien* (Leyden: Brill, 1996); Robert J. Hankinson, 'Body and Soul in Galen', in *Common to Body and Soul: Philosophical Approaches to Explaining Living Behaviour in Roman Antiquity*, ed. by R. A. H. King (Berlin and New York: De Gruyter, 2006), pp. 232–58; Mark Schiefsky, 'Galen and the Tripartite Soul', in *Plato and the Divided Self*, ed. by Rachel Barney, Tad Brennan and Charles Brittain (Cambridge: Cambridge University Press, 2012), pp. 331–49.
2. Michel Foucault, *Archéologie du savoir* (Paris: Gallimard, 1969), p. 58ff.
3. Galen, *On the Usefulness of the Body Parts*, trans. by Margaret Tallmadge May (Ithaca, NY: Cornell University Press, 1968), p. 69. (Galen, *De usu partium* K. II. 3.1.2).
4. Galen, *De usu partium*, K. II. 4, p. 279.
5. In fact, all mathematical treatises before Euclid, that is before the early third century BC, are lost, perhaps because Euclid's work was regarded as definitive. Conversely a long tradition of commentaries on his *Elements* runs from the third century BC onwards. Some of the most renowned commentators are Hero of Alexandria (first century AD), the Neoplatonist philosopher Porphyry (second half of the third century AD), Pappus (fourth century AD), and Simplicius (sixth century). Even though mathematical knowledge continued to develop after the third century BC, Euclid's *Elements* remained a prominent reference. Among the sources of his commentary on Euclid's *Elements*, Proclus mentions Apollonius of Perga, a geometer and astronomer of the end of the third century BC, also known for his writings on conic sections; Geminus of Rhodes, an astronomer and mathematician of the first century BC, and a follower of the Stoic philosopher Posidonius who also wrote, among others works, a kind of encyclopaedia of mathematics, and finally Claudius Ptolemy, a contemporary of Galen, the well-known Alexandrian mathematician, astronomer, geographer and astrologer.
6. Euclid, *Elements*, Book I, trans. and ed. by David E. Joyce <http://aleph0.clarku.edu/~djoyce/elements/bookI/bookI.html> [accessed 28 February 2016].
7. Bernard Vitrac, 'Introduction' in *Euclide. Éléments*, vol. 1 (Paris: PUF, 1990), p. 161.
8. David Joyce, *Euclid's Elements* < http://aleph0.clarku.edu/~djoyce/elements/bookI/defI13.html> [accessed 28 February 2016].
9. Joyce asserts that 'implicit to the concept of figure (σχῆμα) is the ambient plane *or* space of the figure'. Ibid.
10. Ibid.
11. Topology is a twentieth-century branch of mathematics which deals with spaces that keep their properties under continuous deformations (stretching, bending). Two main properties of the topological space are compactness and connectedness.
12. Joyce, *Euclid's Elements*.
13. Ibid.
14. Ibid.
15. In his case, this includes his astronomical knowledge as well.
16. Claudius Ptolemy, *Geography*, I. 1. *Ptolemy's Geography: An Annotated Translation of the Theoretical Chapters*, trans. by J. Lennart Berggren and Alexander Jones (Princeton, NJ: Princeton University Press, 2000), p. 57. Berggren and Jones translate *geographia* as 'cartography' in accordance with the restricted sense that Ptolemy defines this word in this chapter. Regional cartography represents Ptolemy's *chorographia*. Other Greek authors, such as Strabo, use *geographia* to mean a written geographical work. I have altered their translation, replacing 'cartography' with 'geography', in order to stress the difference between regional and general perspectives and drawn and written geography.
17. Strabo, *Geography*, I. 1. Strabo, *The Geography of Strabo*, vol. I, trans. by H. C. Hamilton (New York: The Macmillan Co., 1903), p. 7. < http://www.archive.org/stream/MN40035ucmf_2/MN40035ucmf_2_djvu.txt> [accessed 28 February 2016].
18. Ibid., p. 128.
19. Polybius, *Histories*, I. 2. 7; I. 4. 3. Polybius, *The Histories, Book 1–2*, trans. by W. R. Paton, rev.

by Frank W. Walbank and Christian Habicht (Cambridge, MA: Harvard University Press, 2010), p. 11.
20. Polybius, *Histories*, I. 4. 1–3. Ibid.
21. Ptolemy, *Geography*, I. 3.
22. Strabo, *Geography*, II. 1. 29–30; *The Geography of Strabo*, p. 127.
23. Polybius, *Histories*, I. 4. 7–11; Polybius, *The Histories of Polybius: Translated from the Text of F. Hultsch*, trans. by Evelyn S. Shuckburg (Cambridge: Cambridge University Press, 2012), pp. 4–5.
24. C. R. Whittaker, *Roman Empire: A Social and Economic Study* (Baltimore, MD: Johns Hopkins University Press, 1994), pp. 33–38.
25. Tacitus relates that, in a book of instructions, Augustus would have given Tiberius as a command 'that the empire should be confined within limits'. But Whittaker interprets that as a *counsel to consolidate* after the rebellion of the Pannonian auxiliaries and the losses of Varus' legions in Germany in AD 9. Later, Hadrian became unpopular for withdrawing from Mesopotamia. In the second century AD, Commodus proclaimed his wish of going 'as far as Oceanus', and Septimus Severus created the slogan of the *propagatio imperium*. Whittaker, *Roman Empire*, p. 37.
26. Edward Luttwak, *The Grand Strategy of the Roman Empire from the First Century AD to the Third* (Baltimore, MD: Johns Hopkins University Press, 1976). To Luttwak's mind, grand strategic underlying concepts organized a centralized plan and a long-lasting rational politics of Roman frontiers from the early to the late Empire.
27. C. R. Whittaker, 'Mental Maps and Frontiers', in *Rome and its Frontiers: The Dynamics of Empire* (London and New York: Routledge, 2004), pp. 66. Nicolet more positively noticed that Augustus somehow *inventoried the world* through explorations and travels, mapping, geographical works, population census, land register, demarcation, road construction and underlined their administrative utility. Claude Nicolet, *L'Inventaire du monde: géographie et politique aux origines de l'Empire romain* (Paris: Fayard, 1988).
28. Whittaker, p. 66 (my emphasis).
29. François Jacques, 'L'Emprise romaine sur l'Empire', in *Rome et l'intégration de l'Empire 44 av. JC–260 ap. JC*, Tome 1: *Les Structures de l'Empire romain*, ed. by John Scheid and François Jacques (Paris: PUF, 1990), pp. 161–207.
30. Galen, *On natural faculties* I. ix. 20–24. Galen, *On the Natural Faculties*, trans. by Arthur John Brock (Cambridge. MA: Harvard University Press, 1916), <http://www.perseus.tufts.edu/hopper/text?doc=Perseus:text:1999.01.0256> [accessed 28 February 2106].
31. Galen, *On natural faculties* I. x. 1–63.
32. Galen, *On the Natural Faculties*, K 2, 193. 19–194. 10.
33. Galen, *On the Natural Faculties*, K 2. 194.
34. Galen, *De sanitate tuenda*, K 6. 62. l. 6–19. To almost achieve auto-sufficiency, it would be necessary not only our innate constitution to be the best, and, thanks to controlled diet and exercise, suitable substance to be supplied from the outside in order to replace what flows out, but also us to withdraw ourselves from any economic and social life. To put it briefly we should close in on ourselves as most as possible what remains just an hypothesis or an elusive goal.
35. Galen explains that good proportion (*summetria*) of qualities (wet, dry, hot, cold) provides with a healthy constitution, but that balance is continuously broken. In fact there are intrinsic and inevitable causes of such a disruption and others that are not inevitable and that arise from our own behaviour toward the outside. The innate qualities differ in proportion and mixture but, for every human being, the progressive action of dryness, at the beginning, is responsible for the genesis of the body and of all its parts, and, over time, as all the organs become even drier, affects their function and their vitality. They become more and more feeble and restricted. This state is called old age. It is impossible to escape that process because it is that of human condition, going from birth to death. Conversely we can avoid evitable damages by supplying regularly other substances that replace what has regularly flowed away. It is the function of nutriment and drink (Galen, *De sanitate tuenda*, K 6. 3–7).
36. While questioning Luttwak's 'grand strategy' thesis, Isaac Benjamin claims that, at least for the East, the necessity of supplying the armies with food and other materials was the local impulse

to extend the military empire rather than a conscious central logic and consistency. Benjamin, *The Limits of the Empire: The Roman Army in the East*, rev. edn (Oxford: Clarendon Press, 2000), pp. 372–426.

CHAPTER 4

The Mediterranean Novel Defying Borders

Adrian Grima

In what follows, I will address the representation of the Mediterranean as a shared open space of human and cultural exchange which has no significant internal borders.¹ In particular, what concerns me is the loose category of the 'Mediterranean novel', narratives that not only unfold at sea or are set in some part of the region but also communicate this Mediterranean imaginary. I do not argue or assume that there is such a thing as 'Mediterranean literature', either as a genre or as a corpus, nor that there is some elusive kind of novel native to the Mediterranean region and written by its inhabitants. What I discuss rather is literature that deals explicitly with the Mediterranean. This is a conceptual boundary that I have set for myself and that allows me to focus on literature that represents the Mediterranean as a region or culture, as a shared space in history and in the present. If there is a 'Mediterranean literature', it exists in so far as it deals with the sea and region in a relatively comprehensive, if often critical, way. The novels I will examine include Malika Mokeddem's French novel *N'zid* (2001) and Ġużè Bonnici's Maltese novel *Lejn ix-Xemx* [Towards the Sun] (1940), as well as novels that form part of the genre of 'Mediterranean noir', namely Jean-Claude Izzo's *Les Marins perdus* [The Lost Sailors] (1997), and Massimo Carlotto's *Cristiani di Allah* (2008).

A conception of the Mediterranean as a common space of human and cultural exchange based on a shared history and cultural identity goes back to the early nineteenth century, when it was posited by Saint-Simonians like Michel Chevalier and Emile Barrault as a place that defies borders, that crosses the lines that separate one political, geographical or cultural reality from another, that brings together the East and West.² In Arabic, there is a different conception of the Mediterranean (Sea) and this is exemplified by the names that have been employed for this sea,³ but this is not reflected in European translations of seminal works like Ibn Khaldûn's fourteenth-century classic introduction to history called *The Muqaddimah*, where the term 'Mediterranean' is employed freely by translators and commentators.⁴ The European imaginary of the Mediterranean has been an attempt as well to establish a regional border, to delimitate a shared space in and around the Mediterranean Sea. What is implied by the elusive term 'imaginary' is that it is much more about invention than definition: this is a Mediterranean that is 'imaginable', but, as

Predrag Matvejević and Michael Herzfeld have shown, no less real for being so.[5] The Mediterranean imaginary is not born out of nothing: it has its roots in history, place and time, and ideology; it reflects the beliefs and interests of those who created and continue to promote it. It has historical roots firmly planted in the deep soils of European delusions of grandeur and superiority, but it is also an imaginary that some Mediterranean or Mediterraneanist writers have sought to reappropriate by problematizing and reconstructing it.[6]

I will begin with a brief discussion of the concept of the 'imaginary' as inspired by the ideas of Cornelius Castoriadis and a consideration of the Mediterraneanist ideas of Gabriel Audisio, one of the main figures behind the *École d'Alger* of the 1930s and '40s. Audisio was aware that his Mediterranean was as much an empirical reality as a utopia, but he saw the utopia of today as the oxygen of the future.[7] There are glimpses of this Mediterranean utopia in the novels that I deal with later in this paper, as well as in *La Traversée* [The Crossing], a documentary film about the ferry crossing between France and Algeria, a country that features in a number of these texts. Most of the film's protagonists inevitably come up against a liminality of borders that conjure up memories and reopen personal and inherited wounds. Bonnici's adventure novel, written at the onset of the Second World War, sees the Mediterranean Sea as a space of community and adventure and ignores their lands and cultures of origin, all the while constructing his ideal Mediterranean community of men on a corsair ship that prospers by specializing in the questionable arts of stealing and killing. In another vein, Mokeddem's novel concerns a female Ulysses of mixed identity drifting in the Mediterranean Sea at the turn of the twenty-first century, though she remains fully aware of the contradictions underlying this reappropriation of Ulysses in a Mediterraneanist narrative and challenges them by making her awareness evident to the reader. My reading acknowledges how the Mediterranean Sea has proven to be both an open space of exchange, albeit illicit, reinforcing the idea of the sea as defying borders, and the locus of a comfortable sense of loss. Leading with these reappropriations and reworkings of the Mediterranean narrative, the paper returns to the fundamental issue of the invention of the dominant Eurocentric imaginary of the region, because the invention of this Mediterranean raises questions about those who have created it and those who refuse to question it.

A Mediterranean Imaginary

As an imaginary, the 'Mediterranean' implies creation. What we call 'reality' and 'rationality', Castoriadis claims in *The Imaginary Institution of Society*, 'are the works of the imaginary'.[8] The imaginary has to do with 'the human capacity to conceive meaning' and therefore has 'an irreducibly creative dimension'.[9] Castoriadis sees the creation of things that are radically new as a creation arising out of the inherent potentials of the imaginary. For Castoriadis, the imaginary is what takes human consciousness beyond what is immediately perceptible. On the other hand, 'Every thought of society and of history itself', he writes, 'belongs to society and to history.

Every thought, whatever it may be and whatever may be its "object", is but a mode and a form of socio-historical doing'.[10] In other words, although the Mediterranean imaginary often involves defying mental borders, its constant creation and recreation has its roots in place and time.

Castoriadis identifies the imaginary with poïesis, creative production that transforms and continues the world. History is essentially poïesis, that is, 'creation and ontological genesis in and through individuals' doing and representing/saying', which are also 'instituted historically, at a given moment, as thoughtful doing or as thought in the making'.[11] The imaginary is when we want to talk about something invented, whether this refers to a 'sheer' invention or a 'slippage', a shift of meaning in which available symbols are invented with significations other than their normal or canonical ones. With respect to invention or slippage, one can assume that the imaginary is separate from the real, whether it claims to take the latter's place, as in the case of a lie, or makes no such claim, as in the case of a novel.[12] Either way, history is impossible and inconceivable outside of the productive or creative imagination.[13]

Literary narratives like Mokeddem's *N'zid* and Bonnici's *Lejn ix-Xemx* write culture by inventing a language that redraws the boundaries of imaginable worlds and by providing what Gabriele Schwab calls 'thick descriptions of the desires, fears, and fantasies that shape the imaginary lives and cultural encounters of invented protagonists'.[14] Literature is a medium that '*writes* culture within the particular space and mode of aesthetic production'; it *makes* culture.[15] Literature can remake language and the world, as Mokeddem does when she allows Nora to appropriate the Mediterranean Sea. Her Mediterranean imaginary defies geographical borders and semantic boundaries.

The Marseilles-born Mediterraneanist Audisio (1900–1978), who was a great influence on the young Albert Camus, spent an important part of his life in Algeria and was a key figure in what he coined, in the 1930s, the 'École d'Alger'. Audisio, whose idea of the Mediterranean was constructed in a colonial milieu, espoused and promoted a more benevolent version of the French colonial narrative of a shared Mediterranean culture. In *Amour d'Alger* (1938) he described himself as 'a child of the Mediterranean' who loved Algeria.[16] Audisio, whose father was Italian and mother partly of Romanian origin, described himself as 'an authentic Mediterranean',[17] a definition which must be set against the background of his definition of the Mediterranean race as mixed and 'impure'.[18] From a racial point of view, writes Audisio, if the Mediterranean can give a lesson to the world, it is precisely that of '*rassemblement par affinités*', bringing people together by affinities, a lesson of 'free aggregation', of a community that exists '*despite*' (Audisio's emphasis) the differences in blood ('*les cloisons du sang*'), and that rises above national frontiers.[19] In the early 1900s, talk about a 'Mediterranean race' was not uncommon. In 1912, R. N. Bradley, building on Giuseppe Sergi's work,[20] rallied the support of the hard sciences to argue, 'beyond the region of doubt', in favour of the existence of 'a great pre-Grecian' Mediterranean race, that occupied the whole basin of the Mediterranean and beyond, and possessed 'a high degree of culture'.[21] On the other hand, Audisio was not interested in identifying a single Mediterranean race: in *Sel de la mer* he produced what Liauzu describes as a eulogy of 'bastardy' or '*bâtardise*',[22] thus highlighting the multiple character of the Mediterranean 'race' and taking down all walls within the region.

As an 'imagined, constructed space', the Mediterranean encourages a sort of 'lyricism, romanticism or essentialism',[23] which is evident in Audisio's romantic characterizations of the Mediterranean as inspired by French colonialism. He himself acknowledges his belief in what he calls the '*incontestable romantisme méditerranéen*',[24] or unquestionable Mediterranean romanticism. According to Audisio, if one were to write a Mediterranean constitution, the first article would proclaim the rights and equality of all races. He himself even declares his Mediterranean citizenship on the condition that it be shared by all peoples of the sea, including the Jews, Arabs, Berbers, and Blacks.[25] In this he was reacting against an imperialist conception of the Mediterranean as essentially Latin, inspired by an ideology that had imposed a much vaunted, supposedly all embracing '*pax romana*'. The French and Italian colonialists of the early twentieth century, who chose to see themselves as privileged descendants of the great Roman Empire that 'united' the whole of the Mediterranean, refused to question what Audisio saw as the great myth of Roman peace and order.[26] The Latin order they wanted to (re)impose was not an attempt to erase borders and allow for some benign reincarnation of *mare nostrum*: it was rather an attempt to impose borders between peoples and cultures, between the colonizers and the colonized, between their superior Mediterranean culture with its Latin origins and the myriad cultures of the 'natives' on the southern shores of the Mediterranean. This was done under the pretext of a mission to civilize the natives, a '*mission civilisatrice*' that would once again bring together the Mediterranean but effectively imposed a new racist order.

The 'mind borders' imposed on the Mediterranean by French and Italian imperialists were not the only ones. Despite the attempt of writers like Audisio to construct a shared narrative of the region that countered that of more colonially minded '*algérianistes*' like Jean Pommier and Louis Bertrand, a narrative that would 'translate their Algerian realities as faithfully as possible',[27] they only managed to close this 'Orient' inside the same system of representations that Edward Said highlighted, namely the one in which the West objectifies this part of the world through its arts and sciences.[28] In *L'Algérie littéraire* [Literary Algeria] (1943), Audisio found no reason to even refer to Algerian literature in Arabic.[29] Against the very real backdrop of the distortions of the *mission civilisatrice* of the occupiers and the '*influence nefaste de la colonisation*' or bad influence of colonization on the customs of the colonized,[30] the writers of European origin of the École d'Alger failed, in the eyes of native intellectuals, to narrate the real Algeria, '*l'Algérie authentique*'.[31] Sayeh argues that Algeria became their 'personal province', an expression she borrows from Said, a space where the Europeans let their imaginary gallop freely.[32] In the writings of many of the writers of the École d'Alger, including Camus,[33] the presence of the Maghrebis is hidden. Whether these *pied-noir* writers were aware of it or not, the invisibility, the nonexistence of the natives in their own country is evident in their writings.³⁴ The French culture of the Algerians of European origin was reinforced, distinguishing itself from the metropolis, the centre, which it saw as a kind of secondary self.³⁵ The Orientalism of these writers allowed them to set themselves apart from their compatriots in France, as well as native Algerians.

Audisio wanted to show that the borders between the countries in North Africa and the Mediterranean were artificial, given that languages, peoples and civilizations had mixed within it.³⁶ Yet he had no doubt that the Mediterranean was actually a 'continent', and that for the people of this sea, there is only one true homeland, or *'patrie'*, and that is the sea itself.³⁷ Writing in the same period (1949), Fernand Braudel saw the region as a physical unit marked indelibly by climate and history which imposed its uniformity on both landscape and ways of life.³⁸ The 'Mediterranean complex should have taken its rhythm', argued Braudel, 'from the uniform band of climate and culture at its centre', a 'force operating at the centre' that affected all movements into the Mediterranean and out of it.³⁹ Braudel drew attention in particular to what he sees as the 'identical or near-identical worlds' on 'the borders of countries as far apart and in general terms as different as Greece, Spain, Italy, North Africa,' worlds that live by the same rhythm, defying physical and political borders. Its people and goods 'move from one to another without any need for acclimatization', and this 'living identity implies the living unity of the sea'.⁴⁰ Nevertheless, the fact that he identified the three southern European countries by name, but referred to North Africa in general terms, almost as if it were one country, is an indication of his critical vantage point.

The genesis of Braudel's unifying conception of the Mediterranean lies in the French colonial experience. Braudel, whom Borutta and Gekas describe as 'the founder of Mediterranean history',⁴¹ laid the groundwork for this most important book in colonial Algiers, 'in close contact and intense exchange with eminent protagonists of the French "colonial school"'; and his conception of Mediterranean history was 'a by-product of colonial entanglements in the Mediterranean'.⁴² In Algiers, he was involved in 'the historical legitimation of the French colonial empire in North Africa'.⁴³ Although his book, a veritable act of faith in the region, was hailed as a highly original work, its genesis could not be disassociated from the French colonization of North Africa and a French geopolitical concept of the Mediterranean. In fact, Borutta and Gekas argue that 'It was the colonial Mediterranean that "chose" a brilliant scholar, not vice versa'.⁴⁴ Their reading of the modern Mediterranean is that of a colonial sea, 'a maritime space of colonial interactions and entanglements that transcended continental and national boundaries',⁴⁵ and that was to leave its legacy on every discourse on a shared Mediterranean space. Audisio, on the contrary, did not hide his affinities with the colonial project: in *Sel de la mer*, he draws up a list of 'heroes' of colonization, which includes doctors and priests, soldiers, colonial officials, the colonists themselves, and teachers in remote areas, whose lives are 'discreetly heroic'.⁴⁶ What inspires him is what he sees as the youthfulness of the Mediterranean: the peoples and the races who live on the shores are full of life and are *'vigorously transported by the rhythm of modern life'*.⁴⁷ This is a far cry from Juann Mamo's uncompromising portrayal of the

Mediterranean as chronically backward in his irreverent novel, and it suggests that Audisio's enthusiasm was also a direct result of the French occupation of Algeria. There is a sense of adventure in this narrative of French *colons* of the early twentieth century who are eager to discover (their) Algeria, while the Algerian immigrants and their descendants in France of the early twenty-first century 'return' to their land of origin with mixed feelings and a marked sense of disorientation.

Invisible Borders, Borders Defied

In the documentary *La Traversée* [The Crossing] (2014), which depicts a ferry crossing from Marseilles to Algiers, one of the passengers, the actor and theatre director El Yamine Bendib (Ben), discusses his mixed French-Algerian identity: every time he finds himself caught in the in-between — here it happens to be on the Mediterranean Sea — it causes an upheaval. '*Et à un moment donné, je me retrouve — comme ici, sur ce bateau — en perdition complète*' [And at a given moment, I find myself — like here, on this ship — completely lost].[48] On his way to Algeria, a country he left at a very young age, he feels neither Algerian nor French. He describes frontiers as 'the most bizarre' thing. For Ben, it is impossible for him to identify the precise moment when he crosses the border between Algeria and France. The essential idea is that it is perceived as a sense of loss, as well as a voyage back in time,[49] which is laden with memories of how his Algerian father crossed the same sea in the opposite direction, to seek full citizenship in France, because the French colonial system in Algeria undervalued and even devalued him.[50]

Literature and the cultural imaginary play a crucial role in the fashioning of cross-cultural encounters like the ones experienced by the passengers in *La Traversée*. Inspired by Edward Said, Schwab writes about how those travelling to different countries and coming into contact with other cultures routinely bring along 'the baggage of a cultural imaginary formed by literary or artistic accounts' of the cultures encountered.[51] The first time people travel to a different country is never really the first time they have 'visited' it, and this is even more so the case for the Algerian émigrés in France who travel back to their country of origin, or Mokeddem's protagonist Nora who slowly recovers her memory while she sails from port to port in the Mediterranean. The liminality of borders inevitably conjures up memories and reopens personal and inherited wounds. In this space of loss, on the ferry between the North and South of the Mediterranean, Ben reflects on his own hegemonic border crossing: 'I understood that if my school or university culture were francophone, with Latin or Western references, "*de chair et de sang et de sensibilité*" [in flesh, blood and sensibility], I wouldn't be less than those on the other side of the Mediterranean'.[52] The Mediterranean marks, in effect, this great divide, and crossing it only highlights it. It is the ultimate border, but also a separation wall, an apartheid wall, another Melilla or Ceuta border fence. The shores of the Mediterranean, writes Erri de Luca in the 'Geographical Note' to his poem *Solo andata* (2005), are divided in two, those of departure and those of arrival, but '*senza pareggio*', they don't balance each other out — there are more beaches and more nights of embarkation than disembarkation; less lives make it to the other shore.[53] For migrants, past and present, the Mediterranean is far more than just an imaginary border.

Ben sometimes envies one of his brothers, a wheat farmer, who has never left Algeria. His brother's points of reference are clear. Since there is no 'rupture' he is not at odds with himself. Ben, on the other hand, permanently doubts where he belongs. He wonders whether if to be free one needs to belong to nothing. For Ben, this is why, perhaps, the idea of being in the middle of the sea, between two shores, means that, for a moment, one is neither here nor there.[54] This is probably why he welcomes his sense of loss, because it is something that belongs to him. He dilutes it to the extent that he can in the water of the Mediterranean, but ultimately 'it is me'.[55] Looking at the sea, El Yamine Bendib sees it a bit like a 'blank page'. '*C'est pas banal, la Méditerranée!*', he says, acknowledging that it is shared by many people for whom it is merely a border. For Ben, if it is any kind of border, it is one that is very elastic, a border that 'lasts long'.[56] Despite its 'resistance to fixed determination', the 'very category of 'the Mediterranean' construed as a single entity', writes Edwige Tamalet, remains 'remarkably persistent'.[57] Its waves never change; they are indifferent to the destiny of peoples. The Mediterranean has witnessed the passing of many peoples, but it has remained the same. 'Human history lies on the surface', says Ben.[58] It just flows. It leaves marks that are immediately erased.

In her review of *La Traversée*, Cécile Mury acknowledges that the Mediterranean becomes an invisible frontier, floating between worlds: 'Dans le vrombissement des moteurs, le bouillonnement des vagues, la Méditerranée devient une frontière invisible, en flottaison entre les mondes'[In the roar of engines, the foaming of waves, the Mediterranean becomes an invisible border, floating between worlds].[59] This definition reflects the double interpretation of the Mediterranean as both border, albeit invisible in nature, and a space that defies borders. This is the freedom that Mokeddem's Nora experiences as she sails from one port to another without crossing borders, or rather ignoring them completely. Olivier Seguret also observes how the ferry in *La Traversée* serves as a floating platform for 'confidences off-shore',[60] offshore confessions, unguarded self-revelations. On this 'floating extraterritorial plot', Seguret notes that 'the question of roots floats around in all its absurdity'.[61] Indeed, most of the travellers portray themselves as locked in a double immigration, with the 'Mediterranean corridor' ferrying them from one end to the other.[62]

La Traversée clearly offers a more problematic vision of the Mediterranean than that proposed by Audisio in *Sel de la mer*, despite the fact that he too must have experienced a condition of multiple identities, as French, as an Arabic-speaking pied noir,[63] who was both Algerian and passionately Mediterranean. People like Audisio constituted a cultural and linguistic mix that was in the process of becoming the norm in Algeria,[64] a Creole and mixed country,[65] a synthesis of the Mediterranean races cemented by French culture.[66] The political geography of the École d'Alger in which the Mediterranean imaginary featured prominently focused on life on the coast and ignored the interior of the Maghreb and underestimated the opposition to any sort of reform in colonial circles.[67] The whole Mediterraneanist project fell through after the Vichy years and World War II and after the massacre at Sétif in 1945 which marked the beginning of the Algerian war of independence. Liauzu contends that the rapid falling apart of the literary group of Algiers reveals that it never could have taken root;[68] indeed, the poet Jean Sénac was one of the very few Europeans in Algeria to take the side of the colonized Algerians in their struggle for independence.[69] When the historical circumstances and ideology that gave birth to the French colonial Mediterranean imaginary, and nourished it, changed, the narrative all but disappeared, but the borders it claimed to defy or even erase did not.

Redrawing the Map, A Liberating Imaginary

Bonnici's protagonist Duminku Calleja would certainly agree that not belonging to a country, not being tied to a land, allows for more freedom. The captain of the corsair galleon *Nostra Señora*, Our Lady, has no homeland, nor do the members of his crew. Their names and surnames, Rodrig Gonzaga, Ġorġ Karakis, Barabba, and the Muslim slave Babu, suggest that they come from different Mediterranean lands, but they do not seem to belong to any one of them. What they do belong to is the community on board their ship. Likewise, in Izzo's *Les Marins perdus* (1997), when the crew of the Aldébaran sit down to eat, 'even though they weren't at home, they were on common ground. All from the same country. The Mediterranean'.[70] Bonnici's *Lejn ix-Xemx*, though written in 1940, months before his untimely death, and published in 1958, is a romantic historical novel set in 1701, almost two hundred years into the rule of the Knights of St John's in Malta. Breaking from an important convention of the genre, where Malta is the undisputed home of the protagonists, the only true 'homeland' of Bonnici's protagonists is the Mediterranean Sea.

In the context of a Maltese literature that has focused on issues of national mythology and rarely referred to the Mediterranean, the two mentions of the Mediterranean in Bonnici's rather unorthodox novel are noteworthy. The first is significant: in a particular scene of the novel, Duminku Calleja takes out 'a large map of the Mediterranean' from the cupboard in his cabin, spreads it out on the table before him in order to consult it, then folds it carefully and puts it back in its place.[71] The way Bonnici describes this otherwise ordinary task suggests that the corsair more than just cares for the map: his bonding with the Mediterranean finds expression in the way he delicately handles the image of his sea. His affection for this map is in a way similar to that of Diamantis, the Greek first mate of the commercial freighter in Izzo's novel who has a 'passion for sea maps and ports'.[72] The Atlantic and Pacific, Diamantis says, are 'seas of distance', the Adriatic 'a sea of intimacy' and the Mediterranean 'a sea of closeness'.[73] With a third-century Roman route map, the *Peutingeriana*, spread out in front of him, Diamantis reminisces about his father's passion for maps. When his father bought it he spread it out on the table, 'like a treasure', and then he took Diamantis, who was then four years old, on his knees and told him 'a story about mythical times'.[74] By the age of twelve he had realized that 'mapmaking asks all the important questions about the sea and the land. In other words, about the world, and the way we look at the world'.[75] When things turn decidedly sour towards the end of the novel, Diamantis packs his things haphazardly, but he makes sure not to forget his sea map or his notebook'.[76]

Diamantis tells Abdul Aziz, the Lebanese captain of the *Aldébaran*, that 'Every time we sail, we redraw the map of the world'.[77] Sailing is like literature: it invites readers to practise 'a wilful engagement in artifices of psychic writing, cultural memory, and future-oriented speculation'.[78] We long for 'imaginary maps' that help us 'to navigate the unfamiliar terrain'. Despite the fact that these imaginary ethnographies are haunted by the ghosts of the past, the direction of these maps or ethnographies 'is always toward an emergent future'.[79] The problem of the impounded *Aldébaran* is precisely that it has been deprived of a future, leaving its present to the mercy of these 'traumatic eclipses' and ghosts of the past. At one point Diamantis sits on his bunk and opens the notepad containing the reflections he has made from studying Mediterranean Sea maps, including '*The reason the sea routes are not easy to define may be that they are interwoven with stories: the maps on which they are marked may have been imagined, the writings that go with them invented...*'.[80] Before carefully putting his maps away, he writes, '*The Mediterranean isn't only a geography. It isn't only a history. But it's more than just a place we happen to belong to*'.[81] For Diamantis, the Mediterranean imaginary is liberating, but Izzo's novel is also about how he is being deprived of it.

In *The Lost Sailors*, both Abdul Aziz and Diamantis are struggling, within the confines of their freighter, with personal problems they have long refused to face. The captain sees the Mediterranean as the symbol of the commercial and emotional web in which he is caught; the first mate sees in the Mediterranean his escape route from the strings that tie him to failed relationships, reconnecting him, at the same time, to fond memories of his childhood and the passion for maps and for the Mediterranean that his father passed onto him. The Mediterranean allows him the possibility to redraw his own map. Izzo's Abdul Aziz does not share Diamantis's passion for the Mediterranean. Perhaps the roots of his contempt lie in his frustration as the captain of a sequestered ship, and his subsequent loss of sense of purpose and authority. Perhaps they lie also in his difficult relationship with women, and with home. The fact remains that he sees the Mediterranean as the sea that wove threads around Odysseus 'like a fucking spider's web', and 'Penelope was the fucking spider'.[82] In Circe's arms and Calypso's bed, he was still tied to Penelope, to routine, and to domestic life. 'The ocean liberated men from spider women. From Penelope. From Penelope and Cephea'.[83] The renegade corsair Redouane, the autodiegetic narrator of Carlotto's *Cristiani di Allah*, which is set in 1541, sees the Mediterranean Sea as 'an old closed sea' on which, whether you like it or not, you end up landing on one shore or another.[84] But the corsairs of the Mediterranean still feared the unknown waters beyond the Straits of Gibraltar.[85] Within their region, despite the fact that Christians and Muslims continued to fight each other for supremacy,[86] they moved from one side to the other of the religious and power divide with a certain ease, confident that wherever they go and whichever flag they fly, they could pull it off. The boundedness of the Mediterranean was predictable, perhaps stifling, but also reassuring.

The fluid map of the Mediterranean is also central to Mokeddem's *N'zid* (2001), the story of a modern-day female Ulysses, Nora, who lives in Paris, and whose parents are the Irish Samuel and the Algerian Aïcha. Nora has temporarily lost her memory, but when she finds herself alone on a boat somewhere in the Mediterranean, the sea itself is no secret for the boat, or for her (*'la Méditerranée n'a pas de secret pour le bateau. Pour elle non plus'*).[87] Nora is exasperated because she would like her boat to fly, if only she knew where to go. She puts aside her logbook and instead brings out her map of the Mediterranean, scanning the names of the countries. She is frustrated because the erasure of her memory immobilizes her, but at the same time it liberates her, allowing her to choose where to go. The map of the Mediterranean transmits the feeling that the whole of the region lies at her fingertips, that political borders count for nothing. This returns us to Bonnici's *Lejn ix-Xemx* and its second reference to the Mediterranean, made when a tempest sweeps the Middle Sea,[88] sinking a galleon of the Knights of St John and threatening to sink Duminku's galleon as well. The freedom afforded by the Mediterranean Sea comes at a price, but Duminku Calleja and his crew seem to be well aware of and relatively at ease with its constant danger and precariousness. They find in the Mediterranean the kind of adventure Izzo's Abdul Aziz identifies with the ocean and they don't see the Middle Sea at all as a web that entraps them. In this literature, the unpredictability of the Inland Sea adds to its narrative and dramatic potential.

The protagonist of *N'zid* experiences a comfortable sense of loss in the Mediterranean Sea. Her memory loss is partly unsettling and disorienting, but being able to sail from one port to another in relative freedom is mentally and spiritually liberating. That loss of memory and place comes across as the price one has to pay to erase borders and start afresh, but this is illusory. Something violent has happened in Nora's life — the big bruise on her face is testimony to that — and she has lost all her memory. But it is forcefully coming back, and as the boundaries between the present and past fade, she has to deal with a lot of unfinished personal business festering against the violent background of collective conflicts. Nora appropriates the Mediterranean Sea, her *'patrie matrice'* or motherland,[89] and is appropriated by it. She sees the sea as her best protection from the events on land,[90] but it cannot erase her past or shield her forever from it.

While Nora is sailing the Mediterranean Sea, her *'passion nomade'*,[91] which derives also from the Algerian desert, gets the better of her and allows her to ignore borders, making of her a nomad without a tribe. As a nomad of the waters she loves departures just as much as she loves arrivals, escapes as well as returns.[92] Nora's liberating Mediterranean is an all embracing, determined, rebellious goddess.[93] The sea is her accomplice when she passes through and embraces, at one go, Greece and Turkey, Israel, Palestine and Lebanon, France and Algeria. 'Sa *Méditerranée*', writes Malika Mokeddem's narrator, *'est une déesse scabreuse et rebelle que ni les marchands de haine ni les sectaires n'ont réussi à fermer'* [Her Mediterranean is a dangerous and rebellious goddess who neither the merchants of hate nor the sectarians have managed to stop].[94] One drop at a time, the sea fills her and soothes her pain; it distances her from the land and the borders that separate men and women from each other, from their lands and from themselves, and, at the same time, takes in the sky, continuing her wandering with what is effectively the comfort of the 'indolence of insomnia'.[95] Nora's Mediterranean Sea is an 'immense heart' which beats with the same rhythm as her own heart, with that of her own father-mother, uniting the north (Ireland) and the south (Algeria). She is part of the sea, her motherland. '*Patrie matrice*'. Flux of the exiles. The sea of the Mediterranean is the blue blood of the globe between its lands of exodus.[96] But her memories are not far away: they evoke her country and her own exile. Nora explains that one must first belong to a place in order to be a stranger elsewhere.[97] Being nowhere, being in a non-place condemns her to non-being, but places can turn into prisons. For nomads, fleeing, going elsewhere is a necessity in order not to lose everything. 'What the others call exile to me is deliverance', Nora contends.[98] The dilemma, rather, lies in the fact that it is the act of leaving that establishes place, a place that requires leaving, or the possibility of leaving and crossing the imaginary fault line.

Inventing another Mediterranean

When Audisio wrote about his Mediterranean, like the travellers in Eastern Europe he 'brought along and gave free rein to imaginative and philosophical preconceptions'.[99] The image that emerged from the accounts of those travellers was 'often conditioned by an element of fantasy'. Indeed, Larry Wolff argues that the Eastern Europe was constructed by 'the combined conceptions of 'travellers in the imagination' and 'imaginative travellers' like Voltaire, who was 'powerfully influential in mapping Eastern Europe on the mind of the Enlightenment', but had never in his life travelled farther east than Berlin.[100] Inventing the Mediterranean, like inventing Eastern Europe, required an important dose of imagination and continues to say a great deal about those who created it and why.

After the First World War, the organization of pan-Mediterranean meetings in North Africa sought to implant an all-embracing Mediterranean identity that would run parallel to, or supplant, 'national/imperial configurations', but proved to be 'mainly the work of elites in the metropoles'.[101] Even among the various and sundry communities of early twentieth-century Tunisia, which had the potential to melt into one community that rose above 'national' interests, there is little evidence, beyond instances and spaces of '*convivencia*', that a sense of 'Mediterranean-ness' was able to take root.[102] The borders and boundaries suggested by narratives of the nation or religion held their ground. Gużè Bonnici's uncharacteristically unpatriotic adventure novel, written at the start of the Second World War, proposes the Mediterranean Sea as a space of community, adventure and fortune and chooses to ignore the origins of the community of men (only men) on his galleon. It is notable that it is a corsair ship, after all, and that his crew ultimately prosper through acts of stealing and killing. By 1940 standards, at least, if not by those of the early eighteenth century, the period in which the events of the novel are set, one cannot ignore the profound moral contradictions in this position. Perhaps what this seemingly naive Mediterranean adventure novel suggests, in a period of war no less, is that utopias have to learn to coexist with usurpation and violence.

Nor does Mokeddem's Nora create her Mediterranean out of nothing. The way she conjures up a free and shared Mediterranean space suggests that she is also inspired by the ideal created by the Saint-Simonians in the first half of the nineteenth century and given a new lease of life by the writers of the École d'Alger a hundred years later. Audisio's Ulysses is the '*prototype inaltérablement vrai de l'homme méditerranéen*' [The unalterably true prototype of the Mediterranean man], a quintessential Mediterranean man,[103] in a constant state of creation.[104] It is the kind of freedom that Audisio identifies with Ulysses and his intelligence that Nora seeks and wishes to claim.[105] Mokeddem's Mediterranean is, nevertheless, an ideal that is fully aware of its own deep historical and current contradictions. Nora needs her Mediterranean in order to deal with the bruises of the present and the past, to redesign and reappropriate the desert she has left behind, the desert of her mother and lover, simultaneously a site of freedom and boundedness. The borders of her Mediterranean imaginary are those that she chooses to frame according to her own story and the larger narrative in which she finds herself. Her Mediterranean is an escape from, and alternative to, the administrative, ideological and cultural borders that overpower and bruise her.

Notes to Chapter 4

1. Thanks to Mohamed-Salah Omri, Maria Tatar, Mourad Yelles, and Marina Warner for sharing thoughts with me on an earlier version of this paper.
2. Michel Chevalier, *Système de la Méditerranée. Religion Saint-Simonienne. Politique Industrielle* (Paris: Globe, 1832; repr. 2006); Emile Barrault, *Occident et Orient: études politiques, morales, religieuses pendant 1833–1834 de l'ère chrétienne, 1249–1250 de l'hégyre* (Paris: Desessart, 1835).
3. Bogusław R. Zagórski, 'Sea Names of the Arab World as a System', *Onomastica*, 57 (2013), 205–28 (pp. 212–13, 218) [accessed 7 July 2016].
4. A case in point is 'the only complete English translation of the Muqaddimah', by Franz Rosenthal, first published in 1958; Bruce B. Lawrence's 'Introduction to the 2005 Edition' immediately places Ibn Khaldûn, a 'Mediterranean scholar', within a 'Mediterranean location' and among 'Mediterranean Muslims'. Ibn Khaldûn, *Muqaddimah: An Introduction to History*, trans. by Franz Rosenthal, ed. by N. J. Dawood, new intro. by Bruce C. Lawrence (Princeton, NJ: Princeton University Press, 2015), pp. vii–xxv (p. vii).
5. Predrag Matvejević, *Mediterraneo: un nuovo breviario*, trans. by Silvio Ferrari (Milano: Garzanti, 1991); Michael Herzfeld, 'Practical Mediterraneanism: Excuses for Everything, from Epistemology to Eating,' in *Rethinking the Mediterranean*, ed. by W. V. Harris (Oxford University Press, 2005), pp. 45–63.
6. Adrian Grima, 'L'arte della traduzione e la costruzione di un altro Mediterraneo', in *Paesi e popoli del Mediterraneo*, ed. by Bruno Amoroso, Gianfranco Nicolais and Nino Lisi (Cosenza: Rubbettino, 2009), pp. 173–86 (p. 74).
7. Gabriel Audisio, *Sel de la mer* (Paris: Gallimard, 1936; repr. 2002), p. 123.
8. Cornelius Castoriadis, *The Imaginary Institution of Society*, rev. edn, trans. by Kathleen Blamey (Cambridge: Polity, 1997), p. 3.
9. Hans Joas, 'Review Essay: Institutionalization as a Creative Process: The Sociological Importance of Cornelius Castoriadis's Political Philosophy'. *American Journal of Sociology*, 94.5 (March 1989), 1184–99 (p. 1192) [accessed 20 May 2014].
10. Castoriadis, *The Imaginary Institution*, p. 3.
11. Ibid., pp. 3–4.
12. Ibid., p. 127.
13. Ibid., p. 146.

14. Gabriele Schwab, *Imaginary Ethnographies: Literature, Culture, and Subjectivity* (New York: Columbia University Press, 2012), 'Introduction'.
15. Ibid.
16. Gabriel Audisio, *Amour d'Alger* (Alger: Edmond Charlot, 1938), pp. 9–10.
17. Audisio, *Sel de la mer*, p. 94.
18. Ibid., p. 118.
19. Ibid., p. 119.
20. Namely Giuseppe Sergi, *The Mediterranean Race: A Study of the Origin of European Peoples* (London: Walter Scott, 1901).
21. R. N. Bradley, *Malta and the Mediterranean Race* (London: T. Fisher Unwin, 1912), p. 29.
22. Audisio, *Sel de la mer*, p. 165.
23. Julia A. Clancy-Smith, *Mediterraneans: North Africa and Europe in an Age of Migration, c. 1800–1900* (Berkeley: University of California Press, 2011), p. 11.
24. Audisio, *Sel de la mer*, p. 95.
25. Ibid., p. 119.
26. Ibid., pp. 112–14.
27. Samira Sayeh, 'From Algeria to France and Back: The Changing Literary Identity of Mouloud Feraoun, Mohammed Dib and Mouloud Mammeri' (unpublished doctoral dissertation, Pennsylvania State University, 2005), pp. 62–63.
28. Edward W. Said, *Orientalism* (London: Penguin, 1995) pp. 85–86.
29. Nicole Tuccelli, 'Présentation', in *L'Algérie littéraire*, by Gabriel Audisio (Marseille: Jeanne Laffitte, 2012), pp. 7–31 (p. 29).
30. Sayeh, 'From Algeria', p. 82.
31. Ibid., p. 65.
32. Ibid., p. 66.
33. Claude Liauzu, 'Gabriel Audisio, Albert Camus et Jean Sénac: entre Algérie française et Algérie musulmane', in *Confluences Méditerranée*, 33 (Spring 2000), 161–71 (p. 166) [accessed 4 April 2015].
34. Najib Redouane, 'La Littérature maghrébine d'expression française au carrefour des cultures et des langues', in *The French Review*, 72.1 (October 1998), pp. 81–90 (p. 81) [accessed 1 April 2015].
35. Sayeh, 'From Algeria', p. 66.
36. Tuccelli, 'Présentation', p. 14.
37. Gabriel Audisio, *Jeunesse de la Méditerranée* (Paris: Gallimard, 1935; repr. 2002), p. 15.
38. Fernand Braudel, *The Mediterranean and the Mediterranean World in the Age of Philip II*, vol. 1, trans. by Siân Reynolds, 2nd edn (London: Fontana, 1966), p. 231.
39. Ibid..
40. Ibid..
41. Manuel Borutta and Sakis Gekas, 'A Colonial Sea: The Mediterranean, 1798–1956', in *A Colonial Sea the Mediterranean, 1798–1956/Une mer coloniale la méditerranée de 1798 à 1956*, special issue of *European Review of History/Revue européenne d'histoire*, ed. by Manuel Borutta and Sakis Gekas, 19.1 (2012), 1–13 (pp. 1–2).
42. Ibid., p. 2.
43. Ibid..
44. Ibid..
45. Ibid..
46. Audisio, *Sel de la mer*, p. 181.
47. Audisio, *Amour d'Alger*, p. 76.
48. Elisabeth Leuvrey, *La Traversée* (Shellac Sud, 2014), p. 43 (booklet accompanying the DVD).
49. Ibid., p. 56.
50. Ibid., pp. 45–46.
51. Schwab, *Imaginary Ethnographies*, ch. 2.
52. Leuvrey, *La Traversée*, p. 48.
53. Erri De Luca, *Solo Andata* (Milan: Feltrinelli, 2005), Kindle file, 'Nota di geografia'.
54. Leuvrey, *La Traversée*, p. 49.

55. Ibid., p. 52.
56. Ibid., p. 56.
57. Edwige Tamalet, 'Modernity in Question: Retrieving Imaginaries of the Transcontinental Mediterranean' (unpublished doctoral dissertation, University of California–San Diego, 2009), p. 7.
58. Leuvrey, *La Traversée*, p. 58.
59. Ibid., p. 63.
60. Ibid., p. 64.
61. Ibid., p. 64.
62. Ibid., p. 64.
63. Liauzu, 'Gabriel Audisio', p. 166.
64. Audisio, *Jeunesse*, p. 112.
65. Liauzu, 'Gabriel Audisio', p. 165.
66. Audisio, *Jeunesse*, p. 112.
67. Liauzu, 'Bagriel Audisio', p. 165.
68. Ibid., p. 165.
69. Ibid., p. 165.
70. Jean Claude Izzo, *The Lost Sailors*, trans. by Howard Curtis (New York: Europa, 2007), ch. 24.
71. Ġużè Bonnici, *Lejn ix-Xemx* (Malta: Klabb Kotba Maltin, 1974), p. 92.
72. Izzo, *The Lost Sailors*, ch. 12.
73. Ibid..
74. Ibid., ch. 3.
75. Ibid., ch. 3.
76. Ibid., ch. 27.
77. Ibid., ch. 3.
78. Schwab, 'Introduction'.
79. Ibid..
80. Izzo, *The Lost Sailors*, ch. 11.
81. Ibid., ch. 11.
82. Ibid., ch. 24.
83. Ibid., ch. 24.
84. Massimo Carlotto, *Cristiani di Allah* (Rome: Edizioni e/o, 2008), p. 126.
85. Ibid., p. 156.
86. Ibid., p. 150.
87. Malika Mokeddem, *N'zid* (Paris: Seuil, 2001), p. 21.
88. Bonnici, *Lejn*, p. 131.
89. Mokeddem, *N'zid*, p. 25.
90. Ibid., p. 158.
91. Ibid., p. 164.
92. Ibid., p. 184.
93. Ibid., p. 69.
94. Ibid..
95. Ibid., p. 135.
96. Ibid., p. 25.
97. Ibid., p. 161.
98. Ibid., pp. 161–62.
99. Larry Wolff, *Inventing Eastern Europe: The Map of Civilization on the Mind of the Enlightenment* (Stanford, CA: Stanford University Press, 1994), p. 90.
100. Ibid., p. 90.
101. Clancy-Smith, *Mediterraneans*, p. 419.
102. Clancy-Smith, *Mediterraneans*, p. 347.
103. Gabriel Audisio, *Ulysse ou l'intelligence* (Paris: Gallimard, 1946), p. 55.
104. Ibid., p. 54.
105. Ibid., p. 172.

CHAPTER 5

Infra-materiality and Opaque Drifting

Caroline Bergvall

Þ

My most recent project DRIFT started when I stumbled across an obsolete letter: the runic and anglo-saxon sign, the thorn sign: Þ, now only active in Irish and Icelandic, and unreadable to most others. Or readable only as an indexical marker, the mark of an ancient or dead language, unreadable otherwise. The initiatory qualities of tripping, of falling over became the leitmotif of the project's first piece 'Noping': 'You trip over some Þing nearly makes you fall over' and also a pretext for a seemingly innocent autobiographic turn: 'I went looking for my Nordic roots in the English language and found this sign. A p attached to a long stick, or a type of hoop'. This 'thorn' letter became a sign of absence and of disappearance. I tripped some more over its protruding root and fell deeper into historic soils, deep nightmarish matter, dream-like consciousness. Signing off on absence was bringing up all sorts of ghosts. Charting a course through ancient historical, anglo-saxon and irish sea poetry, medieval travel documents, and viking sagas inevitably took place more or less in parallel with the news of an ill-fated crossing of migrants across the mediterranean sea's political waters, a disaster that came to be known as the 'Left-to-Die' Boat Case (April 2011).[1]

The work developed slowly into a text, into a performance with a musician, into a moving textmass with a digital artist, into drawings and prints. Back and forth between writing, vocal strategies and performance and historic research, this project would keep on asking questions about the handling and processing of the artistic and poetic material in relation to the human dimensions being presented. Developing the various poetic languages of the piece, it was dauntingly clear how these ancient literary journeys were being echoed in the harrowing and unsung, unwillingly documented, disasters of contemporary crossings such as the 'Left-to-Die' boat case. Distinctions between present, future and past times were challenged. History functions as a complex time loop. It can dredge up events seemingly wide apart by running them through a very fine sieve. An implicit notion of 'poetic time' was activated: open vibratory chains of linguistic connection between historic and contemporary languages were set up; verbal declensions were activated. It sought to cover vast ground from ancient tales to current mediatized lives through a complex network of mixed temporalities and mixed art practices.

> Cold gesprung weary worn were my feet frost
> bound in the ice-blinding clamour of kulla
> city sank further seafaring is seafodder heart
> humbling Could scarcely move or draw my
> breath cursed with nightmares gewacked by
> seachops gave up all parts of me on gebattered
> ship Yet a hungor innan mind stole me to more
> weird comas let me let me let me let me freeze
> Blow wind blow, anon am I
>
> Song 2

Writing in an interdisciplinary or transdisciplinary fashion is reflective of my interest in multiple languages, in the power relations between languages, and in thinking about language across various modes of literacy and experientiality. A lot of my recent work is engaged in thinking about how languages cohabit, survive, are prohibited, become dominant, infiltrate or irremediably dominate one another, not only on a syntagmatic axis, in geopolitical proximities, but also paradigmatically, by virtue of deep vertical drops into etymologies, syntactical development or other transformative surges of change within a language's history. This crossing into a range of language soils and environments by way of artistic processes is a way of pushing at questions of power and translatability, of voicing and ghosting, of being and remembering, of empathizing and stripping bare. On this occasion, it asked for more than I had bargained for. The more inter- or transdisciplinary my methods became the more they pressed against borders of knowledge, of practice, of suffering.

Drift had started quite casually from a tiny incident, a stumbling, not even a falling over. Yet it jolted me to the core. It threw me into the mysteries of anglo-saxon writing, a language and an epoch I knew very little about. An experience of intense disorientation became the edge, the limit against which my knowledges and my life started to push. It put everything into question, it threw everything out to sea. It boiled down to questions of methodology and ideology: translatability and opacity, access and cultural unavailability, love and loss. Direction, navigation, journeying out, getting lost, finding a new direction, seeking a steady course, an 'orientation' for oneself and with others, these became *Drift*'s central narrative motifs.

In the 'Log' of the project I wrote: 'Desire's opacity is the longing that gives the courage to depart, to set out. It lends the harshest sweetness to the most total risk. It is as opaque as it is luminous and precious. The intensity of its luminosity always much depends on the political times one lives in and how much darkness is imposed as light. To measure the light at what is needed in order to make out other objects in the night. How much freedom can be retained and explored from dwelling in the dark, how much work can be released when making it out into the light. How much release when making out the nature of darkness and light, and walking into it' (*Drift*, pp. 149–50).

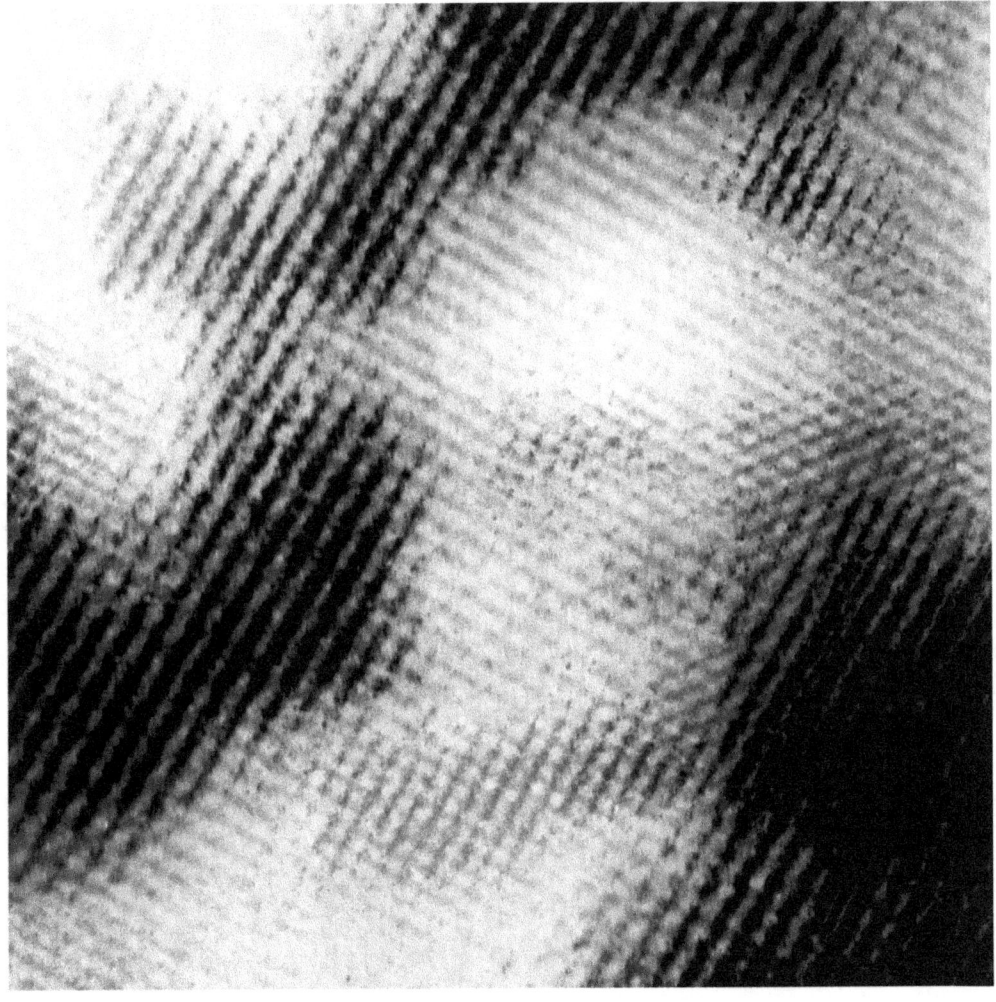

I started to use the original tenth-century poem 'The Seafarer' not only as support for my linguistic excavations and translative elegiac meditations on solitary sailing/flailing/failing, but also increasingly as a way to delve into the unmoored dimensions of contemporary identity, of which the doomed horrors of current sea-bound migrants. This brought home yet again that creating methodological relays of activities when attempting to peer into other epochs through their material signs was far more than a powerful and humbling reminder of one's place in the layers and times of the world. A transhistoric practice provides its own form of contemporary engagement. It generates an actual friction between historic investigation and contemporary witnessing. A palpable connection is made between archaeological work and forensic investigation, between investigating ancient drama at their sometimes horrific residues and piecing together current crimes from unyielding signs at the scene.

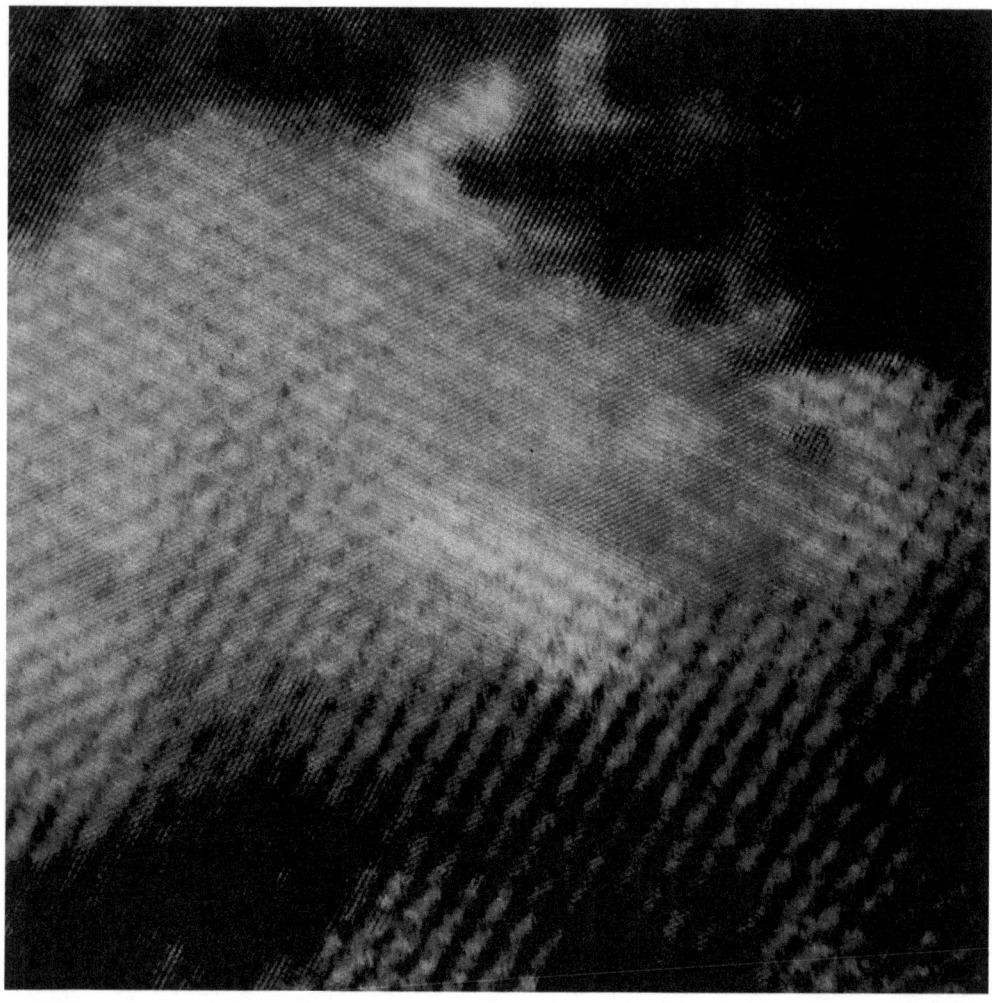

The methodologies of the Left-to-Die report, which brought the case to widespread political attention, were developed by the research group 'Forensic Architecture' at Goldsmiths University. This varied group of researchers has tried for a while to answer these questions by dealing with a whole range of violent acts, harmful and unlawful, engineered and hidden by states. Both their fieldwork and their findings' analysis are inherently interdisciplinary. They use human testimonies, on-the-ground interviews, as well as the most contemporary digital modelling and spatial technologies from tools often used by maritime and military forces to reconstruct the events they're examining: 'What happens to the "era of the witness" when a crime is no longer visible to unmediated human perception? What happens when the evidence has been made untraceable? Will the era of scientific model come to replace human testimony in adjudicating humanitarian claims?' writes Anselm Franke in the seminal group work *Forensis: The Architecture of Public Truth* (2014; p. 507).

Infra-materiality and Opaque Drifting 71

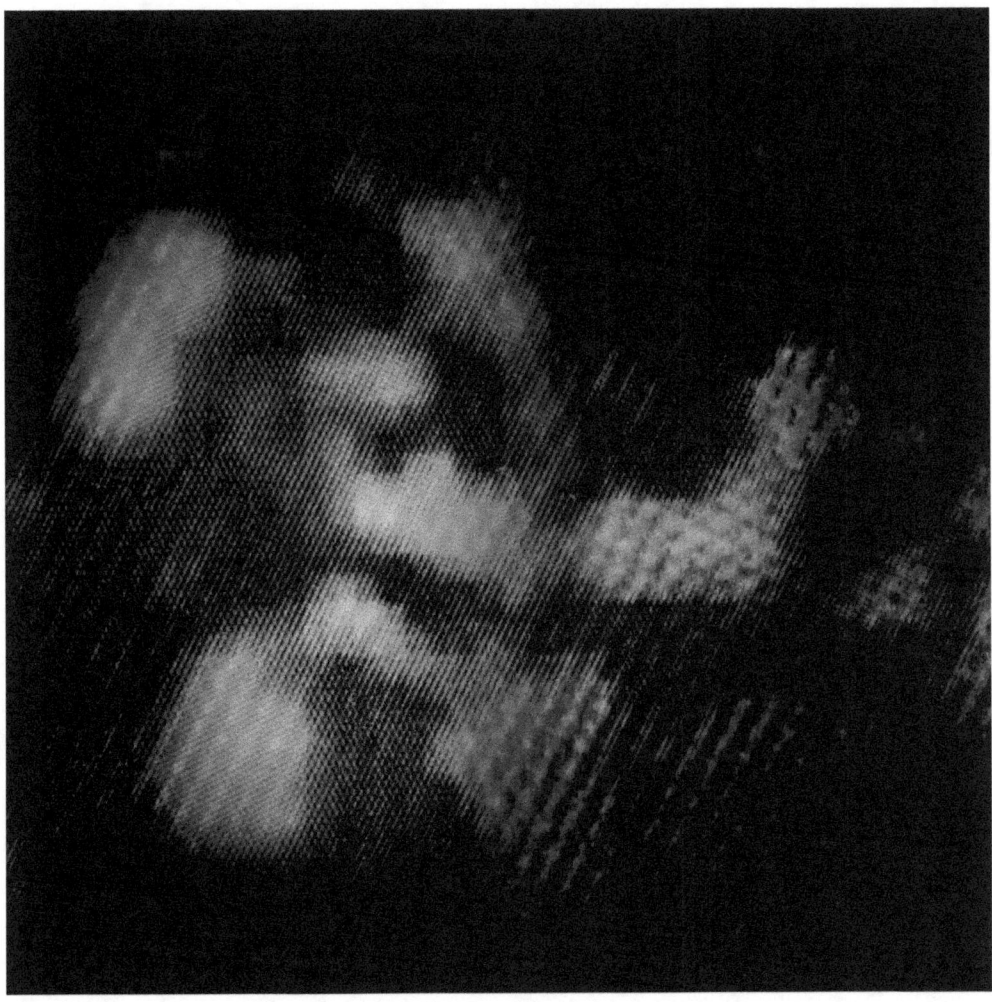

For the book I invited the photographer Tom Martin to reflect on the image that has been widely circulated online: the image of the zodiac of migrants at the start of their journey, photographed by a French military helicopter. Tom has worked as a photographer for international charities, in war-zones and countries ravaged by conflict. He is also keenly interested in old printing processes. The question I ask of him here is how one might unpack the cruel scandal that this image reveals and that is 'about to' take place. How one might imagine and hold visually the memory and the reality of these passengers beyond morbid voyeurism. How one might activate both inquisitiveness and empathetic connection not only in a forensic but also in an experiential way. So that seeing can be radically slowed down and the viewing of the news item can be experienced as a material, opaque, inescapable trace of observed and shared life. He developed a series of macro images, which each seek to respond to this call. They are unreadable, yet potentially decipherable. They remove representation from the viewing. Yet the intense colours bring up a

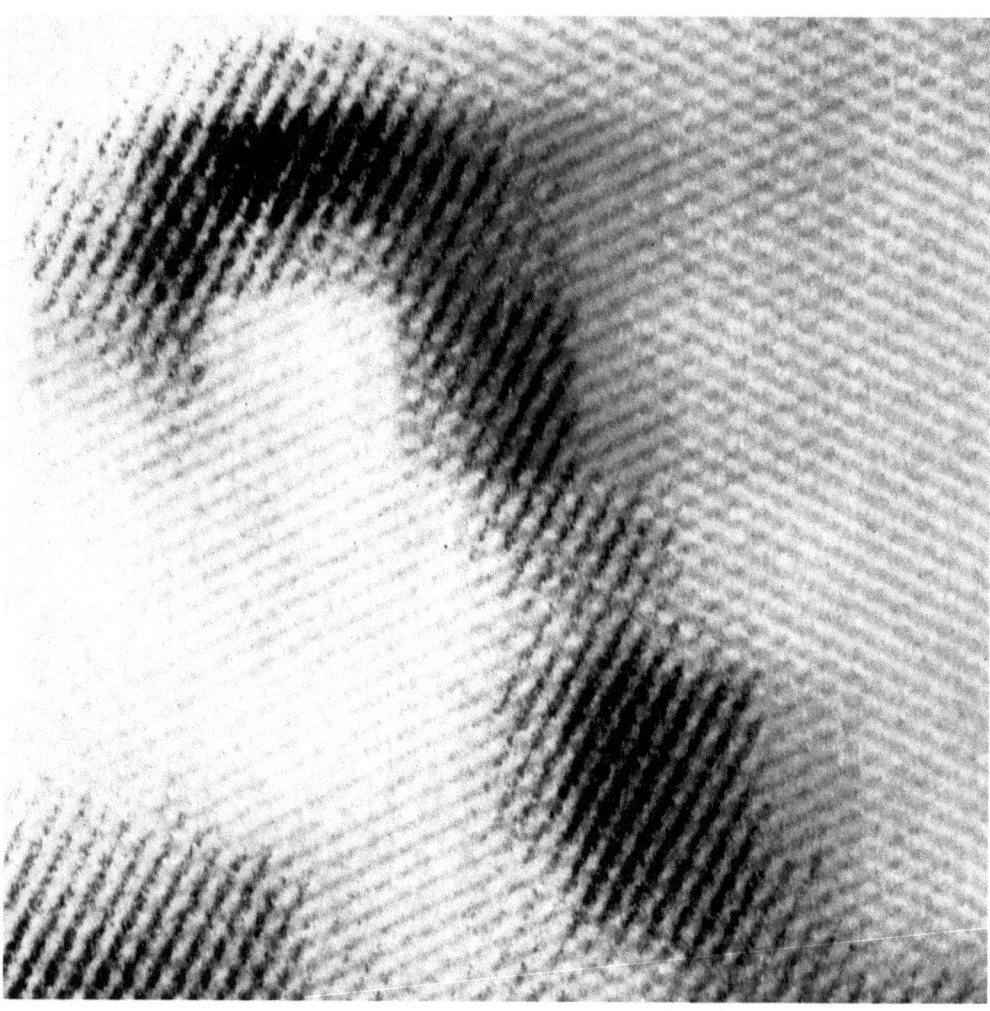

peculiar sense of rawness and fragility. Not being entirely sure of what I'm looking at, they make me feel a bit nervous of what is perhaps hiding here. They open up the viewing process to analysis while also detecting other media traces at the heart of the image: the yellow dots of location sensors embedded in the image processing itself.

These images remind me of the way the 'forensic research' scholars define the technologies they deploy. They do not simply create a new representation of the sea but rather they constitute a new sea altogether, one which is simultaneously composed 'by matter and media' (*Forensis*, p. 667). The remarkable documentary *Nostalgia for the Light* by the Chilean Patricio Guzmán is a powerful example of how mixing media and working transhistorically can release forbidding though fugitive testimonial matter. It meditates on the confluence between the desert of Atacama, the driest desert in the world, the research in astronomy into the oldest galaxies being done there, the Pre-Columbian rock drawings found there, and early twentieth-century open graves of miners and workers. Rather than diminish their significance, as though paling in this layering of time's many events, this complex and resonant accumulation from the past highlights the plight of a few women seen still stubbornly hunching down in the dust, picking up small bones like gold-diggers, still looking for the scattered remains of their loved ones, some of the many thousands summarily executed and hidden about the desert by Pinochet's troops in the 1970s. This becomes a profound act of resistance, which imbues its powerful and deeply moving human testimony across all the layers of the film.

Seeking to create a temporally complex matter of past and present texts to compose and reconstitute 'hafville' (an ancient icelandic term meaning 'sea-loss') in my own project meant that acts of witnessing would stretch across times and epochs. Looking for the 'voices' (signs) of current disappeared passengers gave 'voice' simultaneously to lost apparitions from the ancient past of voyagers and quest literature. A quote I used as the epigraph to one of my chaucerian works, *Alyson Singes*, also impressed itself on these thoughts. It stems from Christa Wolf's profound, transhistoric meandering and anti-nuclear novel *Medea*: 'Do we let ourselves go back to the ancients, or do they catch up with us? No matter. An outstretched hand suffices. Lightly they cross over to us, our strange guests who are like ourselves. We hold the key that unlocks all epochs, sometimes we use it shamelessly, darting a hasty glimpse through the crack of the door, keen on quick, ready-made judgments; yet it should also be possible to get closer, a step at a time, awed by the taboo, unwilling without great need to wrest away a secret from the dead. Confessing our need — we should begin with that' (p. 1).

The work of the French historian Michel de Certeau is particularly relevant here. Indeed, his approach is often that of a tracker of verbal remainders, material smudges, fugitive collective tracks, or 'lapses' as he calls them, which interrupt the smooth functioning of the authoritative text within inscriptive culture. There is in his writing a struggle to make voices and bodily presences seep through the official and eradicating stamp of the omniscient history machine. He describes it in this way in his classic collection *The Practice of Everyday Life*: 'The voice insinuates itself

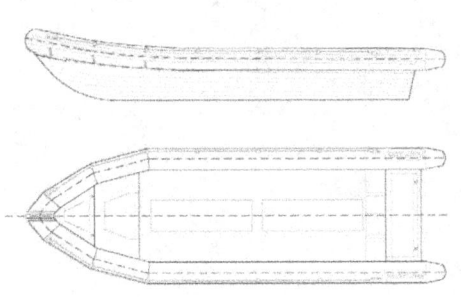

Dimensions	
Overall length	11900 mm
Overall Beam	3770 mm
Internal Length	9600 mm
Internal Beam	2600 mm
Weight Empty	2500 Kg
Buoyancy Collar diameter	550mm

Capacity	
Max No. of Persons	25 Persons
MaxPayload incl. fuel*	3720 Kg
Floor Board Usable Area	22.2 m2
Buoyancy Volume	3758 L

into the text as a mark, a trace [...] an indiscreet ghost [...] a metonymy of the body'. In a previous essay I had come to understand this idea of 'indiscreet ghosts' as a type of infra-materiality (p. 155). A notion I keep very close to Duchamp's fugitive and potent idea of the 'infrathin', this performative friction of bounds between objects in motion, or the inner-outer spaces of some of Rachel Whiteread's negative objects. Small seemingly unimportant or simply illegible elements in a text turn out to be disturbing and revelatory because they do not seem to belong. Or because they belong exceedingly to it. They point to an interiority that is not fully traceable yet is entirely contained in the text's or the object's intrinsic matter. They rub against the reading process. They actualize what is gone in embedded and performative ways. Like indistinct spoors, or lingering afterimages, they call up unexplored, disallowed parts of ourselves and our un/shared histories. In the context of *Drift*, pursuing material traces of both evidence and of invention encourages both a performance of recitation (and mouthing) and of excavatory imagination. It can offer itself up as an impossible salvaging or restitutive operation: 'I wish I could tenderly lift from the dark side of history, voices that are anonymous, slighted — inarticulate' wrote famously the American poet Susan Howe who has always been committed to following histories' indiscreet and accidental revelatory traces (*The Europe of Trusts*, p. 14). Reclaiming the experience of singular lives alongside larger collective investigations provokes a pendular effect between far and close, which can favour various kinds of empathetic identification at both a personal and a collective level. During my performance, my verbatim recitation of sections of the 'Left-to-Die' report based on the archaeological and forensic work became a form of witnessing. It entered into the audience's public consciousness by way of an archaic, experiential

performance. In the book the text is written in white on black page, both a funerary gesture and a hint at the luminous constellations showing the way on the darkest nights.

Note

1. Charles Heller, Lorenzo Pezzani and Situ Studio, *Report on the 'Left-To-Die Boat'* (Centre for Research Architecture, Goldsmiths, University of London, 2012). This chapter includes the following images in order of appearance: *Wake*, Macro Exploration, 2014, Tom Martin; *Passenger*, Macro Exploration, 2014, Tom Martin; *Passengers*, Macro Exploration, 2014, Tom Martin; *Passenger 2*, Macro Exploration, 2014, Tom Martin; Zodiac boat model in *Report on the 'Left-To-Die Boat'*, p. 50; Zodiac constellation, Caroline Bergvall and Pablo Lavalley in *Drift* (2014).

CHAPTER 6

❖

Minding Orientalist Margins: Colonial Nomos and Jonathan Scott's Revision of *The Arabian Nights*

Claire Gallien

In 1811, the booksellers of Paternoster-Row, behind St Paul's Cathedral, London, received the new six-volume edition of the *Arabian Nights Entertainments*, 'carefully revised, and occasionally corrected from the Arabic' by Jonathan Scott. It had taken more than a decade for the publication to reach their bookshelves (Scott had started his work in the final years of the eighteenth century). Indeed, in the preface for the 1811 edition, the orientalist avers that in 1800 he began his translation of the manuscript, procured by Sir Edward Wortley Montague in Egypt.[1] In fact, in 1798, he had already published a table of contents of the Montague manuscript, on which his revision is based, along with two specimens of tales in the second volume of the miscellany *The Oriental Collections* edited by Sir William Ouseley.

The discovery of the Montague manuscript of the *Nights* excited the community of British orientalists because its quality meant that it could serve as the basis for a new translation in English derived directly from Arabic sources. Sir William Ouseley was amongst the many enthusiasts, calling it 'the most perfect copy of the *Arabian Nights*, which has yet been imported into England (perhaps into Europe)'.[2] All previous English editions of the *Nights*, the so-called Grub-Street translations, harked back to the beginning of the eighteenth century and were based on Antoine Galland's French version, which was published in twelve volumes between 1704 and 1710. However, doubts had long been expressed concerning the authenticity of the French orientalist's sources, and his many departures from the texts in his possession were criticized amongst scholarly circles — so much so that the need for a new translation in English directly from the Arabic had grown stronger. At a time of political tensions with France, the Montague manuscripts and Scott's attempts would address this need and permit the establishment of an English version of the *Nights*.

Despite his initial excitement the manuscript turned out to be a real disappointment for Scott, hence the protracted publication. He declared in the preface to the 1811 edition that he found very little difference between the seven volumes of the Montague manuscript he perused and Galland's translation, and was generally appalled at the licentiousness of the *Nights* and dismissive of its poetry:

> Having relinquished the design of retranslating such tales as are given by M. Galland, the original of which appeared in Mr. Montague's MS., the editor began upon the remainder; but vexatious indeed as his disappointment as an orientalist, who had fancied that in seven volumes of Arabic copy of the 1001 Nights he possessed a treasure which would amply repay the labour of research, on discovering upon perusal that far the greater part of them was unfit to appear in an English dress. [...] Among the whole he judged those only *at all* worth translation which form the sixth volume of this edition; M. Galland had already selected all the best.[3]

In the end, Scott followed Galland in both the selection of tales and the order in which they were presented. He merely modernizes the English version, so that the first five volumes do not sound archaic or dissonant in relation to the last volume, which is comprised of the tales newly translated from the Montague manuscript. Finally, he appended elucidatory notes to all six volumes. Thus, on the face of it, Scott's endeavour is confined to a careful revision and occasional correction of Galland's, with the addition of an introduction on Islam, of endnotes, and of a sixth volume of new tales. Galland's standards of taste, which defined his approach to the corpus, were not challenged by Scott; and Galland's voluntary omissions were reproduced in Scott's version, including the erasure of all verses from the narrative of the tales. The new sanitized version of the *Nights* indicates a double submission of the Arabic text — first, at the hands of Galland and then, through Scott's mediation — and obliterates all traces of the struggle of the orientalist grasping with its structure and meaning.

The edited pages are neat and seamless, with unspoiled margins, and can be read in two complementary directions: the first would link this cleaning-up with the history of the book, and compare it with modern editing which systematically removed marginal 'dirt' from the page and also shifted commentaries and references from margins to footnotes;[4] the second reading would relate it to the question of the 'colonial order'.[5] According to this second direction, the pages of the edited volumes could then be interpreted literally as marking the illusion of a total control of the orientalist over his material, and symbolically as textual equivalents for the colonial fiction of a peaceful submission of colonized people under European civilizing rule. The unruly Arabic text is thus brought back within the frame and fold of an orientalist fiction.

The preservation of the Montague manuscript in the Oriental Collections of the Bodleian Library allows for a different story to be told. If we *mind* the borders of this seven-volume manuscript, traces of a struggle between the orientalist and his material emerge. These annotations bordering the Arabic text or inscribed over it are of various sorts. They include corrections of orthographic misspellings, indications concerning the number and title of the tales, words underlined with their translations in English in the margin, passages crossed out, or hypertextual links with other tales from Persian and Indian corpuses. They all indicate attempts to appropriate the Eastern material. In naming chapters and paragraphs in the margins, Scott fragments the on-going flow of stories lined up one after the other

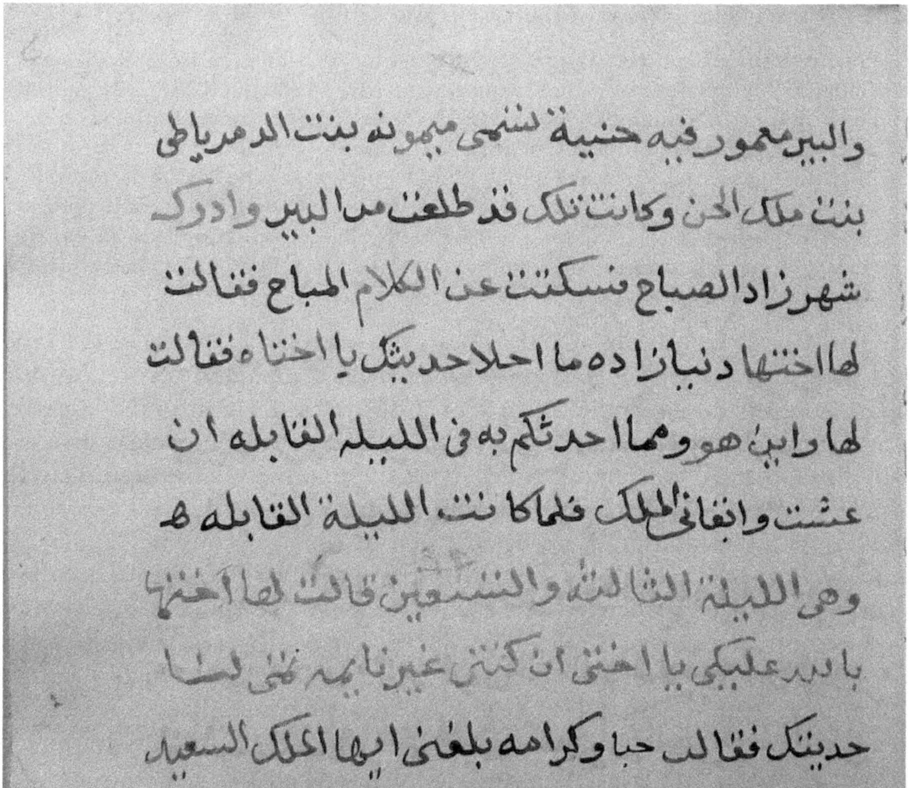

والبير معمور فيه جنية تسمى ميمونة بنت الدمرياطى بنت ملك الجن وكانت تلك قد طلعت من البير وادرك شهرزاد الصباح فسكتت عن الكلام المباح فقالت لها اختها دنيازاده ما احلا حديثك يا اختاه فقالت لها وابن هو ومما احدثكم به فى الليلة القابلة ان عشت وابقانى الملك فلما كانت الليلة القابلة وهى الليلة الثالثة والتسعين قالت لها اختها بالله عليكى يا اختى ان كنتى غير نايمة تمى لنا حديثك فقالت حبا وكرامه بلغنى ايها الملك السعيد الموفق الرشيد صاحب الراى السديد ان ميمونة الجنية طلعت من البيرات فى البرج نور وضوء يشعل بغير العادة وهى عامره منذ سنتين ما عهدت منها فتعجبت من ذلك وقصدت النور فرأته خارج عن القاعة فدخلها فوجدت الخادم نايم وران سرير وعليه هيبة انسان نايم وشمعه وفانوس موقود

FIG. 6.1. MS Bol. Or. 551, fol. 6ʳ *Alf layla wa layla* (Bodleian Library, used with permission)

by the scribe and he reorganizes his material according to Galland's template; in cutting out 'unpleasant' and 'indecent' passages, he revises them so that they appear in a garb deemed proper for an European audience.

Literary critics today should mind the borders of these annotated manuscript volumes and also, by extension, the borders of the translated text, including the preface and the endnotes, because they offer a unique understanding of the functioning of Eurocentric perspectives as forced upon Eastern material, revealing a relation to an object of study defined by rational operations, including reframing, selecting, restructuring. These actions are common, to a certain extent, to all editors, but his praxis does not take place in a vacuum; it is articulated to the colonial nomos, which is based on a fundamental opposition between passion and reason, colonized and colonizer. While the scribe lends his pen to an unimpeded flow of stories, the translator-editor cuts through and clarifies. In fact, with all sorts of notes left by the orientalist on its borders, the manuscript reveals signs of a struggle, as though the Arabic text had not yet been entirely domesticated and was evading the grasp of the scholar.

Colonial tropology has made extensive use of the metaphor of the hunt. Yet, the fact that the Eastern material remains fundamentally elusive, retaining as it does in the volumes under study the fluidity of orality, is not perceptible when the literary critic confines herself or himself to publications, where textual struggles are erased in order to make room for fictions of seamless editions. Furthermore, the selection and re-ordering process, taking place on the pages of the manuscripts, is not random; rather, textual interventions are directed by implied ideological, moral and aesthetic borders, which this article aims to unpack. In other words, minding textual borders enables us to understand the violence but also the resistance built in this encounter between orientalists and their objects of study and to read beyond the sanitized version offered in published editions.

Jonathan Scott and the Montague Manuscripts

The Montague manuscripts are not unknown to literary critics working on eighteenth-century Orientalism. Fatma Mahmoud-Moussa played a crucial part in bringing them to academic attention in her own study of the English novelist William Beckford.[6] Indeed, her focus on the manuscripts allows her to retrace the convoluted history of their circulation and to excavate Beckford's sources of inspiration for his novel *Vathek*; but it falls short of considering the manuscript as an object of enquiry in and of itself. My contribution goes a step further in that specific direction of revisiting the value of the manuscript, by articulating the main text with the borders annotated by Scott, and by comparing the manuscript source with the published translation.

The manuscript in the Bodleian Library consists of seven consecutive volumes (from MS Bodl. Or. 550 to MS Bodl. Or. 556) composed by 'Umar al-Safti in the year 1764–1765'[7] and is accompanied by an eighth volume (MS Bodl. Or. 557) written in English by Scott, which includes a table of contents for the seven volumes as well

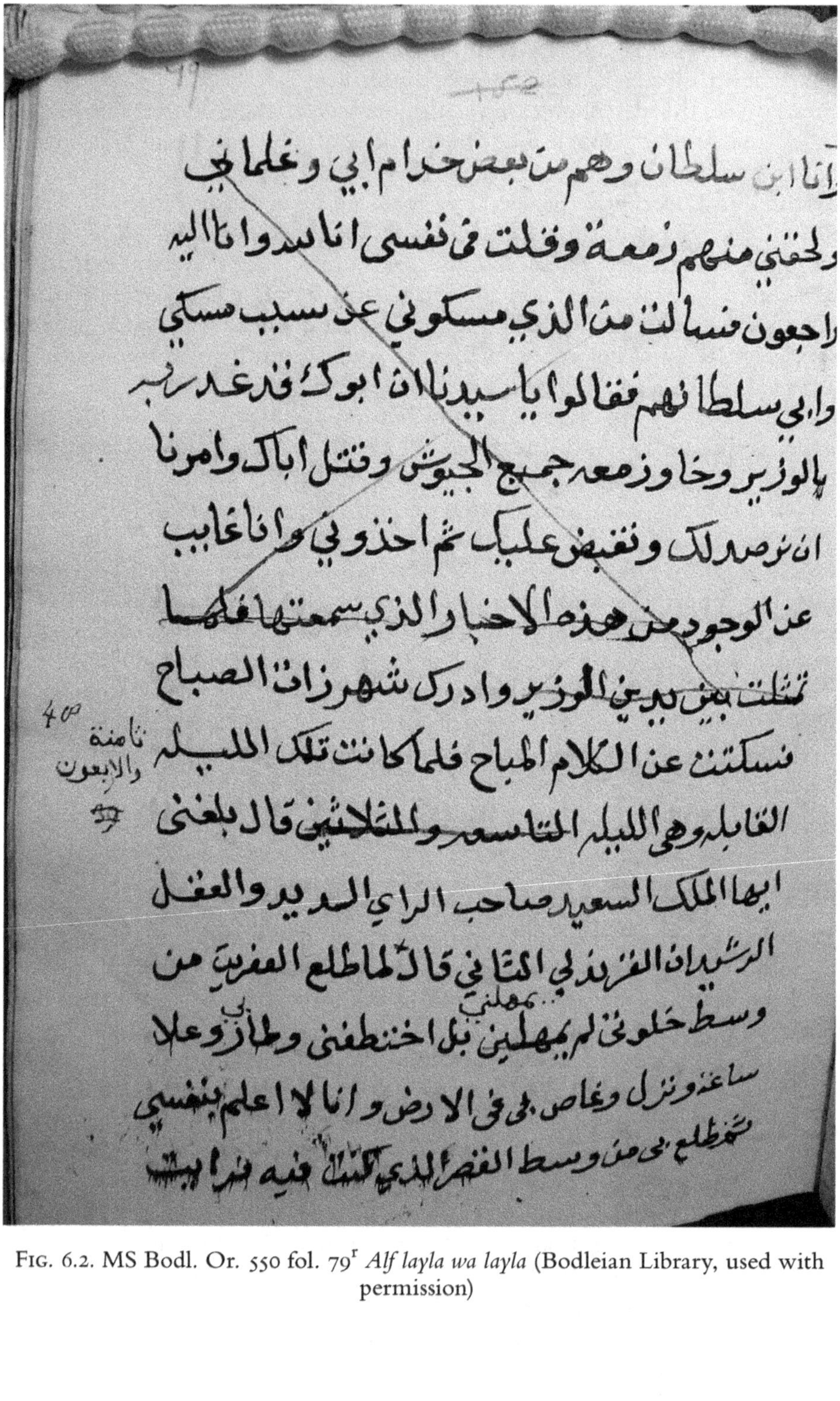

أنا ابن سلطان وهم من بعض خدام أبي وغلمانه
ولحقني منهم جماعة وقلت من نفسي أنا أسير إليه
راجعون فسألت من ذا الذي مسكوني عن سبب مسكي
وأبي سلطان لهم فقالوا يا سيدنا إن أبوك قد غدر به
الوزير وخان وجمع جميع الجيوش وقتل أباك وأمرنا
أن نرصدك ونقبض عليك ثم أخذوني وأنا أأيب
عن الوجود من هذه الأخبار الذي سمعتها فلما
مثلت بين يدي الوزير وأدرك شهرزاد الصباح
فسكتت عن الكلام المباح فلما كانت تلك الليلة
القابلة وهي الليلة المتاسعة والثلاثين قال بلغني
أيها الملك السعيد صاحب الرأي السديد والعقل
الرشيد ان الفريد ابي المنا في قال لما طلع العفريت من
وسط حلوني لم يمهلني بل اختطفني وطار وعلا
ساعة ونزل وغاص بي في الأرض وأنا لا أعلم بنفسي
ثم طلع بي من وسط القصر الذي كنت فيه فرأيت

FIG. 6.2. MS Bodl. Or. 550 fol. 79ʳ *Alf layla wa layla* (Bodleian Library, used with permission)

as comments. The seven volumes were composed for Edward Wortley Montague, son of the eminent female traveller and travel writer Lady Mary Wortley Montague, during the young Montague's stay in Egypt and were kept in his library in Rosetta until his death in 1776. Montague's will stipulated that his Oriental library should be bequeathed to his son Mas'oud, later renamed Fortunatus. The library followed Mas'oud to England were it remained until his death in 1787.[8] A family friend, John Dolben, sold the books and manuscripts at auction, through Leigh and Sotheby,[9] including the manuscript of the *Alf layla wa layla* which was purchased by Professor Joseph White, Laudian Chair of Arabic at Oxford.[10] Scott provides some details of the circulation of the manuscript after White's acquisition in MS Bodl. Or. 557, with the same details reproduced by Ouseley in *The Oriental Collections*. What these accounts reveal is that Professor White later gave the manuscripts to Scott on the understanding that he would hand them to the Bodleian Library when his work was completed. Scott perused the manuscript volumes in the final years of the eighteenth century and finally sold them to the curators of the Bodleian in 1802.[11]

Of this final episode, Fatma Mahmoud-Moussa explains quite dismissively that Scott was actually pleased to dispose of the manuscript volumes in this way because he was not proficient enough in Arabic to translate the whole manuscript: 'He was far from competent for such a task and one would guess he had not really read the MS, or fully understood the tales, at the time when he drew up the Table of Contents for the *Oriental Collections*'.[12] This understates Scott's linguistic proficiency, given that he had entered the military service of the East India Company in 1769 and devoted all of his spare time to the study of Persian, Arabic, Hindustani, and Indian history. In 1783, he was appointed private Persian translator to the governor-general Warren Hastings, was elected member of the Asiatic Society of Bengal soon after its inception in 1784, and became professor of Oriental languages at the East India College, Haileybury in 1802. His publishing career was also very successful, encompassing a history of Mughal India in *A Translation of the Memoirs of Eradut Khan, a Nobleman of Hindostan* (1786), *An Historical and Political View of the Decan* (1791), and *Ferishta's History of Dekkan from the First Mahummedan Conquests* (1794), and the translation of romances, like *Bahar-Danush, or, Garden of knowledge* (1799, in three volumes), and the *Tales, Anecdotes and Letters, Translated from the Arabic and Persian* (1800).[13] In other words, it seems fairer to say that if Scott decided not to persist with the translation of the manuscripts it was due to the lack of interest that these represented for the scholarly community and for the general reader rather than to a lack of competence. This dwindling interest is also clearly established by the fact that the first manuscript volume is far more heavily annotated than the others.

Scott did not spontaneously rediscover the *Nights* ten years later either. His decision to move forward with the revision and publication stems from a request of his publishers Longman and Co. who desired 'to print a new edition of Galland, with some alteration of style and elucidatory notes',[14] and who applied directly to Scott for this. However, Scott's disposal of the Montague volumes and the opportunistic attitude of the publishers who were thinking about how new tales directly translated from the Arabic would attract a substantial number of readers to their new edition, should not be taken for granted and should not dictate the terms of our own approach. Rather, I suggest that, no matter how marginal and uninteresting or unbecoming they have been described so far by orientalists and critics, they are of paramount value if one's attention is focused on the articulation between colonialism and orientalism. If the focus is placed on the published material, and on its position and impact in the history of the European reception of the *Nights*, then the Montague volumes are indeed of little interest, but if we understand translation not as an end result but as a process, and thereby scrutinize its operations, then what has been relegated to the margins of literary history and silenced by Scott and his publisher becomes central. What Gérard Genette argued in *Paratextuality* and which I also use as an important point of entry for this reflection, even if his primary concern was printed material, is that margins indeed have a lot to disclose about how readers, writers, editors, translators enter a text and, in the case that concerns us here, they reveal a struggle between the orientalist and his object of study.[15] They bear the traces of his interventions and of the text's evasions, and that is why this border matters.

The Colonial Nomos

My use of the term *colonial nomos* is an implicit reference to Paul Gilroy's development on the notion of the *racial nomos*, where 'race' refers primarily to 'an impersonal, discursive arrangement, the brutal result of the raciological ordering of the world' and the 'nomos' describes the 'legal, governmental, and spatial order that [...] is now reviving the geopolitical habits of the old imperial system in discomforting ways'.[16] Similarly, I contend that the orientalist approach to Eastern material is framed by a *colonial nomos*, which results in the confident implementation of a textual order inspired by colonial paradigms. The capacity and feeling of entitlement of colonialism and imperialism to reorder the world from the perspective of the colonizer and then turn it into an object of visual, political, and material consumption, as was powerfully described by Timothy Mitchell in *Colonising Egypt* (1988), also applies to Scott's use of the Eastern text in the case under study. He approached the manuscript neither from the position of the antiquarian looking at its preservation, nor from that of an editor, conscientious in the production of a reliable edition, but rather from the perspective of an orientalist intent on publishing a new edition of a book of tales that would renew a fashion for fables of the East and sell well on the European book market.

The question of the constitution and preservation of the Montague Oriental library is not part of the present study even though it deserves further attention on the part of the critic of orientalism and colonialism because it was claimed that it involved acts of extortion and bribery. The English diplomat Nathaniel Davison, deputed by the Royal Society in his capacity of archaeologist to accompany Edward Wortley Montague in Egypt and report on their expeditions, sent a note back to the Royal Society in which he stated that he could not purchase a very fine Qu'ran in Cairo 'for it is in the principal mosque, and the imam would not steal it for me under four hundred sequins, or 1200'.[17] This form of knowledge acquisition was so much the norm at the time that it did not have to be kept secret, even from the members of the Royal Society. Actually, it was the Royal Society itself which encouraged the practice and drew advantage from it.

The *colonial nomos* provides both the tools through which Scott's interventions may be operated and the moral and ideological backing vindicating these operations on the Eastern text. His attitude is not singular but, as I argued elsewhere, it is quite indicative of an eighteenth-century pragmatic approach towards Eastern texts, which would generally be subjected to all kinds of transformations, selections and reordering, before reaching a still confined book market of orientalist productions.[18]

The first step taken by Scott when confronted with the manuscript is to try and make sense of it, and the initial move lies in the uncovering of its structure. Indeed, in the case of the Montague manuscript, the original text functions without borders so to speak. At the micro-level, and as is often the case with Arabic texts of the classical period, no punctuation marks are introduced; rather, they are replaced by grammatical markers such as the *wa* or the *fa* which have no other function in this case but to indicate a break in the syntax and a move to the next sentence. Interestingly enough, punctuation marks became the norm in the Arab world towards the end of the nineteenth century, during the *nahda* (renaissance) period, when countries such as Egypt fell under the indirect rule of the British and the French and opened themselves to European, and in particular French, cultural influences.[19]

Even if the use of punctuation marks becomes systematic towards the end of the nineteenth century, a punctuation system in classical Arabic literature existed as well, but its use was less frequent and not systematized. Thus, a late eighteenth-century manuscript, like the Montague manuscript, bearing no punctuation mark is not in itself a scribal oddity but it certainly indicates a form of cultural distinction from European influence. Since, the manuscript was produced at a specific request from Montague, we could argue that the insistence not to use any punctuation reveals non-conformity with European standards, whether the scribe knew of them and decided not to apply them or whether he was simply not familiar with them.

It would be precipitate to link typography with subaltern agency without further knowledge of the scribe's intentions, because we also find traces of what could be interpreted as subaltern compliance when the ink colour is changed to red for every phrase indicating the beginning or the end of a new night.[20] Indeed, the change of ink colour does not occur at the very beginning — rather, it becomes systematic later on, from vol. II onwards. What is fundamental here is the interpretation Scott gives for this distinction. The non-partition is understood as a form of disorder and his initial intervention on the text lies in the super-imposition of a clearly delineated structure that corresponds to the orientalist's notion of order and clarity.

Thus, pen in hand and with a copy of Galland's translation of the *Arabian Nights Entertainments* sitting on his desk, Scott underlined the night numbers and rewrote them in numerical format in the margins, correcting the Arabic, when it did not match his own calculation. He also underlined elements corresponding to the title of tales as known in Galland's edition, rewriting the name of the tale in English below or beside the Arabic script. For example, MS Bodl. Or. 554, fol. 46^v (see appendix) indicates the beginning of the story of Haroun al-Rashid. This clarification allows him then to devise a table of contents, reproduced in MS Bodl. Or. 557. The Arabic text is dismembered, its structure laid bare, so as to correspond with a type of ordering easily recognizable by future European readers, bearing in mind that Scott was initially devising this table for the Bodleian curators. However, he is not going through the whole seven volumes with the sole intention of producing a table of contents. His primary objective in perusing the volumes is to ascertain the need for revisions and additions to Galland's edition. Indexing the tales is thus a means to gauge Galland's deviations from what orientalists at the time initially assumed to be a definitive version of the corpus. Yet, Scott's measuring goes the other way round. Instead of using the Montague manuscript as a point of reference to which Galland's *Nights* would be compared, the manuscript becomes the tenor and is described solely through its conformity to and departure from the vehicle of Galland's edition.[21] Reverting to analogical thinking, which compares the unfamiliar to the familiar, Scott's endeavour promotes Galland's version as *the* reference text, to which the Arabic manuscript is compared.

Such procedures are in total opposition to the Arabic oral tradition which accounts for the dispersal of and large variations in the corpus. This fact was very well known at the time in Europe. When Ouseley introduced Scott's specimen translations of the first two tales of the *Arabian Nights* cycle, he described the various versions extant, and more precisely a Syrian manuscript belonging to James Russell and an Indian manuscript belonging to James Anderson, and concluded that 'no two copies of the Arabian Tales are to be found exactly alike'.[22] Despite being acquainted with the fundamental heterogeneity of the corpus, Scott and his publishers were still intent on producing a definitive edition. Such an edition is thus an Orientalist creation in the sense that it has no Eastern counterpart. It is, as Edward Said defined Orientalism, an image without a referent, a discourse producing its own imagined system of reference.[23] Orientalists thus produced a textual equivalent to the political principle directing the *colonial nomos* and according to which the East cannot represent itself but has to be represented, whether politically or textually, by others, preferably colonizers. Despite his awareness of these differences in the literary traditions, not only did Scott persist in comparing the versions but he also looked at and evaluated the Arabic manuscript by comparing it to a European translation in French.

Placed side by side, the table of contents of the MS Bodl. Or. 507 and Scott's 1811 edition reveal a different arrangement of the tales, which indicates that, when a discrepancy occurred between the two, Scott would disregard the Arabic manuscript and follow Galland's division, with the exception of the last volume, which consisted of the new tales of the Montague corpus which Scott judged to be proper and interesting to include. This decision is premised on the fundamental belief in the authority of the orientalist over the Arabic material, as articulated by Scott in a letter to Ouseley: 'The other tales [...] appear like pearls strung at random on the same thread. Yet, [...] if they are truly Oriental, it is a matter of little importance to us Europeans, whether they were strung on this night or that night'.[24] In other words, order comes from Europe and Eastern texts clearly do not know how to behave. Their unruly, undomesticated state may, nevertheless, be subjected to orientalist authority, whether at the hands of Galland or of Scott.

As a case in point, in the first manuscript volume (MS Bodl. Or. 550) we observe a series of differences between the order followed in the manuscript and the order followed in the 1811 edition. Generally speaking, Scott ignores the tales that are not already present in Galland's edition and disregards the order given in the manuscript in favour of Galland's ordering of the tales. For example, 'The story of the ox, ass, merchant, dog and cock' and 'The story of the envious man, and of him that he envied' are omitted in the manuscript but because the stories are in Galland, Scott puts them back in his edited version. On a more controversial note, Scott also follows Galland in including the cycle of stories of Sindbad the Sailor even though their authenticity was under dispute at the time, with a number of orientalists believing that Galland had actually forged them.[25] Disregarding their problematic status and the fact that the Montague manuscript quite predictably does not include them, Scott interpolated the cycle, as Galland did before him, between 'The story of the second sister' and 'The story of the tailor and the hunchback'.[26] Conversely, the manuscript includes 'The story of the old man and the mule,' but since it is not in Galland's version, it is omitted in the 1811 edition.

It could be argued that the preference given to Galland's rendition over the original manuscript is not a simple case of deference versus indifference but that Scott was disappointed by the quality of the Arabic manuscript and changed his plan from publishing a new translation to editing a mere revision, with additions. However, the crucial aspect to take into consideration here is that the published edition conceals the marks of these textual interventions. There are no endnotes, even, to indicate the reason for the disappearance, whereas the reader may refer to the endnotes for anthropological details drawn from the tales. In fact, the explanation lies in the border, i.e. in the manuscript, which he used for the preparation of the translation. As such, MS Bodl. Or. 557 includes a footnote which reads for 'The story of the old man and the Mule': 'Omitted by Galland or not in his copy. It is however too licentious for publication, being a very free detail of the amours of an unfaithful wife'.[27]

This comment, and others of its kind[28] are indications that European moral etiquette prevailed over closeness to the original when the two clashed. The same was true for standards of taste. Scott has no appreciation for the passages in verse included in the *Nights*. He only interprets them as infelicitous interruptions in the narration,[29] whereas, from an Arabic perspective, these passages corroborate the poetic skill and literary knowledge of the storyteller. Abdelfattah Kilito comments on the use of poetic citation in classical Arabic writings and underscores its ingenuity:

> [...] contrary to what one might first think, it is far from being an antidote to

> the indolence of writers who lack inspiration. According to Ibn 'Abd Rabbih, selecting texts is more difficult than composing them! The difficulty comes from the fact that the selected wording must be impressive in itself while being pertinently integrated in the context in which it is used. From citation to plagiarism sometimes involves only one step, and — all things considered — plagiarism is an art, but rare are those who excel at it.[30]

From a classical Arabic perspective, plagiarism is an art, and the poet is expected to demonstrate his skills by emulating and surpassing his predecessors. This interpretation dates back to the pre-Islamic poetical contests around the Ka'abah, or those taking place at major caravan fairs, and refers also to the inimitable nature of Qu'ranic verses. Apart from the Qu'ran all other poetry is to be surpassed through imitation. By taking out the quotations and the passages in verse, Galland and Scott thus disregarded a central notion in classical Arabic literature — the art of imitation (*mu'aradah*) — and redirected the text of the *Nights* towards a compliance with modern European aesthetic judgement, according to which such passages were merely deemed abstruse and redundant.

In his article 'Poetry and the Arabian Nights', Geert Jan van Gelder reminds us that genres combining prose and poetry already existed in early Islamic literature but that the *Arabian Nights* is notable in that narrative verse is not employed — the narrative remains in prose but it contains a large amount of non-narrative poetry. This poetry is unequally distributed in the corpus; some stories contain none, others little, and others still are riddled with poems. Josef Horovitz counted up to 1250 poems in the Macnaghten edition of the *Nights* and was able to find the sources for about a quarter of them.[31] His findings show that pre- and early-Islamic poetry is little represented and that the great majority of the poetry quoted dates back to the Abbasid and post-Abbasid periods, with poems from al-Mutanabbi (d. 965) and Bahâ' al-Dîn Zuhayr (d. 1258). Van Gelder indicates that the presence of classical poetry is all the more notable since, by the time the first corpuses were compiled, non-classical poetic forms (such as *zajal*, *mawâliyâ*, and *kân wa kân*) had already made their way into polite literary circles. The choice of classical poetry and the fact that the poetry included varies from one corpus to the other, makes it clear that the compilers and copyists used it to prove their sense of poetic taste, their extensive knowledge of the poetic tradition, and their own skills in the art of emulation.[32]

The poems inserted may influence the course of events present in the plot, by mollifying a ruler for instance; but in the overwhelming majority of cases poetry is inserted as an interlude, which is why Western readers tended to view it as superfluous, or even ludicrous, when, for instance, characters express themselves in verse as they are about to die. Since the orientalists of Scott's generation and before looked at it from a European perspective they only saw in that poetry ornaments or unacceptable departures from the rules of verisimilitude. To an Arab audience, however, the poetry was crucial in creating empathy with the characters and thus taking the plot onto an altogether different plane of universal emotions and truths, whether that poetry took the form of *zajal* (love poetry), *hikam* (wisdom poetry), or *mithal* (proverbial lines). Divesting the *Nights* of these lines restricts the corpus of its aspiration to highbrow and universal literature.

Scott is not totally unaware of this but his belief in the impossibility of producing translations of Arabic poetry that would be acceptable and pleasurable to an English reader was so strong that he preferred to omit all poetic quotations,[33] as had Galland before him: 'such omission (at least in the humble opinion of the editor) is not to be regretted; for he thinks, that for the European reader their insertion would have been an intolerable interruption to the narrative'.[34] Scott spells out the reason for such distaste and argues that the metaphors, lacking reference, remain not only obscure but also unpoetic, and that, on the other hand, notes and comments would unduly burden the text. Paraphrase is an option but risks swelling the text out of proportion.[35] Scott chose to simply wield his authority as European translator and editor and delete all poetry from the corpus.

It seems then that only two options were available to the translator — either writing over, i.e. paraphrasing, or deleting — and that Scott chose the second option in order to facilitate reception. In so doing, the translator builds for himself a reputation of reliability and trustworthiness, assuring his readers that he would not trick them into believing they are reading Arabic poetry when in fact it is his paraphrase they are engaging.[36] Finally, this recourse to the old adage of the untranslatability of poetry may also merely have meant that Scott was trying to homogenize the text so that it would conform to a European idea of narrative and to the classical separation between prose and poetry. This practice had been initiated by Galland who systematically either erased the poetic passages contained in the *Nights* or transformed them into prose and integrated them to the plot.[37]

Textual Resistance

The manuscripts collected by Montague are not only of value to contemporary literary critics for the evidence they provide of colonial interventions on the text but also for the indications they bear of textual resistance to and evasion from the colonial *nomos*. After decades during which Galland's version of the *Nights* monopolized its Western European reception, various manuscripts were collected which either confirmed or departed from the corpus of the *Nights* as set up by Galland. On top of Galland's collection in the Royal Library in France, Scott mentions the existence of manuscripts of the *Nights* preserved in the Vatican Library, in the British Museum, in university libraries, in private collections, and also the copies brought back from Aleppo by Alexander Russell, as well as a fragment that he procured for himself in Bengal and which he translated separately in 1802.[38] This variety in the corpus and its capacity to morph into various shapes is acknowledged by the translator:

> The original Arabian Nights consisted of a far smaller number than the 1001 in thirty six parts; and that upon the original stock various novelists of the Moosulmaun world have engrafted their performances. Hence no two copies procured in different kingdoms or provinces will probably be found to accord, but each vary as the popular tales of this or that country have been added to the original portion.[39]

These conclusions put the emphasis on the elusive nature of the text and recognize that the quest for a definitive edition is by nature an abortive one. Scott highlights the patchiness and the ungraspable nature of the corpus by providing further descriptions of fragments found in Christ Church's library:

> The MS. commences with a continuation of the adventures of Ummir bin Naomaun, his consort Aberwezeh, and the princess Nozut al Zummaun; but they are not concluded in the volume, which is in small quarto, of considerable thickness. This tale does not appear in Galland's, neither in Dr. Russell's copy, in that of Mr. Wortley Montague, or in the fragment procured in Bengal by the editor.[40]

The long list of negative statements does not, strictly speaking, suffice to exclude the fragment from the corpus and yet, beyond the acknowledgment of its existence, Scott seems at a loss as to what to do with this extraneous matter. If today literary critics praise the accretive and open-ended nature of the corpus of the *Nights*,[41] in Scott's time, and as we understand from his own declarations, the objective of the orientalist was to produce a 'complete' and 'perfect' version. Yet, as he revised the Montague manuscript, he was confronted with a text that evaded his grasp, with the numbering of the *Nights* not matching his own calculation, with undecipherable words, and with portions of text missing. For instance, the scribe indicates the beginning of the fourth Night on both fol. 16^v and fol. 24^v (MS Bodl. Or. 550). Scott initially misses the error and later amends his own note in the margin to replace '4th' by '5th' on fol. 24^v. Blank pages also constitute a source of anxiety for the translator, who indicates an irrecoverable defect in the manuscript on fol. 78^v (MS Bodl. Or. 550): 'The beginning of the 2'd Collinder's Story is wanting here'. On the following page, Scott crosses out the top half, which corresponds to the end of a story that never started (MS Bodl. Or. 550 fol. 79^r; see appendix).

Blank pages may also play tricks with the reader, as when Scott warns that there is 'No hiatus here; the story being regularly continued in the next page' (MS Bodl. Or. 552, fol. 134^v; see appendix). Scott embarks on a 'struggle for certainty' and attempts to frame the manuscript by putting his own annotations and marks around the main text.[42] However, like a colonial governor, Scott is now confronted with what may appear a messy and evasive reality. With regard to the first volume, Scott notes:

> [It is] very carelessly transcribed, especially in the division of the Nights. Many corrections are inserted in the margin but not regularly &, as frequently, the division of nights has been neglected; I found it impossible to mark the succession as has been done in the other volumes, which are very correctly written and it is probable by a different scribe.[43]

The expression 'to be at a loss' marks the ultimate dependence of the orientalist towards the scribe and the fact that his translation relied on the vigilance and accuracy of the latter. These indications on the progress of translation being challenged and impeded are obviously eluded in the published version, which records only the work in its completed form, and not in its fragmented and unruly state.

On a larger scale, when several number of nights go missing, Scott records the lapse created in the narration, for instance with the third volume, which 'contains

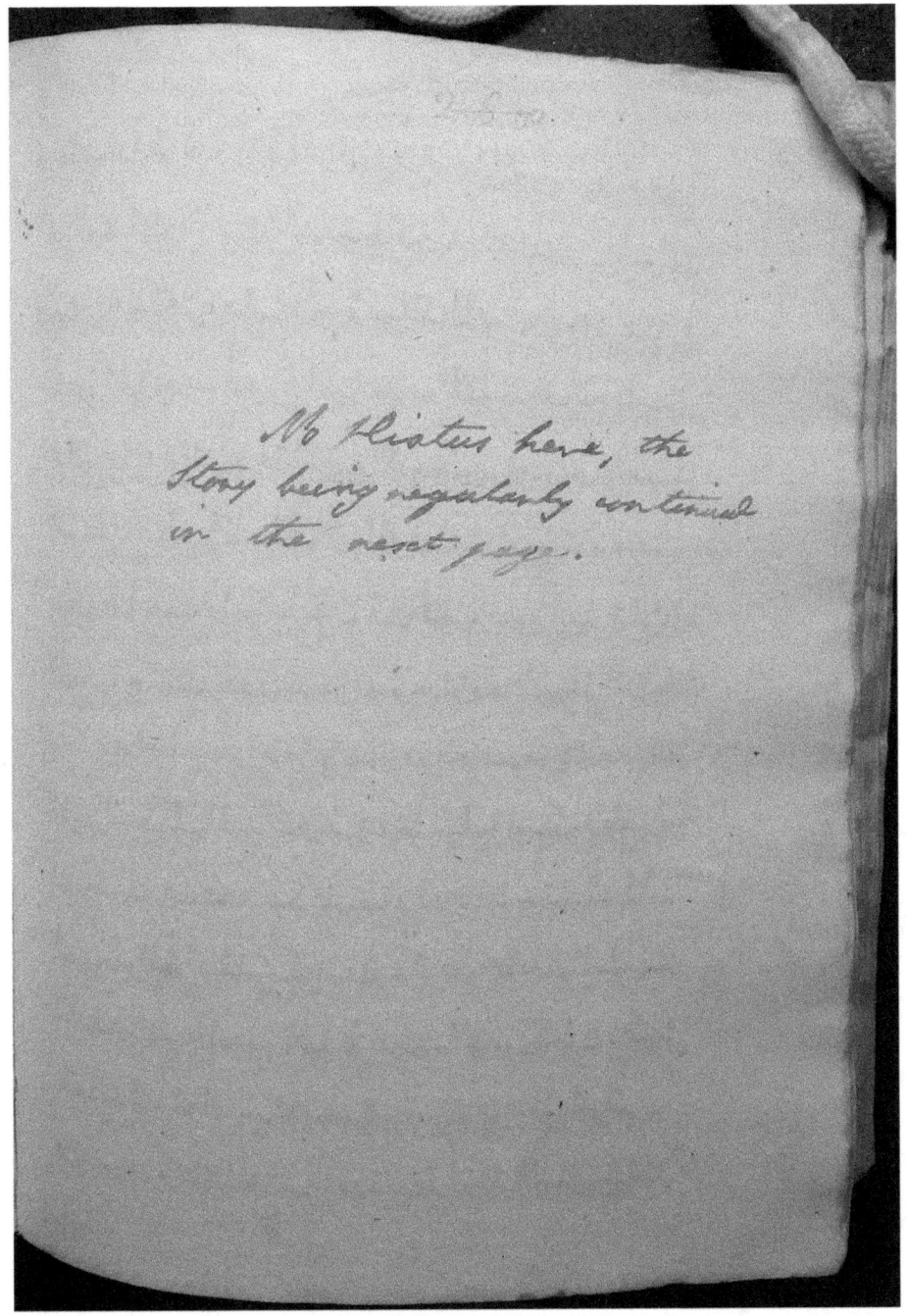

Fig. 6.3. MS Bodl. Or. 552, fol. 134ᵛ *Alf layla wa layla* (Bodleian Library, used with permission)

456 pages, including from Night 306 to Night 425, so that here an Hiatus occurs of 140 Nights, which however may I hope with little trouble be fitted up'.[44] The precarious, uncertain, and empirical nature of the work involved in dealing with ancient manuscripts is highlighted here, along with the confidence expressed by Scott in mending the 'deficient' text. His assured tone may well be accounted for by the fact that he is addressing in these pages the curators of the Bodleian to whom he was actually selling the volumes. Further on, he explains where he thinks the missing pages may have gone:

> On discovering this Hiatus it suggested itself to my mind that possibly another unbound volume, as well as the second, might have been left unmarked in the sale Catalogue and disposed of. Upon writing to Dr White on the subject I was favoured with the following reply.
>
> 'One to two bundles of unbound Arabick Manuscript of the same size and handwriting as the second Volume of the Arabian tales were purchased by an Agent, for Mr Beckford of Fonthill, and I have no doubt whatever, but that the deficient part of your tales is the be found in his Possession.'
>
> Not having the honour of being known to Mr Beckford, I could not take the liberty of requesting a sight of his purchase. Did he know the circumstance he would, I imagine, readily permit a transcript to be made, which I should have great pleasure in doing for the use of the Bodleian if the Curators could not procure a better Copyist than myself.
>
> If Dr Nutshell would allow his Copy of the Arabian Nights to be transcribed also, as well as his other Oriental manuscripts, they would be a desirable acquisition to the Library.[45]

The initial certainty that the gap in the narration of the *Nights* be fitted up with 'little trouble' seems to be contradicted by the lines that follow which again underscore the caution employed by Scott, who uses the negative epistemic through the verb 'suggested', the adverb 'possibly', and the modal 'might', and details a somewhat arduous journey to the missing bundle, via Fonthill and Beckford's agent. Thus, the Arabic manuscript does not easily lend itself to orientalist control and, contrary to the image of an essentialized and monolithic other, it does not come as a whole.

Conclusion: What Edward Said Could Not Say

By way of a conclusion, I would like to go back to Timothy Mitchell and the conceptual frame developed in *Colonising Egypt*, which underpins this essay. As with the nineteenth-century colonial process entailed in modernizing Egypt, Scott's procedure is one of re-ordering of the Arabic text (or of stringing the unstrung, to paraphrase Scott) so that it can be circulated on the European book market as an 'enframed' cultural object legible to Western readers — the first readers being the curators of the Bodleian Library who had purchased the volumes and for whom Scott devised the explanatory table of contents (MS Bodl. Or. 557). Mitchell also analyses the presence of Egypt as an object of consumption 'reframed' within the perimeter of the World Exhibition as indicating the attempt of colonial ideology to circumscribe its object, and by doing so to posit a clear demarcation between what

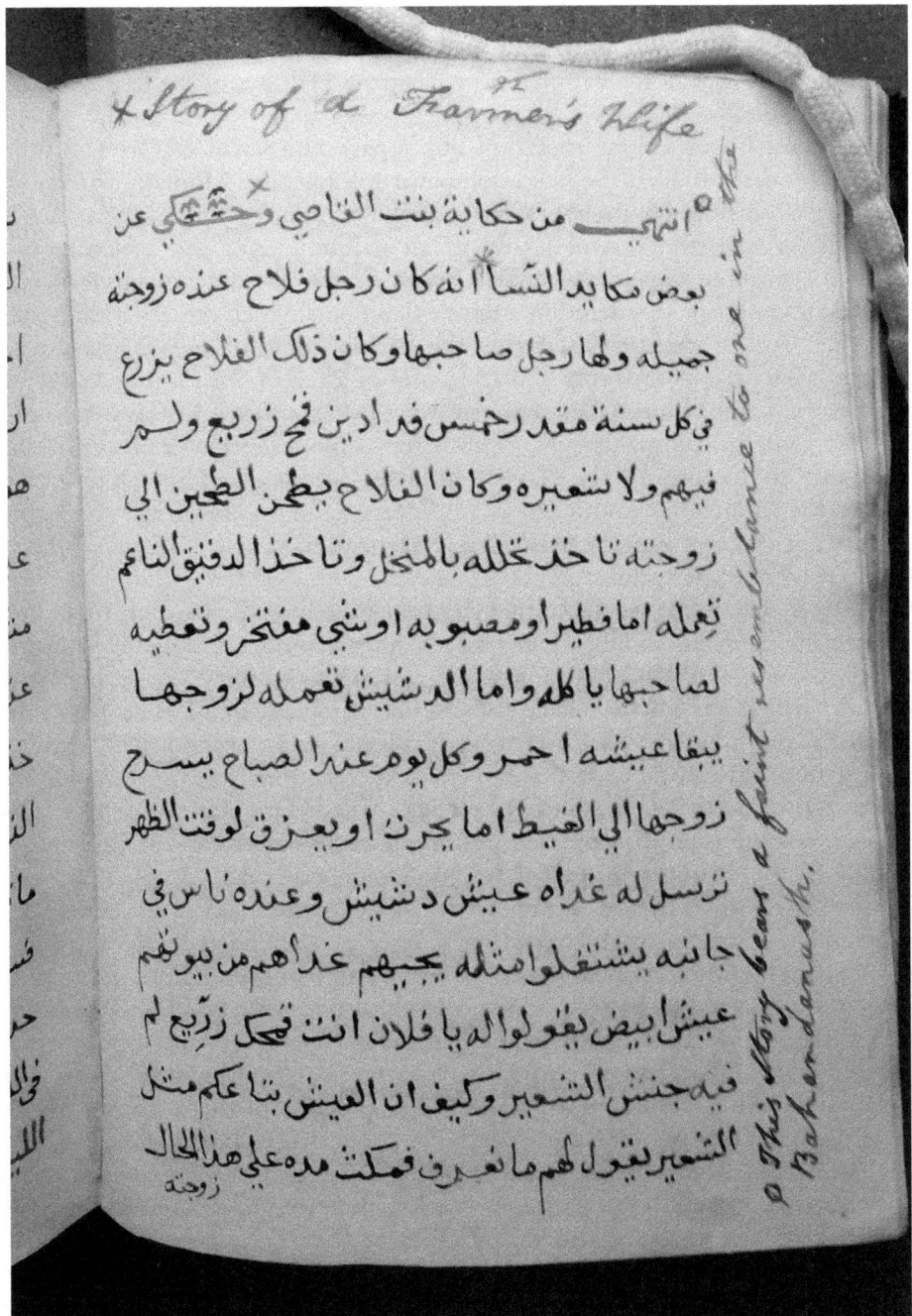

Fig. 6.4. MS Bodl. Or. 554, fol. 46ᵛ *Alf layla wa layla*
(Bodleian Library, used with permission)

it includes as representation and what it excludes as the 'real' world outside. The purpose of the colonial modernizing project was to have 'real' Egypt conform with its 'imagined' European recreation, and what would fall out of the frame would be declared illegible.[46]

This process is not unique to Egypt but is part and parcel of Orientalism as a form of discourse. Indeed, Scott's attempt to reframe the Montague manuscript of the *Nights* corresponds to the same logic of circumscribing, structuring, and excluding. As with the careful layout of an exhibition, or the structure of the barracks for the new Egyptian modern army, or the planning of modern Cairo, the Arabic manuscript is ordered in a table of contents which creates what Mitchell called 'the effect of structure', securing the establishment of a disciplinary power, capable of operating within this structure, and of a realm of meaning and truth.[47] Similarly, the manuscript makes sense so long as it conforms to the structure. As Mitchell wrote, 'to colonize Egypt, to construct a modern kind of power, it would be necessary to "determine the plan".'[48] Equally, I understand Scott's project as it applies to the Montague manuscript as an ordering and streamlining process intent on producing a recognizable version of the *Nights*, aligned with Galland's *Urtext* and with the readers' expectations.

On the other hand, if we agree that in order to 'colonize' the text it is requisite to 'determine the plan,' should we necessarily infer that once the plan is determined the text is colonized? Our position as contemporary literary critics may follow two lines, which are not exclusive, but rather complementary. The first line of analysis, the one followed by Edward Said, offers a study of published texts, once the translation and editing process are over, and determines how these domesticated editions reflect a larger hegemonic project called Orientalism, which served European colonialism, directly, by providing information or intelligence, and indirectly by supporting imperial and racist ideologies.

This line of analysis has produced extremely stimulating studies and has highlighted the structures and effects of power as embedded in knowledge and literature. But it also reproduces the orientalist gesture of keeping out of the picture the Eastern other, on the back of which orientalist discourse was elaborated. In the present case, the line between the in and out, the perimeter separating the world-as-exhibition and the 'real' world outside, falls between the Arabic text as manuscript and the Arab text as published translation. The purpose of this essay was to work beyond the boundary of order and with the material that had been precisely left out of the published edition. By focusing on the manuscript, which had served as the basis of Scott's revised edition of the *Nights*, I wanted to catch a sight of orientalism in the making and examine the various sites of textual encounters between the orientalist and the Arabic text. It was then possible to observe acts of textual domination and 'enframing' as well as spaces of textual evasion, when the material itself escaped his grasp and understanding.

These margins not only bespeak of the structuring effect of colonialism but also of more genuine scholarly engagements with the text, as, for instance, when Scott identifies, from fol. 105^r to fol. 110^r of MS Bodl. Or. 550, the Arabic metres of *basît, kâmil, tawîl, khafîf, wâfir, sarî*', and *mujtatha*, in the poetic passages included in the *Nights*. Thus, when observed from the vantage point of the revised edition, Scott's relation to Arabic poetry seems highly dismissive; but when examined from the margins of the manuscript, what comes out is a genuine interest for and appreciation of its intrinsic qualities. This is probably what Edward Said could not say, or fully engage with conceptually, as his critical reading relied on the edited and monolingual versions of Orientalism, on texts that were both already polished and policed, and not on the messy, unruly, agonistic, and sometimes unpredictable borders, where orientalist encounters were taking place, and where Orientalism was done and undone.

Notes to Chapter 6

1. *The Arabian Nights Entertainments, Carefully Revised, and Occasionally Corrected from the Arabic, to Which is Added a Selection of New Tales, Now First Translated from the Arabic Originals. Also an Introduction and Notes, Illustrative of the Religion, Manners and Customs, of the Mahummedans*, trans. by Jonathan Scott, 6 vols (London: printed for Longman, et al, 1811), I, p. xi.
2. *The Oriental Collections: Consisting of Original Essays and Dissertations, Translations, and Miscellaneous Papers*, ed. by Major Sir William Ouseley, 3 vols (London: printed for Cadell and Davies, 1797–99), II, p. 26.
3. *The Arabian Nights Entertainments Carefully Revised*, I, p. xv.
4. For further explanation on the shift from medieval and early modern to modern editing practices, and from marginal glosses to footnotes, see Evelyn B. Tribble, *Margins and Marginality: The Printed Page in Early Modern England* (Charlottesville: University Press of Virginia, 1993) and *The Margins of the Text*, ed. by D. C. Greetham (Ann Arbor: University of Michigan Press, 1997).
5. I borrow this expression from Timothy Mitchell who talked of the reordering of 'the world-as-exhibition' under the colonial gaze. See Timothy Mitchell, *Colonising Egypt* (Cambridge: Cambridge University Press, 1988).
6. In her article on William Beckford's literary engagement with the *Arabian Nights*, Mahmoud-Moussa observes that the Montague manuscripts, which Beckford perused and partially translated, have long been dismissed by orientalists, such as Hermann Zotenberg, and literary critics, such as Mia Gerhardt and Nikita Eliseef. She advocates a closer analysis of the manuscripts for the light they shed on Beckford's masterpiece *Vathek*. See Fatma Mahmoud-Moussa, 'A Manuscript Translation of the "Arabian Nights" in the Beckford Papers', *Journal of Arabic Literature*, 7 (1976), 7–23 (p. 7).
7. See the colophon bearing the signature of the scribe and the date of the 18th of the month of Safar 1178H (1764–65AD) in Oxford, Bodleian Library, MS Bodl. Or. 556, fol. 205^v.
8. Jonathan Curling, *Edward Wortley Montagu, 1713–1776: The Man in the Iron Wig* (London: Andrew Melrose, 1954), pp. 179–81, 185, 203, 226; Mahmoud-Moussa, 'A Manuscript Translation', pp. 11–14.
9. Edward Forster mentioned the sale in his preface to his 1802 revision of Galland's *Nights*: 'In the catalogue of Oriental manuscripts belonging to Mr. Montague and sold by auction in 1787 was one called, "The Arabian Tales", of one thousand and one nights, in *six volumes complete*'; *The Arabian Nights in Five Volumes*, trans. by Edward Forster (London : printed for Miller, 1802) I, XI.
10. Isobel Grundy, 'Montagu, Edward Wortley (1713–1776)', in *Oxford Dictionary of National Biography* <http://www.oxforddnb.com/view/article/19013> [accessed 6 August 2015].
11. See for reference MS Bodl. Or. 557, fol. 2^r and *The Oriental Collections*, II, 26; See also *The Arabian Nights Entertainments Carefully Revised*, I, p. xi.
12. Mahmoud-Moussa, 'A Manuscript Translation', p. 9.
13. Michael J. Franklin, 'Scott, Jonathan (1753–1829)', in *Oxford Dictionary of National Biography* <http://www.oxforddnb.com/view/article/24900> [accessed 11 August 2015].

14. *The Arabian Nights Entertainments Carefully Revised*, I, p. xvi.
15. Gérard Genette, *Paratexts: Thresholds of Interpretation*, trans. by Jane E. Lewin (Cambridge: Cambridge University Press, 1997).
16. Paul Gilroy, *Postcolonial Melancholia* (New York: Columbia University Press, 2005), p. 39.
17. This report dated 13 March 1766 is reproduced in Curling, p. 185. The Montague-Davison expedition is also related by Isobel Grundy in her entry on 'Montagu, Edward Wortley (1713–1776)' for the *ODNB*.
18. See Claire Gallien, 'Les Orientalistes britanniques de la fin du XVIIIe siècle et la création du canon littéraire indien', in *Problèmes d'histoire littéraire indienne*, ed. by Claire Joubert and Laetitia Zecchini, special issue of *Revue de Littérature Comparée*, 4 (Oct.–Dec. 2015), 405–17. The orientalists often complained of the conditions in which they worked and the cold responses of editors and booksellers who did not wish to commit themselves to publishing orientalist monographs and translations, given the small number of people who were likely to buy their books. This resistance explains, to a certain extent, why orientalist scholarship was largely published through subscriptions and in the format of anthologies, offering selections as appetizers to test the readers' response before going for larger and more costly publications.
19. Punctuation marks were introduced as a complete system by Ahmad Zaki Pacha, Head of the National Library and Archives in Egypt, at the end of the nineteenth century. See Aḥmad Zakī Bāshā, *al-Tarqīm wa-'alāmātuh fī al-lughah al-'Arabīyah*, 2nd ed (Beirut: Dār al-Bashā'ir al-Islāmīyah, 1987).
20. The expression which is usually marked in red ink in Arabic is '*fa lamâ kânat al-laylah al-qâbilah wa hya al-laylah ... qâlat ...*' meaning 'and on the following night, which was the [number] night, [name of the story-teller] said'. See MS Bol. Or. 551, fol. 6^r in the appendix for an example.
21. I borrow the terminology to I. A. Richards, *The Philosophy of Rhetoric* (Oxford: Oxford University Press, 1936).
22. *The Oriental Collections*, II, p. 26.
23. There are many places in *Orientalism* where Edward Said expounds on this idea, starting in the first pages of the introduction, where, for instance, he writes: '[...] the phenomenon of Orientalism as I study it here deals principally, not with a correspondence between Orientalism and Orient, but with the internal consistency of Orientalism and its ideas about the Orient [...] despite and beyond any correspondence, or lack thereof, with a "real" Orient.' In Edward Said, *Orientalism* (New York: Random House, 1978), p. 5.
24. *The Oriental Collections*, II, p. 26.
25. 'In Galland, succeeding the last story, are the seven voyages of Sindbad the Sailor, which do not appear in either of these volumes and I am inclined to think, that as they do not exist in Dr Russell's manuscripts, neither would they be found in the Copies of the Vatican or Paris Libraries, nor in that part of M W Montague's Arabian nights purchased by Mr Beckford. Enquiry on this point from the Curators of the Bodleian would doubtless meet a satisfactory reply from the foreign Librarians. If made, and my supposition should prove just, I should then hazard a conjecture, that the voyages of Sinbad never were written in Arabick, but one of the ingenious fabrication of Mr Galland, built upon "An account of India and China by two Mahomeddan travellers in the ninth century, translated from the Arabick by Renaudot". This work has been rendered from the French into English. M. Galland probably used a copy of the Arabick journal of the travellers for his foundation of the voyages of Sinbad and added many incidents from Marco Polo and other early travellers to the East. Mr Holes' ingenious remarks on the Voyages of Sinbad strengthen my "Conjecture"' (MS Bodl. Or. 557, note 5, fols 7–9). See Richard Hole, *Remarks on the Arabian nights' entertainments* (London: printed for T. Cadell, 1797). The charge of forgery was disproved in 1802 when Scott discovered a separate manuscript of the Sindbad tales in the library of Christ-Church College, Oxford: '[Oxford Dec 13th 1802. Since writing the above I have met with the Story of Sindad in the xtchurch Library. The Arabick has been almost literally translated by Galland excepting some poetical quotations which he has omitted. The tale however in the MS has a regular introduction as if a work of itself so that I suppose Galland inserted it as part of the Arabian Nights, if it was not in his Copy, but this is a point of little consequence now We possess the Arabick original. Scott]' (MS Bodl. Or. 557, note 5, fol. 9).

26. It has now been established that the Sindbad tales were not forgeries but that they came from a separate tradition dating back to sometime between the ninth and thirteenth centuries. In 1701, Galland bought two separate manuscripts, translated them, and then inserted them in his *Arabian Nights*. Galland later bequeathed the Sindbad manuscripts to the Royal Library (Paris, Bibliothèque Nationale, MS Ar. 3645–46). See Ulrich Marzolph, 'Sindbad der Seefahrer', in *Enzyklopädie des Märchens. Handwörterbuch zur historischen und vergleichenden Erzählforschung*, ed. by Kurt Ranke and others, 14 vols (Berlin: de Gruyter, 1975–), XII (2007), pp. 698–707; Mia Gerhardt, *The Art of Story-telling* (Leiden: Brill, 1963), p. 241; and Muhsin Mahdi, *The Thousand and One Nights* (Leiden: E. J. Brill, 1995), pp. 17–20. It has also been proved that Galland was actually not the first one to have inserted the Sindbad tales into the *Arabian Nights* corpus. Rather, the French orientalist Victor Chauvin traced a seventeenth-century Turkish manuscript of the *Nights* which includes the Sindbad cycle; see Victor Chauvin, *Bibliographie des ouvrages arabes ou relatifs aux Arabes: publiés dans l'Europe chrétienne de 1810 à 1885*, 12 vols (Liège: H. Vaillant-Carmanne, 1892–1922), p. 201; and also Hande A. Birkalan-Gedik, 'The Thousand and One Nights in Turkish: Translations, Adaptations, and Issues', in *The Arabian Nights in Transnational Perspective*, ed. by Ulrich Marzolph (Detroit, MI: Wayne State University Press, 2007), pp. 201–20 (p. 205).
27. MS Bodl. Or. 557, fol. 5.
28. One instance of this occurs in the Porter's cycle of stories, where Scott underlined that he favoured Galland's condensed version and excluded many passages for fear of 'offending modesty.' See MS Bodl. Or. 557, fol. 7.
29. The poems 'would to the European reader have been wearisome digressions from the narratives, instead of being considered as illustrative improvements to them'; in *The Arabian Nights Entertainments Carefully Revised*, I, p. xiv.
30. Abdelfattah Kilito, *Arabs and the Art of Storytelling* (Syracuse, NY: Syracuse University Press), p. 7.
31. Josef Horovitz, 'Poetische Zitate in Tausend und eine Nacht', in *Festschrift Eduard Sachau zum Siebzigsten Geburtstage*, ed. by Gotthold Weil (Berlin: Reimer, 1915), pp. 375–78.
32. See Geert Jan van Gelder, 'Poetry and the Arabian Nights', in *The Arabian Nights Encyclopedia*, ed. by Ulrich Marzolph and Richard van Leeuwen (Santa Barbara, CA, Denver, CO, and Oxford: ABC Clio, 2004), pp. 13–17.
33. Carole Boidin stated in her contribution to the dictionary of early modern French translations that Arabic poetry had long failed to attract the attention of translators and that it was only late in the eighteenth century that the first Arabic poems were translated, hence Galland's choice not to translate the poetry contained in the *Nights*. Before that, Arabic literature was restricted to two genres — tales and fables on the one hand, proverbs on the other. See Carole Boidin, 'La Poésie arabe', in *Histoire des traductions en langue française XVII–XVIIIe siècles*, ed. by A. Cointre and Y-M Tran-Gervat (Paris: Verdier, 2014), pp. 1096–1106.
34. *The Arabian Nights Entertainments Carefully Revised*, I, p. xii.
35. Ibid., I, pp. xii–xiii.
36. Ibid., I, p. xiv.
37. See Boidin, 'La Poésie arabe', p. 1103.
38. *The Arabian Nights Entertainments Carefully Revised*, I, p. iii.
39. Ibid., I, p. ix.
40. Ibid., I, p. x.
41. Malcolm C. Lyons introduces his late translation of the *Nights* by affirming that 'It represents accretive literature, changing from place to place and from age to age, and so there can be no "perfect" text.' See Malcolm C. Lyons, *The Arabian Nights*, 3 vols (London: Penguin, 2010), I, p. xxii.
42. John E. Wilson borrows from Pierre Bourdieu in *The Logic of Practice* (1990) in order to analyse the opposition between colonial rule and indigenous organization, in other words between abstract and a priori governance versus local *habitus* based on 'learnt but unarticulable forms of knowing, [...] habitual practice, not conscious, rationalizing thought'. See John E. Wilson, *The Making of a Colonial Order: Information, Uncertainty and Law in Early Colonial Bengal* (Cambridge: Centre of South Asian Studies, University of Cambridge, 2004), p. 2.

43. MS Bodl. Or. 557, fol. 4.
44. Ibid., fol. 12.
45. Ibid., fols 12–13.
46. Mitchell, p. 33.
47. Ibid., p. xv.
48. Ibid., p. 33.

CHAPTER 7

❖

Image, Text, and Conflict: Willie Doherty's 'At the Border'

Rosie Lavan

In a BBC broadcast in 1978, Susan Sontag said that 'photography gives us an unearned relation to the past'.[1] But it is also true that through photography we have inherited a relationship with the past, which presents evolving challenges amid the consistently evolving pressures of the contemporary moment. This essay will consider the nature of and negotiations with that relation as it is constructed in the work of the contemporary photographer and video artist Willie Doherty. Twice nominated for the Turner Prize, Doherty was born and still works in the city of Derry in Northern Ireland, and over the past thirty years he has examined, and creatively disrupted, the idea of the border which is implicit in all his work. The focus of this discussion will be 'At the Border, a series of four photographs made in 1995, approached via contemporary texts that have sought to document, theorize or otherwise confront the Irish border. (These images appear at the end of the essay.) The border in Doherty's work emerges as a critical challenge, forcing confrontation not only of the representative challenges it poses, but also of questions about the developing, post-conflict discourse in Irish cultural studies.

In any territory which has, like (Northern) Ireland, been defined through division, there is a risk that received opinion might trump the complexity of historical detail and lived experience — that, in other words, the routinely summoned idea of the border will be left unchallenged and overdetermined. Before considering the conceptual and semantic problem of the border as Doherty examined and represented it in the mid-1990s, it is worth offering a brief account of the historical, political and affective circumstances which attend it on all sides. This now-invisible line was first drawn in the Government of Ireland Act 1920 to separate the six north-eastern counties (Antrim, Armagh, Derry, Down, Fermanagh, and Tyrone) from 'so much of Ireland as is not comprised' by them.[2] The border was formalized by partition in the Anglo-Irish Treaty of 1921, signed to bring the Irish War of Independence to an end. The Treaty established the Irish Free State but it also precipitated the Irish Civil War, a further phase of conflict at the end of an exhausting period of violence and unrest, which is currently being revisited in the much-debated 'decade of centenaries'.[3] As this book goes to press, the Irish border is the subject of extensive political discussion in the wake of Brexit: it is the United Kingdom's only land border with the European Union.

The creation of the border neglected the ancient division of Ireland into four provinces — 'Ulster', both constitutionally in the 1920 arrangement, and rhetorically in unionist diction and standard journalese, did not encompass the counties of Cavan, Donegal, and Monaghan, which remained in the political South. If the border firmly established Northern Ireland as a state within the United Kingdom, administrative borders within Northern Ireland could still be mutable: manipulation of constituency boundaries consistently returned unionist representatives to power from 1922 onwards, even in majority Catholic/nationalist areas. In addition, despite the abolition of the so-called business and university votes in the rest of the United Kingdom under the Representation of the People Act 1948, the administration in Northern Ireland retained these provisions for elections to its devolved Stormont government, and so 'one man, one vote' became a key demand of the Northern Ireland Civil Rights Association in the 1960s, which was met in the Electoral Law Amendment Act 1968.[4]

The emergence of the civil rights movement has been attributed in part to the major changes which were effected when the reforms introduced by Westminster governments of the 1940s were subsequently implemented in Northern Ireland: the Education Act 1944 was, despite unionist opposition, finally translated into the Education Act (Northern Ireland) 1947, and the provisions of the Welfare State laid down by Clement Attlee's post-war Labour administration also extended to Northern Ireland, throwing differences with the economically straitened Republic into sharp relief. By the 1960s the standard of higher education in the North was greatly improved and, crucially, the number of Catholics attending university had undergone a sharp increase, effectively creating a new social category — what Seamus Heaney would call, ironizing his own experience, 'the newly upwardly mobile eleven-plus Catholic'.[5] This shift, Roy Foster writes, 'would be of great importance in the radicalization of student opinion during the late 1960s'.[6] At the turn of the decade the progressive resolve of the civil rights campaign was overtaken by violence of mounting frequency and intensity, and in time a renascent IRA refocused attention on the territorial dispute which had first flared in the early 1920s.

In August 1994, the IRA declared a ceasefire, and loyalist paramilitaries followed; the peace was fragile and interrupted but it did enable the Belfast, or Good Friday, Agreement to be reached. In the two decades since the 1998 Agreement, Northern Ireland has been gradually and not always comfortably settling into a new post-conflict phase. The economic implications of the border — once a line for smugglers to cross; later the north wall of the extraordinarily prosperous Celtic Tiger Ireland — were much examined, by regional development agencies, economists, and shoppers exploiting the relative value of pound or euro. The prominent economic historian Cormac Ó Gráda and economist Brendan Walsh co-authored a paper titled 'Did (and does) the Irish border matter?' in 2006 to examine the 'partition effect' in economic terms and warn against 'great expectation about the possible economic gains from dismantling the barriers erected between the two parts of Ireland after 1922'.[7] Leaving to one side its 'salutary warning', the paper is material evidence of the vast body of literature on the future implications of the border which has been generated — the Institute for British-Irish Studies at University College Dublin, founded in 1999, having made a significant contribution to this.[8]

The ideological, political, and religious identities which might, broadly speaking, be arranged on either side of the Irish border have been consistently asserted, challenged, represented, and misrepresented — most notably in media coverage of the Troubles in Northern Ireland. The ready phrase 'divided Ireland', which of course has historical applications that precede the actual division of the country, is axiomatic, and while the island plays host to one of the most notorious north-south divides, it hardly needs to be restated that speaking of Northern Ireland in terms of any unity is undermined by the stubbornly dominant fissures — Protestant/Catholic, unionist/nationalist, and loyalist/republican — which make up this 'divided society'. In David Lloyd's words: 'Within the border, borders proliferate, tesserating the interfaces and defiles of power and subjection that hold the state in place.'[9] Its internal division, indeed, has been taken as the definitive characteristic of the whole.[10]

Division is one thing, the actual dividing line quite another. As Lloyd's essay on Allan deSouza's Irish border photography makes clear, the representation of the border itself has been far more complicated — in its bare actuality, and as a fact and a force which conditions life on either side of it. In the recollective prologue to his essay, Lloyd writes:

> When I call the border to mind, I still imagine it as a broad green landscape, unmarked except by the road cutting across it. Though it is tracked now by watchtowers and patrols, helicopters and military vehicles, the lasting image is still that of this banal tract of murky green, more or less indistinguishable from the run of the country around it. How can you tell you have crossed? How can you tell there is anything there at all?[11]

We can only tell when we are told, to play on the verb which so fascinates Lloyd in his essay. In 1987, the photojournalist Mike Abrahams pictured Peter Caraher and his family in a field on their farm, sited on that broad green landscape in south Armagh. One half of the family stand to the left of the image, the other stand to the right of a large gap — the space where the border 'is' — and technically in County Monaghan in the Republic of Ireland. Writing about the border as it is seen and unseen in this image in 1991, Trisha Ziff proposed it as an example of the 'structured absences' which recur in pictures from the North. 'It is often the case in images from the North of Ireland that what is significant cannot be seen or photographed', she argued.[12]

Over fifteen years after Ziff was writing and nearly a decade after the Good Friday Agreement, the contemporary photographer Donovan Wylie was also in south Armagh, taking pictures which would form part of his acclaimed series *British Watchtowers* (2007).[13] For over a year, Wylie went across Northern Ireland photographing the British Army's borderland watchtowers — crudely Foucauldian military structures dating from the mid-1980s, technologically sophisticated and strategically positioned to enable the army to survey the land and the people beneath. Wylie made this series as the British Army was in the process of demolishing the towers and so these photographs are, Colin Graham notes, 'in essence, images of future empty spaces'.[14] Linking *British Watchtowers* to Wylie's earlier work *The Maze* (2004), a series of meticulous images of the Maze/Long Kesh prison before it was demolished, Graham writes, 'Wylie uses the demolition of the built environment (of surveillance in *British Watchtowers*, and of incarceration and surveillance in *The Maze*) to contemplate larger issues in contemporary Northern Ireland, to wonder what future the past has.'[15] A line of division in itself, and a synecdoche for other divisions so long taken to be definitive, the border is a singularly charged subject for visual artists in Northern Ireland, inevitably pointing towards those larger issues Graham identifies, but also allowing more fundamental questions to be posed and faced in representation: questions around division and coherence, past and future, and seen and unseen.

'UNSEEN' was chosen as the title for a retrospective of Doherty's work held at the City Factory Gallery in Derry in 2013 as part of the city's year as a UK Capital of Culture.[16] Through his own distinct practice, Doherty has persistently examined and exposed the implications and limits of the activities of looking and seeing, and the inherent instability of interpretation which follows from them: his work is perplexing and unsettling because it is never certain exactly what we are supposed to 'see' and understand when we look at it. In a career which has been marked by definite phases, a consistent strategy of Doherty's has been to disrupt the formal and generic boundaries and capacities of the media in which he works, disrupting and confusing in turn the experience of the onlooker as they regard his photographs and films. He came to prominence in the 1980s with a series of photographs — often, but not exclusively, black and white — over which sans serif text in block capitals appeared, to pre-empt or interrupt our apprehension of the image beneath. 'The Blue Skies of Ulster' (1986) is a noted example of these so-called 'photographs with text': the words 'We shall never forsake the blue skies of Ulster for the grey mists of an Irish republic', once spoken by Ian Paisley, founder of the hardline Democratic Unionist Party, are overlaid in an appropriately loyalist shade of blue across a landscape scene rendered indistinct by the mist held at bay by Paisley's words. Another, 'God Has Not Failed Us' (1990), can be usefully set alongside 'The Blue Skies of Ulster': the text follows through with the Biblical resonance familiar from Paisley's Free Presbyterian oratory, but the scene — an empty street in the working-class, Protestant, Fountain area of Derry — undermines the Paisleyite conviction.[17] If God has not failed the 'us' who are implied in this depopulated but still domestic city setting, someone else has.

The juxtaposition of these images indicates Doherty's persistent interest in the rural and (or as opposed to) the urban. In more recent video work, including the films 'Buried' (2009) and 'Remains' (2013), landscape and memory are explored: long tracking shots or forensic close-ups force us into an interrogative relationship with the images we encounter. That relationship bears the invitation, or onus, to interpret but this is neither straightforward nor necessarily welcome. During *Art of the Troubles*, a major exhibition at the Ulster Museum in 2014, both films were screened alternately in the kind of black box space usually constructed for video installations, but this familiar gallery arrangement served to augment what was unfamiliar and menacing about the films: to cross the threshold into a space so dark that it was impossible to gauge its dimensions, or to be sure how many other people were already inside, was to find oneself quite literally lost in atmospheric uncertainty, even before the possible truths implied by the films began to play out in image and imagination.[18]

Image is, of course, also about repute. Doherty's photographs with text are an example of the ways in which artists in Northern Ireland since the 1980s have reacted against, challenged, or undermined, the conventionally unchallenged relationship between text and image in print journalism. The fraught press coverage of the conflict has been a source of dismay and contention at least since Eamonn McCann appealed against it in *The British Press and Northern Ireland* (1971).[19] After the introduction of the Broadcasting Ban in 1988, Doherty's interest extended to the dynamic between the image and the spoken word. The ban, introduced by the Thatcher government, famously prohibited the voices of spokespersons of paramilitary organizations in Northern Ireland, and the political parties associated with them, from being heard on television and radio: their words were always 'spoken by an actor'. In the audio/slide installation 'They're All the Same' (1991) and the video installation 'The Only Good One is a Dead One' (1993), Doherty picked up received observations about the figure of the terrorist who had been so definitively cast in Thatcher's Britain, not so much to make a political point as to expose the partialities and inconsistencies of this strategy of media non-representation, suspended as it was between the grave and the absurd. In 'The Only Good One is a Dead One' two videos were simultaneously projected onto the gallery walls at right angles to one another, while a voiceover monologue consistently switched between passages which implied that the speaking man was victim, stalker, and/or assassin. It was impossible to see both videos at the same time; in that work, as Carolyn Christov-Bakargiev has observed, there was 'no position for the innocent bystander [...] everyone has a designated position from the perspective of the person who is killing'.[20] Seamus Heaney's watchman, reimagined after Aeschylus's *Agamemnon* in his post-ceasefire sequence 'Mycenae Lookout', took this point further: regarding Cassandra, the 'camp-fucked' emblem of a country's guilt, he concludes that there is 'No such thing | as innocent | bystanding | [...] | No such thing | as innocent.'[21] Writing of Doherty's oeuvre more generally, Christov-Bakargiev has valuably argued that: '[his works] all attempt to address areas of the mind and of our daily surroundings in which evidence is proof only of a lack of knowledge (and power), and of doubt.' Through the techniques Doherty adopts — i.e. his exaggerated use of cinematic tropes, voiceovers mimicking the omniscient documentary commentator, his overlaid text on photographs — Christov-Bakargiev suggests that 'he does not intend to shy away from the world, but rather to enhance our awareness of the constructed nature of images, even the most documentary, so as to formulate a new kind of individual perspective or agency, able to shape and modify consciousness by attributing value and importance to what could be defined a *fallible gaze*.'[22] Crucially, our own 'fallible gaze' at the image is always one that has been conditioned by an encounter with written or spoken words.

The relationship between language and image — or, more specifically, the uneasy agency which language attains when it is deployed in interpretation of the image — is a central interest of Gabriel Gee's discussion of the visual arts in a broader but still Derry-based context. Gee's focus is on the catalogues produced by the Orchard Gallery in Derry which, from its establishment in 1978 until its closure in 2003, played a key role in supporting and promoting the work of contemporary artists in Northern Ireland — Doherty included — and in bringing contemporary British art to the region.[23] It was also active in publishing, as Gee explores, gathering commentaries from artists and commissioning work from a range of critics and art historians. In a separate context Matthew Reynolds has revisited the encounter between the verbal and the visual text, resisting the tendency to regard the visual as always necessarily more complex than the verbal. 'Written texts too can be stubbornly illegible, weirdly silent, "meaningless" artifacts where all our best attempts at understanding fall apart', he argues.[24] As Gee's argument examines, the written texts produced by the Orchard were under a particular compound pressure, operative in an environment in which text and image are consistently deployed to contrary political ends, and responding to works by artists seeking to subvert and confound expectations across media: 'Much of the commentators' deciphering throughout the Orchard Gallery history can be understood as an effort to mediate the blurring of aesthetic signifiers by artists keen on avoiding the narrowness of clear-cut statements.'[25] In the case of Doherty's photographs with text the matter is all the more acute. Quite deliberately he deals in 'clear-cut statements', incorporating them into his work and thereby foreclosing their use in interpretations of it, and thereby allowing them to bear all the stubborn, weird freight Reynolds recognizes in the written text through the subversive combination with the visual. Verbal and visual meet in Doherty's photographs to expose their mutual instability; it is more an act of confrontation than mediation.

Language in and in relation to Doherty's still and moving images, then, is both effective and affective, in mimicry of the speech acts through which the conflict in Northern Ireland was — and to an extent continues, in its aftermath, to be — articulated. Amid the politically and personally fraught demarcations which conditioned communication during the Troubles, J. L. Austin's explicit and implicit performatives could function alongside one another depending on who was speaking or who was listening. The 'subtle manoeuvrings' in conversation of which Heaney wrote in his famous poem 'Whatever You Say Say Nothing' were enough to determine religious and political identity.[26] The words 'Whatever You Say Say Nothing' had appeared on a poster displayed in republican communities reminding people that 'Loose-talk [sic] costs lives' — urging people to be careful of what they said and to whom, via the ironic co-option of an injunction originally issued by the British during World War Two.[27] It is posters like these which Colm Tóibín notices on the wall of the office of the Sinn Féin councillor he meets in the border town of Crossmaglen in south Armagh, towards the end of his account of his walk along the border in 1987: 'Behind him in his office were posters warning people not to speak to strangers. "This Brit Could Be Standing Beside You" and "Loose Talk Costs Lives" were the slogans.'[28] Heaney refers to the 'the famous Northern reticence', 'the tight gag of place and times', but what he is really targeting is the coded economy of speech: whatever you say, you are always saying something. The ironized activity of not saying might be related to the unspoken activity of not seeing, which Begoña Aretxaga observed in *Shattering Silence* (1997), her feminist-ethnographic study of women in working-class republican areas of Belfast. The women she interviewed in these districts explained that they were routinely subjected to sexual harassment and, in some cases, abuse by members of the British Army and the since disbanded Royal Ulster Constabulary. Faced with such behaviour, their aversive, self-protecting strategy was, simply, not to see the men who did it. Aretxaga recorded that:

> They have become very skillful [*sic*] at ignoring both the words and their source, to the point that a view of the streets of Catholic West Belfast in 1988 could have left an outsider with the impression of having seen wandering ghosts rather than actual uniformed bodies. The conspicuous military presence is erased in a deliberate act of public non-recognition.[29]

To see something is to acknowledge its existence; to confer upon it the legitimacy of recognition. To say something is more akin to the wilful infinitive of vision, to look, which implies the deliberate direction of sight.

Contortions of agency and interpretation follow from these key verbs and their operations in encounters with Doherty's work. But what his images and videos consistently remind us is that interpretation is based on, and charged by, memory. In a recent discussion of Doherty and other contemporary visual artists from Northern Ireland, Fionna Barber has written:

> Within this context, the ways in which art works to produce its meaning — through metaphor, symbol, and suggestion — become means whereby levels of destructive experience can be glimpsed, even if only obliquely. The almost unrepresentable lurks there at the edge of vision, within events remembered in a city's streets long ago, or even beneath the need to retain in language the character of a community's collective identity in the face of imminent change.[30]

Barber's terms are usefully generative here: the 'almost unrepresentable' is analogous to the saying of nothing, allowing for the curious fact that what we might foreclose in language as being 'unrepresentable' can and may yet be admitted into representation — even if only to lurk there, 'almost', by inference. Valuable too is her recognition of what language is required to retain, or rather, what language has become, under that threat of 'imminent change', custodian of. Pursuing this point to the furthest reach, of course, leads us to the language politics of contemporary Northern Ireland — where the Irish language, and increasingly Ulster Scots, have been used as channels through which to revive identities both shared and separate. More closely pitched to Barber's argument, though, are the points advanced by Richard Kirkland at the beginning of his *Identity Parades: Northern Irish Culture and Dissident Subjects* (2002). He notes that 'the fact that the normative "two traditions" version of Northern Irish culture has proved incapable of reimagining the sectarian polarities of the province is now almost axiomatic'. Published just four years after the Good Friday Agreement, Kirkland's work sought instead to offer a critical perspective which 'encounters the cultural manifestations of identity politics not with the aim of locating their obsolescence but rather with the objective of tracing their implicit inner contradictions'.[31]

These arguments take us back to the provocatively 'clear-cut statements' which are written across or beneath Doherty's images. Were we to test them before returning to Doherty we might look to other words and other pictures. Both loyalist and republican have their affirmatives in slogans familiar from gable-end walls: 'No Surrender', and *'tiocfaidh ár lá'*, the Irish phrase, attributed to the hunger striker Bobby Sands, meaning 'our day will come'.[32] Such statements are always open to oppositional challenge within Northern Ireland (the inevitable 'other' side is always ready to refute), but, more interestingly, once these statements are removed from their original context their meanings are dissolved. Questions become possible: no surrender from what? Whose day will come? Doherty's work made such questions possible in the years at the end of the conflict: if it was rooted in its context it was, and is, also deliberately transgressive of it. In a 2003 examination of the word/image dynamic in Doherty's work, Paul O'Brien was ready for new questions: 'For me, the questions raised by Doherty's work escape the Protestant/Catholic duality to raise issues concerning the political construction of that duality in the first place. If one query raised by the work is "which side are you on?" another possible question is "why either?"'[33] Such questions come all the more strongly to the fore now that that conflict is no longer the context that went without saying, thanks to the media-driven notoriety of the Northern Ireland in which the works were first made. And the points Kirkland and Barber are making, too, about the post-conflict future of identities which were so firmly and — for those who claimed them, so affirmatively — set during that conflict reveal the strange, transitional, and vulnerable zone in which the critic must now encounter and assess these issues.

The space for interpretation in the gap between text and image has not always been welcomed. Writing in 1998 of Doherty's 'Border Incident' (1994), which features the image of a burned-out car on an empty country road, the sociologist Bill Rolston argued that '[a]lthough the photograph conveys imprecise, unspecified menace, we need something more.'[34] His analysis required that the image, and by extension the photographer, function responsibly within the context of conflict in order that 'we' might in turn interpret and gauge it with fully informed moral care. He concludes: 'The challenge to photographers is to aid victims and survivors in their struggle for truth and justice. Thus the indeterminacy of Doherty's photograph — its openness to many interpretations — represents a retreat from political responsibility into a postmodern aesthetic. A photograph that can tell different truths is of little value in the endeavour to overcome past repression and abuse.'[35] It is a heavy weight for Doherty to bear, and an ethical argument that grants the making and reception of art little licence in the fray. The understandable urge for righteousness makes arguably unfair demands, but in so doing it serves importantly to remind us of what is put at stake in cultural and theoretical engagements with the North. The resemblance borne by what is represented by the artist and analysed by the academic to what happened is bound to be provocative, because what happened is always debatable.

Kirkland is among a number of cultural and literary critics who have, since the Good Friday Agreement, attended closely to a range of texts, sources and media in their investigations of post-conflict Northern Ireland. Photography has often been a focal medium, offering a rich narrative of development in representations of the North. Colin Graham is a leading voice in this area, and in his book which accompanied a major exhibition in Belfast in 2013, *Northern Ireland: 30 Years of Photography*, he narrated his own changing perspectives on the variant capacities and ambitions of different forms of artistic expression — namely literary writing and photography — to represent Northern Ireland since the late 1990s. He did so with a degree of self-examination, noting the

> [. . .] very specific conviction that I had around the turn of the millennium [. . .] that Northern Irish writing [. . .] was unable to register the changes which were taking place in the North in the wake of the Downing Street Declaration, the IRA ceasefires and then the Good Friday Agreement. My diagnosis was simple and, in retrospect, completely wrong. What I thought was that the Troubles had worn a conceptual and ideological path which Northern Irish writing (poetry, novels and drama) had difficulty leaving. This path was defined by an elevated, intelligent, refined form of liberalism, a middle ground that disavowed sectarianism and looked towards a 'shared' future (or a shared past).[36]

While Graham is writing in the wake of the Troubles, it is salutary to test his observations in consideration of two works produced during the conflict — Seamus Heaney's poem 'The Other Side' which was published in his collection *Wintering Out* (1972), and Doherty's photograph of the same title, 'The Other Side' (1988). Heaney's poem recalls his Catholic childhood on a farm in County Derry, and the Protestant neighbour who would wait politely outside their front door before calling on evenings when he could hear the Heaneys saying the Rosary. The poem, which concludes with the grown man Heaney's new uncertainty in relating to this old acquaintance now the Troubles have aggravated the difference between them, is a legible account of identity politics in Northern Ireland at the time: indeed, Heaney included it in a radio programme titled 'Otherness' which he presented for the BBC Northern Ireland Schools Service in 1974.[37] Even as the poem admits the potential of sectarian difference, it can still occupy the middle ground which would later concern Graham, because it lends itself to well-intentioned readings which wish to recover from its portrayal of dialogue between the two clearly recognizable 'sides' the possibility for the culture of mutual respect from the past for the future. Doherty's 'The Other Side' shows a view across a city — which is his own city, Derry — but the sides are made unsteady by the text which announces that 'West is South' and 'East is North'. The compass points in Northern Ireland have traditionally exerted more than a directional pull: for example, Republican West Belfast, Loyalist East Belfast, and even leafy South Belfast all have their particular associations. In this image of Derry, Doherty seeks to emphasize the disruption — which is not only political and social, but also fundamentally logical — which the border between Northern Ireland and the Republic enacts. West is made South and East North by the border which runs almost vertically between counties Donegal and Derry. There can be no middle ground here, nor can this be read as a straightforward articulation of sectarian difference, because whichever way we look, the divisions, encoded within the directional words, are persistently reversed or upturned.

It is of course significant that throughout his career Doherty has returned to explore and depict the city of Derry, a city with nomenclatural problems, to borrow Dennis O'Driscoll's wry phrasing.[38] The most basic act of representing Derry — writing its name — is questionable. James I made it Londonderry in 1613, but it is conventionally and habitually shortened, either in resistance to that colonial name-change or simply for convenience. That weary nickname which Derry/Londonderry earned during the Troubles, 'Stroke City', is still eloquent in conveying a sense of the identities of the place. This compromise is still observed by the contemporary Google Maps, and it had to be negotiated by the marketing team tasked with creating a new, brand identity for the place during its year as a UK city of culture in 2013. In this branding the city's name was rendered as Derry~Londonderry 2013. Before this translation, Graham had suspected and deconstructed the motives and effects of the rebranding of Belfast shortly after the city council unveiled a heart-shaped B, which cost them £180,000, as its new civic logo in 2008. He was particularly concerned with the way that B, which stood for '"warmth" and "friendliness"', bore the past:

> [...] the final version of the 'B' which was chosen is not meant to reflect directly on the 'history' of the city. Quite the opposite in fact. What it does instead is to package that history, de-particularize it, and then collapse and encompass the past into terms palatable for tourism [...] All of which, of course, has the added side-effect of cleansing the past of all the obviously negative connotations of the city, while turning the city's self-image fully outwards, primarily to its potential visitors, and with the secondary implication and hope that its citizens will be persuaded of the indisputable naturalness of what the 'B' tells them about the city they live in. The resultant insensitivity of this branded future to the actual past is not just in its attempt to brand conflict out of the city's image, but additionally, for example, in its symbolic erasure of the wider memory of Belfast.[39]

A different past posed, and arguably engendered, different problems in Derry~Londonderry. Here, the tilde represented separation as an elegant little wave, more aesthetically dynamic and vital than the forward slash of the old Stroke City on which the past leaned so heavily. In this branding, though, the various grammatical and mathematical functions of the symbol simultaneously performed a range of roles which were each appropriate for the position it occupied between the two names. As a diacritic in use in early printing, a superscript tilde indicated the contraction of a word, and centuries of history are contracted within the name of a place whose utterance might indicate political or ideological conviction. In mathematical logic the tilde is chiefly used to signal that one value is not equal to another, but it can also indicate equivalence. Like West and South and East and North in Doherty's 'The Other Side', Derry is not equal to Londonderry, and vice versa. Yet in the optimistic branding which constructs the city's shared future, they are made equivalent.

In his 'At the Border' series, Doherty presents and anticipates conceptual, theoretical and technical features of his practice which can be traced elsewhere in his work. The early diptych 'UNDERCOVER/UNSEEN' (1985) points the way to these post-ceasefire images; 'UNSEEN', a black-and-white image of a road leading out of Derry, bears under its title word the legend 'TO THE BORDER'. Ten years later, 'At the Border', we would seem grammatically to have arrived, but the destination is indeterminate. As in the images 'Border Incident' (1993), 'The Outskirts' (1994), and 'Border Road' (1994), the landscape between north and south is rural, marked — if not marred — by the road that runs through it. These three earlier images were all stealthily didactic in their assertions of the prior occurrence of some form of menacing activity at the border: the wrecked car, swerving skid marks, and charred road block are all contrived to make us question what that might have been. The 1995 images, by contrast, are almost entirely devoid of the evidence of human activity: with the exception of the car headlights emerging from the darkness in second picture, 'At the Border II (Low Visibility)', the landscapes are apparently empty, filled only by what we deduce from the accompanying captions. Those captions, too, echo other aspects of Doherty's earlier work: the pendant present participles of the second and fourth images ('waiting' and 'trying') recall the 'waiting', 'enduring', 'dreaming', and 'believing' applied to various images of Derry in the photographs-with-text of the mid- to late 1980s. In a later video work, 'Ghost Story' (2007), text and image are made more dynamic, but the implied activity remains uncertain. Once again the focus is on the road: the camera moves along the neat tarmac strips which surround Derry city, while a voice — that of the actor Stephen Rea — narrates memories and observations, all charged by the uncanny intersection of the unfamiliar and the remembered. 'Ghost Story' and the border photographs of the 1990s were among works gathered in *Willie Doherty: Requisite Distance*, an exhibition which ran in the US in 2009 and 2010. In the accompanying catalogue, Charles Wylie argued that 'Ghost Story' 'can be seen as Doherty's summation of his media work to date [...] a powerful work of art that suggests how events, especially traumatic ones, are remembered through a scrim of pictures and words dimly illuminated by the faulty subjectivity of memory itself'.[40] 'Ghost Story' is a work of the aftermath; from Wylie's valuable assertion we can work back to 'At the Border', not necessarily a summative work but certainly and transitional one, before the properly post-conflict scrim had fallen.

Once again, the grammatical governance of language in the captions which accompany the four photographs in Doherty's 'At the Border' series is crucial in the visual interpretation of them. The four photographs are titled: 'At the Border I (Walking towards a Military Checkpoint)'; 'At the Border II (Low Visibility)'; 'At the Border III (Trying to Forget the Past)'; and 'At the Border IV (The Invisible Line)' (Figs 1–4). Each of these titles is instructive, seeming to indicate what we see, but the instructions are undermined by the images themselves. The series title common to each image is ostensibly straightforward in placing the image with the

Fig. 7.1. Willie Doherty, 'At the Border I (Walking towards a Military Checkpoint)' (1995). By kind permission of the artist and Matt's Gallery.

Fig. 7.2. Willie Doherty, 'At the Border II (Low Visibility)' (1995). By kind permission of the artist and Matt's Gallery.

Fig. 7.3. Willie Doherty, 'At the Border III (Trying to Forget the Past)' (1995). By kind permission of the artist and Matt's Gallery.

Fig. 7.4. Willie Doherty, 'At the Border IV (The Invisible Line)' (1995). By kind permission of the artist and Matt's Gallery.

locational preposition 'at'. But 'at', as the *OED*'s headnote to its entry explains, 'is used to denote relations of so many kinds, and some of these so remote from its primary local sense, that a classification of its uses is very difficult'. In the first definition ventured by the dictionary, 'at' is:

> The most general determination of simple localization in space, expressing, strictly, the simple relation of a thing to a point of space which it touches; hence, usually determining a point or object with which a thing or attribute is practically in contact, and thus the place where it is, when this is either so small as to be treated as a mere point, or when the exact relation between the thing and the place is not more particularly expressed by the prepositions close to, near, by, about, on, in, over, under, etc., all of which may at times be covered by at.[41]

The complex 'At' of the captions promises to locate us, but under pressure the word can neither fix nor be fixed. The effectiveness of the caption, then, is diminished, and the images escape from the words which would hold them. 'At the Border I' (Fig. 1) recedes into a 'point of space': this picture of the road cutting through the countryside, itself cut through by the white hyphens of road markings, extends towards its vanishing point. It is the first of four pictures 'at' a border we cannot see, but we find Ziff's structured absences both in the image and in the caption. These accompanying words suggests that there is action within or behind the image: in parentheses, someone is 'walking' towards a military checkpoint, in a present tense which might read as an imitation of documentary representation, or of the permanent present tense of photographic recall: arrested in — or by — the image, this unidentified, unseen subject is always 'walking towards a military checkpoint'.

The verb of the first image, 'walking', leads towards that of the caption to the third image, 'Trying to Forget the Past' (Fig. 3), where the participle again suggests an actor — though here the activity could be collective, we are trying, or they are trying, to forget. Another placid scene is undercut by the implications of the words which accompany it: the green land and the pale sky have formed the backdrop to scenes far less calm than this. It is difficult to forget the 'past' when so many incidents during the Troubles took place, to echo Doherty, at the border. Both the possibility of forgetting and the obligation to remember attended the end of the conflict, symbolized if not finalized by the 1994 ceasefires. Ian Hunt has suggested that in this series, 'we are faced with works that pull a perplexing aesthetic appeal from their subject, and the possibility of a vista, of seeing beauty for what it is even at this location'.[42] What Hunt misses, though, is Doherty's play on the banal which is manifest in the third photograph: the dawn scene signalling the new beginning at which the past might be left behind. It is not that easy. Nor is the possibility of 'seeing beauty' in this image entirely straightforward: the road which cuts through the foreground pre-empts the landscape which extends diagonally beyond it. This photograph can be read in anticipation of the controversy which emerged around the image chosen to illustrate the front cover of the text of the Good Friday Agreement, sent to every home in Northern Ireland ahead of the referendum in May 1998. As Aaron Kelly has explained, the unfortunate implication in this picture of a sun setting on an old day, rather than dawning on a new one, led the Belfast photography magazine *Source* to investigate its provenance: as there are no west-facing beaches in Northern Ireland it could not have been taken there. Richard West's discovery that the stock-image photograph had in fact been taken on a beach in Cape Town, South Africa — introducing new comparative contextual resonances — was, understandably, a spur to cynicism.[43]

The second and fourth images in 'At the Border' retain their focus on the road, but their parenthetical subtitles are free of verbs. Instead they announce issues around sight and seeing: the 'Low Visibility' of 'At the Border II' (Fig. 2) is made all the more menacing because we can see some things — the curved tyre marks on the road which suggest a vehicle may have swerved to avoid danger; the rectangle lozenges of the car headlights in the background which seem to be directed towards us. If the verbs of I and III suggested an actor behind the lens which took these pictures, that actor is no longer alone. 'At the Border IV' (Fig. 4) apparently returns to the scene of the first image, and 'The Invisible Line' is at once disingenuous and accurate. That broken white line on the road which leads our eye to the patch of sky is visible; the line which is not is the one this series would suggest we are standing on: the border itself.

In 1986 Colm Tóibín set out to walk along the Irish border, from west to east. He documented his experiences in the book *Walking along the Border*, which included Tony O'Shea's photographs. The title shares its present participle with 'At the Border I' and the activity of that verb being carried out along the no-place of the border is suggestive enough. It is unfortunate that less than a decade later Tóibín's book was repackaged, minus O'Shea's photographs, with the title *Bad Blood: A Walk along the Irish Border*, complete with a bloodstained cover design, which carelessly sensationalized the subject. Tóibín begins his uneasy journey by walking from Derry in Northern Ireland across the border to the town of Lifford, in the Republic's County Donegal. Looking back Graham noted that Tóibín's first steps were enough to mark him as an outsider in border country: 'The border is a place which is not meant to be stopped at or pondered, so when a camera, or a writer, pauses and looks at it, the photographer, or writer, adopts the position of an alien presence or a recorder of evidence.'[44] In regarding Doherty's images 'At the Border', the onlooker assumes a comparably alien presence, not as a recorder of evidence but as one who is forced — by the accompanying text — to adopt the role of interpreter. But our gaze is, to borrow Christov-Bakargiev's adjective again, always fallible, and the evidence before us proves nothing.

Sontag's articulation of the visual-historical transaction with which this essay began is rhetorically satisfying, but it demands extension at the conclusion of this discussion. Sontag sensed, but did not clearly attribute, culpability in our 'unearned relation with the past': the question of agency is diluted. What we confront in Doherty's video and photographic art is contrived, deliberately produced; what we read into it is no more innocent, and is still shaped and informed by competing stakes, whether these emerge from the opposition of political perspectives or the representative capacities of different media. Writing after Jean Fisher's 1990 analysis of Doherty's photographs with text for the Orchard Gallery, Gee offers a valuable formulation: our reading of those landscapes of the early work, both rural and urban, 'is guided and misguided by textual devices'.[45] The landscapes of the 'At the Border' series might seem straightforwardly rural, but they might more accurately be described as utopic — in the proper, etymological sense of the word. These are no places, and yet context would guide us towards fixing them as *the* place, the definite article pointing us towards Northern Ireland. That same work of guiding and misguiding is performed by the text which accompanies the images, but these captions issue a very different challenge to the onlooker than that presented by the overlaid text on the earlier work. 'At the Border' might be seen as a bridge between media in Doherty's work: with the text no longer on the photographic image but beneath it, the reaction between image and imagination in these works is analogous to that prompted by the video works. If there is 'nothing' there then that nothing is something, 'almost unrepresentable', as Barber would have it, and allowed for by the grammatical activity, or the muted inference, of the captions' words. The curators of UNSEEN, the 2013 exhibition of Doherty's work at the City Factory Gallery in Derry, explained that the title was chosen in reference to Doherty's self-conscious method of using his camera in a context where it was imperative for him to avoid undue attention and to minimize the risk of being mistaken for a photojournalist or a tourist. Doherty's unseen practice makes a self-conscious and consistently questionable practice of seeing itself; it confirms and denies at once.

Acknowledgement

Thanks are due to Willie Doherty and Matt's Gallery, London, for permission to reproduce the 'At the Border' series in this essay.

Notes to Chapter 7

1. 'It's Stolen Your Face', *Omnibus*, BBC, 23 November 1978, extract used in Martin Scorsese dir., 'The 50 Year Argument — *The New York Review of Books*', *Arena*, BBC Four [television], 29 June 2014.
2. The Government of Ireland Act 1920 was repealed with the Northern Ireland Act 1998, as a result of the Belfast/Good Friday Agreement reached that year. Facsimile of the 1920 Act available online at <http://www.legislation.gov.uk/ukpga/1920/67/pdfs/ukpga_19200067_en.pdf> [accessed 30 March 2015].
3. See 'Decade of Centenaries', the official site giving full details of the ten-year programme of events backed by An Roinn Ealaíon, Oidreachta agus Gaeltachta (the Department of Arts, Heritage and the Gaeltacht): <http://www.decadeofcentenaries.com/> [accessed 30 March 2015].
4. See, for example, Brendan Lynn, 'Introduction to the Electoral System of Northern Ireland': <http://cain.ulst.ac.uk/images/posters/ira/index.html> [accessed 28 March 2015].
5. Cited in Neil Corcoran, *Seamus Heaney* (London: Faber, 1986), p. 19.
6. R. F. Foster, *Modern Ireland 1600–1972* (London: Penguin, 1989), p. 584. Foster notes that in 1961 22 per cent of the student population at Queen's University Belfast were Catholics; by 1971 the figure was 32 per cent.
7. Cormac Ó Gráda and Brendan M. Walsh, *Did (and does) the Irish border matter?* Working Papers in British-Irish Studies, no. 60 (Dublin: Institute for British-Irish Studies, University College Dublin, 2006), n.p.

8. Brendan Lynn has compiled a list of IBIS publications for the University of Ulster's CAIN resource: <http://cain.ulst.ac.uk/bibdbs/ibispubs.htm> [accessed 28 March 2015].
9. David Lloyd, *Irish Times: Temporalities of Modernity* (Dublin: Field Day, 2008), p. 129.
10. Relentless focus on the dominant fissures of, have tended to occlude or delay attention to other issues in Northern Irish society — most obviously class, of central importance to the conflict; gender; and race and ethnicity — which are increasingly receiving salutary cross-disciplinary attention in the academy.
11. Lloyd, *Irish Times*, p. 129.
12. Trisha Ziff, 'Photographs at War', in *The Media and Northern Ireland: Covering the Troubles*, ed. by Bill Rolston (Basingstoke: Macmillan, 1991), pp. 187–206 (pp. 195–96). Mike Abrahams's picture of the Caraher family, 'The Invisible Border/South Armagh', was reproduced with her essay; Ziff, 'Photographs at War', p. 195.
13. *British Watchtowers* was exhibited at Belfast Exposed, 25 May to 3 August 2007. See <http://www.belfastexposed.org/exhibition/british_watchtowers> [accessed 30 March 2015]. See also Donovan Wylie and Louise Purbrick, *British Watchtowers* (Göttingen: Steidl, 2007).
14. Colin Graham, *Northern Ireland: 30 Years of Photography* (Belfast: Belfast Exposed and the Mac, 2013), p. 131.
15. Graham, *Northern Ireland*, p. 131.
16. Willie Doherty, UNSEEN, curated by Robert Klassnick and Pearse Moore, City Factory Gallery, Derry, 27 September 2013–4 January 2014. See <http://www.cityofculture2013.com/event/willie-doherty-unseen/> [accessed 30 March 2015].
17. These and other images can be viewed online at <http://williedoherty.com/>.
18. *Art of the Troubles*, Ulster Museum, Belfast, 10 April to 7 September 2014.
19. Eamonn McCann, *The British Press and Northern Ireland* (London: Northern Ireland Socialist Research Centre, 1971).
20. Carolyn Christov-Bakargiev, 'A Fallible Gaze: The Art of Willie Doherty', in *Willie Doherty: False Memory* (London: Merrell; Dublin: IMMA, 2002), p. 13.
21. Seamus Heaney, *The Spirit Level* (London: Faber, 1996), p. 31.
22. Christov-Bakargiev, p. 11.
23. Gabriel N. Gee, 'The Catalogues of the Orchard Gallery: A Contribution to Critical and Historical Discourse in Northern Ireland, 1978–2003', *Journal of Art Historiography*, 9 (December 2013), 1–25 (p. 3); <https://arthistoriography.wordpress.com/number-9-december-2013/> [accessed 30 April 2015]. I am grateful to Niamh NicGhabhann for alerting me to this article.
24. Matthew Reynolds, *Likenesses: Translation, Illustration, Interpretation* (Leeds: Legenda, 2013), p. 6.
25. Gee, 'The Catalogues', p. 3.
26. Seamus Heaney, *North* (London: Faber, 1975; repr. 2001), pp. 52–55.
27. See 'Loose Talk', Examples of Irish Republican Army (IRA) posters, collected by Martin Melaugh for the University of Ulster CAIN (Conflict Archive on the Internet) Web Service: <http://cain.ulst.ac.uk/images/posters/ira/index.html> [accessed 28 March 2015].
28. Colm Tóibín, *Bad Blood: A Walk along the Irish Border* (London: Picador, 2010), p. 170.
29. Begoña Aretxaga, *Shattering Silence: Women, Nationalism, and Political Subjectivity in Northern Ireland* (Princeton, NJ: Princeton University Press, 1997), p. 131.
30. Fionna Barber, 'At Vision's Edge: Post-Conflict Memory and Art Practice in Northern Ireland', in *Memory Ireland*, ed. by Oona Frawley, 4 vols (Syracuse, NY: Syracuse University Press, 2011–14), vol. III: *The Famine and the Troubles* (2014), pp. 232–46 (p. 246).
31. Richard Kirkland, *Identity Parades: Northern Irish Culture and Dissident Subjects* (Liverpool: Liverpool University, 2002), pp. 2–3.
32. See, for examples, the first volume of Bill Rolston's definitive work on the murals: Rolston, *Drawing Support: Murals in the North of Ireland* (Belfast: Beyond the Pale, 1992), pp. 9, 36.
33. Paul O'Brien, 'Willie Doherty: Language, Imagery and the Real', *Circa*, 104 (Summer 2003), 51–54 (p. 52).
34. Bill Rolston, 'All in the Mind? Photographing the Border', *Eire-Ireland* 33.3–4/34.1 (Fall/Winter 1998/Spring 1999), 245–54 (p. 246).

35. Rolston, 'All in the Mind?', p. 253.
36. Colin Graham, *Northern Ireland: 30 Years of Photography* (Belfast: Belfast Exposed and the MAC, 2013), p. 18.
37. 'Otherness' was made as part of the first series of *Explorations*, a literary programme for secondary school students originally broadcast in 1974, written and presented by Heaney and produced by David Hammond. For extended discussion of *Explorations*, see Lavan, '*Explorations*: Seamus Heaney and Education', *Irish Review*, 49–50 (Winter 2014/Spring 2015), 54–70.
38. Dennis O'Driscoll, 'Heaney in Public', in *The Cambridge Companion to Seamus Heaney*, ed. by Bernard O'Donoghue (Cambridge: Cambridge University Press, 2009), pp. 56–72 (p. 56).
39. Colin Graham, 'Gagarin's Point of View: Memory and Space in Recent Northern Irish Art', *Irish Review*, 40–41 (Winter 2009), 104–13 (p. 105).
40. Charles Wylie, *Willie Doherty: Requisite Distance* (New Haven, CT: Yale University Press, 2010), p. 36.
41. 'At, *prep.*' *OED* Online. Oxford University Press, September 2014 [accessed 9 September 2014].
42. Ian Hunt, 'Familiar and Unknowable: Works by Willie Doherty', in Willie Doherty, *Somewhere Else* (London: Tate, 1998), p. 48.
43. Aaron Kelly, 'Geopolitical Eclipse', *Third Text*, 19.5 (2005), 545–53 (p. 547).
44. Graham, *Northern Ireland*, p. 120.
45. Gee, 'The Catalogues', p. 7. He is discussing Jean Fisher's 'Seeing beyond the Pale: The Photographic Works of Willie Doherty', in Willie Doherty, *Unknown Depths* (Cardiff; Derry: Orchard Gallery, 1990).

CHAPTER 8

The Mother Tongue as Border

Anne Isabelle François

Une langue n'est pas seulement un système de signes, c'est un système
de valeurs; et ce n'est pas seulement une vision du monde, c'est une
production de monde.
FRÉDÉRIC WERST, Ward Ier et IIe siècle, 2011

Der Papagei sprach noch bloß seine Muttersprache.
GEORG CHRISTOPH LICHTENBERG, Sudelbuch J 371

It is evident that we are defined by languages, in everyday life, in literary practice, in translation. Languages in general are a powerful means of determination and assignation, but these linguistic boundaries and ties are charged with particularly strong associations and delimitations when it comes to the idea of the mother tongue. It is therefore interesting to explore the mapping of (linguistic) borders present in the expression 'mother tongue', borders that enclose as well as define, that are interiorized as well as imposed from the exterior. How are the borders conceptualized and metaphorized in terms of family relations and national issues (for instance in the articulation between 'mother language' and 'father land')? In what ways is the notion of 'mother tongue' overinvested with emotional, ideological, political and geographical concerns? The expression itself has become an emotionally charged term, establishing a more intimate, allegedly natural and privileged relationship between speaker and primary language. The emphasis on the 'maternal' element in the metaphor inscribes the speaker in a broader networks of relationships, from kin to nation, thus carrying particular gendered and political meanings.[1] My focus will be on European writing, especially late twentieth-century Western literature, where the metaphor of mother tongue seems to proliferate and seems particularly connected to postcolonial challenges to the nation.

To examine the associations and implications of the notion of mother tongue, shared by a number of languages,[2] shows that it does not so much denominate a concept as function as a common expression. My argument is that the metaphor of mother tongue condenses various territories and defines our relation to language through a series of borders, individual and collective.[3] The mother tongue designates at the same time the idea of a shared language of communication, the political quality of the national language, the affective image of the language of our mother (real or metaphorical), the link between language and roots. The very expression 'mother tongue' declares an obsession with the relationship between the question of origins and that of language. It thereby raises numerous issues related to filiation, legacy, genealogy, belonging, memory, and home, as well as to exile, orphanhood, errancy, dissidence, alienation.[4]

Writers, reinvesting the powerful syntagm and questioning its emotional components, thus underline the ambivalence of the metaphor, ranging from relations of longing or adulation to hatred and the desire to rupture logics of social, national and political belonging by creating other languages — hyphenated or post-monolingual — beyond borders.[5] These creators, especially in contemporary fiction and discourse, tend to break up the false self-evidence of the expression, to estrange and deconstruct the 'mother tongue', this 'language called maternal that is never purely natural, nor proper, nor inhabitable'.[6] The notion appears far less transparent than the reassuring brevity of dictionaries would lead us to believe. Whether metaphor or fantasy, reality or substitute, ideal or impossibility, the 'mother tongue' can become a tool that enables us to understand the ways of minding (and overstepping) the multiple borders and borderlines it contains and expresses. I shall therefore examine what is at stake in terms of *representations, paradigms* and *metaphor* when it comes to the mother tongue, in various twentieth- and twenty-first-century texts,[7] and specifically the idea of the mother tongue as border.

Let us start with two examples that demonstrate the range, contradictions and intricacies invested in the notion of the mother tongue and its tense relation to borders. Marina Tsvetaeva, a trilingual (Russian, French, German) poet, notes, in a letter written in German to the German poet Rainer Maria Rilke in 1926, that, as regards poetry and translation, there is no such thing as a mother tongue:

> Goethe sagt irgendwo, dass man nichts Bedeutendes in einer fremden Sprache sagen kann, — und das klang mir immer falsch... Dichten ist schon übertragen, aus der Muttersprache — in eine andere, ob französisch oder deutsch wird wohl gleich sein. Keine Sprache ist Muttersprache. Dichten ist nachdichten. Darum versteh ich nicht wenn man von französischen oder russischen etc. Dichtern redet. Ein Dichter kann französisch schreiben, er kann nicht ein französischer Dichter sein. Das ist lächerlich.[8]

> [Somewhere Goethe states that nothing worthy can be achieved in a foreign tongue; and that has always seemed wrong to me... Writing poetry is already translating, from one's mother tongue into another language — whether it be French or German. No language is a mother tongue. Writing poetry is transcribing. That's why I cannot understand when one speaks about French or Russian poets, and so on. A poet may write in French, but he cannot be a French poet. It is ridiculous.]

The poet Paul Celan, on the other hand, despite a difficult relationship with German's status as a national language, states in a letter written in the late 1940s to the Yiddish actress Ruth Lackner that the clearly idealized mother tongue is the only means of expressing individual authentic truth: 'Nur in der Muttersprache kann man die eigene Wahrheit aussagen, in der Fremdsprache lügt der Dichter' [You can express your own truth only in your mother tongue; in a foreign language, the poet lies].⁹ Celan draws a definitive borderline between the mother tongue and foreign languages; the opposition between *eigen* [own] and *fremd* [foreign], *Wahrheit* [truth] and *Lüge* [lie] reproduces an unquestioned ontology of a language that is at once one's very own and the primary language.

In literary texts, this notion of the mother tongue is often reinvested in relation to actual family members (parents in general, mothers in particular), in a very literal sense: the mother tongue is the language of origins, of individual roots, the first language, transmitted and learned in the 'nursery' — as Leo Spitzer, after Dante, stresses in his famous linguistic study of the notion.¹⁰ It is also a tongue that can be irremediably lost through displacement (chosen or imposed), through the crossing of geographic and cultural borders. It thus raises a vast range of questions, only a fraction of which can be addressed in this investigation: is there a *unique* mother tongue for each individual? Does the mother tongue exist as such or only as a theoretical fantasy, an ideal construction, an impossible dream? Can it be re-learned, if lost, or even become a conscious choice, a sort of acquired mother tongue, however contradictory the idea?¹¹ What are its functions and uses? How does it relate to the genesis of identity? How does it relate to borders and centres of power? How does it translate the relation between minority languages and national languages?

Contemporary literature of the Western tradition in particular problematizes the notion of the mother tongue, showing how identities are constructed and implemented through mediation and self-definition, where the outcome is a redefinition of spaces, a new mapping and naming, even if the process itself is full of fissures and interstices. Examples of late twentieth-century and contemporary works (novels, plays, novellas, video installations, performances) that explicitly address the notion of the mother tongue include: Elias Canetti's *Die gerettete Zunge* (1977), Josef Winkler's *Muttersprache* (1982), Marlene Nourbese Philip's *She Tries Her Tongue, Her Silence Softly Breaks* (1988),¹² Irena Klepfisz's *A Few Words in the Mother Tongue* (1990), Emine Sevgi Özdamar's *Mutterzunge* (1990), Demetria Martínez's *Mother Tongue* (1994), Vassilis Alexakis's *La Langue maternelle* (1995), Betty Quan's *Mother Tongue* (1998), Rouja Lazarova's *Sur le bout de langue* (1998), Ian McEwan's essay 'Mother Tongue' (2001), Wladimir Kaminer's *Es liegt mir auf der Zunge* (2002), Zineb Sedira's *Mother Tongue* (2002), Nurith Aviv's *Perte, Vaters Land* (2002) and *D'une langue à l'autre: Misafa Lesafa* (2004), Vyvyane Loh's *Breaking the Tongue* (2004), Roger Williams's *Mother Tongue* (2006), Marianna Salzmann's *Muttersprache Mameloschn* (2013) or Conrad Alexandrowicz's *Mother Tongue* (2014). These works engage specifically with the expression 'mother tongue' and its metaphorical potential, as also shown in the striking repetition of the expression 'mother tongue' itself in the titles. Many of these creators come from multilingual backgrounds, or have chosen to write in another language for reasons of geographic displacement, often leading to a poetics of displacement. The texts thus enact a shared obsession: questioning the precarious and problematic relationship between origins and language. They also tend to express what linguists call the process of mother tongue shift: namely, not learning the parents' mother tongue, but rather learning the dominant language of one's adopted country. The texts thus exemplify multiple processes of hyphenation, from mother tongue shift to examples of the intergenerational retention of minority languages which express transitional zones within identities.[13]

This hyphenation and questioning is not confined to postcolonial or migrant literatures, as the case of Josef Winkler shows. Born a farmer's son in 1953 in Austria's southernmost province, Winkler is one of Austria's most notable contemporary writers.[14] His first books are profoundly rooted in his native province of Carinthia (Kärnten). His early narratives — three novels published between 1979 and 1982, *Menschenkind* [*Son of Man*] (1979), *Der Ackermann aus Kärnten* [*The Ploughman from Carinthia*] (1980), *Muttersprache* [*Mother Tongue*] (1982) — describe the childhood and youth of a protagonist in a small village, a protagonist crushed under the weight of a destructive and asphyxiating rural world. Winkler, dubbed as a late avatar of what critics call '*kritischer Heimatroman*' or '*Anti-Heimatroman*', is deeply connected to this maternal language and earth. In 1984 he united the novels as a trilogy under the title: *Das wilde Kärnten* [*Wild Carinthia*], a reference to his native province, but also a hidden reference to his favourite boyhood writer, Karl May, author of *Durchs wilde Kurdistan* [*Across Wild Kurdistan*] (1881–82).

The example of Winkler shows how far the notion of the mother tongue is charged with ethnic and national issues, the idea that group members share a unique language. It is thus crucially linked to dimensions of fatherland and nation, defining a collective identity — varying the metaphor of family, the idea of (legitimate) genealogy and offspring, articulating *mother* tongue and *father*land[15]. In 1920, the philosopher Fritz Mauthner (1849–1923), born in Bohemia,[16] published an essay entitled 'Muttersprache und Vaterland' [Mother Tongue and Fatherland] in which he offers a reflection on the metaphor of the 'mother tongue' and its political uses, in the context of the rise of nationalisms and the reconfiguration of identities throughout Europe. He stresses the risk of linguistic nationalism, when the love of one's own language turns into hatred for other languages.

Mauthner's 1920 essay specifically deconstructs, without eliminating it, the tie between language and identity; it offers an incentive to be cautious of one's own language and the representations it conveys. His analysis emerges from his own upbringing, not unlike Kafka's, in the German-speaking Jewish community of Prague, marked by the plurality of tongues within the same territory: German (*Kultursprache*), standardized Czech, Hebrew, but also Yiddish, *Mauscheldeutsch*[17] or *Kuchelböhmisch*, a sort of Germanized Czech he learned from his nurse. The first chapter of the essay, as well as his *Memoirs* published in 1918, relate his youth and the peaceful coexistence and intermingling of German and Czech, before chauvinistic movements turned them into opponents. It is this upbringing that led him to be interested in languages:

> ein Jude, der in einer slawischen Gegend Österreichs geboren ist [...] lernte [...] genau genommen drei Sprachen zugleich verstehen: Deutsch als die Sprache der Beamten, der Bildung, der Dichtung und seines Umgangs; Tschechisch als die Sprache der Bauern und der Dienstmädchen, als die historische Sprache des glorreichen Königreichs Böhmen; ein bisschen Hebräisch als die heilige Sprache des Alten Testaments und als die Grundlage für das Mauscheldeutsch, welches er von Trödeljuden, aber gelegentlich auch von ganz gut gekleideten

jüdischen Kaufleuten seines Umgangs oder gar seiner Verwandtschaft sprechen hörte.[18]

[[A] Jew, born in a Slavic region of Austria [...] learned [...], strictly speaking, three languages at the same time: German, the language of administration, culture, literature and family life; Czech, the language of farmers and maids, the historical language of the glorious kingdom of Bohemia; a little bit of Hebrew, the holy language of the Old Testament and the basis of *Mauscheldeutsch*, which he heard from wandering Jews, but also on occasion from quite well dressed Jewish tradesmen or even members of his family.]

Mauthner nonetheless considered himself to be deprived of a proper mother tongue, 'as a Jew in a country with two languages', just as he was without a proper 'mother religion', 'as the son of a completely non-confessional Jewish family'.[19] He *chose* to write in (High) German, but this *chosen* mother tongue always remained secondary compared to the 'immediate mother tongue', the 'familiar language' (*Mundart der Heimat*) that alone was able to convey the easy-going feeling of homeliness, safety, joy, and comfort,[20] and yet had to remain estranged in order for one to identify oneself within a larger adopted community. Thus the *choice* of the German language remains in his work both painful and complex: Mauthner states that he possesses no other mother tongue than this 'ink and paper German' (*ein papierendes Deutsch*), a highly artificial mode of expression that he had to *acquire*, but did not 'naturally learn' in the nursery. The idea of mother tongue is therefore invested with a profound nostalgia, a feeling of exile in his own language.

According to Mauthner the love of the mother tongue may be 'one of our strongest and most beautiful feelings',[21] but he denies his own mother tongue (*deutschböhmische Muttersprache*) the status of a proper language, in particular the status of a national language which is able to unite the *father*land. To him, the national language will always remain an artefact, precisely because no one properly *shares* a mother tongue, charged as it is with personal experiences and memories:

> Es gibt nicht zwei Menschen, die die gleiche Sprache reden... Dieser Überlegung liegt der Begriff einer einem Volke gemeinsamen Sprache, der Muttersprache, zu Grunde. Wo ist diese Sprache Wirklichkeit? Wo in aller Welt?... Gemeinsam ist die Muttersprache etwa, wie der Horizont gemeinsam ist; es gibt keine zwei Menschen mit gleichem Horizont, jeder ist der Mittelpunkt seines eigenen.[22]
>
> [No two individuals speak the same language... This conviction is at the foundation of the notion of a common tongue of one *Volk*, the mother tongue. Where is this language reality? Where in the whole world?... The mother tongue is shared in the same way we share the horizon; there are no two individuals with the same horizon, each one is the focus of his own].

Mauthner forcefully writes that just as there is no substitute for food and sustenance, the mother tongue cannot be replaced.[23] It is profoundly unique, but as such it is inadequately equipped to unite the national community. Nonetheless his essay is a heartfelt reminder not to sacralize the mother tongue, precisely because this sacralization cannot be dissociated from the rise of nationalism and is part of the imaginary construction of a national community: 'Man liebt die Muttersprache sogar stärker als man seine Familie liebt, als man seinen Nächsten lieben kann;

man liebt sie wirklich wie sich selbst, wie man nur einen edlen Teil seines Ich lieben kann, wie man sein Auge liebt. Auch sehen wir ja die Welt nur durch unsere Sprache' [You even love your mother tongue more than you love your family, more than you love your neighbour; you truly love her as yourself, as you can only love a noble part of yourself, as you love your eyes. And it is true that we see the world only through our language].[24] This link between mother tongue and fatherland, mother tongue and *Heimat*, leads to the idea of the mother tongue as having a suffocating proximity, a sort of affective determinism that weighs on the individual. The sacralization or adulation of the mother tongue may be pictured even as a harmful imprisonment, leading thus to its rejection, precisely because of its articulation of issues of political and national domination and heritage, as well as familial bonds.

In her 1994 novel *Mother Tongue*, Demetria Martínez shows that the idea of the mother tongue as a key factor of community and unity is an illusion. Her two main characters, a Chicana from New Mexico and a Salvadoran fleeing his country, may speak apparently the same language (hence the title of the book), but the supposed seamlessness of the Latino-Latin American connection, the fantasy of connectedness through the shared language, is shown as a false assumption and even a lie. This idea of the mother tongue as affective determinism, as border, is also expressed in the Indian Bengali American writer Jhumpa Lahiri's first novel, *The Namesake* (2003). One of its central characters, Moushumi, chooses a third language in order to escape from the ties and assignations that come with English and the language her parents, immigrants of the first generation, still speak at home:

> At her parents' insistence, she'd majored in chemistry, for they were hopeful she would follow in her father's footsteps. Without telling them, she'd pursued a double major in French. Immersing herself in a third language, a third culture, had been her refuge — she approached French, unlike things American or Indian, without guilt, or misgiving, or expectation of any kind. It was easier to turn her back on the two countries that could claim her in favour of one that had no claim whatsoever.[25]

French, because it represents nothing to her, is devoid of any emotional link, it becomes a neutral 'third' space,[26] allowing the character to invent her own personal identity.

Atiq Rahimi, born 1962 in Kabul, a political refugee in France since 1984, also sees the choice of another language as a means of freeing himself from ideological forces. Commenting on his first French novel *Syngué sabour, Pierre de patience* (Prix Goncourt 2008), which followed three novels written in Persian, he states in a 2008 interview:

> Ma langue maternelle, le persan, m'impose des tabous, des interdits. La langue maternelle dit l'intime, c'est elle qui nous apprend la vie, l'amour, la souffrance, elle qui nous ouvre au monde. C'est aussi la langue de l'autocensure... Avec le français, j'étais libéré de tonnes de contraintes affectives. Jusqu'en 2002, quand je suis retourné dans mon pays après 18 ans d'exil, j'étais incapable d'écrire en français. Je retrouve donc mon pays, ma culture, ma langue, et là, mystère, je ne pouvais plus écrire en persan.[27]

[My mother tongue, Persian, imposes on me taboos and bans. The mother tongue expresses the intimate; it teaches us life, love, suffering, it opens us to the world. It is also the language of self-censure… In French, I felt freed of tons of affective constraints. Until 2002, when I went back to my country after 18 years of exile, I was incapable of writing in French. Then I find my country again, my culture, my language, and suddenly, mysteriously, I am no longer able to write in Persian].

Rahimi thus decides to cut the umbilical cord, in order to avoid, out of love, a quasi incestuous relationship with the Persian language: 'Ne serait-ce que le mot "maternel": il crée trop de liens. Adopter une autre langue, le français, c'est choisir la liberté. On ne se marie pas avec sa mère!' [Take only the word 'maternal': it creates too many ties. To adopt another language, French, is to choose freedom. You're not supposed to marry your own mother!]. Rahimi forcefully states a necessary and salutary severance to free himself and his writing from the constraints imposed by Persian, but it also implies a sense of primal loss. His discourse is very ambiguous in that he claims that writing in French releases him from the ideological baggage of the mother tongue, but the reasons he gives appear more emotional and psychological, as if the different levels were inextricably tied — implying that this severance from the 'maternal' is not as natural or evident as he may claim ('you're not supposed to marry your own mother').

When we examine the ways in which artists handle the physical, psychic, and emotional separation from their mother, both symbolic and real — motherland, mother figures, mother tongue — we observe a spectrum of experiences ranging from intense love to fear, guilt, anger, outright hatred, and even feelings verging at times on what Adrienne Rich calls '*matrophobia*', or the wish to be purged 'of our mothers' bondage'.[28] Outright hatred of the mother tongue is thus explicitly expressed, for instance, by James Joyce, Jean Genet and Thomas Bernhard, another Austrian author who aims at violently tearing the mother tongue out of him, leading to systematic strategies of poetic and linguistic estrangement, as Mathias Verger has recently shown in his comparative analysis of these three major writers.[29] The issue of filiation thus appears crucial in these writers' reinvestment and affective mapping of the notion of the mother tongue, set against an ideological framework that seems to condemn and banish texts not aiming at reinforcing the legitimacy of a national literature. The articulation of the mother tongue and fatherland is also designed to impose the necessity of producing legitimate offspring/texts. If there is an attempt to sire children otherwise (with another mother, i.e. another language), then these texts will be bastards. Since the mother tongue is, according to this kind of political representation, conceived as natural, any tampering with it — any infidelity — is seen as unnatural, impure, monstrous and immoral. Thus, it is 'natural' law which requires monogamous relations in order to maintain the 'beauty' of the language and in order to insure that the works are authentic. In such an ideological reasoning, the reference to bastard children makes clear a concern over the purity of the mother tongue, but also a concern with the paternity of texts, from kin to nation, in any case a very charged connection to national, ethnic and gender issues. Mathias Verger demonstrates how Joyce's, Genet's and Bernhard's poetic practices directly reject and refute the national and ideological claims embedded in the notion of the mother tongue.

Freeing oneself from the mother tongue may therefore be envisioned as a form of liberation as well as treason. It may also describe a mixed relation to a language that is both one's own and also estranged, especially in a colonial context. John Skinner, in a well-known book, uses the expression 'stepmother tongue' to describe colonized peoples' relationship of love and hatred to the English language, the tongue of the oppressor and dominator.[30] It adequately expresses, by enriching the metaphorical net, the modalities of affect at the core of linguistic use and feeling. As in traditional fairy-tales, the stepmother, an evil if fascinating queen, rejects the adopted offspring only to be overpowered by it — as is, according to Skinner, the case with New Anglophone Fiction, which encompasses writing from Scotland to Australia and South Africa. The same image is used by Hédi Bouraoui, Francophone Canadian writer born in Tunisia, in his 'Letter to the French Language' (1994) sent from Québec, where he directly addresses his 'dear stepmother [*marâtre*]'. Feeling rejected by an official and restrictive apprehension of French language as national language, he glorifies the 'treason' enacted by the various other 'illegitimate sons' of this cruel stepmother, those of African, Caribbean, Ontarian or Vietnamese origins. True to the French Republic's motto (*'liberté, égalité, fraternité'*), Bouraoui envisions a future based on a new definition of the French language: one embracing all Francophone expressions, a transformation from 'stepmother tongue' to 'fraternal tongue' — whether the original mother be willing or not.[31]

Marlene NourbeSe Philip's 1989 poetry collection *She Tries Her Tongue, Her Silence Softly Breaks* addresses this issue, especially the conflicting and tense relation to a language, English, that is forever linked to past and present offenses, namely slavery, eugenics, colonialism as well as gender oppression and forced silencing. This complex set of issues leads the Caribbean-born poet to particularly brilliant, anguished and obsessive word-plays, bending and restating the expression 'mother tongue' itself, its various layers of meaning and affect, in the poem 'Discourse on the Logic of Language', which expresses the impossibility and yet possibility to write in English and to 'possess'[32] a language:

> English
> is my mother tongue.
> A mother tongue is not
> not a foreign lan lan lang
> language
> l/anguish
>   anguish
> — a foreign anguish.
>
> English is
> my father tongue.
> A father tongue is
> a foreign language,
> therefore English is a
> foreign language
> not a mother tongue.

> What is my mother
> tongue
> my mammy tongue
> my mummy tongue
> my momsy tongue
> my modder tongue
> my ma tongue?[33]

The chant-like refrain of this long, complex text, combining prose, poetry and various discourses, its main riff, fabulously musical and rhythmic, shows the potent elasticity of the expression 'mother tongue'. The text progresses via repetition, with subtle and powerful variations revolving around the central pun 'l/anguish' ('language + anguish') that picks up resonances from the surrounding discourses. As Evie Shockley writes in her foreword (2014) to the poetry collection: Philip takes an expression 'and hold[s] it up to the light to see what it obscures, what it refracts, what it illuminates; can blow air into it to hear its song, its call, its howl; can crack it open'.[34] From an intersectional perspective, gender and racial issues appear inextricably linked in the poem as well as in the metaphor of the 'mother tongue', especially in the tension between 'father tongue' (the White Euro-Christian male canon) and 'mother tongue' (Black African female).[35]

At the opposite end of the spectrum, in an oft-quoted passage from *Étrangers à nous-mêmes* [*Strangers to Ourselves*], 'The Silence of Polyglots', Julia Kristeva describes the inevitable return of linguistic determination. However long the linguistic exile, a polyglot will never manage to shed him- or herself entirely of the mother tongue. It may leave him or her for a time, but without ever totally deserting him or her, turning him or her into an imperfect polyglot, condemned to silence because of the inability to be completely him- or herself in another language. Kristeva writes that this hovering mother tongue leaves behind a hole, a void even, a chasm that cannot be filled:

> Ne pas parler sa langue maternelle. Habiter des sonorités, des logiques coupées de la mémoire nocturne du corps, du sommeil aigre-doux de l'enfance. Porter en soi comme un caveau secret, ou comme un enfant handicapé — chéri et inutile — ce langage d'autrefois qui se fane sans jamais vous quitter. Vous vous perfectionnez dans un autre instrument, comme on s'exprime avec l'algèbre ou le violon. Vous pouvez devenir virtuose avec ce nouvel artifice qui vous procure d'ailleurs un nouveau corps, tout aussi artificiel, sublimé — certains disent sublime... Mais l'illusion se déchire lorsque vous vous entendez, à l'occasion d'un enregistrement par exemple, et que la mélodie de votre voix vous revient bizarre, de nulle part, plus proche du bredouillis d'antan que du code d'aujourd'hui.

> [Not speaking one's mother tongue. Living with resonances and reasoning that are cut off from the body's nocturnal memory, from the bittersweet slumber of childhood. Bearing within oneself like a secret vault, or like a handicapped child — cherished and useless — that language of the past that withers without ever leaving you. You improve your ability with another instrument, as one expresses oneself with algebra or the violin. You can become a virtuoso with this new device that moreover gives you a new body, just as artificial and

sublimated — some say sublime. You have a feeling that the new language is a resurrection: new skin, new sex. But the illusion bursts when you hear, upon listening to a recording, for instance, that the melody of your voice comes back to you as a peculiar sound, out of nowhere, closer to the old spluttering than to today's code.][36]

Inscribed in the polyglot's deepest self, incorporated through his or her voice, forever imprinted in sonorities and resonances, the mother tongue resurfaces despite him- or herself. It belongs to the body's nocturnal memory (*la mémoire nocturne du corps*). This deep-rooted mother tongue is for Kristeva something that belongs to the linguistic unconscious of each individual.[37]

In contemporary literary texts, the metaphor and realities of the mother tongue are more often than not explicitly related to the figure of the actual mother.[38] Thus, maternal bodies and mother tongue may be linked with another paradise, nostalgia for a cultural past, the pleasures of innocence, or the evanescent bliss of complete belonging. Jamaica Kincaid, American writer of Antiguan descent, literalizes the expression of the mother tongue in her 1990 novel *Lucy*. Her eponymous young heroine states: 'My past was my mother; I could hear her voice, and she spoke to me not in English or the French patois that she sometimes spoke, or in any language that needed help from the tongue; she spoke to me in language anyone female could understand'.[39] As an au pair for an affluent family in New York, nineteen-year-old Lucy desires to 'put as much distance' between herself and her mother as she can, her mother's love having become a 'burden': 'I had come to feel that my mother's love for me was designed solely to make me into an echo of her; and I didn't know why, but I felt that I would rather be dead than become just an echo of someone. That was not a figure of speech'.[40] It is in order to escape this fate of turning into a mere echo or stutter that she leaves these origins behind, crossing a border with multiple coordinates (from childhood to adulthood, from Antigua to the United States, etc.). In the novel, Lucy's mother as well as the mother tongue is constantly associated with the customs and landscapes of her island home of Antigua, with the rain forest and sun-drenched rivers or the wisdom of an herbalist.

This link with the mother and all she represents can lead to a dreadful sense of loss, a forced tearing apart. In the last pages of his 1966 book *Le Polygone étoilé* [*The Star-Shaped Polygon*], the Algerian writer Kateb Yacine tells how the father of the main character, who will become a writer himself, wants to persuade his son to go to a French school, although the father himself is a fine Arab scholar. And the son narrates how, in front of his mother, he embraces his father's desire, viewing it in retrospect as a capitulation and even a matricide as well as a symbolic suicide:

> Ma mère était trop fine pour ne pas s'émouvoir de l'infidélité qui lui fut ainsi faite. Et je la vois encore... un soir, d'une voix candide, non sans tristesse, me disant: 'Puisque je ne dois plus te distraire de ton autre monde, apprends-moi donc la langue française...' Ainsi se referma le piège des Temps Modernes sur mes frêles racines, et j'enrage à présent de ma stupide fierté, le jour où, un journal français à la main, ma mère s'installa devant ma table de travail, lointaine comme jamais, pâle et silencieuse... Jamais je n'ai cessé, même aux jours de succès près de l'institutrice, de ressentir au fond de moi cette seconde

rupture du lien ombilical, cet exil intérieur qui ne rapprochait plus l'écolier de sa mère que pour les arracher, chaque fois un peu plus, au murmure du sang, aux frémissements réprobateurs d'une langue bannie, secrètement, d'un même accord, aussitôt brisé que conclu... Ainsi avais-je perdu tout à la fois ma mère et son langage, les seuls trésors inaliénables — et pourtant aliénés!

[My mother was too subtle not to be moved by the infidelity that had been done to her. And I still see her... one evening, in an innocent voice, not without sadness, saying to me: 'Since I am no longer to distract you from your other world, teach me the French language...' Thus the trap of Modern Times closed in on my frail roots, and I am now infuriated at my stupid pride, the day when, holding a French newspaper, my mother sat down in front of me at the worktable, further away than ever, pale and silent... Never, not even in those days of success in the eyes of the (French) schoolteacher, have I ceased to feel deep within me that second rupture of the umbilical cord, this internal exile that no longer brought together the schoolboy and his mother except to wrest them, each time a bit more, away from the murmur of blood, from the reproaching shivers of a banished tongue, secretly in an agreement as quickly shattered as concluded. ... Thus I had lost at once my mother and her language, the only inalienable and yet alienated treasures![41]

In this powerful and beautiful passage — which closes a book that offers a mosaic of fragments, mirroring a hybrid and multifaceted identity — the narrator again varies the notion of the mother tongue. Turning to the French language, at his father's initiative, he transforms his mother and her tongue into receding ghosts: although sitting in front of him, she appears 'further away than ever, pale and silent'. As in Elias Canetti's *Mutterzunge*, the passage describes a second linguistic birth, but unlike Canetti, this leads to an inexorable distancing and estrangement from his mother and the first 'umbilical' language, the child even replacing the 'blood' ties with a surrogate mother figure, the female schoolteacher (*institutrice*). Yacine finally underlines the inextricable entanglement between the actual mother and the 'banished tongue', ending on a paradoxical formulation ('the only inalienable and yet alienated treasures') stating both the primal status of the 'maternal tongue' and its irretrievable loss as first language and as tongue of the mother, charging the whole passage with a lingering expression both of guilt and longing.

Family — and child-mother-father constellation — is also at the core of the trilogy *Das wilde Kärnten* [*Wild Carinthia*], by Josef Winkler, the Austrian writer I introduced near the start of this essay. He tells first of the child's resistance to the law of the father, before trying, in *Mother Tongue*, to find a fantasized union with the mother, narrating a sort of return to a prenatal time. He thus relives, in an imagined womb, the time before his birth spent contemplating the exterior world.[42] The first-person narrator finally replaces his actual parents with a symbolic father and mother, an artist who taught him painting when he was seventeen and a peasant woman of Ukrainian origin in whose house he lives for some time whilst finishing his book. With these two substitutes, real human relations become possible: contrary to his mute mother, the peasant woman constantly talks to him, and contrary to his father, the artist respects him and opens him to a new world, the one of art. The world of childhood seems to be banished with Winkler rejecting his father's violence and his mother's silence, forcefully rupturing the genealogical chain as a sort of linguistic therapy, as a conscious return of the repressed:

> Mutter, warum muss ich dich und meinen Vater immer wieder ansprechen? Warum kann ich nicht erzählen wie jeder andere, beschreiben wie jeder andere beschreibt? Als wollte ich einen Brief in Romanform schreiben, aber es sind keine Briefe, die ich schreibe, keine Erzählungen, Gedichte, oder Sprechstücke, es ist die Sprache, die während meiner Kindheit abgewürgt und stumm gemacht worden ist. Diese unterdrückte Sprache ist aufgebrochen, wie sie abgewürgt wurde, mit derselben Kraft, der Liebe und des Hasses.
>
> [Mother, why do I have to address you and my father over and over again? Why can't I tell as everyone else, describe as everyone one else describes? As if I wanted to write a letter in form of a novel, but I do not write letters, I do not write tales, poems, or plays, I write the language that has been throttled, stifled and muted when I was a child. This choked language bursts open, just as it was throttled, with the same power, the power of love and of hate.][43]

The final series of verbs ('throttle', 'stifle', 'burst open') expresses the violence experienced in childhood, the imposed aphasia, as well as the consecutive linguistic catharsis, a tearing apart and outburst of the mother tongue that holds all the power of primal emotions. The utterance becomes a liberating physiological reaction, nausea and logorrhoea, one of infinite iteration.

The assimilation between the mother tongue and the figure of the mother can also lead to the fear of ultimate loss and a desire to reconnect to both the mother and 'her' language. This is at the core of Vassilis Alexakis's *La Langue maternelle* (Prix Médicis 1995), a novel written in Greek which the author himself then translated into French. Again, the way Alexakis describes his relation to Greek is charged with affective issues — betrayal, infidelity, sense of loss, just as in a love story, even more so since in French 'language' is a feminine word (*she*). In his autobiographical book *Paris-Athènes*, Alexakis writes:

> Je me suis rendu compte que j'avais pas mal oublié ma langue maternelle... Mon grec s'était sclérosé, rouillé. Je connaissais la langue et pourtant j'avais du mal à m'en servir... Je me suis rendu compte aussi que la langue avait énormément changé, que je l'avais quittée... Il a donc fallu que je réapprenne, en quelque sorte, ma langue maternelle: ça n'a pas été facile, ça a pris des années, mais enfin, j'y suis arrivé. Je continuais cependant à écrire en français. Je le faisais par habitude et par goût. J'avais besoin de parler de la vie que je menais ici.[44]
>
> [I realized that I had forgotten my mother tongue... My Greek was sclerotic, rusted. I knew the language and yet I had trouble using it... I realized that the language had changed a lot, that I had left it [*her*]... Therefore I have had, in a way, to learn my mother tongue anew; it hasn't been easy, it took years, but finally, I got there. I still wrote in French though. I did it out of habit and inclination. I needed to talk about the life I led here [in France].]

He adds:

> Non seulement je m'étais beaucoup éloigné de ma langue, mais elle s'était elle-même éloignée de celle que j'avais apprise... Je devins attentif à son évolution, enregistrai les gens dans les cafés comme je l'avais fait à Paris. Je constatai,

non sans agacement, qu'elle avait adopté beaucoup de mots étranger... Je ne lui pardonnais pas d'avoir eu des faiblesses pour ces mots moi qui n'avais cessé de la tromper avec une autre langue'.

[Not only had I drifted away from my language, but my mother tongue had itself [*herself*] drifted away from the language I had learned... I paid more attention to its evolution, recorded people in cafés as I had done in Paris. I noted, not without some annoyance, that it [*she*] had adopted a lot of foreign words... I, who had constantly been unfaithful to it [*her*] with another language, could not forgive it [*her*] for having had weaknesses for these words'.][45]

The son who has himself adopted a new language, who has had a long love affair with the French language, thus resents his mother tongue for having done the same, for having changed and been 'unfaithful' to him. The way Alexakis describes his relationship to Greek is thus embedded in a family story and affective entanglements, and appears moreover inseparable from his actual relations to his parents and their deaths.

He goes on to say in an interview that he possesses two languages that have their specific uses: one for laughs (French), one for tears (Greek).[46] The novel written in Greek after his mother's death is his first attempt at reconciliation with the language of his origins:

À la mort de ma mère, j'ai écrit, en grec d'abord, *La langue maternelle*. C'était un retour vers le grec. Il s'agissait de faire la paix avec les mots grecs, les mots de ma mère. La mort de mon père, en revanche, m'a entraîné dans une langue étrangère. J'ai eu le sentiment que le grec m'avait trahi. Je n'étais plus l'enfant de personne dans cette langue. Aller vers une autre langue, c'était une manière de retrouver l'enfance.[47]

[When my mother died, I wrote *La Langue maternelle*, first in Greek. It was a return to Greek. My aim was to make peace with the Greek words, my mother's words. My father's death on the other hand had led me to a foreign language. I had had the impression that Greek had betrayed me. I was no longer anyone's child in that language. To go towards another language is a way of finding your childhood again.]

Alexakis thus equates each parent with one language: personal evolution towards or away from his childhood coincides with the practice of a particular tongue. It is furthermore striking that he can appear to be a child, his mother's child, in one language only: in Greek, his mother tongue.

The main character in the novel, upon returning to his native country, starts what he calls an exercise in his mother tongue (*exercice sur ma langue maternelle*), collecting in a notebook forty words starting with the letter epsilon so as to mark the different stages of his journey. This attempt to re-engage with his mother tongue merges more and more with a process of mourning. Unwilling and unable to accept the loss in communication with his deceased mother, the narrator projects this incapacity onto his mother tongue. At the end of the journey he comes to realize that all that he values — his life, destiny and meaning — are enclosed within his collection of words starting with the letter epsilon: *enigma*, the god Hermes (protector of travellers), *ego*, *ethnikismos* (nationalism), '*e, e*' (an onomatopoeia expressing suffering), *ekpatrisménos* (expatriate), *éleuthéria* (freedom), *épistrophi* (return), *elpida* (hope), but also loss, *ellipsi*, loss of his country *ellada*, loss of his mother tongue, *ta ellènika*, all present in the fundamental loss of his mother. He thus feels free to re-engage with his mother tongue, with the culture he left behind, with his roots, free to acquire, to seek, to find (*eurisko*), to possess what he misses or what he has lost. The novel ends with the hero's visit to the graveyard where his mother is buried:

> Je me suis penché et j'ai soufflé la poussière. J'ai songé une fois encore à l'epsilon. Le nom de ma mère, Marika Nicolaïdis, ne comporte pas cette lettre. Ni le mien d'ailleurs. J'étais certain pourtant que le mot qui me manquait pour compléter mon cahier était là, quelque part. J'ai regardé le gravier qui forme une mince bordure autour des géraniums. Deux oiseaux picoraient un peu plus loin. J'ai soudain pensé au mot *ellipsi*, le manque. 'Tu nous as manqué, Marika', ai-je pensé.
>
> [I bent over [the tomb] and blew away the dust. I thought anew about epsilon. My mother's name, Marika Nikolaidis, does not contain this letter. Mine neither by the way. I was nevertheless convinced that the word I was missing to complete my notebook was there, somewhere. I looked at the gravel that forms a narrow border around the geraniums. Two birds were pecking a bit farther away. I suddenly thought of the word *ellipsi*, lack. 'We've missed you, Marika,' I thought.[48]

The main characters in these texts thus act as interested archaeologists, constructing collaborative and personal histories as the product of digging. To negotiate subjectivity, they have to learn to deal with the delimitations and borders entailed in particular by the mother tongue and its affective dimensions. The narratives are anchored in the lived experiences of identity. Often stories of origin, they aim at reconstructing, restoring, and renaming.

Finally, Emine Sevgi Özdamar's first book *Mutterzunge* (1990), deals with this issue in a setting where the notions of borders and crossing are physically materialized within the text, namely by the Berlin wall. The acclaimed book[49] ranges amongst cultural productions of Germany's 'Others', i.e. works by ethnic or immigrant non-German writers of Germany such as Franco Biondi, Rafik Schami or Herta Müller. Özdamar is a Turkish-born writer living in Germany and writing in German. The major focus of her work is language as rite, ritual, mode of survival, and comfort zone in an inhospitable environment. The narrative texture is woven with highly idiomatic and metaphorical Turkish expressions and colloquialisms as well as proverbs, elements of folklore, songs and fragments of religious Muslim texts, which appear in deadpan German translation. Her book is dedicated to her mother[50] and subdivided into four parts. The first two in particular, '*Mutterzunge*' and '*Großvaterzunge*', vary the resonances and potentialities of the common expression. The titles are linguistic creations that sound quite strange in German: *Mutterzunge* is a literal translation of the English 'mother tongue', the French *langue maternelle*, or the Turkish *anadil*, but it is not at all usual in a German that uses the term '*Muttersprache*', mother language. The tongue itself occupies a striking position, both in its literal sense — as organ, part of human anatomy — and in its metaphorical sense — as language. The linguistic creation is justified by Özdamar in the opening of the book: 'In meiner Sprache heißt Zunge: Sprache. Zunge hat keine Knochen, wohin man sie dreht, dreht sie sich dorthin. Ich saß mit meiner gedrehten Zunge in dieser Stadt Berlin' [In my language tongue means: language. Tongue has no bones, wherever you twist and bend it, it twists and bends. I sat with my twisted tongue in this city Berlin].[51] The noun *Zunge* is picked up again only a few lines on and is connected with the word *Mutter* (mother), repeated four times: 'Wenn ich nur wüsste, wann ich meine Mutterzunge verloren habe. Ich und meine Mutter sprachen mal in unserer Mutterzunge. Meine Mutter sagte mir...' [If only I knew when I had lost my mother tongue. My mother and I once spoke in our mother tongue. My mother said to me...].[52] The opening of the book thus sets the tone of what is to come, varying the fabric and texture of the common expression, enriching the German language with an ever-expanding series of neologisms (*Mutterzunge, Muttersätze, Großvaterzunge*, &c.). The first-person narrator, wondering how and when she lost her mother tongue, sets out on a quest to regain it, but also to acquire other languages: Arabic (her grandfather's tongue) and German. This quest, and crossing of (linguistic, national, identity) borders, is also materialized and enacted by her crossing back and forth from East to West Berlin.

The text is interspersed with foreign words (foreign for the German reader) and Özdamar provides quite literal and grammatical translations of Turkish and Arabic expressions. However, she simultaneously demonstrates that the lived cultural, social, and moral history of a people often remains embedded in an irreducible untranslatability. The memory of the (m)other tongue cannot be erased and thus transfigures its new medium.[53] In 'Großvater-zunge', the second story of Berlin, the narrator remarks: 'In der Fremdsprache haben Wörter keine Kindheit' [In a foreign tongue words have no childhood].[54] Özdamar thus implicitly criticizes Kemalist reforms for erasing all traces of the Islamic Ottoman culture, creating a vacuum in which modern Turks struggle to define a cultural identity.[55] Her book, a dialectic of levitation desired and privation actually suffered, is typical of the inhabitants of shifting borders and geographies. Names, identities, and histories that expired along with passports and visas can be flown back to life through the potent medicines of memory: language, image and script.

> Ich werde zum anderen Berlin zurückgehen. Ich werde Arabisch lernen, das war mal unsere Schrift [...] [M]ein Großvater konnte nur arabische Schrift, ich konnte nur lateinisches Alphabet, das heißt, wenn mein Großvater und ich stumm wären und uns nur mit Schrift was erzählen könnten, könnten wir uns keine Geschichten erzählen. Vielleicht erst zu Großvater zurück, dann kann ich den Weg zu meiner Mutter und Mutterzunge finden. Inschallah.[56]
>
> [I will go back to the other Berlin. I will learn Arabic; it used to be our script [...] [M]y grandfather only knew Arabic writing, I only knew the Latin alphabet. So if my grandfather and I were mute, if we could only communicate by way of writing, we would not be able to tell one another stories. Maybe start by going back to grandfather, then I will be able to find my way to my mother and my mother tongue.
> *Inch Allah*.]

For Özdamar, memory is not a work of mourning. Her text crosses borders, shaping new languages, underlining the fundamental necessity of generational transmission and transmissibility.

My concluding remarks concern the fundamental ambivalence in the idea of mother tongue as border, its securing stability but also its imprisoning dimension and therefore the need to both mind and cross this border. As a metaphor, the expression 'mother tongue' is neither monolithic nor uniform (a metaphor never is); it works as a border in the sense that it can constrain while permitting crossing. The expression of mother tongue condenses a tight net of interconnected determinations, offering therefore a good number of borderlines. It provides a potent symbolic force for the writers I have discussed above. In their works, we witness a need to demythologize the illusion of the 'motherland' or 'mother-country' or 'mother tongue' as a parallel movement to discover, create and give birth to new forms and new languages of expression. These artists express a conflicting desire to reject and at the same time fuse with their mothers; they show the expectations we project onto the mother tongue as well as the need to assign it meaning.

This is particularly potent in hyphenated or 'post-ethnic' writing, the enterprise bearing a particular relationship to contexts of displacement and postcolonial settings. Estranging the associations embedded in these terms, many artists try to negotiate the diverse cultural and political forces that interact with a heightened intensity today. Thus, many Turkish-German women writers such as Özdamar are aware that exile has fostered among their compatriots a sense of exaggerated nationalism, ethnicity and religion. Their fractured narratives mimic the configurations of dream and memory and resist the notion of an idealized native history as well as a unified sense of nation, ethnicity, and religion among the displaced residents of Germany. They remain outside of the cultural ethos of the lost homeland and the never-to-be-gained host country, searching for a third territory, an alternative space of writing and *willed* memory. Their writing is thus hyphenated in time and place as well as in language. Suspended between histories and geographies, between identities and languages, their work resists both the temptation of nostalgia and a false sense of assimilation. It is this characteristic in particular that may ultimately, according to Trinh T. Minh-Ha, define contemporary writing and creation: 'Whether we choose to concentrate on another culture, or on our own culture, our work will always be cross-cultural. It is bound to be so [...] above all because of the heterogeneous reality we all live today, in postmodern times — a reality, therefore, that is not a mere crossing from one borderline to the other or that is not merely double, but a reality that involves the crossing of an indeterminate number of borderlines, one that remains multiple in its hyphenation.'[57]

Notes to Chapter 8

1. In a diachronic perspective, this ideological shift in the term 'mother tongue' coincides with the historical constellation of the emerging nation-states. Cf. Einar Haugen, 'The "mother tongue"', in *The Influence of Language on Culture and Thought*, ed. by Robert L. Cooper and Bernard Spolsky (Berlin: de Gruyter, 1991), pp. 75–84.

2. Latin: *lingua materna*; French: *langue maternelle*; German: *Muttersprache*; Spanish: *lengua materna*; Portuguese: *língua materna*; Italian: *lingua madre* or *lingua materna*; Dutch: *moedertaal*; Swedish/Danish: *modersmål*; Norwegian: *morsmål*; Czech: *mateřština*; Slovak: *materinský jazyk*; Croatian: *materinji jezik*; Turkish: *anadil*; etc.
3. See Andrée Tabouret-Keller, 'La Langue maternelle, un carrefour de métaphores', in *Langues dépaysées, Diasporas* 2 (CNRS: Université Toulouse-Le Mirail, 2003), pp. 21–35; Paul Ricœur, *La Métaphore vive* (Paris: Seuil, 1975); Barbara Agnese, 'Konstruktion und Metapher: der Metapher-Begriff zwischen Sprachphilosophie, Literatur und Wissenschaft', in *Konstruktion und Verfremdung*, ed. by Barbara Agnese and Friedrich G. Wallner (Wien: Braumüller, 1999), pp. 45–57.
4. See Robert Nisbet, 'Genealogy, Growth, and Other Metaphors', *New Literary History*, 3 (1970), 351–64; Carlo Ginzburg, 'Family Resemblances and Family Trees: Two Cognitive Metaphors', *Critical Inquiry*, 30.3 (2004), 537–56; François Noudelman, *Les Airs de famille: une philosophie des affinités* (Paris: Gallimard, 2012).
5. See Jacques Derrida, *Le Monolinguisme de l'autre* (Paris: Galilée, 1996); Marc Crépon, *Langues sans demeure* (Paris: Galilée, 2005); Yasemin Yildiz, *Beyond the Mother Tongue: The Postmonolingual Condition* (New York: Fordham University Press, 2012).
6. Derrida, *Le Monolinguisme de l'autre*, p. 117: 'la langue dite maternelle n'est jamais purement naturelle, ni propre ni habitable'.
7. My investigation is part of a larger project on the mother tongue as metaphor. One of the ambitions of this work in progress is to establish a relevant corpus of texts in contemporary literature of the European tradition. The various examples presented in this essay are only a selection of this ongoing project. They have been chosen for their expressivity and their argumentative value.
8. Rainer Maria Rilke and Marina Zwetajewa, *Ein Gespräch in Briefen*, ed. by Kostantin M. Asadowski (Frankfurt am Main and Leipzig: Insel, 1992), pp. 76–77; also quoted in Daniel Heller-Roazen, *Echolalias: On the Forgetting of Language* (Cambridge, MA: MIT Press, 2005), p. 177; all translations are mine unless otherwise indicated. Cf. Johann Wolfgang von Goethe, *Sämtliche Werke II.1*, Abt. Briefe, Tagebücher und Gespräche, ed. by Karl Eibls et al. (Frankfurt/Main: dtv, 1991), p. 196: 'Wer in einer fremden Sprache schreibt oder dichtet, ist wie einer der in einem fremden Hause wohnt'.
9. Quoted in Israel Chalfen, *Paul Celan: eine Biografie seiner Jugend* (Frankfurt/Main: Insel, 1979), p. 148; also quoted in Myriam Suchet, *L'Imaginaire hétérolingue: ce que nous apprennent les textes à la croisée des langues* (Paris: Classiques Garnier, 2014), p. 51. Celan also refers to an aphorism by Jean Paul that underlines the link between mother tongue and original language: 'Sprache-Lernen ist etwas höheres als Sprachen-Lernen und alles Lob, das man den alten Sprachen als Bildungsmitteln erteilt, fällt doppelt der Muttersprache anheim, welche noch richtiger die Sprach-Mutter hieße' (Paul Celan, *'Du musst versuchen, auch den Schweigenden zu hören': Briefe an Diet Kloos-Barendregt*, ed. by Paul Sars (Frankfurt am Main: Suhrkamp, 2002), p. 99).
10. Leo Spitzer, 'Muttersprache', *Monatshefte für deutschen Unterricht*, 36.3 (March 1944), 113–30; Leo Spitzer, 'Muttersprache und Muttererziehung', in *Essays in Historical Semantics* (New York: S. F. Vanni, 1948), pp. 15–65. Cf. Dante, *De vulgari eloquentia*, 1.1.2–3, *Opere minori* I, ed. by Pier Vincenzo Mengaldo and Bruno Nardi (Milan and Naples: Ricciardi, 1996), pp. 28–33. Dante famously writes in the opening lines of his essay that the first language (*prima locutio*) is the language of children, the language we speak without rules, by imitating our nurse (*...vulgarem locutionem asserimus quam sine omni regula nutricem imitantes accipimus*).
11. Cf. Elias Canetti, *Die gerettete Zunge: Geschichte einer Jugend* (Zurich: Erben, 1977), p. 90: 'eine spät und unter wahrhaftigen Schmerzen eingepflanzte Muttersprache'. Thus Canetti, in his linguistic autobiography, irrevocably links the mother tongue and his mother, whilst telling the story of his second linguistic birth, a sort of inception, pregnancy and delivery in reverse, since it is the son who experiences the pains of labour and finally gives birth to the German 'mother tongue' (with thanks to Nicola Gardini for reminding me of this reference). As for Aharon Appelfeld, he calls Hebrew his 'adopted mother tongue' <http://www.theparisreview.org/interviews/6324/the-art-of-fiction-no-224-aharon-appelfeld> [accessed 9 August 2015].

12. With thanks to Costanza Ferrini for sharing this reference.
13. See for instance Guillermo Gómez-Pena, 'Bilingualism, Biculturalism, and Borders', in *English is Broken Here: Notes on Cultural Fusion in the Americas*, ed. by Coco Fusco (New York: The New Press, 1995), pp. 147–58 (p. 157): 'I am very interested in subverting English structures, infecting English with Spanish, and [...] finding new possibilities within the English language that English-speaking people don't have. [...] When I make the choice to work in English, Spanish, Nahuatl, or Caló, I am expressing those transitional zones within my identity that are a part of my life as an intellectual and as a border citizen'.
14. He received numerous awards, including the most prestigious awards in German-language literature, such as the 'Ingeborg-Bachmann-Preis', the 'Großer Österreichischer Staatspreis für Literatur' and the 'Georg-Büchner-Preis'.
15. Cf. Pierre Boutan, 'Langue(s) maternelle(s): de la mère ou de la patrie?', *Revue de didactologie des langues-cultures*, 130.2 (2003), 137–51.
16. Mauthner was a writer and a journalist; he is the author of an important philosophical work that he defines as *Sprachkritik*. Cf. Jacques Le Rider, *Fritz Mauthner: scepticisme linguistique et modernité: une biographie intellectuelle* (Paris: Bartillat, 2012); Helmut Henne, *Fritz Mauthner: Sprache, Literatur, Kritik* (Tübingen: Niemeyer, 2000); Pascale Roure, *L'Écriture critique: enjeux politiques, littéraires, épistémologiques et philosophiques de la critique de la langue de Fritz Mauthner* (unpublished doctoral thesis, Université Paris-Sorbonne, 2015).
17. Cf. Hans Peter Althaus, *Mauscheln: ein Wort als Waffe* (Berlin: De Gruyter, 2002).
18. Fritz Mauthner, *Prager Jugendjahre: Erinnerungen I* [1918] (Frankfurt am Main: Fischer, 1969), p. 30.
19. Mauthner, *Prager Jugendjahre*, p. 50: 'Wie ich keine rechte Muttersprache besaß als Jude in einem zweisprachigen Lande, so hatte ich auch keine Mutterreligion, als Sohn einer völlig konfessionslosen Judenfamilie'.
20. Fritz Mauthner, *Beiträge zu einer Kritik der Sprache* 3, augmented edition (Leipzig: Meiner 1923), p. 227: 'Wir alle haben an dem Gebrauche unserer Muttersprache eine tiefe Freude'. His thoughts coincide with Jean Améry's definition of mother tongue and *Heimat* as safety and homeliness in his famous essay: 'So wie man die Muttersprache erlernt, ohne ihre Grammatik zu kennen, so erfährt man die heimische Umwelt. Muttersprache und Heimatwelt wachsen mit uns, wachsen in uns hinein und werden so zur Vertrautheit, die uns Sicherheit verbürgt' (Jean Améry, 'Wieviel Heimat braucht der Mensch?', in *Jenseits von Schuld und Sühne: Bewältigungsversuche eines Überwältigten* (Stuttgart: Klett, 1980), pp. 83–84).
21. Fritz Mauthner, *Wörterbuch der Philosophie: neue Beiträge zu einer Kritik der Sprache* (Leipzig: Meiner, 1923–24), p. 526: '...die Liebe zur Muttersprache als eines unserer stärksten und schönsten Gefühle'.
22. Fritz Mauthner, *Beiträge zu einer Kritik der Sprache* 1 (Leipzig: Meiner, augmented edition 1923), p. 26.
23. Fritz Mauthner, *Muttersprache und Vaterland* (Leipzig: Dürr & Weber, 1920), p. 19.
24. Mauthner, *Muttersprache und Vaterland*, p. 52.
25. Jhumpa Lahiri, *The Namesake* (London: Fourth Estate, 2003), p. 214. Lahiri has written her most recent nonfiction book, *In altre parole* (2015), in Italian (translated into English by Ann Goldstein as *In Other Words*).
26. Also in the sense Homi K. Bhabha who defines the 'third space' as enabling other positions to emerge, the space of negotiations, of translations, of in-betweenness, of hybridity.
27. Interview with Martine Laval for *Télérama*, 22/11/2008. <http://www.telerama.fr/livre/atiq-rahimi-je-ne-crains-pas-de-dire-la-barbarie-ou-la-decadence,36049.php> [accessed 9 August 2015].
28. Adrienne Rich, *Of Woman Born: Motherhood as Experience and Institution* (New York: Norton, 1976), p. 236.
29. Mathias Verger, *La Haine de la langue maternelle: une lecture de James Joyce, Jean Genet, Thomas Bernhard* (unpublished doctoral thesis, Université Paris 8, 2013). Verger claims, for instance, that the fact that Bernhard was an illegitimate child, informs his representation of the mother tongue. Cf. for instance: Graciela Trabajo, 'Langue maternelle, haine-amour, exil', in *Faut-il*

avoir la haine?, ed. by Olivier Le Cour Grandmaison (Paris: L'Harmattan, 2001), pp. 123–29.
30. John Skinner, *The Stepmother Tongue: An Introduction to New Anglophone Fiction* (Basingstoke and London: Macmillan, 1998); John Skinner, 'Contemporary Scottish Novelists and the Stepmother Tongue', in *English Literature and the Other Languages*, ed. by Ton Hoenselaars and Marius Buning (Amsterdam: Rodopi, 1999), pp. 211–20; Mehmet Yaşin, *Step-mother Tongue: From Nationalism to Multiculturalism Literatures of Cyprus, Greece and Turkey*, World Literature Series (London: Middlesex University Press, 2000).
31. Hédi Bouraoui, 'Lettre à la langue française', *La Toison d'Or*, 35 (1994), 42–43. For Bouraoui, this linguistic rape (*'avec ou sans ton consentement'*) is the only means to give new life to a moribund, sterile, academic language, through hybridization and creativity.
32. Cf. Jacques Derrida, Jean Birnbaum, *Apprendre à vivre enfin* (Paris: Galilée/Le Monde, 2005), pp. 37–39.
33. M. NourbeSe Philip, 'Discourse on the Logic of Language', in *Prismatic Publics: Innovative Canadian Women's Poetry and Poetics*, ed. by Kate Eichhorn and Heather Milne (Toronto: Coach House Books, 2009), pp. 149–52 (p. 152).
34. Evie Shockley, 'Her Tongue Tries She (or How NourbeSe Philip Breaks English to Fit Her Mouth)', in M. NourbeSe Philip, *She Tries Her Tongue, Her Silence Softly Breaks* (Middletown, CT: Wesleyan University Press, 2014), pp. ix–xiv (p. ix).
35. It would be worthwhile to analyse further the metaphor 'mother tongue' *vs.* 'father tongue' — for instance in Akira Mizubayashi's *Une langue venue d'ailleurs* (2011), Roland Barthes' *L'Empire des signes* (1970), Ursula K. Le Guin's 'Bryn Mawr Commencement Address' (1986), Rosario Ferré's novels and poems in English or Antoine Berman's notion of 'maternalité' of language (*Jacques Amyot, traducteur français*, 2012) — but it would by far exceed the scope of my present inquiry.
36. *Étrangers à nous-mêmes* (Paris: Fayard, 1988), p. 32; Julia Kristeva, *Strangers to Ourselves*, trans. by Leon S. Roudiez (New York: Columbia University Press, 1991), p. 15.
37. See also Hannah Arendt, 'Was bleibt? Es bleibt die Muttersprache', *Gespräche mit Hannah Arendt* (Munich: Piper, 1964); <http://www.rbb-online.de/zurperson/interview_archiv/arendt_hannah.html> [accessed 4 September 2014]. Cf. Marc Crépon, 'La Langue sans communauté: Améry, Adorno, Arendt et la langue maternelle', *Rue Descartes*, 26 ('Ce que les philosophes disent de leur langue') (1999), 117–40; Barbara Cassin, *La Nostalgie: quand donc est-on chez soi?* (Paris: Librairie Arthème Fayard/Pluriel, 2015), pp. 85–132.
38. Cf. Anne-Emmanuelle Berger, 'L'Idole maternelle en régime poétique bourgeois', in *Du Féminin*, ed. by Mireille Calle (Sainte-Foy, Grenoble: Le Griffon d'argile, Presses universitaires de Grenoble, 1992), pp. 203–20; Kate Cummings, 'Reclaiming the Mother's Tongue: Beloved, Ceremony, Mothers and Shadows', *College English*, 52.5 (1990), 552–69.
39. Jamaica Kincaid, *Lucy* (New York: Farrar, Straus and Giroux, 1991), p. 90.
40. Kincaid, *Lucy*, p. 36. Cf. Françoise Kral, 'Langue maternelle, résurgence et affect dans la littérature diasporique anglophone', *L'Atelier*, 1 (2009), 96–108.
41. Kateb Yacine, *Le Polygone étoilé* (Paris: Seuil, 1997), pp. 183–84, cf. Anne-Emmanuelle Berger, 'The Impossible Wedding: Nationalism, Languages and the Mother-tongue in Post-Colonial Algeria', in *Algeria in Others' Languages*, ed. by Anne-Emmanuelle Berger (Ithaca, NY: Cornell University Press, 2002), pp. 60–78.
42. Josef Winkler, *Das Wilde Kärnten* (Frankfurt am Main: Suhrkamp, 1995), p. 673. On the mother tongue as a womb, a liquid environment that nurtures and nourishes, see also Rita Wong's 1998 poem 'Write Around the Absence': 'live | half-submerged | in the salty home of | my mother tongue' (in *Prismatic Publics: Innovative Canadian Women's Poetry and Poetics*, ed. by Kate Eichhorn and Heather Milne (Toronto: Coach House Books, 2009), p. 354). Wong, a Canadian poet of Chinese origin, conveys in this striking image both the idea of the mother tongue as an ocean — international waters, untamed, unchartered, unclaimed, free of national borders — and the risk of drowning, the necessity to navigate constantly between her languages, English and Cantonese.
43. Winkler, *Das Wilde Kärnten*, p. 291.
44. Vassilis Alexakis, *Paris-Athènes* (Paris: Seuil, 1989), pp. 12–13.

45. Alexakis, *Paris-Athènes*, p. 191
46. Vassilis Alexakis, 'Une langue pour rire une langue pour pleurer', *Synergies Monde* 5 (2008), 29–30.
47. Quoted in Josyane Savigneau, 'L'Enfance', *Le Monde*, 20 September 2002.
48. Vassilis Alexakis, *La Langue maternelle* (Paris: Gallimard/Folio, 2006), p. 412.
49. It was enthusiastically reviewed in the *New York Times Book Review* and named by *Publishers Weekly* as one of the best works of fiction published in 1994. Cf. Charlotte Innes, 'Turkish-German Stories, review of *Mother Tongue*, by Emine Sevgi Özdamar, trans. by Craig Thomas', *New York Times Book Review*, 25 September 1994, p. 1.
50. The dedication reads: '*Für meine Mutter Fatma Hanim*'. M. NourbeSe Philip's poetry collection *She Tries Her Tongue, Her Silence Softly Breaks* bears an analogous dedication: 'For all the mothers'. For a comparative study of these two writers, see Sabine Milz: 'Comparative Cultural Studies and Ethnic Minority Writing Today: The Hybridities of Marlene Nourbese Philip and Emine Sevgi Özdamar', *CLCWeb: Comparative Literature and Culture* 2.2 (2000): <http://dx.doi.org/10.7771/1481-4374.1071> [accessed 9 August 2015].
51. Emine Sevgi Özdamar, *Mutterzunge. Erzählungen* (Berlin: Rotbuch, 1990), p. 7.
52. Özdamar, *Mutterzunge*, p. 7.
53. Cf. *(M)Other Tongues: Literary Reflexions on a Difficult Distinction*, ed. by Juliane Prade (Cambridge: Cambridge Scholar Publishing, 2012). Özdamar uses in particular one metaphor to express her poetic project: her creation is properly tailored by those who 'sew their Turkish clothes out of German materials [*aus deutschen Stoffen ihre türkischen Kleider nähen*]' (Özdamar, *Mutterzunge*, p. 90).
54. Özdamar, *Mutterzunge*, p. 42.
55. Cf. Jale Parla, 'The Wounded Tongue: Turkey's Language Reform and the Canonicity of the Novel', *PMLA*, 123.1 (2008), 27–40. Parla highlights the drawbacks of the language reform during the Kemalist regime and underscores how literature — as well as other cultural institutions — was affected by the language reform.
56. Emine Sevgi Özdamar, *Mutterzunge*, p. 12. The issue of transmissibility, linked to issues of language, script, and to gender issues in a matrilineal set-up, is also at the core of British-based artist Zineb Sedira's 2002 installation *Mother Tongue*. It shows 3 videos: '*Mother and I*', '*Daughter and I*', '*Grandmother and Granddaughter*', each woman speaking in her own language (Arabic, French, English), although grandmother and granddaughter can hardly communicate because of the linguistic barriers. See also the artist's following works: *Mother, Father and I* (2003) and *Retelling Histories: My Mother Told Me* (2003). Cf. Joseph McGonagle and Zineb Sedira, 'Translating Differences: An Interview with Zineb Sedira', *Signs*, 31.3 (2006), 617–28.
57. Trinh T. Minh-Ha, *When the Moon Waxes Red: Representation, Gender and Cultural Politics* (New York: Routledge, 1991), p. 107. Trinh T. Minh-Ha, born in Hanoi, brought up in South Vietnam during the war, before migrating to the USA in 1970, is a filmmaker, writer and literary theorist. She may be best known for her films *Reassemblage* (1982) and *Surname Viet Given Name Nam* (1985).

CHAPTER 9

❖

The Edge of Thought: Extended Cognition and the Border between Mind and World

Michael Wheeler

Minds in Space

Where is the mind? If we understand this question literally — that is, as requiring something like spatial coordinates as an answer — some people will complain that it's simply preposterous. Psychological phenomena, such as thoughts, chains of reasoning, emotions and feelings, are just not the right sorts of 'things' (they will say) to have such coordinates. Indeed, when Roberta Flack and Donny Hathaway posed the immortal question 'Where is the love?', they didn't expect an answer of the form 'two metres to the left of the door, just above the sofa, with a volume about the size of a football'. And it's not only great soul singers who will be queuing up to pour scorn on the idea that mind literally has spatiality. The frowning line of naysayers will also include a motley assortment of philosophical heavyweights, including the much-maligned substance dualists, who hold that mind is a non-physical entity which is distinct from the material world and so certainly not extended in space, and a range of thinkers who, despite their differences, would all be moved to protest, perhaps with a Heideggerian, Rylean, or later Wittgensteinian swagger, that even though substance dualism is a confused doctrine, to think of a mind as a spatially locatable entity is to commit a kind of logical error in one's use of the very concept of mind.

All that said, and with apologies to Roberta, Donny and their philosophical friends, I think our opening question is not only perfectly reasonable, but has a surprising and controversial answer. Here's a quick and dirty argument for why it is reasonable. Substance dualism is officially unpopular with most philosophers and scientists, and a natural (and naturalistic) alternative is to claim that minds are (in some way) realized in the physical world, rather than in some non-physical substance. But if minds are (in some way) realized in the physical world, then (in some sense) they must take up space. And if minds (in some sense) take up space, then (in some sense) it must be reasonable to ask where in space they are. QED. Well, not quite. My irritating use of qualifying parenthetic phrases in the foregoing argument emphasizes just how under-specified that argument is. Nevertheless, the key point is, I think, secure enough: if we are interested in the realizers of psychological states and processes, and if those realizers are physical elements on a metaphysical par with doors, sofas and footballs (if one dislikes the 'thing-y-ness' of these examples, one can simply switch to examples of physical systems, networks, or even flows), then it is perfectly reasonable to wonder where in space those realizers are, just as it is perfectly reasonable to ask about the spatial position and extent of more pedestrian physical phenomena. In other words, if the question 'where is the mind?' is interpreted as meaning 'where are the physical elements that realize psychological states and processes?', then it isn't preposterous at all. Indeed, one could press the point about realizers while also thinking that, in some psychological contexts (such as that of revealing the intentions of a lover whose commitment is in doubt), it would be an inappropriate way of addressing a 'where' question. Nevertheless, once the focus *is* on realizers, it seems that we can meaningfully talk about minds that take up space.

One consequence of this state of affairs is that it also makes sense to conceive of any particular mind as having some sort of spatially locatable outer limit that marks the border between mind and world — the edge of thought, as one might put it. But, of course, given that such a border exists, there is, in principle anyway, room for genuine disagreement over just where in space it is. That's the 'where' issue that this chapter addresses.[1]

Extended Cognition

It is time for us to re-ask our opening question, but this time without all the defensiveness. Here we go. Where is the mind? More specifically, where is the edge of thought, the border between mind and world? One answer with plenty of contemporary momentum (see below) is that the mind-world border is stationed at the sensory-motor interface between the organic body and the beyond-the-body environment. For present purposes, I am not going to fuss over the genuine distinction that exists between saying that the mind is located in (or perhaps is co-located with) the brain or central nervous system, and saying only that the mind is located inside the skin. Whether we go for skull or skin as our mind-world border, what we confront is a version of a view that some philosophers call *vehicle internalism*. To explain: in the present context, the term 'vehicle' is practically equivalent to the term 'realizer'. According to vehicle internalism, then, psychological states and processes are realized by physical machinery that is always inside the skull or skin. I would fearlessly risk my treasured collection of early punk rock singles on the bet that, right now, vehicle internalism is overwhelmingly the default view in cognitive neuroscience, cognitive psychology, developmental psychology, cognitive-science-friendly philosophy, and indeed in many further disciplines and communities (including some situated in the wider humanities). Indeed, given all those 'pictures of the brain thinking' that have been produced over the past few years by modern neuroimaging techniques, one might reasonably wonder where else the material machinery of mind could possibly be. So any answer to our 'where' question that departs from vehicle internalism surely counts as surprising and controversial, although of course it won't surprise, or attract passionate disagreement from, everyone.

Just such an answer has been defended in and around cognitive science recently by advocates of the so-called *hypothesis of extended cognition* (henceforth *ExC*).[2] Rejecting vehicle internalism, fans of ExC endorse the competing position of vehicle *externalism*. In other words, according to ExC, the physical machinery of mind *sometimes* extends beyond the skull and skin. More precisely, if ExC is true, then there are actual (in this world) cases of intelligent thought and action, in which the material vehicles that realize the thinking and thoughts concerned are spatially distributed over brain, body and world, in such a way that certain external (beyond-the-skull-and-skin) factors are rightly accorded fundamentally the same cognitive status as would ordinarily be accorded to a subset of your neurons. Eye-catching examples of external elements that advocates of ExC often take to have such cognitive status include smartphones, tablets and at least some instances of wearable computing, but, in the end, nothing much hangs on such feats of contemporary technological wizardry. Less fancy items such as notebooks (the old-fashioned kind), tally sticks and abacuses would, under the right circumstances, do just as well.

Of course, on all (sane) views, there is a sense in which minds reach beyond the skin, in that they secure epistemic contact with what our thoughts are (typically) about, namely the external world. As Heidegger puts it:

> We do not represent distant things merely in our mind [...] so that only mental representations of distant things run through our minds and heads as substitutes for the things. If all of us now think, from where we are right here, of the old bridge in Heidelberg, this thinking toward that location is not a mere experience inside the persons present here; rather, it belongs to the nature of our thinking of that bridge that in itself thinking gets through, persists through, the distance to that location. From this spot right here, we are there at the bridge — we are by no means at some representational content in our consciousness.[3]

One could mistake turns of phrase such as 'thinking [...] persists through [...] the distance to [a remote] location' as endorsements of ExC, but, of course, jettisoning the idea that thinking cannot reach beyond a veil of inner representations (which is what Heidegger is up to here) is not, in and of itself anyway, sufficient to establish ExC, since ExC concerns not the correct characterization of the intentional or epistemic reach of thought, but rather the location of its underpinning physical machinery.[4]

To highlight more clearly what one ought to mean when one claims that the machinery of mind is extended, consider the way in which a skilled bartender may achieve the successful delivery of a large and complex order of drinks.[5] Fulfilling such an order can strike the casual observer as a relatively daunting task, especially if the memory-relevant resources available to the bartender are thought to be restricted to inner storage and recall. However, it is a fortuitous fact that different kinds of drink often come in differently shaped glasses. (Think of cocktails.) The cognitive ecology of the bar is thus characterized by some relatively persistent physical structures (the differently shaped glasses), plus some culturally established norms (the specificity of kind of drink to shape of glass). What novice bartenders learn to do, under the tutelage of their experienced colleagues, is to retrieve the correct glass for each drink as it is requested, and to arrange the differently shaped glasses in a spatial sequence that tracks the temporal sequence of the drinks order. From the perspective of the purely organic cognitive resources available, what the bartender has learnt to do, in replicating this culturally transmitted practice, is to exploit her physical environment in order to outsource complexity and so reduce the burden on inner processing. In effect, she transforms what might have been a highly challenging memory task into a simpler (roughly) perception and association task.

This is a compelling example of what Andy Clark has dubbed *cognitive niche construction*, the process by which human beings build external structures that, in combination with culturally transmitted practices, transform problem spaces in ways that promote (or sometimes obstruct) thinking and reasoning.[6] As such, it is at least an example of what is now commonly called *embedded cognition* — cognition that itself remains wholly internal, even though it exhibits subtle and complex patterns of causal dependence on the beyond-the-skin environment. The advocate of ExC wants to go further than this, however, by demanding that it's not merely that the bartender's successful delivery of the drinks order depends *causally* on her non-neural bodily movements (the manipulation of different glasses so as to produce an order-tracking spatial arrangement), as well as on material environmental structures (the actual spatial arrangements of different glasses). Rather, those non-neural bodily movements and material environmental structures are themselves revealed to be genuine *constituents* of the realizing physical machinery of the cognitive trait of memory. If this second interpretation is correct, our distributed embodied-bartender-plus-glasses system is a paradigmatic case not of embedded, but of extended, cognition. The border between mind and world has been relocated to a point beyond the skin.[7]

Perception, Action, Mind, World

In this chapter I am not going to present arguments in direct support of ExC.[8] Instead, I am going to describe a seemingly powerful objection to the extended view and then show how responding to that objection eventually leads us to say something that is (with respect to the orthodox view in and around cognitive science anyway) profoundly unexpected about the border between mind and world. The worry in question is nicely expressed by David Chalmers (ironically, of course, one of the original architects of ExC) in the following short passage. 'It is natural to hold that perception is the interface where the world affects the mind, and that action is the interface where the mind affects the world. If so, it is tempting to hold that what precedes perception and what follows action is not truly mental.'[9] Here is the picture that Chalmers describes as 'natural' and 'tempting'. Where perception is the focus, there are events and states of affairs that occur in the world, and these (conceptually, and perhaps typically temporally too) come before the experiences of, and the beliefs about, those worldly states of affairs that occur in the mind, and that are produced via perception. Perception is thus the world-to-mind channel by which certain beyond-the-mind happenings generate certain psychological happenings. Where action is the focus, there are desires and related thoughts about how to satisfy those desires that occur in the mind, and these (conceptually, and perhaps typically temporally too) come before the changes to the states of affairs in the world that occur so as to satisfy those desires, and that are produced via action. Action is thus the channel by which certain psychological happenings generate certain beyond-the-mind happenings. Put all this together, and that's why the border between mind and world is located at the perception-action interface.

This is indeed an intuitively compelling picture, but how, exactly, does it generate an objection to ExC? Consider, once again, our complexity-outsourcing bartender. An attentive observer might be moved to make two observations about the bartender's order-delivering activities: (i) prior to the empty glasses being placed physically in their appropriate spatial positions, the bartender plausibly has various order-related desires, and thoughts about how to satisfy those desires, that kick-start and organize her bodily movements; (ii) prior to making the right drinks, the bartender must look at the glasses before associating their particular shapes with specific kinds of drinks. The first of these observations provides an example of Chalmers' mind-to-world action channel, with bodily movement understood as the border crossing between mind and world, while the second provides an example of Chalmers' world-to-mind perception channel, with visual sensing understood as the border crossing between world and mind. But if this analysis is correct, then the relevant beyond-the-skin elements, namely the glasses in their spatial arrangements, are on the *wrong side* of the perception-action interface to count as realizing vehicles of the bartender's cognitive states and processing. Those external elements scaffold, but they do not realize, bartender-cognition. In other words, our brain-body-environment drinks-order system is an example of an embedded, rather than an extended, mind.

How should the fan of ExC respond? In their classic treatment, Clark and Chalmers[10] argue that the correct reply to the foregoing sort of worry is to claim that although our intuitive inclinations are to categorize an organic agent's use of her eyes as perception and her intentional deployment of bodily movements as action, those inclinations are not always reliable. Indeed, to assume that they are always reliable would be to beg the question against ExC. To explain: in effect, Clark and Chalmers suggest that although the perception-action interface may constitute the border between mind and world, that interface is not always co-located with the organic sensorimotor boundary. Thus, and to apply this suggestion to our bartender example, from an extended mind perspective, the bartender-plus-glasses assemblage constitutes a cognitive system in its own right, so the salient events that involve the bartender first moving the glasses into sequence and then looking at the sequentially ordered glasses all happen *inside* that cognitive system. But if that is right, and if the perception-action interface fixes the border between mind and world, then the organic sensorimotor boundary cannot be co-located with the perception-action interface. The latter has to be at the edge of the cognitive system, not inside it. So how are we to think about the bartender's deployment of bodily manipulations to move the glasses around and her use of her eyes to access information about the glasses? The idea is that, in comparison with ordinary cases of inner cognition, we should think of these occurrences as more akin to wholly internal information processing — as cases of internal memory recall and introspection perhaps — than to the world-to-mind and mind-to-world events that are indicative of perception and action. In response to the obvious complaint that the bartender's access to the glasses involves a distinctive phenomenal experience that is not present in the case of wholly inner processing, Clark and Chalmers appeal to the science fiction example of Arnold Schwarzenegger's Terminator character, as depicted in the James Cameron film. Information that the Terminator retrieves from his memory is presented to him in his conscious visual field. The fact that this access system presumably has an accompanying visual phenomenology does not seem to prevent it from realizing the Terminator's memory, so why should it have that sort of consequence in the case of our distributed bartender-plus-glasses system? The answer, Clark and Chalmers suggest, is that it shouldn't.

It is hardly news to note that the defence of ExC just canvassed involves a good deal of revision of our natural way of thinking about the border between mind and world. Of course, we should not be afraid of such revisionism, where it is mandated, but it is hard to dispel the thought that there is something suspicious about a position that decouples the perception-action interface from the sensorimotor interface. And it is just such a decoupling that Clark and Chalmers seem to be recommending. After all, no challenge is offered to the thought that the bartender uses her visual sense to access the shapes of the glasses, and it is hard to know what sort of argument could convince us that this is not what is going on. So, if these genuinely sensory events take place inside the cognitive system, and if the perception-action interface is located at the border between mind and world, and if ExC is true, then the perception-action interface must have been decoupled from the sensorimotor interface. Under these circumstances, it strikes me that the revision to our intuitive framework that is demanded of us by the defence of ExC under consideration should at least make us feel uncomfortable. What we certainly don't have, anyway, is a clear victory for ExC. So where do we go from here?

Extended Sensing

Let's say that we hang on to the thought that the perception-action interface and the sensorimotor interface move around in tandem, and that together they locate the border between mind and world. Is there anything which might give us reason to conclude that the mind-world border, so conceived, is sometimes stationed beyond the skin, meaning that ExC is true? The answer, I think, is yes. Consider cases of what is known as *sensory substitution*. This phenomenon occurs when technological augmentation enables one sensory modality to support the kind of environmental access and interaction ordinarily supported by a different sensory modality. The seminal work in this area is Paul Bach y Rita's research on tactile-vision sensory substitution (henceforth TVSS).[11] In this work, blind subjects were equipped with a head- or shoulder-mounted camera that conveyed information, from video images, via the activation of an array of vibrators located on the subject's back, abdomen or thigh. After a short period of adaptation, those TVSS subjects who actively controlled the information received, either by manipulating their bodies or by manipulating the camera, were able to make reliable judgments about things such as the number, relative size and position of distal objects in three-dimensional space, and perform actions such as reaching out and picking up objects. TVSS subjects have also been successful at making perceptual judgments involving effects such as looming and object occlusion, and (this time with image-sourced information transmitted via vibrators on the tongue) have reported experiencing illusory movement effects such as the waterfall illusion.[12] TVSS is not the only form of sensory substitution. For example, in auditory-vision substitution,[13] video images from a camera are converted into sounds (e.g. the vertical positions of pixels may be correlated with different audio frequencies) and conveyed to the subject via headphones. Again after short periods of adaptation, subjects equipped with such devices have been able to localize, and to recognize the shapes of, distal objects in three-dimensional space.

There are some challenging empirical and conceptual issues raised by sensory substitution, and, to clear the way for the lessons that I want to draw from the phenomenon, we need to remark on two of them. First, given that TVSS subjects are perceptually sensitive to distal objects, and because of the phenomenal reports supplied by these subjects, one might wonder whether one ought to say that the perceptual access in question is a form of vision or, alternatively, that it is 'simply' vision-like. This threatens to plunge us headlong into a murky debate over how to individuate the senses.[14] For present purposes, however, we can safely ignore this debate, since we need only the weakest substantive claim in the vicinity, namely that sensory substitution devices support a mode of sensory access to the world that is not the same as the mode of the proximal stimulation that they employ. So, in the case of TVSS, the claim would be that even though the proximal stimuli in play are tactile in character, the observed perceptual sensitivity is not correctly categorized as one of touch, even if it isn't vision. Given the distal character of the observed perceptual access, and given that touch is a way of accessing external elements by coming into physical contact with them, it certainly seems uncontentious to say this much. And we need this much because anything less than a technology-driven change from one perceptual modality to another is unlikely to send us reaching for ExC. Consider, for example, the fact that poor eyesight may be improved by putting on the right spectacles. This is a case of a technology-driven transformation in perceptual performance *within* a single sensory modality. But spectacles are most naturally interpreted as modifying the causal inputs to the relevant psychological machinery (by bending light rays), rather than as part of that machinery. After all, the proximal sensory channel here is already set up so as to support distal perceptual sensitivity prior to the augmenting technology being added. By contrast, in, say, TVSS, the proximal sensory channel is not already set up so as to support distal perceptual sensitivity. Such sensitivity becomes possible via that channel only once the augmenting technology is added. The contribution made by the technology is thus more likely to motivate the claim that the psychological capacity itself is partly realized by the augmenting technology.

The second issue on which I need to comment is that thinkers such as Alva Noë, Mirko Farina and Julian Kiverstein have argued that sensory substitution provides the raw material for an argument in support of what we can call the hypothesis of extended phenomenal consciousness.[15] For the uninitiated, phenomenal consciousness is the *what-it's-like-ness* of experience, such as what it's like for me to see green, taste spaetzle, or, as I'm doing right now, listen to Public Service Broadcasting. If the hypothesis of extended phenomenal consciousness is true, then although the machinery that realizes conscious phenomenal experience includes, and maybe necessarily includes, neural elements, it is not restricted to such elements. There will be cases in which that machinery additionally includes not only non-neural bodily elements, but also elements located beyond the skull and skin. Whether extended phenomenal consciousness ever occurs, and even if it does whether sensory substitution provides supporting evidence for it, are vexed questions.[16] However, this is another debate that, for present purposes, we can happily put aside, because as long as there is a distinction *within* the class of the psychological, between, on the one hand, conscious mental states and processes, and, on the other, unconscious or nonconscious mental states and processes, it is, in principle, possible to develop ExC as a claim about the latter while simultaneously holding that phenomenal consciousness is realized entirely in the brain. If this is the right way to divide things up, then while ExC is true (as a restricted claim about unconscious or nonconscious mental states and processes), the hypothesis of extended phenomenal consciousness is false. In the present context, what this means is that even if the psychological machinery that realizes the conscious perceptual experiences enjoyed by TVSS subjects is wholly neural, the underlying psychological machinery that realizes the process by which one sensory modality supports the kind of environmental access and interaction ordinarily supported by a different sensory modality may include all sorts of processing routines of which the subject is not conscious, and thus may be extended so as to encompass the skin-external augmenting technology. There's nothing especially mysterious about this disassociation. After all, my conscious registering of some item of information recalled from my organic memory may occur in some particular group of neurons, but that conscious registering may be supported by access and storage mechanisms elsewhere in the brain, mechanisms of which I remain unaware, even though they partly realize the psychological process of remembering that's going on.

We are now in a position to make what is, with respect to the received view in and around cognitive science, a bold but exciting claim, one that I cannot hope to defend fully here. Given that the shift in perceptual modality that sensory substitution involves (e.g. from touch to a modality that is certainly not touch and which bears at least some similarities to vision) depends crucially on the contribution of the skin-external augmenting technology, and given that we have resolved not to be distracted by questions regarding the locations of the vehicles of the subject's conscious experience, it seems that sensory substitution is at least in the right ballpark to count as an example of extended sensing, and thus, if we maintain the co-location of sensing and perception, of extended perception. If this is the correct interpretation of sensory substitution, then the advocate of ExC can agree with Chalmers that the mind-world border ought to be stationed at the perception-action interface, because, according to the proposed model, it is that very interface that has been shifted outwards, beyond the skin, to the periphery of the augmenting technology. And if the border between mind and world has been relocated to a point beyond the skin, then ExC is true.

Beyond the Container

I have just suggested that Chalmers' objection to ExC may be met, because sensory substitution should be understood as an example of extended sensing. But this is not the final resting place of my argument. To bring that final destination into view, we need to reveal an unexpectedly conservative facet of ExC, as presented so far. To achieve this, let's start not with ExC, but with our old friend vehicle internalism. Even though vehicle internalism has it that cognition takes place in the brain, which makes it metaphysically opposed to substance dualism, and even though Descartes' philosophy is perhaps the historical pinnacle of substance dualism, nevertheless the fact is that vehicle internalism, as standardly developed, has a decidedly Cartesian heritage. As Jennifer Hornsby points out:

> philosophers of mind have come to see Cartesian dualism as the great enemy, but have underestimated what they have to contend with. Taking the putatively immaterial character of minds to create the only problem that there is for Descartes' account, they marry up the picture of the person with the picture of her brain and settle for a view of mind which, though material in its (cranial) substance, is Cartesian in its essence.[17]

There are a number of dimensions along which the Cartesian legacy of orthodox vehicle internalism may be laid bare,[18] but here I want to focus on an aspect that intersects with our present interest in borders. In the movement of thought through which philosophers, psychologists, neuroscientists and others took the Cartesian mind and shoehorned it into the body/brain, the seductive idea that the perception-action interface is the border between mind and world became allied with a view of the edge of the body/brain as a kind of physical container within which the mechanisms of mind are housed. Of course, the container is not impermeable: as we have seen, structure flows into the container via perception (so that inner thought comes to reflect the external world) and out of the container via action (so that the external world comes to reflect our inner desires). Nevertheless, it encloses, in a fixed way, the material mechanisms of thought, just as the realm of immaterial substance 'encloses', in a fixed way, the immaterial mechanisms of thought in Cartesian substance dualism.

It is at this juncture that a profoundly conservative dimension of ExC, as we have encountered it so far, is revealed. Consider: from what we have just seen, how much damage is caused to the Cartesian cognitive container by the arrival of the extended mind? Plausibly, the answer is 'not much'. The container has become enlarged, of course, so that the border between mind and world is no longer stationed at the edge of the brain or body, but at the other side of a notebook, smartphone, arrangement of glasses, or TVSS device. Nevertheless (this line of reasoning goes), that border still acts as container for our psychological mechanisms in a remarkably familiar way. Of course, it's not entirely familiar. The cognitive container is now one that gets bigger and smaller. For example, expert users of TVSS devices routinely experience distal objects and states of affairs in the world via the substituting (not-touch) perceptual modality. However, with conscious, deliberate effort, those users are sometimes able to refocus their conscious attention, so that they experience the *proximal* sensory inputs, that is, tactile experiences of the vibrations taking place on the surface of their skin.[19] Here one should not be distracted by the fact that we have resolved not to think of sensory substitution as supporting the hypothesis of extended phenomenal consciousness. The shifting of conscious attention here 'merely' provides evidence that the mind-world border, as located by the functionally defined sensorimotor (perception-action) boundary, may shift dynamically, between a position located at the skin and one located beyond it. The resulting picture is thus one of a dynamic container, one that grows and shrinks as skin-external elements become incorporated into, and divested from, the cognitive system, during its ongoing activity. Still, a rubbery container remains a container, something that confines, encloses, and constrains. And, as framings of the mental go, this simply doesn't do justice to the fact that out our cognition-realizing materiality doesn't merely provide a channel by which we achieve epistemic and practical access to a world beyond us, it also plays a conceptually prior role in constructively founding both (a) the world, as an intelligible place that may be accessed epistemically and practically by us, and (b) us, as beings who are essentially of that world. In short, we need to get beyond the container model, if we are to turn sensing into sense-making.

Heidegger has his eye on this very prize when he rejects (what is tantamount to) the container model, with the following words: 'the perceiving of what is known is not a process of returning with one's booty to the "cabinet" of consciousness after one has gone out and grasped it'.[20] And indeed it is Heidegger who, I think, offers us some of the conceptual resources that might enable cognition to escape from the Cartesian container, in that he supplies us with an account of spatial borders in general that may be used to generate a new account of the mind-world border in particular.

According to Heidegger, spatial borders are not limits or enclosures. Rather, they are productive events — what he calls *horizons* — that establish sites for sense-making. As he puts it:

> A space is something that has been made room for, something that has been freed, namely within a boundary [...] A boundary is not that at which something stops but, as the Greeks recognized, the boundary is that from which something

begins its essential unfolding. That is why the concept is that of *horismos*, that is, the horizon, the boundary.[21]

Straightaway, any Heidegger scholars out there will no doubt be clamouring to complain that when Heidegger conceptualizes space in this way he is concerned not with mathematically describable physical space — the kind of space with which we have been concerned up to now — but rather with the space that is relevant to sense-making, or what we might call *existential space*, the collection of spaces in which we dwell. Heidegger calls such existential spaces *locales*. A bridge, for example, brings a locale into existence by establishing a 'passage that crosses'.[22] Heidegger claims explicitly that physical space is an abstraction from existential space, and furthermore that once one thinks in terms of physical space, one has lost all sight of locales.[23] But it seems to me that this final move ought to be challenged, because it's hard to resist the thought that locales are realized in physical space. Indeed, Heidegger himself describes the locale founded by the bridge as encompassing the banks of the stream (while also transforming them into banks that *lies across from each other*) as well as the surrounding earth (while transforming it into *landscape*). The best way to express this point, I think, is to say that the borders of locales are both mathematically and existentially spatial.[24]

Of course, minds — even spatial ones — are not locales. Indeed, because the contours of how we find ourselves in the world will partly be determined by the psychological structures that we bring to the sense-making party, it seems that minds are implicated, at a fundamental level, in the very founding of locales. But this fact does not make a consideration of locales irrelevant to our present concerns: we are pursuing the idea that a Heideggerian account of spatial borders might help us to free ExC from the clutches of containerism about the mind. Locales give us a clue as to how this might work, since they embody an account of such borders not as enclosing or limiting surrounds, but as horizons — productive events in histories of sense-making. To see what matters, we need to take two steps. First, it is a feature of Heidegger's account of human sense-making that mind and world co-emerge as interdependent functions of each other.[25] So, just as minds will be implicated, at a fundamental level, in the very founding of locales, so locales will be implicated, at a fundamental level, in the very founding of minds. Minds, too, are productive events in historical flows of sense-making. Second, if we keep this co-emergence picture in view, Heidegger's work is arguably in the nearby background when Christine Battersby recommends a shift from containers to event-horizons in our conceptualization of the edge of the body. Inspired also by the science of self-organizing dynamical systems, in which global form arises not from external or executive control, but in an autonomous, emergent fashion from nonlinear causal interactions between lower-level elements, Battersby writes as follows:

> [F]orms are not fixed things, but temporary attestations in continuous metastable flows, potentialities or evolutionary events. If we think about boundaries, then [...] the boundaries of bodies need not be thought as the edges of 'three-dimensional containers into which we put certain things [...] and out of which other things emerged'. The boundary of the body can also be

thought as an event-horizon, in which one form (myself) meets its potentiality for transforming itself into another form or forms (the not-self). Such a body-boundary entails neither containment of internal forces nor repulsion of/ protection against external forces. Those who are aware of themselves as centred 'inside' an insulated container — free from contamination by the threatening other which is located on the 'outside' — are captured by an illusion generated by the mechanisms of ego-protection, as well as by spatial models inherited from a classical science which is now no longer compelling.[26]

For Battersby, then, the bodily boundary is not an inert territorial wall between self and other that is traversed or breached, but rather an active site of production — that from which the self, as a relational form, begins an unfolding into (a realization of) possibilities. To say that the self is contained within the bodily boundary is to ignore the fact that the self is essentially a function of that boundary, a boundary which is itself only a more or less temporary, more or less stable structure in a dynamic and historically evolving flow.

In a manner, all I wish to add to Battersby's (if I am right) Heidegger-influenced horizonal account of the edge of the organic body is the claim that a similar horizonal approach may be profitably adopted toward yet another spatial boundary, namely the edge of thought. That too is a productive event that allows the mind to unfold in many different forms, some extended and some not. So neither skull nor skin constitutes a container for the mind. In fact, nothing does. Moreover, there is no single, fixed edge of thought coinciding with the skull or skin. Thought has many edges, or, if you prefer, it has a moving, shifting edge. Put another way, there is no single, fixed, mind-world border coinciding with the organic sensorimotor interface. In different circumstances, that border is founded, refounded and refounded again, as skin-external elements become incorporated into, and divested from, the cognitive system, during its ongoing activity. This amounts to what John Sutton has dubbed a 'deterritorialized' view of cognition, a view 'which dissolves individuals [and individual minds] into peculiar loci of coordination and coalescence among multiple structured media' and which analyses the 'boundaries [between inner and outer, natural and artificial] as hard-won and fragile developmental and cultural achievements, always open to renegotiation'[27]. Importantly, this deterritorialized picture does not require us to struggle against the intuitive pull of the idea that the mind-world border is located at the perception-action interface, for, as we have seen, that very interface, reconceived as a productive event-horizon on the model of spatial borders recommended by Heidegger and Battersby, is itself a dynamic, moving structure. So, where is the love? Sometimes it's over here, sometimes it's over there, and sometimes it really is two metres to the left of the door, just above the sofa, with a volume about the size of a football.[28]

Notes to Chapter 9

1. In my opening paragraph, I suggested that thinkers such as Heidegger, Ryle and the later Wittgenstein were representatives of a nonspatial view of mind. But now that we have separated out questions about physical realizers from other questions in the vicinity of cognition, it might seem that although these thinkers were themselves focused on a level of analysis separate from realization, a level at which thinking of psychology in terms of spatiality is, as they might argue, misguided, nevertheless their philosophical frameworks might, without violence, be mined for insights about, or for guidance regarding, questions about realizers. And, in a sense, that's precisely what I shall do later in this chapter, by calling on Heidegger. However, as a matter of good methodology, it seems abundantly clear that one should begin by being suspicious of any analysis that appeared simply to *read off* a view about realizers from a view pitched at an altogether different level of analysis. For more on this sort of issue, see e.g. section 4 of Michael Wheeler, 'The Revolution will not be Optimised: Radical Enactivism, Extended Functionalism and the Extensive Mind', *Topoi* (2015), SpringerLink Online First, DOI: 10.1007/s11245-015-9356-x.
2. The original presentation and case for ExC was in Andy Clark and David Chalmers, 'The Extended Mind', *Analysis*, 58.1 (1998), 7–19; see also Andy Clark, *Supersizing the Mind: Embodiment, Action, and Cognitive Extension* (New York: Oxford University Press, 2008). For a more recent collection that places the original Clark and Chalmers paper alongside a range of developments, criticisms and defences of ExC, see *The Extended Mind*, ed. by Richard Menary (Cambridge, MA: MIT Press, 2010). Throughout this chapter, I will use the terms 'mind' and 'cognition' interchangeably. Although this irritates some people, it strikes me as standard practice in cognitive science. From this perspective, 'extended cognition' and 'the extended mind' are alternative names for the same view.
3. Martin Heidegger, 'Building, Dwelling, Thinking', in Heidegger, *Poetry, Language, Thought*, trans. by Albert Hofstadter (New York: Harper and Row, 1971), pp. 145–61; reprinted in Martin Heidegger, *Basic Writings*, ed. by David Farrell Krell (London: Routledge, 1978), pp. 343–63. Quotation from p. 358 of the Krell edition.
4. I say 'in and of itself' here because I don't rule out the possibility that additional arguments might take us from an analysis of the structure of, say, intentionality to ExC. For arguments in this area — minus the antirepresentationalism — see Mark Rowlands, *The New Science of the Mind: From Extended Mind to Embodied Phenomenology* (Cambridge, MA: MIT Press, 2010). For the view that rejecting any sort of robust representational account of basic cognition is a key step in securing something like ExC, see: Daniel D. Hutto and Erik Myin, *Radicalizing Enactivism: Basic Minds without Content* (Cambridge, MA: MIT Press, 2010); Daniel D. Hutto, Michael D. Kirchhoff and Erik Myin, 'Extensive Enactivism: why Keep it all in?', *Frontiers in Human Neuroscience*, 8.706 (2014), 1–11. For a critical response to the latter, antirepresentational view, see Wheeler, 'The Revolution will not be Optimised'.
5. See King Beach, 'The Role of External Mnemonic Symbols in Acquiring an Occupation', in *Practical Aspects of Memory*, ed. by M. M. Gruneberg and R. N. Sykes (New York: Wiley, 1988), pp. 342–46.
6. Beach's analysis of bartender behaviour is developed as an example of cognitive niche construction by Clark in his *Supersizing the Mind*; see also Michael Wheeler and Andy Clark, 'Culture, Embodiment and Genes: Unravelling the Triple Helix', *Philosophical Transactions of the Royal Society Series B*, 363 (2008), 3563–75.
7. My chosen way of expressing the difference between embedded cognition and ExC, that is, in terms of a causal-constitutive distinction, is due originally to Fred Adams and Kenneth Aizawa, *The Bounds of Cognition* (Malden, MA and Oxford: Blackwell, 2008), although it is now widespread in the literature.
8. The most-discussed argument for ExC, which is based on what is called the parity principle, is to be found in the original Clark and Chalmers treatment of the issue. For alternative pro-ExC arguments that claim various advantages over parity-based considerations, see e.g.: Richard Menary, *Cognitive Integration: Mind and Cognition Unbounded* (Basingstoke: Palgrave Macmillan,

2007); John Sutton, 'Exograms and Interdisciplinarity: History, the Extended Mind, and the Civilizing Process', in *The Extended Mind*, ed. by Richard Menary, pp. 189–225; Michael Wheeler, 'Revolution, Reform, or Business as Usual? The Future Prospects for Embodied Cognition', in *The Routledge Handbook of Embodied Cognition*, ed. by Lawrence Shapiro (Abingdon and New York: Routledge, 2014), pp. 374–83.
9. David Chalmers, Preface to Andy Clark, *Supersizing the Mind*, p. xi.
10. Clark and Chalmers, 'The Extended Mind'.
11. See, canonically, Paul Bach-y-Rita, *Brain Mechanisms in Sensory Substitution* (New York: Academic Press, 1972). For a more recent treatment, see e.g. Paul Bach-y-Rita and Stephen W. Kercel, 'Sensory Substitution and Augmentation: Incorporating Humans-in-the-Loop', *Intellectica*, 2.35 (2002), 287–97.
12. If one stares at a waterfall for a while, and then looks at any stationary rocks at the side of the waterfall, the rocks will appear to be moving upwards.
13. Malika Auvray, Sylvain Hanneton, Charles Lenay, and Kevin O'Regan, 'There is Something out There: Distal Attribution in Sensory Substitution, Twenty Years Later', *Journal of Integrative Neuroscience*, 4 (2005), 505–21.
14. For a fresh take on this difficult issue, see Fiona Macpherson, 'Taxonomising the Senses', *Philosophical Studies*, 153.1 (2011), 123–42.
15. See: Alva Noë, *Action in Perception* (Cambridge, MA: MIT Press, 2004); Alva Noë, *Out of Our Heads: Why you are not your Brain, and other lessons from the Biology of Consciousness* (New York: Hill and Wang, 2009); Julian Kiverstein and Mirko Farina, 'Do Sensory Substitution Devices Extend the Conscious Mind?', in *Consciousness in Interaction: The Role of the Natural and Social Context in Shaping Consciousness*, ed. by Fabio Paglieri (Amsterdam: John Benjamins, 2012), pp. 19–40.
16. For critical discussion, see e.g.: Andy Clark, 'Spreading the Joy? Why the Machinery of Consciousness is (probably) still in the Head', *Mind*, 118.472 (2009), 963–93; Michael Wheeler, 'Not What it's Like but Where it's Like: Phenomenal Consciousness, Sensory Substitution and the Extended Mind', *Journal of Consciousness Studies* 22.3–4 (2015), 129–47; Michael Wheeler, 'Extended Consciousness: an Interim Report', *The Southern Journal of Philosophy*, 53, Spindel Supplement (2015), 155–75.
17. Jennifer Hornsby, 'Physicalist Thinking and Conceptions of Behaviour', in *Subject, Thought, and Context*, ed. by Philip Pettit and John McDowell (Oxford: Oxford University Press, 1986), pp. 114–15.
18. For example, in the principle that perception, thought and action are conceptually and functionally distinct, and in the claim that intelligent action is always governed by reason. See Michael Wheeler, *Reconstructing the Cognitive World: The Next Step* (Cambridge, MA: MIT Press, 2005).
19. See Noë, *Out of our Heads*, p. 62.
20. Martin Heidegger, *Being and Time*, trans. by John Macquarrie and Edward Robinson (Oxford: Blackwell, 1962), p. 89.
21. Heidegger, 'Building. Dwelling, Thinking', p. 356.
22. Heidegger, 'Building. Dwelling, Thinking', p. 355. In truth, my brief gloss on the notion of a locale barely hints at the complexity of Heidegger's account, which involves what he calls the 'gathering of the fourfold' (earth, sky, divinities and mortals). I do not have the space here to explore this intricate notion. For my interpretation, see Michael Wheeler, 'Martin Heidegger', in *The Stanford Encyclopedia of Philosophy*, ed. by Edward N. Zalta, section 3, <http://plato.stanford.edu/entries/heidegger/> [accessed 4 September 2015].
23. Heidegger, 'Building. Dwelling, Thinking', p. 357.
24. For critical commentaries on Heidegger's account of space that go well beyond the very swift criticism that I offer here, see e.g.: Hubert L. Dreyfus, *Being-in-the-World: A Commentary on Heidegger's 'Being and Time', Division 1* (Cambridge, MA: MIT Press, 1991), chapter 7; Jeff Malpas, 'Heidegger, Space and World', in *Heidegger and Cognitive Science*, ed. by Julian Kiverstein and Michael Wheeler (Basingstoke: Palgrave Macmillan, 2012), pp. 309–42. These commentaries concentrate mostly on the account of space given by Heidegger in *Being and Time*, but the criticisms lodged plausibly generalize to the account he gives in 'Building, Dwelling, Thinking'.

25. Put *very* crudely, the picture in *Being and Time* is that Heideggerian worlds are structured by the interests and concerns of socially embedded human beings, while the activities of individual human beings are to be interpreted in terms of the structures and possibilities that such beings inherit within such worlds.
26. Christine Battersby, *The Phenomenal Woman: Feminist Metaphysics and the Patterns of Identity* (London: Routledge, 1998), p. 52.
27. Sutton, 'Exograms and Interdisciplinarity', p. 213.
28. My thanks go to two anonymous referees whose comments on an earlier version of this chapter enabled me to make improvements.

CHAPTER 10

On Entanglings: Disciplines, Materiality and Distributed Cognition

Peter Garratt

The mind is increasingly theorized as an entity not set apart from life but something realized within it, integrated with a lived world that it reciprocally reconfigures — even as something spread out and radically distributed over assemblages of bodily and extra-bodily structures and resources. Mind and world are seen as porous or mutually enfolding; human agents and environmental objects smear into one another. Seeing them this way, as contingent meshes of ideation, agency and material formations, has lately driven theorizing in different quarters as part of distinct programmes and critical projects, within and across fields including science studies, geography, anthropology, archaeology, literary studies, philosophy and cultural theory. A commitment to dynamic relational ontology, for example, motivates thinkers identified with posthumanism and the new materialism (such as Donna Haraway and the feminist physicist Karen Barad), while the 'extended mind' view — which proposes that the mind is not localized intra-cranially, so cannot not be said to stop where our 'bioprejudices' guess it must, at the skull or skin boundary — has its roots in philosophical functionalism and a marked return to Continental phenomenology (exemplified by the work of Andy Clark, Michael Wheeler and Mark Rowlands).[1] These theorists work sometimes in complementary modes but, on the whole, conceive of their own engagements and purposes in distinct ways, channelled through their own intellectual heritage, concepts, rhetorics and styles. All the same, through them — and through other hybrid thinkers — several related stories of dynamic cognitive-material co-mingling now get told.

If quite different investments motivate this increasingly common recognition of what William Connelly calls 'our manifold *entanglements* with nonhuman processes, both within the body and outside humanity', it is not impossible to survey this scene critically and see in it the germ of an interpretation of our own contemporary intellectual history.[2] As a way of beginning that task, this chapter asks how we might interpret the heterogeneous shift to a language of entangled states, processes and agents in the twenty-first-century humanities. Entanglement, Connelly's operative term here, has a growing resonance with multifarious positions making up the scene of what can broadly be termed contemporary theory. A simple question that its appearance motivates, especially for a literary critic interested in figures and tropes, is the following one: why has the figure of the tangle or mesh been taken up so readily in quite different areas at roughly the same time, in response to the pressures and possibilities of the contemporary moment? What might be made of a common turn to a vocabulary of meshing and entanglement now evident in relatively remote areas and across typical disciplinary borders — from the medical humanities to ecocriticism, from gender studies to critical animal studies — seemingly in parallel and sometimes betraying little awareness of the shared conceptual imagery? As it turns out, if something like a general orientation can be said to be disclosed by the contemporary figure of entanglement, its most interesting feature as an ascription of living structural interdependence is that it manages to speak simultaneously for quite different theoretical models and for theorists of many stripes. The mesh may be an image of our time, but it gets used as a model or metaphor to support radically different, and even conflicting, sorts of claims.

If it is only starting to become clear what, if anything, is to be gained from the figure of the tangle or mesh, the fact of its emergence and dispersed uptake justifies taking it as an interpretable feature of the critical landscape. Here, then, by way of an initial illustration, are three brief instances where entanglement or meshing help to articulate governing (and invariably self-consciously radical or non-standard) assumptions about mind, world, agency and matter — for contrasting ends, as we shall see. Example one, from the philosopher Andy Clark, comes from one of his neat glosses of the extended mind hypothesis: 'the actual local operations that realize certain forms of human cognizing include inextricable *tangles* of feedback, feedforward, and feed-around loops: loops that promiscuously criss-cross the boundaries of brain, body, and world'.[3] The second example is from the ecocritic Timothy Morton, whose posthumanist environmental framework in his recent book *Hyperobjects* (2013) uses very similar vocabulary to model a theory of material relations, but with a nod to quantum physics: 'Objects entangle one another', Morton says, 'in a crisscrossing mesh of spacetime fluctuations'.[4] Third, Karen Barad's influential *Meeting the Universe Halfway: Quantum Physics and the Entanglement of Matter and Meaning* (2007) develops (as its title promises) a sustained, abstract conceptualization of entanglement, derived from a far more detailed understanding of particle physics than Morton can boast, as part of a project of moving beyond the dead-end dualisms of the 1990s Science Wars, where critical theory was consigned to a place outside the sciences in the form of hermeneutic and ideological critique.[5] Whether gently invoked or rigorously theorized, an operative image of a meshy structure informs how all three examples talk; yet generally these same theorists do not talk to each other.

What is clear, though, is that the mesh or tangle expresses our move into a phase after postmodernism, extending earlier forms of what might be described very loosely as non-Cartesian thinking, especially Derridean deconstruction, while reacting against postmodernism's sceptical distancing of the real through the fecund play of language and signs. This has required rescuing Derrida from linguistic idealism by aligning his early work with a new materialism, while the bogeyman remains Cartesianism, perhaps all too easily.[6] Different contemporary instantiations of entanglement are often bound up with some promised return to vitality, presence, materiality, living systems, and staked on the reintegration of agency and matter, by way of a move against representationalism, both at the semiotic level and with regard to the classical computational model of cognition (that is, internal mental representation). Entanglement, in other words, goes hand in hand with anti-representationalism. This returning figure of thought, echoing Darwin's memorable, emphatic use of the 'entangled bank' image at the end of *On the Origin of Species*, which arguably marks the inception of the metaphor, affirms a simultaneous debt to the life sciences.[7] If one accepts Patricia Waugh's interpretation that this new era after the postmodern is one of complexity and complex thinking, then the figure of entanglement captures a recursive style of thought that reveals the limitations of a causality conceived linearly or mechanistically: 'This shift — from the linear to the non-linear and from analytical reduction to varieties of complex emergence — partly reflects the current reorientation towards the life sciences, the revival of evolutionary thinking and the growing pressure on the sciences, including economics, to leave the laboratory and the model and to enter the world'.[8] No doubt, generally speaking, the mesh and tangle convey a shift to complexity of this kind; and no doubt other figures, such as 'contamination', perform similar work.[9] However, in what follows I want to suggest that this general picture only gets us so far, just as the pervasive tags 'post-' and 'anti-'- and 'non-'Cartesianism only do a certain amount of broad-brush description. In establishing that entanglement is a common motif found repeatedly in — to speak very generally — contemporary theories of bodies, borders and boundaries, I will go on to re-emphasize how differently its figural potential gets exploited, and why this matters for thinking about agency and intentionality.

Inside Out, Outside In

To begin, here is an interesting example of an unexpected, seemingly unacknowledged convergence between ways of talking about the boundaries of the human mind in ecology and current cognitive science. It comes from Morton's recent work *Hyperobjects*, where he introduces the term 'interobjectivity' to account for the arrival of newness and creativity in flat networks of human and nonhuman participants (or objects), or what Bruno Latour would call actants. Suppose we think of Morton writing the very book that we are presently reading:

> What is called subject and what is called mind just are interobjective effects, emergent properties of relationships between enmeshed objects. Some neurons are tied together in a brain, and the brain sits in the skull of a lifeform that is sitting at this computer, typing these words. Mind is not 'in' the brain but rather, to use the Heideggerian term, 'thrown' into the interobjective space consisting of a banker's lamp, skull, computer, and keyboard, as well as fingers, neurons, and Mahler's seventh symphony playing on iTunes, Michael Tilson Thomas conducting the San Francisco Symphony Orchestra, a pair of eyes, a medium sized wooden Danish dining chair covered with black velvet, the muscular system, and so on.[10]

Morton wants to turn things inside out: what begins dismissively, with a renunciation of mind and subjectivity as 'just interobjective effects', then quickly develops into a provocative rendering of the writing act, which not only illustrates some of the ideas of entanglement mentioned above but also has a bearing upon hypotheses and debates in current cognitive science, especially over the extended mind, as I shall sketch. Here, in a brief local example, one can see how similar sorts of moves are being made in ecocriticism and theories of embodied cognition, just as they are in further afield areas of the humanities such as cognitive archaeology and narratology. In the passage, the drift of Morton's thought leads him towards a familiar biological image of structural interdependence ('enmeshed objects') which he exemplifies via the at-hand example of his own immediate interobjective context as a practising writer. When even lightly scrutinized, he suggests, this context turns out to be a highly effective temporary assemblage of heterogeneous elements — neurons, eyes, a human bodily frame, embodied gestures such as finger movements, sounds, furniture, digital technology, even actions once performed by a distant orchestral conductor — which together realize the labour of written composition and result in the words on the page before us. What exactly 'is' thinking here and what has performed it? The invited answer is unlike the one that common sense might give — that words were chosen from inside Morton's private intentional mind, itself located somewhere in his brain, inside his head, and then these words were typed subsequently using a keyboard and computer. Morton's interpretation entails a more radical view of what has gone on.

On this alternative account, the act of writing — a cognitive process — involves many more elements than neural events alone. For one thing, it has important embodied features, not just in the loose sense that the brain has to belong to a living anatomical human body in order to carry out its work on a task like writing, but in the deeper sense that the moving, gestural, proprioceptive body plays an active, constitutive role in the fulfilment of the process itself. Thinking and writing are an enactment, a doing. A second feature is that the physical sensory environment does more than serve as a backdrop or neutral context for this embodied process of cognition. It too supports the realization of thinking/writing: the process is a loop or circuit spread out over brain events, embodied motor actions and sensations, technology and other objects of the room (computer, chair, lamp), further enabled by environmental sensory cues (the played music), without the need for a border to separate those bits located inside Morton's skin from those outside it. The whole assemblage (contingent, dynamic, spread out) constitutes the process.

There is nothing especially new in this suggestion, even if it runs against a supposedly humanistic cliché of the lone writer as meditative, autonomous and inwardly focused. What Morton establishes, using his own terminology, is an idea of mind as distributed over its world rather than purely inward, as pictured by a traditional internalist or computational paradigm. He elicits a familiar meshy image to do this, where the mind is an ensemble of relations rather than a fixed and originating point, and he does so in a way that reproduces some important aspects of Andy Clark's extended mind hypothesis in an ecological context, without engaging directly with Clark at all. Morton's purpose in turning things inside out via a theory of the enmeshed mind is also quite at odds with the direction of travel of Clark and other philosophers and cognitive theorists. For Morton, as will be discussed below, the mesh vividly serves — and indeed somewhat simplistically serves — to abolish the default image of the mind as a centred intentional agent set before a given world of material entities and processes that correlate with human understanding or anthropocentrism. For Clark, on the other hand, a similarly tangled set-up of mind and environment would reveal just how efficiently and opportunistically the mind is able to offload tasks onto available structures lying around it (physical props or even symbol systems) in ways that extend its reach beyond the location of the skull. The point of the first case is to illustrate how agency gets dispersed across the local system, whereas the second case seeks to move the boundary marking where the mind stops out into the world.

Theories of distributed cognition, with which Morton intersects, challenge the standard boundaries of cognition and also the extent to which cognition can be equated with building internal representational models of the outside world. Distributed cognition theories vary considerably on the detail of this, however. Even the embodied, embedded, enactive and extended approaches (4E cognitive science) disagree on important issues, such as whether what we typically count as cognition is distinctive for being realized in a specific type of body; and the lineage of distributed cognition includes sources as diverse as the twentieth-century Russian developmental psychologist Lev Vygotsky and key proponents of biological autopoeisis like Humberto Maturana and Francisco Varela.[11] Different areas of contemporary theory also challenge the reduction of the mind to the brain, especially in an era of neuroscientific imaging and what Raymond Tallis has dubbed 'neuro-mania'.[12] The medical humanities and the recent framework of critical neuroscience are two such areas. Isolating the brain as the seat of mental experience, the so-called organ of the mind, can be traced back at least as far as the empirical work of Franz Joseph Gall and Johann Spurzheim at the start of the nineteenth century, though a new brain-bound model of mental processes has dawned in the era of contemporary cognitive neuroscience. Here, it may be observed that the widely upheld explanatory authority of neuroscientific concepts, such plasticity, and techniques of brain imaging (especially fMRI), have helped transform social understandings of the human person in ways that are neurally focused and lead to 'brainhood'.[13] As Fernando Vidal puts it, brainhood means '*being*, rather than simply *having*, a brain'.[14]

By contrast, the key commitment in distributed cognition entails some claim that thinking does not just happen in the head. Nowhere in contemporary thought is this organismic porosity more pronounced, or centrally at stake, than in 4E cognitive science. Cognitive science, itself a thoroughly mongrel enterprise bridging aspects of AI, linguistics, robotics, philosophy of mind, empirical and evolutionary psychology, and other fields, is increasingly part of new forms of interdisciplinary enquiry in the literary humanities, recently in relation to the 4E picture in particular.[15] Without firmly planting a foot in the 4E literature, Morton's example of his own writing as a distributed, embodied cognitive process touches on all four of the 4Es. Let us leave aside the terms embodied and embedded in order to look in closer detail at the two arguably more contested Es, the enactive and extended. Enactivism downplays the need for mental representations or mentalizing and takes cognition to be skilful, acted engagement with the world, which discloses possibilities for action. Elsewhere in *Hyperobjects* Morton seems to endorse such a view, albeit in fairly rudimentary terms. 'Intelligence need not be thought of as having a picture of reality in the mind,' he reflects, 'but as an interaction between all kinds of entities'. Yet this comes without Morton citing any enactivist philosopher or cognitive scientist, such as Alva Noë, whose influential *Action in Perception* (2004) provides a rigorous account of that basic suggestion, dismantling our intuitive sense that perceiving things is like having a 'snapshot conception' where 'You open your eyes and you are given experiences that represent the scene — picture-like — in sharp focus and uniform detail from the center out to the periphery'. Noë shows that these intuitions — and the philosophical support they have been leant — do not match up with what happens. For example, uniform all-the-way-out detail is illusory, a kind of virtual seeing governed by the availability of visual information enabled by the possibilities of eye and head movements. 'To experience detail virtually [not as a realistic hi-res photo], you don't need to have all the detail in your head', Noë explains. 'All you need is quick and easy access to the relevant detail when you need it'.[16]

Storing rich representations of the world internally, as common sense supposes we do, would be incredibly demanding, using heavy resources of energy and cognition. Enactivism explains how perception (in action) manages to avoid the problem of burdensome resource implications. It supplies a good example of cognitive offloading, where what might be thought of as internal to a person or mind is located in an external environment. Rather than appropriating full informational content, it is enough for the mind to know it has access to the required information through gesture or engagement of some sort. The anticipation of such enacted possibilities becomes functionally the same as, in this example, encoding a complex pictorial representation of a situation. But this way of approaching cognitive offloading and anticipation drives the theory of extended mind, too. The work of Andy Clark has been seminal in this debate. Clark's story of the mind is one in which cognition seeks out ways of extending itself beyond the biological site of the person, into structures, bodies, edifices, technologies, scaffolds in the available surrounding environment. Cognition thus becomes leaky, the bounds of thinking (and perhaps mind itself, even personal identity) radically spread out in changing configurations. In 'The Extended Mind' (1998), co-authored with David Chalmers, he argues that 'If, as we confront some task, a part of the world functions as a process which, *were it done in the head*, we would have no hesitation in recognizing as part of the cognitive process, then that part of the world *is* (so we claim) part of the cognitive process. Cognitive processes ain't all in the head!'[17] Their discussion set off a vibrant series of arguments, rebuttals and refinements to the hypothesis, including fine-grained analysis of their main thought experiment of Otto and Inga.

Clark and Chalmers set up Otto and Inga as superficially different yet revealingly identical cases of cognitive agents seeking to know the location of the Museum of Modern Art, which is on New York's 53rd Street. Inga retrieves this from her memory. Otto, who has a mild degenerative condition affecting memory function, consults his personal notebook (which he always carries with him) where the address of the museum happens already to be written down, and he, too, finds the right information. Both can find the museum. Without going into the thought experiment in finer detail, a key point is that Clark and Chalmers defend the parity of the two cases: nothing other than the external location of Otto's notebook distinguishes it *in use* from the inner neural storage system of Inga's memory. One must conclude, they suggest, that Otto provides a genuine case of an extended cognitive circuit that moves out from the perimeter of his person to encompass a material object that plays a *constitutive* role (not just a causal or supporting one) in the accomplishment of thought.

What wider significance does the case of Otto and Inga have, and cognitive extension for broadly, for entanglement in the sense we have been evaluating here? While noting the quite different terms in which the extended mind debate is configured, the grip it has depends on the notion of an inseparable coupling of material and mental components in a contingent structure. The further notion of cognitive niche construction, elaborating on post-genomic models of biology, provides a related term for designed environments that reciprocally modify agent and surroundings.[18] The work of Clark and Wheeler and Noë is also marked by a turn to Continental phenomenology, often Heidegger and Merleau-Ponty, which help facilitate a break with classic computational cognitive science (the mind as computer) and also the dualisms upon which Cartesian internalism is founded. In some respects, too, the nonhuman is invested with renewed vitality or at least something like the chance to be operationalized agentively in heterogenous couplings that extend beyond the skin. The mind emerges relationally, enmeshed with material and substances that become its vehicles. And perhaps it is no coincidence, as Claire Colebrook has pointed out critically, that a revealing rhetorical pattern — that of healing rifts — runs through the titles of books by these thinkers, as in Clark's *Being There: Putting Brain, Body and World Together Again* (1997) and Wheeler's more recent *Reconstructing the Cognitive World* (2005). Renewal, remaking, integration, repairing disunity, binding together: these terms mark out an important dimension of the new cognitive science (and for Colebrook they depend on a selective reading of Heidegger) in which thought is no longer set critically against a world but unfolds purely relationally from within it.[19]

Yet Colebrook's criticisms of Clark may be said to go too far here, and miss their target. For it is credible to read the extended mind hypothesis not as some drastic fulfilment of post-Cartesian (and posthuman) vitalism but as foremost a story of individual optimization. Colebrook takes the extended mind to mean a radically decentred one (and, as noted, Morton finds the mesh figure attractive for this reason, too, though for different ends). For Clark, she claims, 'Not only is it the case that there is no such thing as mind in itself, for the mind is nothing other than the sense of relation it bears to the world in which it lives; the sense and orientation of the world are not located in the mind'.[20] True, in *Supersizing the Mind* Clark adopts the rhetoric of the mesh and tangle, as when he says that 'neural processes are often productively entangled with gross bodily and extrabodily processes of storage, representation, materialization, and manipulation'.[21] But Clark's position hardly affirms what Colebrook claims, a radical emptying of the mind into emergent forms of relatedness. His thought is not so much that the subject is already caught up in, or constituted by, a prosthetic excess or supplement (despite the catchy title of his earlier *Natural Born Cyborgs*) but instead that the individual cognizer characteristically seeks out opportunities to offload the burden of internal computation onto whatever available bodies or objects or tools it can successfully integrate into its goals, even reshaping its surrounding environment to do so. Far from abandoning an idea of the mind as an originating intelligence or seat of intentional agency, Clark's defence of extended cognition requires a mind with just these attributes. Not for nothing is his prose given to occasional twinges of utopian humanism: 'We self-engineer ourselves to think and perform better in the worlds we find ourselves in. We self-engineer worlds in which to build better worlds to think in. We build better tools to think with and use these very tools to discover still better tools to think with'.[22] Such claims unmistakably part company with just about any of Clark's posthumanist admirers.

But technical optimization and improved efficiencies are not the only point. Clark's picture of the extended mind appears to take its template from standard internalist or 'in the head' definitions of cognition. This can be seen in the way that he devises a 'parity principle' to determine whether or not something external (a hybrid process, a coupling) counts as genuinely cognitive, a heavily discussed area in the philosophical literature. According to this principle, what counts as 'cognitive' can be decided by judging whether or not a process would be taken as such if it happened to go on inside the head rather being part of the external world. To head off the fear that almost anything external might suddenly seem to be capable of counting as part of cognition, Clark imposes some constraining criteria. For an external physical process to count, it must (like Otto's notebook) be treated uncritically and transparently by its user, and be constantly available. In other words, it needs to be trusted in the same manner as an internal process. As Shaun Gallagher has pointed out, this reflects the fact that the extended mind hypothesis invokes a standard Cartesian concept of mental process, indeed a representationalist one, even as it contests the naturalized limit of the skin or skull boundary. A difficulty with this is that Clark means it to apply to all forms of cognition, not just instances of static informational retrieval, like Otto using his notebook: 'One problem with this example is that it frames the discussion with a concept of the mind that the extended mind hypothesis is really trying to challenge', Gallagher notices.[23] And it is not well fitted to the more dynamic picture disclosed by enactivism.

Entangled Agency and the New Materialism

One might say that Clark's hypothesis is an extended kind of internalism, where emphasis falls on drawing a more satisfactory boundary of cognition than the default one given by the biological body. The mind couples itself heterogeneously to its world in a mesh or contingent tangled assemblage in a way that expresses grounded and pragmatic cognitive agency. As I suggest, this needs to be distinguished from the vital materialism of the kind that Colebrook has in her sights. Yet, all the same, the metaphor of entanglement has emerged in parallel in thinkers associated with this new materialism, such as Karen Barad and the political scientist Jane Bennett. For Karen Barad, 'entanglement' develops from a philosophy of science rooted in her reading of Niels Bohr and quantum physics, which she uses to elucidate an 'onto-epistemology' of how entities emerge ('subjects', 'objects', 'nature', 'culture') through a dynamic process of materialization or *mattering* termed, in contrast to interaction, 'intra-action'. Subject and object are disclosed and differentiated only in intra-actions, by an 'agential cut' (*cut* as in impermanent delineation, from the inside, making something visible), and not by any inherent separation, for 'relata do not preexist relations'.[24] Such intra-action, Barad says, 'signifies the mutual constitution of entangled agencies', recognizing how all such agencies emerge from, rather than precede, entanglement. Intra-action unfolds as a process of making and unmaking performed by the constraints and exclusions of 'material-discursive practices' or apparatuses, and in this regard it facilitates a move beyond the antagonism of scientific realism and social constructivism.[25] Practices of observation, say, following Bohr, always participate in what is observed; similarly, culture is constitutively entangled in nature. But, lest this appear like the conventional stance adopted by science studies, Barad's ontologizing opposes the thought that mediation in the form of a cultural-linguistic signifying system produces or constructs its referent. To claim this would be to repeat an error committed by post-structuralist and social-constructivist critique, namely representationalism — engaging with materiality only as it is caught in language or signs, rendering it as 'passive, immutable, and mute, in need of the mark of an external force like culture or history to complete it'.[26]

Only by abandoning the dominant representationalist norms of literary and cultural theory — found even in a feminist 'materialist' like Judith Butler — can justice be done to the vitality of the physical world. The metaphor of 'mediation', which for deconstruction meant assigning vitality or 'play' to language, thereby holding matter at a distance, has 'for too long stood in the way of a more thoroughgoing accounting of the empirical'. For Barad, matter comes to matter as something agential, not passive, 'a doing — a congealing of agency', hence her term *agential realism*, which insists that separateness is not an essential part of the way reality is (though in our habitual anthropocentric perspective it appears to be so).[27] This kind of agency does not express the agency 'of' a person or a body (in other words, agency understood as liberal humanist choice) but rather the deep relational dynamism of the world in its unfolding, the intra-active enactments of that world. To grasp this means decoupling agency from the metaphysics of individualism, and from the Romantic or vitalist tradition of projecting a force that animates matter. If intra-action and agential realism codify a response to the absence of ontological separation in the world — the lack of a Kantian gap between noumena and phenomena, as explained for Barad by theoretical physics — then they also compel a conception of agency not derived from, or bound by, human intentionality ('it is an enactment, not something that someone or something has').[28] In a corresponding sense, the entanglement of the nonhuman and human (and the material-discursive practices that instate their contingent border) make it possible to regard agency as something distributed over entangled phenomena and accordingly across nonhuman forms.

Comparisons with Bruno Latour's thinking about distributed material agency in actor network theory may suggest themselves here, but Barad steps away from Latour precisely on the issue of nonhuman agency, for political as well as ontological reasons (the two being inseparable anyway in her terms). As Barad sees it, although there are important ways in which 'the world kicks back', agentively, as it were, a weakness with actor network theory lies in identifying agency with an actor (either human or nonhuman) without accounting for the political determinations that bear upon 'the framing of agency as a localizable attribution', namely adjudicating in advance what counts as either human or nonhuman (her extended example being a foetus).[29] Despite these tensions, Latour's distributed agency might be read with a slightly different emphasis to recuperate actor network theory through the framework of what the political theorist Jane Bennett calls 'vital materiality'. Bennett, herself in the frontline of a new materialism, proposes that Latour's elaboration of conjoined agency and his use of the terminology of *actants*, not agents, serve to 'pry some space between the idea of action and the idea of human intentionality'; moreover, Latour 'explicitly rejects the categories of "nature" and "culture" in favor of the "collective", which refers to an ecology of human and nonhuman elements'.[30]

Latour is only one (obvious) illustration of how agential realism seems threaded into a cross-disciplinary tangle of related theories today. Another illustrative interrelationship is that between Barad and Timothy Morton's influential work in ecology and ecocriticism. Barad's performative matter and her postulation of an energized, agentive (nonhuman) world have affinities with Morton's quite different posthumanist project of thinking ecology without nature and, more recently, his concept of hyperobjects. Manifest differences between them make such points of convergence all the more compelling. While Morton explores the analogical potential of some ideas in quantum physics — without conversing directly with Barad, it may be noted — the most significant influence on his thought comes from object-oriented ontology, especially the philosopher Graham Harman, whose version of speculative realism contests those western epistemological traditions and philosophies of nature that have neutralized the absolute otherness of objects and the external world by taking their starting point as a centred human subject. Harman, in contrast, discovers the human to be merely one object among other objects — again, after Latour, in a flat network.[31]

This sounds like — and indeed is — more or less the opposite of Barad's vital ontology, which (Harman would say) has the effect of erasing objects from the picture altogether, by forgoing the nature of inherent objecthood for the sake of some underlying relational force whose primacy is explained only inadequately. Object-oriented ontology turns against human exceptionalism, then, in a highly unusual way, by asking what it means for an object to have strictly autonomous, non-relational, static being — a kind of alien or indifferent reality (being for itself) set apart from any instrumentality or recognition by a subject. Take the example of a stick: there is the stick as it exists for humans, the stick that has properties and possibilities to a bounding dog, and the stick that has some nature of its own, one isolable from its human or dog context. For Harman, drawing on Husserl, objects withdraw their nature from us: their full reality is not available to my look or touch but instead coyly retained.[32] Taking this up, Morton's reading of Harman blends these ontological commitments with his own styles of thinking, environmental, poetic, literary-critical, deconstructive (and also phenomenological), leading *Hyperobjects* to a politicized cultural analysis of the posthuman situation which concludes that we have now arrived at the end of (our engrained concept of) the world. The uncanny dissonance of hyperobjects, which for Morton include such varied phenomena as global warming and nuclear waste, or any entity 'massively distributed in space and time relative to humans', is a feature of this loss. The gap between how a raindrop feels on one's upturned palm and the vast spatio-temporal sprawl of global warming would be one illustration of it. Hyperobjects, he says, as weirder instantiations of more modestly scaled objects, refuse to disclose their being *for us*.[33] And in their weirdness they expose the failed anthropocentric expectation that phenomena can be brought into a rightful correlation with the human.

Odd though it seems, the import of Harman's philosophy leads Morton to articulate concerns that partly overlap with those of vital materiality. Morton's hyperobjects are structurally complex phenomena with uncanny properties, and they also supposedly tell us something about objects in general (modestly proportioned ones). As massively distributed entities they cannot be stabilized from one observational standpoint: in the Husserlian sense their reality is withdrawn, as noted; but for Morton they do more than simply behave like outsized, mega aliens that loom threateningly over modernity's conventional means of sense-making. How hyperobjects produce relations and express or mediate agency also matter to the way Morton formulates them. Far from being eerily non-relational, the nature of hyperobjects is to entangle the local with the vastly distant, as in cases like the Styrofoam cup, even if a radical rupture occurs in the subjective attempt to integrate these two scales (holding the cup in my hand and its material non-degradation millennia hence). Transcending locality in this way, and being inherently 'interobjective' as Morton terms it — that is, bound up with other objects — hyperobjects might equally be thought of as meshes of *hyperrelations* that are not open to analytical inspection or representation at the scale of the human observer, in much the same way as Barad's ontology of entangled phenomena.[34] Like Barad's intra-action, they name the breakdown of linear causal patterns in the material configurings of the world: hyperobjects do not exist in classical geometrical space and time, and they lack any discoverable exteriority. They deconstruct materially the metaphysics of an inside/outside split, and they 'force us to acknowledge the immanence of thinking to the physical', as Morton puts it.[35]

What Harman finds suspect about vitalist models is their claim for the primacy of *relations* over things. To begin ontologically with the unit of the relation, as Barad and Jane Bennett do, is to treat relations *as* (pseudo)things. But one could find this relations/things dichotomy to be just as suspect. In a supple review essay of 2012, in which she adroitly responds to the object-oriented theories of both Morton and Harman, Bennett shares her own misgivings about the terms of such a choice:

> But perhaps there is no need to choose between objects or their relations. Since everyday, earthly experience routinely identifies some effects as coming from individual objects and some from larger systems (or, better put, from individuations within material configurations and from the complex assemblages in which they participate), why not aim for a theory that toggles between both kinds or magnitudes of 'unit'? One would then understand 'objects' to be those swirls of matter, energy, and incipience that hold themselves together long enough to vie with the strivings of other objects, including the indeterminate momentum of the throbbing whole. The project, then, would be to make both objects and relations the periodic focus of theoretical attention, even if it is impossible to articulate fully the 'vague' or 'vagabond' essence of any system or any things, and even if it is impossible to give equal attention to both at once.[36]

These throbbings and strivings and swirlings speak of agency: of agentive reconfiguring. One could go further and identify them as terms of desire — a desire always already at work in contingent assemblages and entangled relations of elements — but this would be a posthuman mode of desire more akin to primordial striving than conscious will (for example, Spinoza's idea of conatus) or a principle of self-organization rather than erotic subjectivity. While it is conceivable that Bennett applies this rhetoric to tease out (or simply to tease) the mute solemnity of Harman's cut-off objects, her passage elicits the possibility of something like a shared frame of reference, even a shared purpose, among these theorists, yet one whose idea of vitality is so abstractly impersonal that it becomes difficult in the end to distinguish between it and Bergson's *élan vital*. Despite its attempts to do otherwise, Morton's idea of interobjectivity, for example, best illustrated by hyperobjects, comes close to reprising entanglement as both Bennett and Barad conceptualize it, emphasizing as it does key themes of indeterminacy, ecological interdependence and generalized agency:

> There is no *world*, strictly speaking — no *environment*, no *nature*, no *background*. These are just handy terms for the *n* objects that make it into interobjective relationships with whatever's going on. There is simply a plenum of objects, pressing in on all sides, leering at us like crazed characters in some crowded Expressionist painting. Interobjectivity is the uterus in which novelty grows. Interobjectivity positively guarantees that something new can happen, because each sample, each spider web vibration, each footprint of objects in other objects, is itself a whole new object with a whole new set of relations to the entities around it.[37]

Life belongs to Morton's objects, hyper or otherwise. They press and vibrate. As he explains in his recent *Realist Magic* (2013), Bennett is right in wishing to 'inject a little bit of animism into the discussion', against the mechanistic reification of things, since object matter is not just 'lumps of dullness'.[38] Even Harman's reticent, dark-sided objects exude a negative kind of agentive force, one can surmise. But by bringing forward the lifeform metaphor in this way, Morton opens his view of hyperobjects to the extended dynamics of biological vitality (if not vitalism), even seeming to agree with Barad that 'feeling, desiring and experiencing are not singular characteristics or capacities of human consciousness', once agency has been expunged of its traces of liberal humanist choice.[39] One of the ramifications of these varied attempts at materialist ontology, then, is that emergent structures and temporary assemblages pay no special attention to the boundary marking the perimeter of the human organism, its limit points of inside and outside — the assumed delineations of its mind, body and world. More to the point, Morton's position cannot relinquish ascribing life to lifeless matter, imagining material objects to be at once crisscrossed and enmeshed, relationally situated, and yet always withdrawn and numinous. His theory paints a confusing picture that is at once relentlessly full of force and relations, and yet also somehow entirely impoverished of agency and mystically inert.

Entangling the Literary Humanities?

Agential realism, ecological hyperobjects and the extended mind hypothesis, to name three sites of contemporary theory in the humanities, unexpectedly converge in the way they elicit images of entangled complexity. Yet they exploit this common figure in quite different ways, with little commerce between them. The mesh is used variously to model vital differentiation and indeterminacy, in Barad's terms, or dispersed agency in a network of independent objects (Morton), or how a cognitive agent interacts with external props and tools to form temporary productive alliances (Clark). It is a highly pliable figure, almost emptily suggestive, capable of gesturing at self-organizing systems, at material border-practices and at the agency of individual minds, subtly linked by a turn away from representationalist models of language and cognition, as enactment replaces detachment and embodied involvement displaces postmodern irony, scepticism and distancing. As it has been taken up, the real world has sharply returned to critical and cultural theory at large, kicking back in the guise of critical animal studies, ecocriticism, object-oriented ontology and other outgrowths of posthumanism. In literary studies, a decade of a sometimes unprofitable fascination with objects and things may be coming to an end, having been '(over)dignified' as 'thing theory' in its most philosophical forms, as the classicist Simon Goldhill notes in *The Buried Life of Things*, a book which supplies a good example of the contested ways in which materiality has returned after the heyday of high theory.[40]

So text, language, discourse, representation, subjectivity, and a host of other familiar terms from the last thirty or so years in literary criticism and the humanities generally have been supplanted by a new intense focus on matter, bodies, agency, objects, even realism. Cognitive science has been energized, meanwhile, by its engagement with embodied, sensory, tactile and experiential forms of knowing, where once it drew inspiration from an ideal of disembodied computation. These entanglings can be found in areas of the medical humanities or in cognitive archaeology, for example in the fully worked out Theory of Material Engagement proposed by Lambros Malafouris recently in *How Things Shape the Mind*. Malafouris explores how 4E cognitive science can undergird an understanding of human artefacts in distant cultures.[41] Interesting, innovative historical work on Renaissance literary and dramatic culture has been produced separately by Evelyn Tribble and by Miranda Anderson, demonstrating some of the ways in which the extended mind was instantiated long before the digital and biotechnological cultures of today.[42] But if expressions of mind-matter entanglement come from relatively dispersed intellectual sites, such that links and loops even more extensive and knotted than we might expect now weave their way through the standard disciplinary scene, it is also the case that new forms of interdisciplinary practice are emerging within and beyond the literary humanities that make use of this mobile figure and in the process re-inflect our understanding of interdisciplinarity itself.

Until recently, the venture of interdisciplinarity has frequently been understood in terms of mappable practices of mobility.[43] According to a familiar spatial, geopolitical rhetoric (exemplified by *crossing borders*), what it means to engage with multiple disciplinary frameworks and traditions, or with collaborators in other disciplines, can be understood as an experience of travel and transposition. Whether 'border crossings' speaks of the tourist or the migrant, the phrase implies certain demands of mobility: leaving home, having to disclose one's identity at entry- and exit-points to sovereign states, a process of reaction or adjustment to whatever lies on the other side of the boundary, and so on. This way of grasping interdisciplinary interactions — an idea of lateral movement against a fixed background of stable disciplines — gives rise to further metaphors that shape what it means to exercise interdisciplinary agency: culture shock, contact zones, even acculturation.[44] Produced in these terms, the interdisciplinary researcher is assumed to behave as a passport-wielding citizen embarking valiantly across predetermined zones and thresholds.

A different rubric or schema — one of entanglement — has now begun to emerge in contrast to this once dominant one. Entanglement resists theorizing an interdisciplinary model grounded in such zonal, cartographic conceptualizations. Proposed with varying emphases by Des Fitzgerald, Felicity Callard, Will Viney and Angela Woods, the term quixotically embraces a messy, non-linear, unpredictable form of practising collaboration, one of whose conditions of possibility is to recognize some deep quality of inseparability among its constituents (i.e. agents, bodies, institutions, questions, methods, settings and apparatuses, epistemic frames).[45] To think of entangling disciplines, rather than crossing between them, means eliciting not merely a new set of relational dynamics but a differently constituted venture and performative outcome. Such operationalized and practical entanglement has special features — risk, fragility, complexity, creativity, affective force — which might be explored or lived with in some processual way, rather than ideally overcome for the sake of borders marking out professional specialization. As Fitzgerald and Callard (both social scientists) explain:

> Our use of the term entanglement thus signals our growing suspicion that the central epistemological and institutional problem is not one of whether, or to what degree, disciplinary and epistemic boundaries might be crossed. The pressing question, it seems to us, is how, as human scientists, we are to produce knowledge amid a growing realization that those boundaries are pasted across objects which are quite indifferent to a bureaucratic division between disciplines; and that scholars and researchers of all stripes invariably attend to, and live among, objects whose emergence, growth, development, action, and disappearance do not at all admit of neat cuts between the biological and the social, or between the cerebral and the cultural.[46]

Entanglement, in these terms, would supplant 'today's arid rhetoric of "interdisciplinarity"' (with its 'narrow discursive range') in at least two ways, focusing on the cognitive neuroscientific experiment as a potential paradigm case of such transformed understandings.[47] It would first mean contesting the implications of being governed by the ubiquitous 'inter-' term, where it is assumed that knowledges and methods are brought together from a prior condition of separateness. (Here, since Fitzgerald and Callard are concerned with the relationship of the social sciences and humanities to current brain science, the respective domains are the neural and the sociocultural.) Only a 'recalcitrant fantasy' of their tidy separation and historical seclusion makes possible the particular sense of purpose indicated by boundary crossing, and this has required repressing evidence of rapport, mingling or distributed purpose (shared terminologies, and so on) within and across these domains.[48] Second, the entanglement model conceives of collaboration in practical and experiential terms, as a scene made up of people, bodies, affects, technologies and other material topologies. The novelty of entangling them may produce surprising questions and effects, perhaps unease and tensions, but their relational identities emerge in (and as) concrete participatory actions.

Overlapping concerns can be identified here. Just as entanglement has arisen as a disposition of contemporary academic enquiry (a 'new' interdisciplinary impetus, loosely speaking) it has also begun to name new strategies for unlearning standard partitionings of mind and world, knowing and being, observing and acting. Regardless of whether or not its premises are genuinely new (whatever that might mean), the shift to 'entangled' models of collaboration across disciplines is observable — it is undeniably something happening, and it marks an attempt to reconceptualize interdisciplinary research — and it may even be taken as a commentary upon the possibilities of, and resistances to, the bureaucratic rise of 'interdisciplinarity' as a perceived good (caught up as it is in the politics of the neo-liberal university, as well as in how we address complex phenomena like 'the mind'). It follows from this, too, that taking account of the enworlded mind, or the spreading out of cognitive processes, entails some sort of commitment to (re-)entangling disciplinary traditions, methods and perspectives. In fact, cognitive extension has already been taken up as a way of modelling an interdisciplinary practice.[49] More to the point, mind here becomes an exemplary interdisciplinary object, a phenomenon beyond the grasp of any one discipline — something long recognized by cognitive literary studies.[50]

Whatever the charms of entanglement in these terms, the word itself has an almost vapid capacity to speak of the concerns of the present. What distinguishes it may be little more than its function of pointing to the inseparability of bodies and minds and contexts of action and meaning. Yet it has its grip: the mesh and tangle figure across the span of theory. In many contexts it expresses not just structure per se but force, life, vitality, as well as complex, dynamic reconfigurations of ideas and material structures, though it is given the task of registering agency in the most impersonal terms while elsewhere referencing the scale of individual action. It gathers its own force — that is, its rhetorical force — by appearing to absorb understandings from the biosciences or from quantum physics and indeterminacy or from systems theory — and for this reason alone the literary humanities should be prepared to look especially critically at its figurative dimension. And the literary perspective is important here: rather than being some sort of immense mimetic archive of human cognition, literature itself initiates new ways of thinking and being by virtue of the fact of its own creativity and irresponsibility. Criticism and critical thinking, too, can exhibit similar qualities. Literary experience, such as the experience of reading fiction, can be both intensely involving and detached, simultaneously immersive and recursive, cognitive and affective, embodied and mentalistic, rooted in macro pattern recognition in a text or oeuvre or genre while sensitive to the singularity of an isolated phrase or meaning. In other words, while one might come up with an 'entangled' account of literary construal, such an effort would be redundant from the start since this crisscrossing of states and entities and participant-observers already emerges from the medium itself. Without naively endorsing an entanglement model, then, either as a theoretical rubric or a practice of interdisciplinarity, the literary humanities can be alert to the special advantages of its own modes of understanding when it comes to talking about cognition, materiality and agency in these terms. Literary narratives can, for example, embed a character's and a narrator's and a reader's acts of world-construal in an inseparable tangle, as in Henry James, say; or they can they can render the multimodality of individual sensory experience, something found everywhere in James Joyce; or they can disclose the body's shaping effects on language and perception, and the mind's incorporation of other bodies, voices and presences, as one experiences in writers as different as George Eliot and Virginia Woolf. Literature can register the simultaneity of an experience's constitutive elements, as various as they may be, in a way that unites analytical and aesthetic understanding. Being at ease with entanglement in this sense means that literary studies has a particular opportunity to spread itself out, as it were, in new forms of interdisciplinary encounter with other areas of the humanities and the sciences, not simply to serve as an illustrative resource for existing concepts and hypotheses but to influence the development of these models and shape how contemporary theoretical rhetoric is formulated and thought about beyond the boundaries of any one discipline.

Notes to Chapter 10

1. Some of these thinkers are discussed in more detail below. 'Bioprejudices', referring typically to the assumption that cognition is made up by processes located only inside the skin, is a coinage of Andy Clark in *Supersizing the Mind: Embodiment, Action and Cognitive Extension* (New York: Oxford University Press, 2011), p. xxvi.
2. William E. Connelly, 'The "New Materialism" and the Fragility of Things', *Millennium: Journal of International Studies*, 41 (2013), 399–412 (p. 401).
3. Clark, *Supersizing the Mind*, p. xxviii. Emphasis added.
4. Timothy Morton, *Hyperobjects: Philosophy and Ecology after the End of the World* (Minneapolis: University of Minnesota Press, 2013), p. 65.
5. Karen Barad, *Meeting the Universe Halfway: Quantum Physics and the Entanglement of Matter and Meaning* (Durham, NC: Duke University Press, 2007).
6. For discussion of how Jacques Derrida is read by a new turn to vitalism and materialism, see Claire Colebrook, 'Matter without Bodies', *Derrida Today*, 4 (2011), 1–20. For a more nuanced account of the anti-Cartesian turn in 4E cognitive science see Michael Wheeler's *Reconstructing the Cognitive World: Taking the Next Step* (Cambridge, MA: MIT Press, 2005), especially chapters 1–3.
7. As Gillian Beer observes, 'The emphasis in these final affirmative pages [of *On the Origin of Species*] is on the delicate richness and variety of life, on complex interdependency, ecological interpretation, weaving together an aesthetic fullness'; see Beer, *Darwin's Plots: Evolutionary Narrative in Darwin, George Eliot and Nineteenth-Century Fiction*, 2nd edn (Cambridge: Cambridge University Press, 2000), p. 159.
8. Patricia Waugh, 'Discipline or Perish: English at the Tipping Point and Styles of Thinking in the Twenty-First Century', in *Futures for English Studies: Teaching Language, Literature and Creative Writing in Higher Education*, ed. by Ann Hewings, Lynda Prescott and Philip Seargeant (Basingstoke: Palgrave, 2016), pp. 19–38 (p. 25).
9. See Michael Mack, *Contaminations: Beyond Dialectics in Modern Literature, Science and Film* (Edinburgh: Edinburgh University Press, 2016). Mack acknowledges his sympathies with Barad's entanglement model, and tries similarly to demonstrate a non-dialectical approach to the interdependent emergence of seemingly pure entities like subject/object, nature/culture and science/literature.
10. Morton, *Hyperobjects*, p. 84.
11. See for example Lev Vygotsky, *Thought and Language*, ed. and trans. by Eugenia Hanfmann, Gertrude Vakar and Alex Kozulin (Cambridge, MA: MIT Press, 2012); and Humberto Maturana and Francisco Varela, *Autopoiesis and Cognition: The Realization of the Living* (Dordrecht: Reidel, 1980).
12. Raymond Tallis, *Aping Mankind: Neuromania, Darwinitis and the Misrepresentation of Humanity* (London and New York: Routledge, 2014).
13. See, for example, Lisa Blackman, *Immaterial Bodies: Affect, Embodiment, Mediation* (London: Sage, 2012); and Jan Slaby, 'Steps towards a Critical Neuroscience,' *Phenomenology and the Cognitive Sciences*, 9 (2010), 397–416.
14. Fernando Vidal, 'Brainhood, Anthropological Figure of Modernity', *History of the Human Sciences*, 22 (2009), 5–35 (p. 6).
15. See for example a 2014 special issue of the journal *Style* which sought to establish a new dawn or 'second generation' of cognitive approaches to literature inspired by 4E cognitive theories. Its editors Karin Kukkonen and Marco Caracciolo survey this shift in their 'Introduction: What is the "Second Generation?"', *Style*, 48 (2014), 261–74. Beyond narratology, the AHRC project 'A History of Distributed Cognition' (2014–18) based at the University of Edinburgh is a prominent example of scholars and critics in disciplines such as classics, history and literary studies engaging with aspects of 4E cognitive science in the analysis of culture, texts and artefacts from antiquity to the modern period; see <http://www.hdc.ed.ac.uk/welcome-hdc>.
16. Alva Noë, *Action in Perception* (Cambridge, MA: MIT Press, 2004), p. 35; p. 50.
17. Clark, *Supersizing the Mind*, p. 222. The original paper appears here as an appendix. See Andy Clark and David Chalmers, 'The Extended Mind', *Analysis*, 58.1 (1998), 7–19.

18. On cognitive niche construction, see for example Michael Wheeler and Andy Clark, 'Culture, Embodiment and Genes: Unravelling the Triple Helix', *Philosophical Transactions of the Royal Society: Biology*, 363 (2008), 3563–75.
19. Claire Colebrook, 'Vitalism and Theoria', in *Mindful Aesthetics: Literature and the Science of Mind*, ed. by Chris Danta and Helen Groth (New York and London: Bloomsbury, 2014), pp. 18–29.
20. Colebrook, 'Vitalism and Theoria', p. 40.
21. Clark, *Supersizing the Mind*, p. 169.
22. Clark, *Supersizing the Mind*, p. 59.
23. Shaun Gallagher, 'The Socially Extended Mind', *Cognitive Systems Research*, 25 (2013), 4–12 (p. 6).
24. Barad, *Meeting the Universe Halfway*, p. 140. Her coinages 'onto-epistemology' and 'ethico-onto-epistemology' act as resistance to the separation of knowing and being built into the disciplinary organization of analytic philosophy: knowing never happens in isolation from but always as a part of what is known: 'We are part of the world in its differential becoming' (p. 185).
25. Barad, *Meeting the Universe Halfway*, p. 33; p. 141. Barad rejects the the term 'beyond' to describe her work's relation to the antagonism between realism and social constructivism since it connotes a transcendence at odds with agential realism; moreover, agential realism is not a middle space between them either. 'The point is that agential realism calls into question representationalism, individualism, and other foundationalist assumptions that prop up *both*' (p. 408).
26. Barad, *Meeting the Universe Halfway*, p. 133.
27. Barad, *Meeting the Universe Halfway*, p. 244; p. 210.
28. Barad, *Meeting the Universe Halfway*, p. 33; p. 178.
29. Barad, *Meeting the Universe Halfway*, p. 216.
30. Jane Bennett, *Vibrant Matter: A Political Ecology of Things* (Durham, NC, and London: Duke University Press, 2010), p. 103.
31. See for example Graham Harman, *Tool-Being: Heidegger and the Metaphysics of Objects* (Chicago, IL: Open Court, 2002).
32. See Harman, *Tool-Being*, pp. 1–12.
33. Morton, *Hyperobjects*, p. 1.
34. 'Interobjectivity', one of five delineated qualities of hyperobjects (viscosity, nonlocality, temporal undulation and phasing being the others), is discussed in the final section of Part 1, 'What are Hyperobjects?'
35. Morton, *Hyperobjects*, p. 2.
36. Jane Bennett, 'Systems and Things: A Response to Graham Harman and Timothy Morton', *New Literary History*, 43 (2012), 225–33 (p. 227). There is an allusion to Deleuze and Guattari here in the terms 'vague' and 'vagabond', both of which come in their parsing of Husserl's idea of fuzzy aggregative essences in *A Thousand Plateaus*.
37. Timothy Morton, *Realist Magic: Objects, Ontology, Causality* (Ann Arbor, MI: Open Humanities Press, 2013), p. 122.
38. Morton, *Realist Magic*, p. 101.
39. From an interview with Karen Barad that appears in Rick Dolphijn and Iris van der Tuin, *New Materialism: Interviews and Cartographies* (Ann Arbor, MI: Open Humanities Press, 2012), p. 59.
40. Simon Goldhill, *The Buried Life of Things: How Objects Made History in Nineteenth-Century Britain* (Cambridge: Cambridge University Press, 2015), p. 11.
41. Lambros Malafouris, *How Things Shape the Mind: A Theory of Material Engagement* (Cambridge, MA: MIT Press, 2013).
42. Evelyn Tribble, *Cognition in the Globe: Attention and Memory in Shakespeare's Theatre* (New York: Palgrave Macmillan, 2011); and Miranda Anderson, *The Renaissance Extended Mind* (Basingstoke: Palgrave Macmillan, 2015).
43. For a detailed overview see Julie Thompson Klein, 'A Taxonomy of Interdisciplinarity', in *The Oxford Handbook of Interdisciplinarity*, ed. by Robert Frodeman (Oxford: Oxford University Press, 2010), pp. 15–30. A previous work by Klein, adopting the metaphor of transit in geopolitical space, reflects an emerging rhetoric of interdisciplinarity in the 1990s: *Crossing Boundaries: Knowledge, Disciplinarities and Interdisciplinarities* (Charlottesville and London: University Press of

Virginia, 1996). For an introduction to the more recent configuration of the debate, particularly as it appears from the perspective of the humanities, see Joe Moran's *Interdisciplinarity*, 2nd edn (New York: Routledge, 2010).
44. 'Contact zones', coined by Mary Louise Pratt in a 1990 keynote lecture at the MLA, 'The Arts of the Contact Zone', is used to refer to emergent intercultural spaces, sites of transformation, contestation and transculturation. Pratt went on to define the contact zone as 'the space in which peoples geographically and historically separated come into contact with each other and establish ongoing relations, usually involving conditions of coercion, radical inequality, and intractable conflict'; see Pratt, *Imperial Eyes: Travel Writing and Transculturation*, 2nd edn (London: Routledge, 2007), p. 8.
45. See Des Fitzgerald and Felicity Callard, 'Social Science and Neuroscience beyond Interdisciplinarity: Experimental Entanglements', *Theory, Culture and Society*, 32 (2015), 3–32; Fitzgerald and Callard, 'Entangling the Medical Humanities', in *The Edinburgh Companion to the Critical Medical Humanities*, ed. by Anne Whitehead, Angela Woods, Sarah Atkinson, Jane Macnaughton and Jennifer Richards (Edinburgh: Edinburgh University Press, forthcoming); Callard and Fitzgerald, *Rethinking Interdisciplinarity across the Social Sciences and Neurosciences* (Basingstoke and New York: Palgrave, 2015); and Will Viney, Felicity Callard and Angela Woods, 'Critical Medical Humanities: Embracing Entanglement, Taking Risks', *Medical Humanities*, 41 (2015), 2–7. Also relevant, if less focused on entanglement, is Callard, Fitzgerald and Woods, 'Interdisciplinary Collaboration in Action: Tracking the Signal, Tracing the Noise', *Palgrave Communications*, 1 (July) 2015, 15019. <DOI:10.1057/palcomms.2015.19>.
46. Fitzgerald and Callard, 'Social Science and Neuroscience beyond Interdisciplinarity', p. 21.
47. Fitzgerald and Callard, 'Social Science and Neuroscience beyond Interdisciplinarity', p. 4; p. 6.
48. Fitzgerald and Callard, 'Social Science and Neuroscience beyond Interdisciplinarity', p. 14.
49. See Marco Bernini and Angela Woods, 'Interdisciplinarity as Cognitive Integration: Auditory Verbal Hallucinations as a Case Study', *WIREs Cognitive Science*, 5 (2014), 603–12.
50. By way of explanation, cognitive literary studies has grown into a vibrant and increasingly respected subfield at the intersection of literary theory and criticism, narratology, poetics, linguistics, psychology and philosophy, and mapped expertly by influential figures such as Ellen Spolsky, Alan Richardson and Lisa Zunshine. For an excellent recent overview see *The Oxford Handbook of Cognitive Literary Studies*, ed. by Lisa Zunshine (Oxford: Oxford University Press, 2015). The sections and chapters of this *Handbook* (written by leading experts in the field, and on such topics as historicism, narratology, empathy and other minds, the emotions, neuroaesthetics and quantitative research) help in their own way to illustrate the rather different scope of the present chapter, which gives more attention to 4E cognition (embodied, embedded, enactive, extended) and its relations with, and entanglements in, other strands of contemporary thought and cultural theory.

CHAPTER 11

Cross-Channel Literary Crossings and the Borders of Translatability

Céline Sabiron

'"Now for the land of Rob Roy and Fergus MacIvor — the scenery immortalized by the poetical descriptions of Walter Scott"', exclaims James Starr in Jules Verne's 1877 *Les Indes noires* [*The Underground City or The Black Indies*]. The modern Lowland engineer is referring to the romanticized description of northern Scotland in Scott's historical novel *Rob Roy* (1817), as the group of miners arrive on the borders of the Highlands. '"You don't know this country, Jack?" James asks his companion. "Only by its songs, Mr. Starr, [...] and judging by those, it must be grand"', replies Jack Ryan, a Scottish miner and amateur minstrel, often busy turning the dark legends devised by his superstitious mind into ballads sung to the sound of his bagpipe.[1] The deep and lasting imprint of Scott on Verne's novel is indisputable. Scott's work serves as a 'filter through which Verne's Romantic "vision" of Scotland is expressed', asserts Verne specialist Arthur B. Evans.[2] Starr and Ryan advance in an intertextual landscape-cum-literary patchwork fraught with pieces from Scott's novels *Waverley* (1814) and *Rob Roy* (1817), and poems like *The Lady of the Lake* (1810), with Verne's Loch Katrine redolent of the struggle between King James V and powerful clan Douglas. By setting his novel in Scotland, Verne pays tribute to Scott's literary exploration of the frontier theme. He also proposes an additional figurative crossing of borders since Scotland was sometimes viewed as England's internal colony. It was an even more profitable land for the imperial motherland than India, its Eastern counterpart, thanks to its vast extent of coal mines.

The trope of the 'coal mine' ties to themes and practices of translation, in the sense of both linguistic and non-linguistic exchanges. It can serve as a metaphor for the idea of exploration, so it will be the backbone of this study. As the miner, armed with his pick, digs interconnecting subterranean galleries to obtain combustible minerals, so too does the writer, equipped with his pen, as he seeks the literary fuel feeding his creative imagination. '"Let us cut our trenches under the waters of the sea! Let us bore the bed of the Atlantic like a strainer; let us with our picks join our brethren of the United States through the subsoil of the ocean!"', cries the engineer Starr with passion.[3] The anaphoric repetition of the imperative performative structure 'let us' enacts the perforation of the soil to create axes of communication in almost surgical terms ('cut'; 'bear'; 'join'). Yet, instead of choosing to set sail through the Atlantic, it is across the English Channel that Verne proposes to steer his fictitious characters by embarking them aboard his backward-looking time machine,[4] the steamer aptly named *Rob Roy*. What turned the geographical Channel, a maritime border, into an active axis of circulation between English and French literatures in the nineteenth century? If the Channel enhances exchanges between cultures, it is also an obstacle to communication, as a border separating two countries with two different mother tongues. For the exchange to take place the physical translation must therefore be accompanied by a process of linguistic translation. '"Unhappily, I can read only those works which have been translated into French"', Verne regretfully admits to American journalist Marie A. Belloc in an 1895 interview.[5] Verne's trading and peddling of French and English literatures in *The Black Indies* illustrates the more general issue of the translatability — which is a process of translation between languages and cultures[6] — of literary texts, and in particular novels. I will examine the borders of translatability across the Channel through the two complementary motifs of 'mine' and 'water': 'mine' in its figurative nominal sense of 'mines of resources', i.e. galleries of communication, circulation of texts and ideas, but also its pronominal sense of appropriation, quest for identity ('it is mine'). What remains of a national literature in such international exchanges? 'Water' — one of the main incidents threatening mines — evokes the constant risk of flood, as well as Narcissus and his self-reflection in the water. It is also a means of conveyance, the liquid that allows for the cross-Channel movement of circulation to take place.

My investigation has been informed by recent work on cultural translation and translatability.[7] A particular example would be Margaret Cohen's concept of 'zone', which she borrows from the military and mathematical fields and adapts in her collective work *The Literary Channel* to identify 'patterns of literary transmission and exchange between Britain and France'.[8] The originality of my contribution lies in a reflexion on the role of translation in these poetical channellings.

I. Circulation as Contamination

'Over the Water':[9] *A Risk of Infiltration*

In late eighteenth- and early nineteenth-century Britain, internal boundaries were being removed through union between England and Scotland, in 1707, and between Great Britain and Ireland, in 1800. However external boundaries were very firmly sealed off to prevent any contamination from neighbouring 'degenerate' France. Any political and cultural circulation between the two countries was therefore hampered, France featuring as a threat to the United Kingdom's political peace and moral righteousness.[10] Walter Scott's historical novels, published between 1814 and 1828 but with plots set in the previous century, reflect on this risk of infection through liquid images of water infiltration, from seepage to flood.

The Highlanders reside beyond the Highland Line, which is geologically materialized by the Highland Boundary Fault, splitting Scotland into two. They are compared to 'a stream of rushing water',[11] a raging ocean whose surging waves threaten to flow over the coast and to flood everything in their way. The same watery symbol is used when talking about the French:

> [T]he hitherto silent expectation of the people became changed into that deep and agitating murmur, which is sent forth by the ocean before the tempest begins to howl. The crowded populace, as if the motions had corresponded with the unsettled state of their minds, fluctuated to and fro without any visible cause of impulse, like the agitation of the waters, called by sailors the ground-swell.[12]

The passage highlights the subversive, stifled whisper uttered by an altogether deceitful and unseizable chimeral water monster coming from France as demonstrated by an undercurrent of words with French origin ('murmur'; 'tempest'; 'populace') filtering through the otherwise English paragraph. The French language is gradually coming through, announcing a rising of the linguistic tide and storm, as the noise, first muffled ('silent'; 'agitating murmur') becomes deafening ('howl'; 'swell'). The rhythm of these serpentine sentences conveys the relentless, implacable progress of the treacherous 'French' water waves that eat away the English shore.[13]

The English Channel is a very porous limit and a constant source of concern in *The Antiquary* (1816). The small Scottish port of Fairfort is under the threat of a French invasion during the Napoleonic Empire which seeks to extend its national borders throughout Europe. '"The French will be ower to herry us ane o' thae day"', insists the old prophet Edie Ochiltree.[14] The French irruption is even briefly enacted before being belied. The signal of an impending invasion is given, thus causing panic among the community: '"[t]he French coming to murder us, Monkbarns!" screamed Miss Griselda. "The beacon, the beacon! — the French, the French! — murder, murder! and waur than murder!" cried the two handmaidens like the chorus of an opera.'[15] The disarticulated language with its ungrammatical syntax and paratactic style mirrors the extreme confusion ('[s]uch was the scene of general confusion'[16]) triggered by this false external threat. The language is decomposed to signal the risk of a dismantling of British national borders. The Fairfort community also harbours 'an affiliated society of the *soi disant* Friends of the People.'[17] Through this reference, Scott ironically criticizes the society born out of the French Revolution, which, in the name of freedom, was involved in acts of transgression and contributed to the regime of Terror. The threat of waterborne infection is conveyed through the contamination of the language which is unconstrained in an almost un-British manner, with French phrases like '*soi disant*' and '*insouciance*' seeping through the text. The dissolution of the linguistic barriers testifies to the potential dissolution of political boundaries. The alternating rising and falling tone taken by the women mimics the to-and-fro rocking of the waves — with the dashes embodying the receding water — which turn into a swell through the last long exclamatory scream: '"murder, murder! and waur than murder!"' The houses seem to be bouncing up and down as if tossed about by the sea: 'the windows were glancing with a hundred lights [...] appearing and disappearing rapidly.'[18] The yeomanry takes on watery qualities, as the farmers are said to be 'pouring from their different glens'.[19] It is thus through images of water, be they metaphorical (the raging ocean alluding to the French Revolution) or literal (the risk of a French attack from the sea), that the contamination may occur. Scott's novels bring to the fore an interplay of border and incursion, as one cannot exist without the other.

'A Necessary Contagion'

The Channel served as a limit even if it was one that was full of holes. As Enid Starkie put it, 'in the nineteenth century, France was generally held in universal contempt by the English, except as a playground for frivolous pleasure,'[20] be it debauchery or, worse, adultery, and French literature was deemed debased by its state of depravity. George Sand was thus debunked for her immorality and cynicism, Honoré de Balzac for the coarseness of his plots, while Victor Hugo was labelled as the 'champion of vice, shame and degradation that transgressed the bounds of decency.'[21] If the culture of France had been admired in the seventeenth and eighteenth centuries, it was later desecrated by the outrages of the revolution, the tyranny of upstart Napoleon, and finally by the country's defeat and humiliation in 1815, with the restoration of the Bourbon dynasty through foreign arms. Starkie claims that little was known in England of the new French Romantic movement until the late 1830s, and very little even then. Yet, this statement is a generalization and French literature did seep into English culture through all sorts of little channels, or else there would have been no need for the widespread denunciation of it. In the 1820s the young Elizabeth Barrett Browning was a great reader of George Sand and Madame de Staël for instance,[22] while Eugene Sue was popular in England in the middle of the century.[23] However, the British also felt that very little valuable literature was produced by their neighbours who were almost exclusively focused on trade and above all politics in the first half of the nineteenth century:

> [t]he present state of France, though full of promise with respect to her commercial and political advancement, is not very favourable to the immediate interests of her literature. The minds of a great part of the population are still too unsettled for such calm pursuits [...]. Accordingly we find that [...] there is but little original produced in the department of literature; and the Press is chiefly employed in circulating either new editions of long established works, or translations from the popular writers of other countries.[24]

French cross-Channel influence certainly was a seepage rather than a flood but there were quite a few inevitable cases of infiltration. The Channel was thus a double-sided limit: while it was mostly waterproof on the English side, it proved very porous on the French one.

As shown by Eric Partridge in his 1924 study *The French Romantics' Knowledge of English Literature (1820–1848)*, the French had been absorbing English literature with dazzling speed, so that the circulation of literature across the Channel was one-sided, and mostly composed of translations of volumes by Shakespeare, Byron, Wordsworth, the Lake Poets, and Scott. Scott's novels, and in particular *Guy Mannering, Old Mortality, Rob Roy, Ivanhoe* and *Quentin Durward*, were extremely popular across the Channel.[25] 'The overwhelming evidence from all quarters is that

Walter Scott was not only the most popular Scottish writer among French readers but was simply one of the most successful authors in France. [...] Taking all known records of Parisian "cabinets de lecture" between 1815 and 1830, Scott, with twenty-six citations, is second only to Madame Genlis with twenty-seven, in a list of 172 men and women [all novelists].'[26]

And yet, Scott's work is also very Scottish, with plots revolving round the Union of the two kingdoms of England and Scotland and the subsequent Jacobite Rebellions, followed by the Highland repression organized to pacify the country. Not only do the novels deal with Scottish, and more generally British, history and politics, but they are also culturally and linguistically rooted in Scotland with numerous references to Border culture, Presbyterianism, and the use of a fabricated language (made of Scots and fake Gaelic), especially in dialogues. Despite this very distinct Scottish setting and language, Scott's novels were adapted for the French stage and the opera; they inspired painters liked Eugène Delacroix, Delaroche and Scheffer, as well as imitators.[27] Most of all, they fuelled the imagination of many nineteenth-century French writers in the making: Charles Nodier in his 1822 fantastic short story *Trilby ou le Lutin d'Argail* [*Trilby or the Fairy of Argail*] dealt with the familiar spirits of Scotland through the figure of a goblin named Trilby, modelled on Scott's *Black Dwarf* (1816). One of Honoré de Balzac's earliest novels, *Clotilde de Lusignan, ou le beau Juif* [*Clotilde de Lusignan or the Handsome Jew*] (1822), was also influenced by Scott's *Ivanhoe* and his Jewish protagonist Rebecca. Writing in 1828, Sainte-Beuve commented on this Scott fever in France and declared that his was an 'epoch in which the imitation of Walter Scott was almost a necessary contagion, even for the highest talents.'[28] Although 'contagion' usually means infection, Sainte-Beuve is using it with an awareness of its etymological root, as it comes from Latin *contagionem*, related to *contingere*, which is to 'touch closely'. The term thus implies some contact, a physical exchange, while the qualification 'even' is both a tribute to Scott and an expression of amazement. How could this literary fad from across the Channel have crossed and penetrated French culture not only so quickly but also so profoundly, so much so that a whole generation of French writers even regarded him as French?[29] How can a literary text serve as a common point of reference in defining affiliations within national and transnational frameworks? What is it that makes a text so 'conveyable', so translatable to another language and culture? Scott himself raised the issue in his own journal on his return from his 1826 visit in France, as he could not but acknowledge his incredible and unsuspected popularity across the Channel:

> Ere I leave *la belle France*, however, it is fit I should express my gratitude for the unwontedly kind reception which I met with at all hands. It would be an unworthy piece of affectation did I not allow that I have been pleased — highly pleased — to find a species of literature intended only for my own country has met such an extensive and favourable reception in a foreign land where there was so much *a priori* to oppose its progress (10 Nov. 1826).[30]

The historical context undoubtedly played an important part in Scott's fame on both sides of the Channel. Considering the relative lack of literature produced in France in the 1820s and the national interest in history, and mostly that from the Middle Ages, as well as the anti-revolutionary feeling prevailing during the Restoration period,[31] it is no wonder that Scott's historical novels, and in particular *Ivanhoe* (1820) and *Quentin Durward* (1823) centred on medieval rivalry and set in the twelfth and fifteenth centuries respectively, should have proved so resourceful a mine, to take up Maggin's metaphor, for the French:

> The most popular employment of the learned in France at present seems to be history. It is the mine in which almost every man of talent hath set himself to work [...]. And in the historic mine, to continue my metaphor, revolution is the vein of metal most prized and followed. Vertot seems to reanimate each pen. Mazure has written our Revolution of 1688, and Guigot is busy upon our anterior one; while Thierry has attained the highest success, by his History of the conquest of England by the Normans [...]. With us, who have been a long time wearied by the middle ages, and all that relates to them, such a work would not have the smallest chance of being read. But in France, where the mania of research and historic retrospect is altogether new, not long since, indeed, awakened, for the first time, by the volumes of Sismondi, works on this subject and area are most greedily perused and spoken of.[32]

The French historical context cannot on its own account for Scott's glory on foreign soils, which almost matched his popularity throughout Great Britain, and in particular in England: the first edition of *Waverley*, consisting of one thousand copies, was sold out within two days of publication, and Scott himself was made a Baronet in 1820, and granted a doctor's degree by both Oxford and Cambridge. In order to understand why English literature, and Scott's novels in particular, was such a mine of resources for the French at the time I now turn to a consideration of the borders of translatability from two main spheres, namely the political and the literary.

II. Scott's Novels and the Borders of Translatability

Balance, 'Middlingness', and Juste Milieu

After the fall of the Napoleonic Empire in 1814, France was concerned with questioning itself, its identity, and rebuilding the nation. The restoration period (1814–30) was dominated by French doctrinaires, i.e. royalists who aspired to reconcile monarchy and Revolution, authority and liberty, and who made 'middlingness' the programme of organized political parties.[33] 'Middlingness' — or *juste milieu* in French — is a neologism borrowed from George Eliot's *Felix Holt, the Radical* (1866), chapter 5 of which starts with an epigraph in which the second citizen says '"'Tis a poor climax, to my weaker thought, | That future middlingness."' The just middle was the guiding ideal of the July Monarchy (1830–38), a liberal constitutional monarchy led by King Louis-Philippe. Dominant elements in literature and political rhetoric were marked by Classicism in literature and a concomitant political search for conflict resolution through the triumph of harmony and order.[34] Scott's advocacy of the middle way was embodied by his most radical, least moderate Jacobite protagonist, Hughes Redgauntlet: '"I hoped that some middle way might be found, and it shall — and must.'"[35] The eponymous character's stance seemed attractive in this (French) context, which explains why the French looked up to their nearest neighbours, who shared a similar history and whose constitution was judged to be a source of inspiration and a fit model by which to regulate the ideas of a younger French generation. The mechanism of representative government was still new in France in the 1820s and '30s and the attention of well-educated young men had naturally been directed to British institutions, as mentioned by Scott himself in his 1827 *Life of Napoleon Bonaparte*.[36] Numerous eighteenth-century philosophers and writers, such as Montesquieu (who considered the English Constitution a 'beautiful system' in which 'power stops power'),[37] his disciple, the Comte de Mirabeau, or Voltaire in his *Philosophical Letters* and his *Philosophical Dictionary*, had already demanded an English-like constitutional monarchy. Voltaire, together with Rousseau and the Abbé Prévost, had even found shelter in England after suffering from the atmosphere of intolerance in France and being chased out of their own country. These values of balance, and moderation, already powerful in late eighteenth-century France, had gathered momentum and reached the apex of their popularity in the early- to mid-nineteenth century. Scott's call through his novels for a constitution that achieved a balance between the ultras of both parties did not leave his French readers indifferent, all the more so since, being the theatre of history in the nineteenth century, France was also very receptive to the new subgenre of the historical novel which Scott had invented.

The Waverley Novels as Translation Novels: The Channel versus the 'Prism'[38]

Scott's novels appealed to the French across the Channel, not only on political, philosophical and literary grounds, but also because they were metatextual texts staging the concept of translation and theorizing their own crossing motifs and processes. These works were arguably more easily translatable into the French language and culture because they were translation novels, 'offering an act of simultaneous translation'[39] within the texts through the figure of the English protagonist who carries out an act of translation for the English readership. In *Guy Mannering*, the eponymous English soldier is destabilized by the lexicon and accent of the Lowlanders, as illustrated by the following exchange between him and the owner of an old dilapidated house:

> 'Troth, I ken na, unless ye like to gae doun and speer for quarters at the Place. I'se warrant they'll take ye, whether ye be gentle or semple.'
> 'Simple enough, to be wandering here at such a time of night,' thought Mannering, who was ignorant of the meaning of the phrase, but how shall I get to the place, as you call it?'
> 'Ye maun haud wessel by the end o' the loan, and take the tent o' the jaw-hole.'
> 'O, if you get to easel and wessel again, I am undone! — Is there no boy that could guide me to this place?'[40]

Mannering misinterprets the words 'gentle or semple', i.e. gentleman or commoner, which he understands as 'soft', or 'sweet', another meaning of 'gentle', or 'simple-minded.' The cardinal points are also misconstrued, for 'easel' commonly refers to a wooden frame used by painters while working on their canvasses, and 'wessel' is mistaken for 'vessel', that is a ship, or large boat. Scott resorts to antanaclasis ('gentle', 'semple') and paronomasia (through the pairings of 'semple'/'simple', and 'wessel'/'vessel') in order to open up meanings, and highlight a certain linguistic hybridism and tension. In *Waverley*, this need for translation is signalled in chapter 8, when the eponymous character discovers the village of Tully Veolan on the border between the Lowlands and the Highlands. The whole scene defies definition within English linguistic terms: 'to say the truth, a mere Englishman, in search of the *comfortable*, a word peculiar to his native tongue, might have wished the clothes less scanty, the feet and legs somewhat protected from the weather, the head and complexion shrouded from the sun.'[41] The use of 'in search of', comparisons such as 'less', and adverbs like 'somewhat' testifies to the difficulty at finding the right word to depict what is seen, and to the absence of equivalence in another language ('a word peculiar to his native tongue'). As Alison Lumsden, observes: 'To an English outsider, then, the scene can only be described by what it is not. It requires an almost literal act of translation for its English audience.'[42] It is an act which becomes even more acute when the character moves up to the Highlands, where both Waverley and the reader are quite literally learning a new language, as the protagonist is told that a 'town' refers to a house, the adjective 'innocent' alludes to a simple-minded person, while 'the *dark hag* [...] had nothing to do with a black cat or a broomstick, but was simply a portion of oak copse which was to be felled that day'.[43] Scott plays with a language that is both familiar and foreign; he multiplies the meaning of words by furrowing new channels of meanings, by creating new lexical connections, thereby inventing an artificial language out of Scots and fake or 'corrupt' Gaelic — which he did not himself know, apart from a few odd words. In his aim to come up with a Unionist language that could be shared, he coined more than 1500 neologisms, among them the adjectives 'harrowing',[44] 'upsetting',[45] and 'vocalic',[46] the noun 'Gael'[47] to talk about a Highlander, or the substantives 'stag-hunting',[48] 'hobby'[49] and 'stocking',[50] which are now part of standard contemporary English. With characters speaking different existing languages (Scots, French, Spanish, German, Latin and even Greek, to name but a few) as well as non-existent ones, the only common language seems to be that of translation, since the protagonists must constantly carry out an act of translation to understand one another. The channel image is thus complicated into a prism with refractions going in all sorts of different directions. As to the water metaphor, it gives way to an optical one since the source language is not only English but a wide spectrum of languages. This multilingual and even hybrid English is bound to challenge any translator of Scott's texts who may have to rechannel cultural and linguistic resources, i.e. to undermine them — in the etymological sense of the word which is to 'render unstable by digging at the foundation'.

Translation as a Common Language in a Reterritorialized Space

Translation, this necessary common language between the characters, is spatialized, as Scott's stories usually move into a geographical and linguistic grey zone, a third space, a conjunctive space which preserves the memory of a former disjunction. This in-between space could be seen as a definition of the space of translation which defies all binarism between the source language and the target language. It is both double and bifocal, closed and open, limited and unlimited, finite and infinite. This space emerges in the novels through displacement, the transplantation from a realistic, down-to-earth Scotland into an unknown, foreign, exotic land of the imagination. As *Waverley*'s eponymous protagonist is about to cross the border into the Highlands, the outlines of the landscape are hardly drawn when they are suddenly blurred by the foam over the stream ('foaming stream'[51]) to give it an unearthly, ethereal appearance favourable to Scott's imagination: 'Edward gradually approached the Highlands of Perthshire, which at first had appeared a blue outline in the horizon, but now swelled into huge gigantic masses.'[52] Scott immediately deprives the landscape of any characteristics that would aestheticize it, following the principles of Edmund Burke's theory on the sublime. It is because of the absence of any well-defined limits that the image of the border partakes of the sublime. While Waverley is nearing the outlaw's den on the Highland Line, he sees a light on the horizon: '[t]he light, which they now approached more nearly, [...] appeared plainly to be a large fire.'[53] This very literal description, given in plain, factual style with some indication of time sequence ('gradually'; 'at first'; 'now') is followed by a more figurative depiction marked by a more vivid imagination. This 'sudden figurative leap'[54] generated by the impact with the border aims at blurring an image which had previously been clearly outlined: 'but whether kindled upon an island or the main-land, Edward could not determine.'[55] The fire suddenly turns into a

> red glaring orb [...] rest[ing] on the very surface of the lake itself, and resembl[ing] the fiery vehicle in which the Evil Genius of an oriental tale traverses land and sea. [...] Edward could discover that this large fire, amply supplied with branches of pine-wood by two figures, who, in the red reflection of its light, appeared like demons, was kindled in the jaws of a lofty cavern.[56]

Comparisons ('resembled the fiery vehicle'; 'appeared like demons'), metaphors ('the jaws of a lofty cavern') and hyperboles ('lofty'; 'large'; 'amply') are thus combined to convey an even more sublime image of the landscape. The forbidden is here poetical as Scott experiments with styles and genres. This poetical licence over the border is both transgressive and creative: words are freed from lexical, grammatical and semantic constraints. The writer is embarked on a quest for an asymptotic infinite that he can only come close to without ever reaching it. Scott aims at extending human experience through a liberation of the language which does not abide by any rule or code, and which constantly requires translating. Scotland's space is deterritorialized[57] — and then reterritorialized into an imagined romanticized Scott-land where translation is the only language. Scott's novels thus question the borders of translatability by dealing with the untranslatable and the untranslated, for instance, when the narrator sometimes admits to his powerlessness by using ellipses for words spoken in Gaelic ('[t]he word was given in Gaelic'[58]). This translation process taking place within the original English text is further complicated through the translation of Scott's novels into a foreign language, and in particular French. Whereas the text diffracts meanings by offering different translations for each word or by coining new words within the text, we are going to see that translation conversely tends to polarize meanings and turns the prism back into a channel. As mines of resources circulate across the border, they are undermined, appropriated by the translator who makes them his own ('mine').

III. Translation as Appropriation

The Translator's Aesthetics of Pleasure: Winning over the Target Readership

During the late eighteenth century there was a growing debate between the French and English traditions of translation on one side, and the new German strategy on the other. In 1776 German writer and philosopher Johann Gottfried Herder famously complained that 'the French, who are much too proud of their own taste, adapt all things to it, rather than try to adapt themselves to the taste of another time.'[59] At the time, translation was commonly viewed as an interpretation,[60] i.e. an appropriation or reduction — in a word a domestication — of the foreign text, depending on the linguistic structures and cultural traditions of the target language. The goal of the translator was then to make the text accessible and understandable to a foreign readership; hence the 'conservative and openly assimilationist approach to the foreign text.'[61] Scott's novels were very popular in France, but of course only in translation: most French people could not read the source texts in their original language since English was not taught at school until late in the nineteenth century. In fact, nearly all English-language works until after the Second World War passed first through the medium of the French language and the prism of French thought. French readers of Scott then had to rely on the work of translators, like Auguste Jean-Baptiste Defauconpret (1767–1843), the official conveyor of Scott's voice across the Channel; hence the great influence of translation in the reception of literary works. 'What do we remember of those who translated Goethe and Scott, who were in fact the responsible agents of influence? Histories of the novel tell us of the impact on Europe of Fenimore Cooper and Dickens. They do not mention Auguste Jean-Baptiste Defauconpret through whose translations the impact was made',[62] wonders George Steiner is his seminal book *After Babel*. Defauconpret was very prolific as a translator, getting through 120 translations, or 500 volumes, of English-language fiction between 1816 and 1828, and yet he was not an English specialist, but a former Arts student at the University of Paris. He studied law and for fifteen years practised as a notary. But a reversal of fortune forced him to seek a livelihood in London, where he devoted himself entirely to the pursuit of literature. Although he assisted in the compilation of dictionaries and encyclopaedias and even wrote two historical novels in the manner of Scott, he is now remembered solely for his translation work, which he undertook with his son Charles-Auguste Defauconpret, and a couple of other collaborators. Defauconpret may be best remembered as a translator but he was hardly Scott's only translator; others included Joseph Martin (*Guy Mannering*) as early as 1816, Sophie de Maraise (*The Antiquary*), Henri Villemain, Amédie Chaillot, Gigault de la Bédollières, and Amédée Pichot, with whom Defauconpret collaborated. Yet, the story of how he gained the upper hand illustrates the control that was at stake in the translation economy, which was in keeping with the level of the circulation of goods at the time. Free trade was not put into place before the middle of the nineteenth century, which marked the end of protectionism as exemplified by the 1846 repeal of the Corn Law. Cross-Channel circulation was protected and transactions between the French and English were hardly open-ended, including in the publishing world. Defauconpret managed to become Scott's official French translator after the 1822 Mephistophelian pact that the Faust-like publishers of Scott in London signed with the French publisher Charles Gosselin. It was agreed that Scott's London agents Black, Young and Young would give Defauconpret the proof sheets of Scott's novels straight from the press in exchange for the translator's inviolable secrecy concerning this transaction. The benefit of this secret transaction was that, from then on, every work from Scott's pen came out on the same day in English in Edinburgh and London, and in French in Paris. Defauconpret was thus given priority over his other French and European counterparts, so that he could get his translations on the market long before his rivals. The year 1822 marked a turning point: for the first time French editions of new Scott novels kept pace with the issue of the originals. That is why for Lyons, 'the publishing history of Walter Scott in France can [...] be divided into periods of introduction (1816–20), of consolidation (1820–22), and of great popularity (1822 to 1827 or 1828).'[63] The introduction period is linked to the appearance of the first French edition of Scott's complete works, in the duodecimo format, by Nicolle and Ladvocat, while the consolidation and popularity periods stem from the publishing of Defauconpret's translations and Scott's second visit in Paris in the autumn of 1826.

Defauconpret's aesthetics of translation followed the manner of eighteenth-century translators, absorbing the general sense of the original text but rendering it into the target language in their own terms to adapt to the new readership, as he himself explained in an 1819 letter addressed to the editor of the *Journal des Débats* [*Journal of Debates*] who had accused him of exercising too much liberty in his translation of Lady Morgan's *Florence MacCarthy*:

> Je crois qu'en faisant passer un *roman* d'une langue dans une autre, le premier devoir d'un traducteur est de le mettre en état de plaire aux nouveaux lecteurs qu'il veut lui procurer. Le goût des Anglais n'est pas toujours conforme au nôtre [...]. J'ai donc supprimé quelques détails qui auraient pu paraître oiseux à des lecteurs français et j'ai raccourci les portraits de quelques personnages qui ne sont aucunement liés à l'action. Je me suis permis la même liberté à l'égard d'un auteur dont la Réputation, n'en déplaise à Lady Morgan, est infiniment au-dessus de la sienne en Angleterre. M. Walter Scott, et la manière dont on a accueilli en France *Les Puritains d'Écosse*, *Rob-Roy*, et tout récemment *La Prison d'Édimbourg*, m'a prouvé que je n'avais pas eu tort.[64]
>
> [I believe that in importing a *novel* from one language to another, a translator's first duty is to make it capable of pleasing the new readers that he wishes to

> acquire for it. The taste of the English does not always conform to our own […]. I have thus suppressed some details which might have appeared otiose to the French reader, and I have abbreviated the portraits of several characters that are quite unconnected to the action. I have taken the same liberty with respect to an author whose reputation, *pace* Lady Morgan, stands infinitely above hers in England, Mr Walter Scott; and the welcome accorded in France to *Old Mortality*, *Rob Roy* and only recently, *The Heart of Mid-Lothian*, has proved that I was not wrong.]⁶⁵

Defauconpret, accused of excessive freedom and even rewritings of the author's thoughts in his translation of Lady Morgan's *Florence MacCarthy*, clearly stated his adherence to a classical poetics. The translatability of the Waverley novels across the Channel also stems from the fact that they were not only translated but in parts rewritten to 'please' the new readership and match French tastes. Defauconpret's practice of translation was thus bound to change the nature of Scott's texts which paradoxically stopped being translation novels once they were translated in such a manner. From hybrid multilingual texts they became mostly monolithic and monolingual. At the time the quality of his translations was measured by the number of sales, and not by its relation to the original source text. Following the classical French model of translation as a 'belle infidèle' ('faithless beauty') and taking considerable licence, Defauconpret was less the translator of Scott's texts than the real writer of the French Waverley novels.⁶⁶

Being Scott in disguise across the Channel, Defauconpret could be seen as another of the translator's personae, proceeding to contextual and stylistic rewritings in order to refashion Scott's texts for the French. He practised a high level of textual manipulation on poetical and ideological grounds, since some of his remodelling was politically motivated. His tendency towards simplification, clarification and thus Manichaeism is opposite to Scott's, constantly promoting a middle way through the blurring of antagonistic values or characters in the style of 'Middlingness' and *'Juste Milieu'*. If we compare the following two passages from *Waverley*, the translated text is much more assertive (as seen in my own English translation of Defauconpret's French translation), the act of translation figuratively becoming an act of prosecution: 'si l'ont me traduit devant un conseil de guerre'. 'Traduire' is here used in the metaphorical sense of being brought to justice, as if translating consisted in separating the facts from the fancy, of separating good from bad. The translator also voluntarily omits the context which twists the meaning of the scene, suppresses the modals, modal periphrases and comparisons used by Scott to qualify a statement:

> He might be delivered up to the military law, which, in the midst of the civil war, was not likely to be scrupulous in the choice of its victims, or the quality of the evidence. Nor did he feel much more comfortable at the thoughts of a trial before a Scottish court of justice, where he knew the laws and forms differed in many respects from those of England, and had been taught to believe, however erroneously, that the liberty and rights of the subject were less carefully protected. A sentiment of bitterness rose in his mind against the government.⁶⁷

Si l'on me traduit devant un conseil de guerre, se disait-il, je ne dois m'attendre à aucune indulgence, pas même à l'examen réfléchi de l'accusation dirigée contre moi. Les circonstances où nous nous trouvons lui feront une loi de frapper impitoyablement tous ceux qui paraîtront avoir allumé la guerre civile. Je ne serai pas mieux traité si je parais devant la cour royale d'Écosse ; je sais qu'elle n'est pas très scrupuleuse sur le choix de ses victimes, et que la moindre apparence lui tient de preuve. Ces réflexions le portèrent à détester le gouvernement.[68]

[If I am court-martialled, he said to himself, I should expect no indulgence whatsoever, not even the careful study of the charge levelled against me. The circumstances under which we find ourselves will only and relentlessly empower the law which will then mercilessly strike all those who will seem to have sparked the civil war. I will not be better treated if I appear before the royal court of Scotland; I know it is not very scrupulous about its choice of victims, and that the slightest appearance of guilt serves as a proof. These thoughts led him to the government.][69]

The change of discourse type — from free indirect speech in the source text to direct speech in the target text — contributes to dramatizing the scene and victimizing the hero. The French translation points at a difference of treatments between the English and the Scots, therefore bringing out a feeling of injustice, through the erasure of the additional comment 'however erroneously' inserted by the narrator in the original version to show that the sentiment is groundless. The modal periphrasis 'not likely to' (in 'was not likely to be scrupulous') becomes a standard negation (i.e. 'n'est pas très scrupuleuse') in the target text, and comparatives or the indefinite adjective 'aucune' ('none') are added ('aucune indulgence', when the English text reads 'less carefully protected', and 'la moindre apparence lui tient de preuve', when it is only 'the quality of the evidence' that is questioned in English) to radicalize the tone and bring out the overall state of iniquity reigning in Scotland. The subjectivity of the character's viewpoint, highlighted by the opinion of the narrator filtering through, is completely lost in translation. Defauconpret has also changed the order of the text, and therefore mixed the argument, since the alleged lack of qualm in the choice of victims or quality of the evidence is applied to the Scottish court in the translated passage, whereas it refers to the military law in the original text. The qualified picture drawn by the narrator in Scott's text becomes a black and white image, with scapegoat Waverley on the one hand and the evil tyrannical British government on the other. The last sentence of the paragraph 'détester le gouvernement' [to loathe the government] to translate 'a sentiment of bitterness' is symptomatic of the translator's translation style. Defauconpret's overt radicalism, i.e. his lack of stylistic moderation, is visible in long passages or shorter expressions, as when the 'melancholy day'[70] becomes 'a day of sadness and death' ('jour de tristesse et de deuil') in the translated text, since Edward takes leave of his family to travel up north.

Translation as Manipulation and Rewriting

The translator aims to please the French taste for dramas at the time by suppressing most of the narrative's subtleties and drawing a Manichean picture. He also manipulates the text, changing the titles of chapters — with 'Waverley-Honour: A Retrospect'[71] becoming 'Le Château de Waverley sans tache' ('Waverley's stainless Castle'; my translation) for instance — the level of language, and the use of Scots in dialogue. In the following passage, Edward Waverley is journeying into the Highlands with a guide Donald Bean Lean:

> After journeying a considerable time in silence, he could not help asking, 'Was it far to the end of their journey?'
> 'Ta cove was tree, four mile; but as duinhe-wassel was a wee taiglit, Donald could, tat is, might — would — should send ta curragh.'

This conveyed no information. The *curragh* which was promised might be a man, a horse, a cart, or chaise; and no more could be got from the man with the battle-axe but a repetition of 'Aich ay! ta curragh.'[72]

> Après avoir marché assez longtemps en silence, il ne put s'empêcher de demander s'ils étaient loin du but de leur voyage.
> — La caverne était à trois ou quatre milles, répondit le montagnard; mais le *duinhewassel* étant un peu fatigué, Donald devrait — pourrait — devrait bien envoyer le *curragh*.
> Cette réponse n'apprenait pas grand-chose à Édouard. Le *curragh* qui lui était promis pouvait être un homme, un cheval, une charrette, une chaise de poste; mais il ne put tirer de l'homme à la hache d'armes que les mots: *Aich, ay, ta curragh*.[73]

Through this exchange in direct speech between the Englishman and the Highlander, the narrator wishes to highlight the linguistic barrier separating the two men. Defauconpret does not manage to keep the colloquialism of the language, be it through the lexis or the spelling. His translation is flattened, standardized through the use of a rather formal and grammatical French language, like 'ta cove' translated as if it were 'the cavern' in English, or 'a wee taiglit' being translated as if it were 'a little bit tired'. The specificity of the Highlander's expression is undermined, subdued, so much so that both Waverley and Donald seem to be speaking the same language in the translation, the Scots being reduced to a couple of foreign-sounding words (*duinhewassel* and *curragh*).

The Waverley novels have a particular aptness for translation because, as mentioned earlier, translation is the common language of Scott's protagonists. If the language of the text is already a translated language, it seems to loosen the translator's obligations to the original. This helps to account for Defauconpret's mimetic act and assumed decision to rewrite Scott's texts for a French audience, thus transplanting them into a standardized language easily understandable by his readership, but also into a history and culture that readers could share. The 'Reformed Kirk of Scotland' is for example simply translated as 'l'Église d'Écosse' without any reference to the Protestant Reformation. In *Rob Roy* the translator gets rid of all the criticisms raised against Catholicism, and the sentence '"There are many good men Catholics"'[74] is even inflated to '"D'où vient donc votre prévention contre les catholiques...? Il y a parmi eux de tout aussi braves gens que parmi nous."' ['But where does your prejudice against Catholics come from...? There are as many brave people among them as among us']. Likewise, he omits all religious discussions between Frank and the Catholic Diana Vernon, including their first serious exchange, where Diana ribs Frank for being a 'heretic', and Frank compares nuns to 'imprisoned singing birds.'[75] By bringing Scott's writing into line with the conventions of French Classicism, and by refashioning Scott's protagonists as sentimental heroes, Defauconpret, or Scott's distorted voice across the Channel, inadvertently created a highly influential formal hybrid. This paradoxically caused the French novel to diverge from the example pioneered by Scott himself as it helped give a new lease, within French Romanticism, to the Gothic, but it played a significant role in the evolution from the sentimental to the realistic novel in France. Defauconpret's translation played a major part in the translatability of Scott's works across the Channel, providing the Scottish author with a major French breakthrough and beyond his first major European success.

Conclusion

To conclude, the eighteenth and the first half of the nineteenth centuries contributed to the erasure of national borders, in particular through an increase of literary circulation, transportation ('transport', from old French *transporter* meaning 'carry or convey across') and therefore of translation (from Latin *translatio*, i.e. 'bearing across') across the Anglo-French border. To take up the two complementary motifs of 'mine' and 'water' which opened this article and served as a linking thread throughout my study, the Channel facilitated the circulation of texts and ideas between the two neighbouring countries, allowing mines of resources to be shared, borrowed, and adapted. Yet it was a double-sided limit which was mostly waterproof on the English side and quite porous on the French side in the nineteenth century. Scott's novels use such hybrid multilingual English that they become translation novels, with translation serving as the common language between the characters. It is the Unionist language spoken in a land that is neither Scotland, nor England, but a fluid, in-between, liminal space where creativity can emerge. Yet, when Scott's novels are conveyed across to France and therefore translated into French, they tend to lose their prismatic effects. They are under*mined* because they are rechannelled by the translator who appropriates them. Instead of working like 'a prism' by opening up and diffracting meanings, the geographical Channel is reduced to its core minimal function of channelling literature from one country to another in a rather polarized and therefore reduced way. Far from showing the wide range of meanings in Scott's texts, the Channel in the early part of the nineteenth century only serves to narrow them down, as the translator fails to show the richness of the source text in order to privilege one interpretation which is judged more suitable to the tastes of the receiving culture.

Nevertheless, this impoverishment of Scott's texts eventually proved a richness for French and even European literature, as the French Waverley novels influenced many Romantic writers who modelled their works on the one whom they considered as their master: Alfred de Vigny, Alexandre Dumas — who even translated *Ivanhoe* into French in 1820 — Victor Hugo, Balzac, Jules Verne, or more recently Hergé and *L'Île noire* (1938). Defauconpret's translations have been essential to the development of French historical and maritime novels.

Notes to Chapter 11

1. Jules Verne, *The Underground City or The Black Indies*, in *Works of Jules Verne*, ed. by Charles F. Horne, vol. IX (New York: F. Tyler Daniels Company, 1911), ch. 15, <http://www.gutenberg.org/files/1355/1355-h/1335-h.htm> [accessed 25 January 2016].
2. Arthur B. Evans, 'Literary Intertexts in Jules Verne's *Voyages Extraordinaires*', *Science-Fiction Studies*, 23.2 (July 1996), 171–87 (p. 177).
3. Verne, *The Underground City*, ch. 8, <http://www.gutenberg.org/files/1355/1355-h/1335-h.htm> [accessed 25 January 2016].
4. Verne anticipates H. G. Wells — actually nicknamed the 'English Jules Verne' — and his device journeying into the future two decades later in his 1895 *Time Machine*.
5. Marie A. Belloc, 'Jules Verne at Home', *Strand Magazine* (Feb. 1895), p. 212.
6. *The Translatability of Cultures: Figurations of the Space Between*, ed. by Sanford Budick, and Iser Wolfgang (Stanford, CA: Stanford University Press, 1996).
7. *The Literary Channel: The Inter-National Invention of the Novel*, ed. by Margaret Cohen, and Carolyn Dever (Princeton, NJ: Princeton University Press, 2002); Emily Apter, *Against World Literature: On the Politics of Untranslatability* (London: Verso, 2013); and *The Translatability of Cultures*, ed. by Budick and Wolfgang.
8. *The Literary Channel*, ed. by Cohen, and Dever, p. 3. For cultural exchanges taking place after the 1880, see Andrew Radford and Victoria Reid's edited volume *Franco-British Cultural Exchanges, 1880–1940: Channel Packets* (London: Palgrave Macmillan, 2012).
9. This is a reference to the exiled Stuarts. The Jacobites would refer to 'the King over the water' in order to avoid naming him.
10. Enid Starkie, *From Gautier to Eliot: The Influence of France on English Literature, 1851–1939* (London: Hutchinson, 1960).
11. Walter Scott, *Rob Roy*, ed. by David Hewitt, Edinburgh Edition of the Waverley Novels (EEWN) (Edinburgh: Edinburgh University Press, 2008), p. 261.
12. Walter Scott, *The Heart of Mid-Lothian*, ed. by Alison Lumsden, EEWN (Edinburgh: Edinburgh University Press, 2004), p. 35.
13. Water often figures threatening crowds but it takes on a special significance linked to rebellions, and in particular the French Revolution, when it threatens a border, as in the case of the Highlanders and the French.
14. Walter Scott, *The Antiquary*, ed. by David Hewitt, EEWN (Edinburgh: Edinburgh University Press, 1995), p. 162.
15. *The Antiquary*, p. 349.
16. Ibid., p. 350.
17. Ibid., p. 35.
18. Ibid., p. 350.
19. Ibid., p. 350.
20. Starkie, *From Gautier to Eliot*, p. 17.
21. Ibid., p. 19.
22. 'You have seen the clever letters of young De Stael upon England'. William Maggin, *Blackwood's Edinburgh Magazine, 1824–1900*, 18 (Dec. 1825), p. 717.
23. *The Mysteries of Paris*, trans. by Sir W. Dugdale (London: Edwards' Parisian Repository, 1844); *The Wandering Jew* (London: E. Appleyard, 1845).
24. Thomas Moore, *The Edinburgh Review, 1802–1900*, 34 (Nov. 1820), p. 372.
25. Martyn Lyons, 'Audience for Romanticism: Walter Scott in France 1815–51', *European History*

Quarterly, 14.21 (1984), 26–31. 'By 1824, according to the periodical *Le Globe*, 200,000 copies of Scott's novels had sold in France, and by 1830, according to another source, 1,500,000', Donald Haggis, 'The Popularity of Scott's Novels in France and Balzac's *Illusions perdues*', *Journal of European Studies*, 15.1 (March 1985), 21–29 (p. 21).
26. *Edinburgh History of the Book in Scotland*, ed. by Bill Bell, vol. III: *Ambition and Industry, 1800–1880* (Edinburgh: Edinburgh University Press), p. 436.
27. Louis Maigron, *Le Roman historique à l'époque romantique: essai sur l'influence de Walter Scott* (Paris: Champion, 1912); and Émile Legouis, 'La Fortune littéraire de Walter Scott en France', *Études anglaises*, 24.4 (Oct. 1971), 492–500.
28. Cited in Murray Pittock, *The Reception of Sir Walter Scott in Europe* (London: Continuum, 2006), p. 12.
29. 'Des écrivains étrangers que la France recueillit alors et qu'elle aima, ce fut Walter Scott, et de beaucoup, le plus populaire et le plus français'. Louis Maigron, *Le Roman historique à l'époque romantique*, p. 58. For a list of the French artists, writers, and historians who have been influenced by Scott, see Émile Legouis, 'La Fortune littéraire de Scott en France', *Études anglaises*, pp. 496–500.
30. W. E. K. Anderson, *The Journal of Sir Walter Scott* (Edinburgh: Canongate Classics, 1998), p. 267.
31. 'Sa popularité en France est contemporaine du retour des Bourbons. Elle se propage dans une France légitimiste et monarchique, en réaction contre la crise révolutionnaire, hantée par le regret du passé. Or Walter Scott avait l'âme féodale. Presque seul des grands romantiques anglais, il avait dès le début été hostile à la Révolution française, abominant le bouleversement d'un monde dont il aimait passionnément toutes les traditions.' Émile Legouis, 'La Fortune littéraire de Walter Scott en France', p. 493.
32. William Maggin, *Blackwood's Edinburgh Magazine*, 18 (Dec. 1825), p. 717–18.
33. John P. Farrell, *Revolution as Tragedy: The Dilemma of the Moderate from Scott to Arnold* (Ithaca, NY: Cornell University Press, 1980), p. 18.
34. Robert Howell Griffiths, "Modération et centrisme politique en Angleterre de 1660 à 1800", *Annales historiques de la Révolution française*, 3.357 (2009), 119–42 (p. 124).
35. Walter Scott, *Redgauntlet*, ed. by G.A.M. Wood, EEWN (Edinburgh: Edinburgh University Press, 1997), p. 362.
36. 'Thus loath and late, the French began to cast an eye on the British constitution, and the system of checks and balances upon which it is founded, as the best means of uniting the protection of liberty with the preservation of order', Walter Scott, 1827, *The Life of Napoleon Buonaparte, Emperor of the French. With a Preliminary View of the French Revolution*, II (Edinburgh: Robert Cadell, 1835), p. 376.
37. Montesquieu, *L'Esprit des lois*, XI. 4, 128; XI. 6, 138.
38. My reflexion is based on the concept of 'prismatic translation' coined by Matthew Reynolds, author, among others, of *The Poetry of Translation: From Chaucer and Petrarch to Homer and Logue* (Oxford: Oxford University Press, 2011).
39. Alison Lumsden, *Walter Scott and the Limits of Language* (Edinburgh: Edinburgh University Press, 2010), p. 86.
40. Walter Scott, *Guy Mannering*, ed. by Peter D. Garside, EEWN (Edinburgh: Edinburgh University Press, 1999), p. 6.
41. Walter Scott, *Waverley*, ed. by Peter D. Garside, EEWN (Edinburgh: Edinburgh University Press, 2007), p. 35.
42. Alison Lumsden, *Walter Scott and the Limits of Language*, p. 86.
43. *Waverley*, p. 44.
44. Scott, *The Tale of Old Mortality*, ed. by Douglas S. Mack, EEWN (Edinburgh: Edinburgh University Press, 1993), p. 350.
45. *Rob Roy*, p. 314.
46. *Waverley*, p. 111.
47. Scott, 'The Highland Widow', in *Chronicles of the Canongate*, ed. by Claire Lamont, EEWN, 2 vols (Edinburgh: Edinburgh University Press, 2001), I, 79.

48. *Waverley*, p. 121.
49. *The Antiquary*, p. 87.
50. Scott, *The Black Dwarf*, ed. by Peter D. Garside, EEWN (Edinburgh: Edinburgh University Press, 1993), p. 68.
51. *Waverley*, p. 81.
52. Ibid., p. 34.
53. Ibid., p. 85.
54. Franco Moretti, *Atlas of the European Novel, 1800–1900* (London: Verso, 1999), p. 44.
55. *Waverley*, p. 85.
56. Ibid., p. 85.
57. Gilles Deleuze and Félix Guattari, *Capitalisme et schizophrénie 2: Mille Plateaux* [1st edn 1980] (Paris: Minuit, 2009).
58. *Waverley*, p. 123.
59. Quoted by Susan Bassnett, 'Translating Terror', in *Connecting Cultures*, ed. by Emma Bainbridge (London: Routledge, 2008), pp. 7–18 (p. 10).
60. 'Communication here is controlled by or for the receptors, it is in fact an interested interpretation, and therefore it seems less an exchange of information than an appropriation of a foreign text to serve a purpose in the receiving culture', Lawrence Venuti, *The Translator's Invisibility: A History of Translation* (London: Routledge), p. 20.
61. Mona Baker, *Routledge Encyclopaedia of Translation Studies* (London: Routledge, 1998), p. 242.
62. George Steiner, 'The Claims of Theory', in *After Babel: Aspects of Language and Translation* (Oxford: Oxford University Press, 1975), pp. 248–311 (p. 285).
63. Martyn Lyons, 'Audience for Romanticism: Walter Scott in France 1815–51', p. 30. It is difficult to date the time when Scott lost some of his popularity in France. After 1840 Octave Boistel d'Exhauvillez proposed abridged versions of the most popular novels aimed at a juvenile audience, and in 1848 the publisher Charpentier started an affordable complete edition of Scott's novels which, for the first time, presented each novel in one volume, so they were still very much read in translation throughout the Victorian period.
64. Jacques Béreaud, 'La Traduction en France à l'époque romantique', *Comparative Literature Studies*, 8.3 (Sept. 1971), 224–44 (p. 232).
65. Translated by Paul Barnaby in Barnaby, 'Another Tale of Old Mortality: The Translations of Auguste-Jean-Baptiste Defauconpret in the French Reception of Scott', in *The Reception of Walter Scott in Europe*, ed. by Murray Pittock (London: Continuum, 2006), pp. 31–44 (p. 37).
66. See Céline Sabiron, 'Handing over Walter Scott? The Writer's Hand on the English and French Marketplace', in *Walter Scott: New Interpretations, Yearbook of English Studies*, 47 (2017).
67. *Waverley*, p. 176.
68. *Waverley*, trans. by Defauconpret (Paris: Garnier Frères, Jouvet et Cie, 1883), p. 119.
69. My English translation is based on Defauconpret's French translation of Scott's *Waverley*.
70. *Waverley*, p. 6.
71. Ibid., p. 6.
72. Ibid., p. 83.
73. *Waverley*, trans. by Defauconpret, p. 109.
74. *Rob Roy*, p. 44.
75. Ibid., pp. 102, 104.

CHAPTER 12

❖

A Conversation across Borders: Marcel Proust's *Le Temps retrouvé* and its Translation into Estonian

Madli Kütt

Marcel Proust has given world literature a heritage that crosses borders in many ways.[1] One of his lessons, however, is that borders play a fundamental role in the process of creating a work of art. He uses border processes on different levels, but his main goal is clear: borders create dualities, but in so doing they also create a means of meeting and communicating between these dualities. Proust's use of borders is a systematic and methodical work of research, studying the possible relationships between the two sides, two opposites, between Swann's way and Guermantes' way. Translation, as a border process itself, applies its own borders and relationships onto the world of *La Recherche*, and Estonian translation provides its own significant point of view in that respect. By shifting the emphases, intensifying the visuality of figures, and modifying the subject-object relations, it brings changes in the relationship that the narrator has with the world. Proust's *À la recherche du temps perdu* has been translated into Estonian only in small portions, and rather erratically. Most recently, *Le Temps retrouvé* was translated in 2004 by Tõnu Õnnepalu, a novelist and a poet who is also one of Estonia's best-known authors abroad. In this essay, I have chosen to focus on this particular translation because of its completeness and its recent publication, but most of all because of its particular way of dealing with Proust's border processes.

★ ★ ★ ★ ★

Proust's use of borders can be understood mainly on three levels. The first one is presented by the surface of things, such as the surface of water. For Proust, the problem is that the surface is not transparent, as with water when it is glittering: you know that there is something under the water, but you cannot quite make out what it is.

The surface of things is an appearance, a border blocking our view. That is the reason why Proust's narrator refers to using 'X-ray vision' for his observations — it is not enough for him just to see the world, he needs to reach under its skin:

Fig. 12.1. Photograph by Madli Kütt.

'comme le chirurgien qui, sous le poli d'un ventre de femme, verrait le mal interne qui le ronge. J'avais beau dîner en ville, je ne voyais pas les convives, parce que quand je croyais les regarder je les radiographiais'[2] [like a surgeon who beneath the smooth surface of a woman's belly sees the internal disease which is devouring it. If I went to a dinner-party I did not see the guests: when I thought I was looking at them, I was in fact examining them with X-rays].[3] In the course of becoming a writer, he realizes indeed that a true artist has to see through the surface, to see the underlying meaning: 'La réalité à exprimer résidait, je le comprenais maintenant, non dans l'apparence du sujet, mais dans le degré de pénétration de cette impression à une profondeur où cette apparence importait peu'[4] [The reality that he has to express resides, as I now began to understand, not in the superficial appearance of his subject but at a depth at which that appearance matters little].[5]

But that opposition is not as self-evident, or as categorical, as it may seem. Anne Simon has pointed out that surpassing the level of appearance should not be taken as a sign of devalorization of sensation.[6] On the contrary, the discovery of the deeper layers of reality is always connected to sensing the surface, as she explains through the Proustian figure of the diver: the diver who is swimming under the surface of the water is still connected to the air on the surface, through his breathing tube.[7] Proust needs the surface because that is where the contact happens between the world and the subject. The surface works as a border in both of its main functions, by obstructing the exploration of anything that is behind it, but nonetheless giving the searcher a touching point, the possibility of an opening: 'S'il n'y avait rien tout simplement, il n'y aurait rien à dire et plus rien à savoir. Mais ce n'est pas le cas. On sait, on sent qu'il nous faudrait atteindre et qu'on ne le peut pas' [If there would simply be nothing at all, there would be nothing to say and nothing to know. But this is not the case. We know, we feel that we need to reach for it and that we cannot.][8]

The second border consists of isolating objects and bringing them out of the background, out of the invisibility of the ordinary, just as we know from the famous madeleine passage, where the memory images are compared to a Japanese paper game:

> Et comme dans ce jeu où les Japonais s'amusent à tremper dans un bol de porcelaine rempli d'eau de petits morceaux de papier jusque-là indistincts qui, à peine y sont-ils plongés *s'étirent, se contournent, se colorent, se différencient*, deviennent des fleurs, des maisons, des personnages consistants et reconnaissables, de même maintenant toutes les fleurs de notre jardin et celles du parc de M. Swann, et les nymphéas de la Vivonne, et les bonnes gens du village et leurs petits logis et l'église et tout Combray et ses environs, tout cela qui prend forme et solidité, est sorti, ville et jardins, de ma tasse de thé.[9]

> [And as in the game wherein the Japanese amuse themselves by filling a porcelain bowl with water and steeping in it little pieces of paper which until then are without character and form, but, the moment they become wet, stretch and twist and take on colour and distinctive shape, become flowers or houses or people, solid and recognisable, so in that moment all the flowers in our garden and in M. Swann's park, and the water-lilies on the Vivonne and the good folk of the village and their little dwellings and the parish church and the whole of Combray and its surroundings, taking shape and solidity, sprang into being, town and gardens alike, from my cup of tea.][10]

The images and forms on these Japanese papers, invisible at first, are revealed as they come in contact with water, by being outlined, delimited, taking colour and becoming distinct from the background of the paper. It is important to note that this process, which Alain de Lattre has called *singularisation*, is twofold. According to Lattre, Proust's writing is indeed based on 'le grand principe de séparation', but this principle appears in such a way that it also automatically implies the possibility of a connection. He explains that the singularity of each object, place or character is given not really by its attributes but by the particular connections it retains with other objects, places or characters: 'Les singularités individuelles dont [Proust] fait état n'ont pas, pour se recommander à nous, la forme immédiate de leur apparence; elles s'imposent beaucoup plus étroitement par la sorte de relations dont elles donnent témoignage' [The individual singularities which [Proust] speaks about don't have an immediate form of appearance to offer for us; they establish themselves much more directly through the types of relations of which they give notice].[11] Seen in this light, isolation of the objects is not an end in itself, but a particular and organized method for discovering hidden images, and most of all, for writing.

There are thus two main effects that *singularisation* entails. Firstly, no connection

Fig. 12.2. The singularization process in everyday life. In order to find the gate in the fence, the inhabitants have marked it with a sign saying: "Gate for pedestrians". Photograph by Daniel Allen.

is prone to happen unless there is separation, unless there is one thing that stands out from all the other things. And secondly, singularizing is always a strictly personal process. A singular object is meaningful only for the subject (and through the subject) perceiving it; that is, perceiving its singularity. This means that the method of perceiving the objects in their singularity is used in order to realize how and why things are related, and more importantly, how they are related to the subject. So, if singularization is a sign that there is something hidden, a hidden meaning somewhere inside the thing, under its surface, then this surface becomes a connection point (or a door) between the thing and the subject who perceives it. But this relation is complex and difficult to open. The door is locked and we need a key.

The third level of border processes provides this key. This level concerns time, or more precisely — lost time. There is a border of oblivion between the moments of memory, and the present, a distance that separates the narrator from himself at some other times in the past.

Some have seen this distance as tragic and impassable,[12] others argue that it is part of the method for creating connections.[13] There is really no pathway from one self to the other(s). The road has to be forgotten, and that is where the border lies. It is not possible to go back linearly to recollect the memories — that is one of the major reasons for the narrator's disappointment in *Le Temps retrouvé*, when he tries to recall images from Venice,[14] or understand the meaning of a row of trees by the

Fig. 12.3. Photograph by Daniel Allen.

railway.[15] Distance is a mandatory factor, in Proust's view, because he values highly the involuntary emergence of memories. He even goes so far as to say that this is really the only way to know the true meaning of things, the only way to discover things is to discover them *'malgré moi'* — despite myself. As though you are giving a gift to yourself from the past, an ice cream once bought and forgotten in the fridge, then found again on a hard day's night... But one cannot deliberately forget. That is the complicated bit. One has to give away control over memory completely, and let things happen on their own. So we could say that, in a way, in Proust's view, it's really a blessing to have a bad memory. And the more time has passed, and the more the forgetting is complete, the more there is of the things that come out (the sweeter the ice cream, so to say).

★ ★ ★ ★

Le Temps retrouvé begins with a moment that gives an exemplary idea of how the border works as a separation, a connection point, and a place for discovering meanings. The narrator is in a room in Tansonville, in a country house where he is visiting Gilberte, and looking out of the window. But what happens in the text is much more than a description of things he has before his eyes. Firstly, we can recognize an interaction taking place between inner and outer space, the room itself and the natural scene outside. The inside is compared to a *cabinet de verdure*, a sort of 'indoors outdoors', as the walls have been decorated with garden roses or birds in the trees that seem almost alive while, on the other hand, the narrator's glance moves out of the window towards the park which surrounds the house, with trees and bushes and a body of water. The window functions here as a border point that allows such crossovers and entanglements between the two spaces.

As the inner and outer spaces become more entwined with one another, a second element in the border process is revealed, that of separation. It appears first in the comparison of wallpapers in old and new houses:

> où sur la tenture des chambres, les roses du jardin dans l'une, les oiseaux des arbres dans l'autre, vous ont rejoints et vous tiennent compagnie — isolés du moins — car c'étaient de vieilles tentures où chaque rose était assez séparée pour qu'on eût pu si elle avait été vivante, la cueillir, chaque oiseau le mettre en cage et l'apprivoiser, sans rien de ces grandes décorations des chambres d'aujourd'hui où sur un fond d'argent, tous les pommiers de Normandie sont venus se profiler en style japonais, pour halluciner les heures que vous passez au lit.[16]

> [on the wall-paper in the bedrooms, here the roses from the garden, there the birds from the trees outside join you and keep you company, isolated from the world — for it was old wall-paper on which every rose was so distinct that, had it been alive, you could have picked it, every bird you could have put in a cage and tamed, quite different from those grandiose bedroom decorations of to-day where, on a silver background, all the apple trees of Normandy display their outlines in the Japanese style to hallucinate the hours you spend in bed.][17]

The old-style decorations are clearly in favour, because their elements are isolated from each other, firstly by space — the roses are in one room, the birds in another — and secondly by language, which describes them in a singular form, bringing out 'every rose' and 'every bird' individually. The effect of separation creates, somewhat controversially perhaps, the possibility of a new connection, so that these elements become accessible for the person viewing them — a rose could be 'picked', a bird 'captured and tamed'. The connection between the elements themselves needs to be cut off, in order to allow a connection with the viewer, and that is what makes them real, and (possibly, almost) alive. This is not however the case with the newer buildings, where the decorations present no such isolation. They appear on a silver background and remain part of that background, forming a pattern (of a Japanese style) with multiple pieces, from which nothing stands out on its own, or gains the possibility of a life of its own. Instead, the plurality is perceived as static, unfortunate, and disturbing.

The separation process continues into the next image, by which the narrator describes the view out of the window. This time, the effect is brought on by opposition of colours, doubled by contrast of light and dark. A light green background of scenery is being built up throughout the description: the word *verdure* — a generalizing term in itself — is repeated no less than three times in this short paragraph, and the scene is enriched by other green elements like 'les feuilles vertes [...] étincelants de soleil'[18] [the green leaves [...] sparkling in the sun][19]. Then, his eye is caught by a completely different element, singled out from the rest of the *tableau* by its dark blue colour: the steeple of the church of Combray. It should also be noted that his attention is drawn not to the bright and shiny, but towards that which is in the dark still — it is something that cannot be seen at a first glance, something that has yet to be discovered and brought up from the deep. Thus, thanks to the contrast, the narrator suddenly realizes that the steeple is not part of the general impression of a painting, but is real. It is the steeple itself that comes out of the greenery:

> Non pas une figuration de ce clocher, ce clocher lui-même, qui mettant ainsi sous mes yeux la distance des lieues et des années, était venu, au milieu de la lumineuse verdure et d'un tout autre ton, si sombre qu'il paraissait presque seulement dessiné, s'inscrire dans le carreau de ma fenêtre.[20]
>
> [Not a representation of the steeple, but the steeple itself, which, putting in visible form a distance of miles and of years, had come, intruding its discordant tone into the midst of the luminous verdure — a tone so [dark] that it seemed little more than a preliminary sketch — and engraved itself upon my window-pane.][21]

The explanation of this recognition relies again on the very process of separation. Because of its singularity, the steeple can bring before his eyes the profundity under the surface, the distance of miles and of years. Thus the steeple is real, is itself, and is not a representation, which it would be if it did not have this profundity and stayed merely on the surface of the greenery.

The Estonian translation changes these two images in ways that (among other things) affect the process of separation, which certainly does not have the same intensity, and tends even to disappear. In the first sentence of the description of the wallpapers, the translator omits a part of the text 'assez séparée pour que' which means that the separation is no longer a cause for the possible interaction that the viewer can have with these objects. Instead, the translator turns towards a relationship between the objects themselves, as the effect of *isolation* is translated by an effect of *relation* (the phrase 'isolés du moins' becomes 'üksteist siiski segamata' [without disturbing each other, nonetheless]).[22]

The separation process in the second image does not survive much better in the translation. Firstly, it could be said, figuratively speaking, that in the Estonian paragraph the green is not as green as it is in the original: the word-stem 'roheline' [green] only appears twice, instead of six appearances of 'vert' in the French text, and in one case the colour is left out completely, so that 'les feuilles vertes' [green leaves] become just 'lehed' [leaves]. The colour of the objects forming the background is thus not quite so explicitly stressed as it is for Proust, and becomes more of an occasional tool of description rather than the trigger of a process. Secondly, we could also claim that the blue is not quite as blue either; the syntax of the translated sentence is altered in such a way that it turns around the logic explaining the difference of the colour of the steeple. The steeple is no longer recognized thanks to its contrasting colour; it is recognized first, on its own, and just happens to be also of a different colour. According to the logic prevalent in the translation, it might just as well be of any colour. The contrast between the green and blue no longer plays the same role, and the translator decides here again to leave out the part of the sentence where it was outlined: 'au milieu de la lumineuse verdure et d'un tout autre ton' [its discordant tone into the midst of the luminous verdure]. The border becomes blurred.

One of the reasons why this happens is that the translation gives these figures a more visual value, treating them strictly as descriptions of objects. The translator 'sees' the objects, but does not mind the border between them. The problem here is that the border not only organizes the space but, more importantly, creates the process of discovery which is the purpose of the narrator of *À la recherche*. But if you don't see the border, you may miss out on seeing what's on the other side of it. And thus we could argue that this level of borders as contrasts and separators does not work very well in the Estonian translation. If you don't see the door, you cannot open it.

Still, there might be a way of doing exactly that, and this is the reason why we need to consider the third aspect of borders, the aspect of lost time. As Proust explains through his narrator — if you stumble upon the door unwittingly, *malgré soi*, it opens:

> Mais c'est quelquefois au moment où tout nous semble perdu que l'avertissement arrive qui peut nous sauver, on a frappé à toutes les portes qui ne donnent sur rien, et la seule par où on peut entrer et qu'on aurait cherchée en vain pendant cent ans, on y heurte sans le savoir, et elle s'ouvre.[23]

> [But it is sometimes just at the moment when we think that everything is lost that the intimation arrives which may save us; one has knocked at all the doors which lead nowhere, and then one stumbles without knowing it on the only door through which one can enter — which one might have sought in vain for a hundred years — and it opens of its own accord.][24]

One of the critical changes in this respect is the Estonian translator's tendency to make the speaker's subjectivity somewhat fade behind the scenes, altering its role to be more passive, even more absent, and thus give control away to the outer world. This happens mainly in two ways. Firstly, the translator transposes the subject of action from the narrator to other objects involved in the activity. For instance, where Proust writes: 'la beauté sur laquelle *j'ai superposé* trop d'images, de moins en moins aimées'[25] [the beauty on which *I have* since *superimposed* so many less and less loved images],[26] Õnnepalu translates so that the images overlap each other in their own right and the 'I' subject is entirely missing from the sentence: 'ilu, millele *on ladestunud* nii palju aina vähem armsaid kujutlusi' [the beauty on which so many less and less loved images *have superimposed*].[27] This change is partly consistent with the comparisons made between Indo-European and Finnic languages. Speakers of Finnic languages, such as Estonian, tend to use more impersonal forms and generally pay more attention to the event itself, the action rather than the person doing it, whereas Indo-European languages, such as French, emphasize the subject over the action.[28] Õnnepalu is going along with this tendency and taking it even further of his own accord.

This tendency has a clear impact on translating such a subjective author as Proust. One of the ways this happens can be seen in the following example, where the narrator describes one of his biggest moments of discovery while stumbling upon uneven paving stones: '*je posai* mon pied sur un pavé qui était un peu moins élevé que le précédent' [I put my foot on a stone which was slightly lower than its neighbour] which triggers in him a vivid memory experience, a feeling mixed of 'azur profond' [profound azure], 'des impressions de fraîcheur, d'éblouissante lumière' [impressions of coolness, of dazzling light].²⁹ He keeps repeating the same movement and eventually manages to capture this vision: 'mais si je réussissais, oubliant la matinée Guermantes, à retrouver ce que j'avais senti *en posant ainsi mes pieds*, de nouveau la vision éblouissante et indistincte me frôlait'³⁰ [but if I succeeded, forgetting the Guermantes party, in recapturing what I had felt when I first placed my feet on the ground in this way, again the dazzling and indistinct vision fluttered near me].³¹ However, even though this is clearly one of the moments of unwittingly discovering something, the French sentence still gives the narrator himself as the source of this repeating movement, whereas the Estonian replies with a transposition of the subject of action from the person to his feet, respectively: 'kui mu jalg leidis toetuspinna' [when my foot found the ground]³² and 'kui mu jalad nii astuma sattusid' [when my feet happened to step in such a way].³³ Such a transposition causes the sentence to be no longer about the person, but about his feet, which seem to operate on their own account. It is the foot that finds a place to support itself, as if the owner of the foot had nothing more to do with it than to follow it. In the second sentence, the translator also uses a different verb 'sattuma' [to happen] — whereas the French repeats the verb 'poser' — which further increases the randomness of the event. In addition, the translator leaves out several other references to the first person subject, like 'malgré moi' [despite myself], 'j'avais cru' [I thought] or 'près de moi' [close to me], in the same paragraph.

Another observation, this time on the lexical level, indicates a change towards a more modest, more concealed subject. This happens when Õnnepalu chooses to express the originally neutral actions of the narrator with connotations of surrendering, being oppressed, being directed by others. He is surrendering to his thoughts ('andusin' [surrender] for 'je *faisais* ces reflexions' [I was *making* these reflections]), is forced to make an effort ('sunnitud' [to be forced] for 'l'effort d'adaptation ou d'attention que nous *faisons*' [that effort of adaptation or attention which we *make*]), the ground leads him ('viima' [to lead] for 'le sol de lui-même savait où il devait *aller*' [the solid earth knew of its own accord where it had to *go*]) and Françoise takes him by the hand, rather than just him walking with her ('käekõrval' [taken by hand] *for* 'les rues [...] que je prenais jadis avec Françoise' [the streets [...] which I used to take with Françoise]).³⁴ So in addition to giving more details about the activity, the subject comes across as less decisive, less determined, and less in control. The narrator thus seems to be more willing to accept what the world is giving him, and less willing, at the same time, to take action, to make decisions for himself, preferring rather to go with the flow.

Therefore we can say that the process of discovery, and the relationship with the world in general, happens even more *malgré soi* than in its original version. The important thing here — and this, I believe, is where the dialogic nature of translation lies and where the Estonian translation specifically can give something back to the original Proust text — is that all these changes and tendencies in the translated text make the narrator more open to the involuntary emergence of the past. Proust speaks about letting go of the subject's rational control, but is not entirely able to do so himself because he remains bounded by the French language, which does not allow him to let go. Proust is never going to be able to forget himself entirely, because he can never be free of the 'I' in his expression. (And that's what he is famous for, of course.) But placing Proust's work in such a different language as Estonian enables the process of forgetting oneself and letting the past emerge on its own to happen also on the linguistic level. This is where the change of language can give a text a new way of life, and a way of rediscovering itself in a new form, as the text crosses the borders of languages and literatures. But the Estonian translation is also in a curious situation because the text does not simply cross borders, passing from one side to the other, but rather goes to a place which is itself a border. A glimpse into one of Õnnepalu's novels will provide an insight as to what that might entail.

★ ★ ★ ★ ★

Estonia is a country that is very conscious about its situation on a border and its function as a border. Estonia's identity entails the very notion of border, as it is indeed situated in a transition area in quite a few different ways — geologically (between limestone and sandstone), naturally (Estonia is at the border of many animal and plant species' distribution areas), culturally (between farmers and hunter-gatherers), linguistically (between Finnic and Indo-European languages), etc., not to mention historically and politically — all of them closely linked to each other.

This borderly nature has been recognized by Tõnu Õnnepalu who published in 1993, under the *nom de plume* of Emil Tode, a novel called *Piiririik* (translated by Madli Puhvel into English as *Border State* in 2000 and published this time under author's real name). The novel is presented as a series of letters written by an unnamed narrator, confessing to the murder of his Franco-German lover, Franz. However, in the course of his testimony, the narrator reveals even greater concern about the uncertainty of his own identity, and seems to lose control over it as the writing proceeds. Nothing seems to define him. He never gives away his name. He doubts his origins: coming from an unnamed East European country, one of those 'impoverished, dark countries that helplessly bemoan their stillborn histories',[35] he feels underestimated and unaccepted amongst the Westerners. He is a stranger in a foreign city, constantly uncomfortable, and does not feel secure even when he knows he is in the right place. His bodily identity is rather hidden too. The Estonian language does not use grammatical genders, and other references that would identify the character as a man or a woman are close to none. Some rare hints in the text, as well as the connection between narrator and author, would lead the reader to believe that the character is a homosexual; but even this does not help him to identify himself, but leaves him rather unsatisfied because 'he cannot try all the possibilities and combinations which would be accessible to him in a world without sexual (or geographical) categories'.[36] He is not really sure of the existence of his correspondent, Angelo, nor of his lover, and victim, Franz. 'Where do I even get the notion that this Franz existed as a person?' he asks.[37] It is rather the nothingness of these characters that connects him to them, their inexistence that reminds him of his own inexistence:

> Yesterday on the telephone you said, '*Je suis nul*'. I answered, '*J'adore ta nullité, Angelo.*' I said this was as good as it gets. And after that we were silent for at least a minute. Not even the sound of breathing could be heard. As if the words had become reality and there were two nothings at either end.[38]

His actions are meaningless to him and have no clear outcome. The work he has come to do in Paris, to translate French poetry 'into a language this poetry cannot be translated into',[39] seems doomed to fail and bores him to death. And his other action, the murder he confesses to in the letters and considers part of his identity,[40] is told evasively, through negations, hints and questions.

It is the tale of a man in-between who is dissolving himself, his story, and his characters, by constantly discrediting his own words. Every statement is immediately turned around or questioned: 'In other words, I will tell my story. But what story? I don't have a story.'[41] And so are the borders that would hold the identities together. Although his country of origin is not named, it is clearly recognizable as Estonia, among other things because it is delimited by Estonia's natural borders. But even these borders are immediately blurred: 'all this geography is just a dream, a fantasy, because such a country doesn't exist.'[42] The same happens with the murder to which he confesses but for which, at the same time, he refuses to take responsibility. While studying the mechanisms of identity in *Border State*, D. M. Skerrett concludes that, by living between identities, refusing to define himself, blurring borders and making them strange, dubious and queer, the narrator can achieve a certain degree of freedom.[43] This may well be true. Indeed, he seems to be able to escape from his pursuers because, simply, he does not exist. He stands on the border and disappears in it, and with it:

> A border state is nonexistent. There is something on one side and something on the other side of the border, but there is no border. There is a highway, and a field of grain with a farmhouse under tall, thirsty trees, but where is the border between them? It's invisible. And if you should happen to stand on the border, then you too are invisible, from either side.[44]

Even the letters he writes may not really be his own, as he ends up confessing that they might have been given to him on a data disk, by a ghostly hand that reached out of the river one day. The letters he writes thus come from the other side, are handed to him across the border. However, the encounter (with the mysterious stranger, the underwater author, the real murderer, or just his other self) remains a mystery, never to be explained or repeated. Never again would he get in touch with this hand, even though he keeps going back to the place where it happened. The water remains wild, and its surface an inaccessible boundary:

> I look at the surface of the water as if it were a boundary behind which the real world begins. I wait for your hand to extend from the water, at least for circles to form on the surface, as a sign that I have permission to come. But nothing happens. Only a breeze ripples the water and makes the tall trees rustle above my head.[45]

In contrast to Proust's diver who is himself diving in, reaching across the border to find meaning, Õnnepalu's narrator is expecting the hand to reach out towards him, 'but nothing happens'. The truth is, there is nothing on the other side of this border, because there is nothing really on this side either. Not only does he not see through the surface, there is no reflexion of him in the water either, because he is not on one side or the other. He is living inside the border, becoming part of one: 'I was standing on the boundary. I could not be seen'.[46] As subjectivity is given up and being dissolved, borders become useless and everything on those borders will disappear as well.

* * * * *

Proust's method is singularization, a technique by which he ties together two apparently opposite mechanisms of separation and connection, in one single process. More precisely, it is a process of connection through separation. By identifying the borders, delimiting the details out of the background, he can see and vivify the links that these elements entail. It is important to separate the details from their ordinary, conventional structure, to allow the emergence of new and more personal relations between the subject and the world.

Õnnepalu's *Border State* demonstrates a reversed method, of dissolving borders and trying to break free from predefined frames, to find alternative ways of relating to the world. Instead of singling out details, he blurs boundaries. Where Proust proceeds to bring invisible things forward and out of their background, Õnnepalu's tendency is to make visible things invisible, and even, where possible, non-existent.

These two methods meet and communicate in Õnnepalu's translation of *Le Temps retrouvé*. In this text, these two authors can talk to each other, across borders, but also about borders. On the one hand, we have seen how Õnnepalu's method tends to dissolve Proust's, but on the other, Õnnepalu's approach also reveals some aspects of Proust's method in a different light, and opens perspectives that Proust could not achieve on his own. This is the reason that makes it intriguing, as well as enjoyable, to eavesdrop on their conversation while reading this translation.

Notes to Chapter 12

1. This article was supported by the Estonian Institutional Research Funding grant IUT 34–30: 'Ideology of Translation and Translation of Ideology: Mechanisms of Cultural Dynamics under the Russian Empire and Soviet Power in Estonia in the 19th–20th Centuries'.
2. Marcel Proust, *À la recherche du temps perdu* (Paris: Éditions Gallimard, coll. Pléiade, 4 vols, 1987–89), IV (1989), p. 297.
3. Marcel Proust, *Remembrance of Things Past*, trans. by C. K. Scott Moncrieff, et al., 3 vols (New York: Vintage Books, 1982), III, 738.
4. Proust, *À la recherche du temps perdu*, IV, 461.
5. Proust, *Remembrance of Things Past*, III, 916.
6. Anne Simon, *Proust ou le réel retrouvé: le sensible et son expression dans 'À la recherche du temps perdu'* (Paris: Honoré Champion, 2011), p. 184.
7. Simon, *Proust*, p. 185.

8. Alain de Lattre, *La Doctrine de la réalité chez Proust*, 3 vols (Paris: Librairie José Corti, 1979–85), III (1985), pp. 123–24, my translation for English.
9. Proust, *À la recherche du temps perdu*, I, 47, my emphasis.
10. Proust, *Remembrance of Things Past*, I, 51.
11. Lattre, *La Doctrine*, I (1979), p. 69, my translation.
12. Georges Poulet, *L'Espace proustien* (Paris: Gallimard, 1982), p. 61.
13. 'Le *microscope* trompe et c'est dans la *distance* qu'est le vrai. [...] Rien n'est plus loin que ce qui est plus près. Et rien plus proche — et plus *précis*, par conséquent — que ce qui est touché dans la "distance" où nous savons le mettre' [The microscope is deceiving, and the truth is in the *distance*. [...] Nothing is so far as that which is the closest. And nothing is closer — or, thus, more *precise* — than that which is touched in the 'distance' where we know to put it]. Lattre, III, 207–08, my translation.
14. Proust, *À la recherche du temps perdu*, IV, 444.
15. Ibid., IV, 433.
16. *À la recherche du temps perdu*, IV, 275.
17. *Remembrance of Things Past*, III, 715–16.
18. *À la recherche du temps perdu*, IV, 275.
19. *Remembrance of Things Past*, III, 716.
20. *À la recherche du temps perdu*, IV, 275.
21. *Remembrance of Things Past*, III, 716.
22. Proust, *Taasleitud aeg* [Time regained], trans. by Tõnu Õnnepalu (Tallinn: Eesti Keele Sihtasutus, 2004), p. 15.
23. Proust, *À la recherche du temps perdu*, IV, 445.
24. *Remembrance of Things Past*, III, 898.
25. *À la recherche du temps perdu*, IV, 466, my emphasis.
26. *Remembrance of Things Past*, III, 923.
27. Proust, *Taasleitud aeg*, p. 236.
28. This tendency is explained as one of the differences between Finnic and standard average European languages, in Mati Erelt and Helle Metslang, 'Estonian Clause Patterns: From Finno-Ugric to Standard Average European', *Linguistica Uralica*, 4 (2006) 254–66; Helle Metslang, 'Estonian in Typological Perspective', *Sprachtypologie und Universalienforschung*, 62.1/2 (2009), 49–71; and more specifically in Liina Lindström 'Kõnelejale ja kuulajale viitamise vältimise strateegiaid eesti keeles' [Strategies of avoiding explicit reference to the speaker and the addressee in Estonian], *Estonian Mother Tongue Society Year Book*, 55 (2009), 88–118.
29. Proust, *À la recherche du temps perdu*, IV, 445, my emphasis. For translation, Proust, *Remembrance of Things Past*, III, 899.
30. Proust, *À la recherche du temps perdu*, IV, 446, my emphasis.
31. Proust, *Remembrance of Things Past*, III, 899.
32. Proust, *Taasleitud aeg*, p. 214.
33. Ibid., p. 213.
34. Proust, *À la recherche du temps perdu*, IV, 436. For translation, Proust, *Remembrance of Things Past*, III, 890.
35. Tõnu Õnnepalu, *Border State*, trans. by Madli Puhvel (Evanston, IL: Northwestern University Press, 2000), p. 5.
36. Delaney Michael Skerrett, 'Narratiiv, ülestunnistus, identiteet: Emil Tode "Piiririik"' [Narratives, Confessions, Identities: Emil Tode's 'Border State'], *Keel ja Kirjandus* [Language and Literature], 9 (2006), 728–35 (p. 733).
37. Õnnepalu, p. 25.
38. Ibid., p. 29.
39. Ibid., p. 33.
40. Skerrett, p. 729.
41. Õnnepalu, p. 10.
42. Ibid., p. 5.
43. Skerrett, p. 734.

44. Õnnepalu, p. 97.
45. Ibid., p. 95.
46. Ibid., p. 96.

CHAPTER 13

When Do Different Literatures Become Comparable?

The Vague Borders of Comparability and Incomparability

Xiaofan Amy Li

Although the mushrooming of studies in comparative and world literature in recent years gives the impression that comparison has become an accepted approach, and the claim that cultural differences invalidate comparison has lost much of its purchase, methodological concerns still remain at the centre of comparative literature and greatly influence how the discipline is developing. This is reflected by the constant questioning of comparative literature's status as a discipline. Not surprisingly, attempts to define the aims, methods, and boundaries of comparative literature in the past few decades have revolved around the notion and uses of comparison. Since the 1960s, as Spivak remarks, the term 'comparative' in 'comparative literature' has often been pointed out as a misnomer, for what is at stake in the discipline is not really comparison.[1] Indeed, comparative literature does much more than compare, and heavily involves cultural evaluation (R. Radhakrishnan), 'constant interaction' (Damrosch), or 'dis-parative' encounters that discover radical differences and shift the Eurocentric power balance towards the marginalized postcolonial side (Thomas Claviez).[2] As Robert Young argues, comparative literature is still haunted by the painful question 'What does the comparative do?', resulting in its 'recurring state of crisis'.[3] David Ferris's observation that comparative literature is an 'indiscipline' that 'eschews definition of itself'[4] further highlights the problematics of comparison, showing that it remains a crucial question. It is the aim of this essay, therefore, to clarify the concept of comparison and argue that it is still a fundamental operating logic in comparative literature, although it stays open to re-definitions and new uses. To do this, I will focus on the notions of comparability and incomparability because although comparison is not singular and has different modes and purposes, in any comparative study there is always some notion of what is comparable or not. Nevertheless, the question of when texts become comparable to each other and when they are not is a controversial topic that needs further scrutiny. Here I will take recourse to recent philosophical studies on comparability, demonstrating that they can shed light on how we make comparisons in comparative literature, especially in regard to the problem of evaluation, or the imposition of biased comparative frameworks on different literatures and cultures.

Comparability and the Problem of Incomparables

Much of the discussion about comparability has in fact been advanced by debates about incomparability. Since the 1970s, critics in comparative literature have emphasized incomparability by anchoring their arguments in the poststructuralist view that there exist incommensurable differences between languages and cultures that would make the conceptual framework of any comparison an imposition of the logic of the more powerful on the less powerful. Thus comparison inevitably causes linguistic and interpretative violence. As Andrei Terian proposes, the incomparable was understood as three irreducibles: 'cultural alterity', 'linguistic alterity' (or untranslatability), and 'historical alterity'.[5] Although the notion of absolute difference and the view that it entails mutual unintelligibility between cultures — characteristic of earlier debates during the 1970s–80s — have been convincingly criticized by scholars such as Zhang Longxi and Geoffrey E. R. Lloyd,[6] the concern about doing violence to cultural difference remains urgent in discussions about comparison. These three irreducible alterities, therefore, still have strong advocates who, instead of denying the possibility of any comparison, focus on the ethical and political problems that these alterities pose when they enter into comparison.

To start with, nowhere is cultural alterity more thorny an issue than in comparative studies that involve postcolonial literature. As Spivak observes, postcolonial literature always already engages with the spectre of the colonial master, so that from the very beginning comparison already places the non-Occidental Other in an unequal system of literary exchange and appropriation.[7] In this sense, the comparison is between two incomparable *comparanda* — incomparable because the Other's alterity, if we agree with Levinas (as Claviez argues we should), is not based on 'any quality that distinguish[es] him from me, for a distinction of this nature would precisely imply between us that community of genus which already nullifies alterity'.[8] Thus comparison is already an evaluation that re-affirms existing power hierarchies.

Secondly, linguistic alterity, which has been recently expounded forcefully by Emily Apter's *Against World Literature* (2013) and Barbara Cassin's *Dictionnaire des intraduisibles* (2004), posits the untranslatability of culturally specific expressions and concepts, and in extension, the incommensurability of different languages and literatures. For instance, in Apter's view, different narrative forms such as *midrash* in Hebrew, *monogatari* in Japanese, or *xiaoshuo* in Chinese are 'continually re-translated and mistranslated' when rendered into English terminology that denotes genres such as 'fiction' and 'novel'.[9] Such untranslatables are therefore 'proof of the manner in which some concepts or structures mean, in comparative literature, a limit of "commensurability"'.[10] Apter thus connects incomparability to untranslatability, proposing that just as we should allow untranslatable terms such as *xiaoshuo* 'to stand in their original languages',[11] we should appreciate different literatures in their original languages and forms instead of rendering them into a reader-friendly (i.e. customer-friendly) English that reinforces the commercialization of the global literary market. Apter's notions of the untranslatable and incomparable should, however, be understood as '*infelicitous* to translate/compare' rather than '*unfeasible* to translate/compare'. Her point is not that it is impossible to gain adequate understanding of a term or concept by discussing it in a foreign language (the fact that Apter explains the nuances and problematics of such terms already defeats such a claim), but that untranslatability and incomparability should be invested with the political significance of resisting the global capitalism that reduces different literatures and cultures to an easily digestible uniform idiom.[12] In the case of incomparable linguistic alterity, therefore, the crucial problem is again that of a linguistic power hierarchy that evaluates foreign languages and literatures through the currency of English — the *lingua franca* that allows non-Anglophone literatures into global circulation.

Finally, with regard to incomparability as irreducible historical alterity, Damrosch has maintained that this alterity exists notably in the radical remoteness of pre-modern literatures to contemporary critics and writers. 'The truly foreign literatures are not so much the works of [writers today] elsewhere, but rather the classical works of their own tradition'.[13] According to this view, in our globalized and well-connected world, different literatures and cultures interact much more with each other than with literatures of the past. The impossibility of accessing 'live' historical context leads to a temporal incommensurability which will always pose serious challenges when one compares dyssynchronous literatures, for as comparatists now we cannot but see history through our contemporary eyes, and discuss ancient texts by means of modern languages.

The above versions of irreducibility reflect a concern for the ethics of comparison. The question of comparability between different literatures, instead of denying the feasibility of relating literatures via comparison, is rather about how literatures and cultures can compare in ways that would not perpetuate various power structures, be it Eurocentrism, Anglophone-centrism, global capitalism or our bias towards modernity. Comparability and incomparability are no longer mutually exclusive diametrical opposites, but an oscillating relation that constantly re-negotiates between the inequalities of the *comparanda*. This is evidenced by recent scholarship that explores how incomparables can also be compared. Detienne's *Comparer l'incomparable* (2000) certainly pioneered this approach; more of late, in *Les Nouvelles Voies de comparatisme* (Academia Press, 2010), comparatists repositioned comparability in a scheme of more of less comparable, without an absolutely justified comparability, nor a complete incomparability;[14] in 2013, *PMLA* devoted an issue to comparative theory (vol. 128, no. 3) that probed how comparison could serve as a dynamic, non-superlative dialogue between literatures, and how there could be a 'comparativity' that reveals both the comparable and incomparable.[15]

In sum, contemporary discussions about comparability and incomparability have increasingly indicated that comparison is embedded in a politics of cultural perception and evaluation, and is a dynamic practice that can be shaped in different ways instead of an abstract structure that promises neutrality. Comparability is no longer about surpassing differences (because differences should not be smoothed out), but about exploring differences and how they can be compared in more ethical ways that challenge cultural hegemonies. This reflects a fundamental conflict in comparative criticism: the evaluative and imposing comparison that is pre-disposed to favour one *comparandum* over the other, versus the dialogical comparison that seeks to be non-imposing and treat each *comparandum* on its own terms while our understanding of the *comparanda* can be deepened by their comparison. There is therefore an infelicitous evaluative comparability, and an apposite dialogical comparability. To examine their dynamics and explore how literatures can compare in more felicitous ways, I now turn to some relevant discussions in the philosophy of comparison.

In parallel to discussions in literary criticism, the concept of comparability has also received more philosophical interest recently, in both analytic philosophy and the rising field of comparative philosophy that attests to new interest in expanding the scope of philosophical investigation by bringing in non-Occidental thought traditions for comparative study. But comparative philosophy also has another meaning and use, as Ralph Weber has pointed out: namely, the philosophy of comparison, because the concepts of comparison and comparability still lack extensive philosophical analysis.[16] Indeed, a new strand of philosophy has formed around discussions of comparability, value theory, and cross-cultural comparison of thought systems. Here, Ruth Chang's pioneering edited volume *Incommensurability, Incomparability, and Practical Reason* (Harvard University Press, 1997) is particularly worth mentioning. In this book, philosophers probed questions such as the uncertainty of rational choice when confronted with qualitatively different items (sometimes seen as incommensurable), definitions of comparability and incomparability and the borders that separate them, and the structural characteristics of comparison. These important issues were followed up in 2002 in Chang's monograph *Making Comparisons Count* (Routledge). The philosophical concern with comparison has continued since these major publications and more recently various scholars from comparative philosophy like Weber and Brook Ziporyn have produced further discussions on the topic.[17]

Interestingly, these philosophical studies have revealed a tension between different modes of comparison similar to the above-mentioned conflict between evaluative and dialogical comparisons in comparative literature. This stems from the problematic relation between what Chang and Weber have recently called 'ranking comparability' and 'contrastive comparability'. In Chang's words, 'ranking comparability' is 'the comparability of items, perhaps reasons or alternatives for choice, with respect to some value or normative criteria that yields a ranking of those items' (e.g. comparing a candle-lit room and the same room with dim electric lighting in regard to brightness); whereas 'contrastive comparability' denotes 'the comparability of items where the point of the comparison is not to determine which item is better in a ranking sense but to draw out similarities or differences between items in various respects that help illuminate each or something else to which each or both are related.'[18] Thus, they are two different kinds of comparabilities that enable different comparisons and have their own distinct purposes. The problem is, however, as Weber points out, the distinction between ranking comparison and contrastive comparison is often furtively blurred. 'Ranking comparison, it might then be said, presupposes contrastive comparison, and perhaps the inverse is also true. The first I take for granted (could you rank something without having compared it for its differences?).'[19] Vice versa, in a contrastive comparison, 'the result of a comparison is a relation between the *comparata* on the basis of the chosen respect [i.e. *tertium comparationis*]'.[20] Nevertheless, the result of such a contrastive comparison 'is most often exemplified by relations such as "better than", "equally good", etc. In other words, [...] "ranking" is the very outcome of (contrastive) comparison.'[21] But this is deeply perplexing, because comparative philosophy aims to illuminate certain issues in different philosophical texts and traditions rather than evaluate which *comparandum* is better. Indeed, Weber argues that comparative philosophy has the ethical obligation to 'not be about a ranking sense'; but 'in many ways and certainly in actual practice, it is either surreptitiously or manifestly about ranking.'[22] Weber gives the example of comparing ancient Greek and Chinese philosophy, saying that in the case where the comparatist favours rational arguments over contradictions and correlation, then Chinese thought is disadvantaged by being labelled as 'not logical', or 'lacking abstract concepts'; but in the case where the comparatist thinks contradictions are much more interesting and evocative than rational arguments, then Greek thought would be depreciated on this account.[23] Either way, a latent evaluation and ranking take place. This problem is the same as the one in comparative literature demonstrated above. Dialogical comparison in comparative literature is very similar to Weber's 'contrastive comparison', especially if we remember Natalie Melas's term 'contrastive literature',[24] but if dialogical comparison also starts with certain biased conceptions about literature, then one *comparandum* emerges from the comparison as superior to the other(s). The purpose of contrastive comparison to construct mutual insight between literatures and philosophies is compromised by the underlying evaluation.

At this point we may ask: do ranking comparability and contrastive comparability always have to intertwine? Is there a way to keep them distinct from each other or reposition their relation in a better way? To address this question I will examine more closely in the following sections the conceptualizations of ranking comparability and contrastive comparability, and how they can relate to the political dynamics between evaluative and dialogical comparisons in comparative literature. By way of doing this, I also aim to show that philosophy and literary criticism have much potentiality for cross-fertilization, for the theoretical rigour of the philosophy of comparison can complement and extend literary criticism so that it enriches the understanding of the uses and purposes of comparison in literature.

Ranking Comparability and the Need for Vagueness

Ranking comparability means thinking in terms of degrees of difference. Take the pair 'comparable' and 'incomparable', for instance: we could think of their relation as the comparable gradually decreasing until it becomes the incomparable. That there is no precise cut-off line but rather a graduated spectrum between the comparable and the incomparable can be demonstrated in many cases. For instance, if you compare the sweetness of an apple and an orange, the measurable sugar content in the fruits does not directly translate into perceived sweetness, so you cannot be precise about exactly how much sweeter one fruit is than the other. Nevertheless, as Chang and Joseph Raz have observed, thinking of ranking comparability in terms of a spectrum of degrees involves the Sorites paradox, which poses interesting questions about how comparability and incomparability can be positioned in regard to each other.

To begin with, the Sorites paradox appeared in pre-Socratic debates among logicians around the fifth to fourth centuries BCE, and illustrates fundamentally the type of arguments that use the logic of little-by-little. One of its most famous examples is that of a heap of sand given by Eubulides of Miletus, famous for constructing paradoxes. This is also how the name 'Sorites' came about, for *sōrós* means 'heap' in ancient Greek. Eubulides's question was, if you keep subtracting one grain of sand each time from a heap of sand, when will the heap be no longer a heap? On the other hand, if you start with a grain of sand, and keep adding to it a grain of sand each time, when will they become a heap of sand? The logical puzzle is due to the indeterminacy of the concept of a heap, for it seems that 'no one grain of [sand] can be identified as making the difference between being a heap and not being a heap'.[25] We can also refer to Zeno's paradoxes for more examples of the Sorites argument. Zeno of Elea was renowned for producing contradictions and dialectical arguments. Reputedly, he produced a Sorites paradox about 'arguments against motion', which was recorded by Aristotle in his *Physics* as: 'That which is in locomotion must arrive at the half-way stage before it arrives at the goal'.[26] To give a concrete illustration, suppose I want to go to the train station. Before I can get there, I must get halfway there. Before I can get halfway there, I must get a quarter of the way there. Before travelling a quarter, I must travel one-eighth of the distance; and so on ad infinitum. This scenario poses the Sorites question as the infinite divisibility of a line and the infinite number of tasks one needs to complete when going from one point to another. Since it is impossible to complete an infinity of tasks I can never reach the train station and, in fact, I cannot move anywhere. Therefore Zeno argues, following Parmenides's view that change is impossible, that no motion can really take place.

There have been many attempts in the history of philosophy to solve this paradox, some of which have successfully refuted it,[27] but that is not the concern of the present discussion. Instead, I would like to explore how this paradox reveals that the degrees of difference between comparability and incomparability need to be understood as *vague*. The nuances of difference that a ranking comparison produces do seem to map onto a Sorites spectrum, but then such a spectrum involves an area of uncertainty of ranking or evaluation. Firstly, consider the words we use to describe a ranking comparison: 'more', 'less', 'as ... as' or 'the same'. This terminology puts different items of comparison under a certain perspective of evaluation and then determines how much they weigh against each other. This perspective of evaluation is what Ruth Chang calls 'a covering value':

> Every comparison must proceed in terms of a value. A 'value' is any consideration with respect to which a meaningful evaluative comparison can be made. Call such a consideration the *covering value* of that comparison.[28]

Chang emphasizes that a comparison of different items cannot make sense unless you are comparing them in regard to something. The necessity of a covering value in comparisons means that comparisons must be relative, there is no comparison *simpliciter*. For instance, 'this rod may be greater than that one with respect to length or mass or conductivity, but it cannot be greater, period'.[29] By the same logic, for incomparability, you cannot say items are incomparable *simpliciter*, only incomparable in regard to something. Therefore, saying that apples and oranges do not compare does not say anything meaningful, since the specification of the aspect under which they do not compare is absent. We *can* compare apples and oranges in regard to their vitamin C content per 100g (oranges are richer in vitamin C), their hardness (apples are usually harder), or fruitness (they are equally fruits).

Returning to the Sorites problem, we may translate its logic of little-by-little into comparative situations, which then reveal an area of vagueness on the spectrum of difference. Let us consider the case that Chang proposes:

> If A and B are equally good with respect to V [covering value], then A and B stand in the same value relations to all other items with respect to V. It follows that a small improvement in A with respect to V, no matter how small, makes the improvement A+ of A better than B with respect to V. If an improvement in one item does not make it better than the other, the original items cannot be equally good. That is, it must be *false* that they are equally good.[30]

In other words, if a slight improvement or impoverishment of one item does not make any difference in the comparison (i.e. does not make item A better or worse than item B in regard to V), then these two items are incomparable: they cannot be described by the comparative relationship of 'better', 'worse' or 'equally good'. This argument, which Chang terms the 'Small improvement argument', has the form of a Sorites paradox and shows that ranking is not always measurable or linear. As Chang suggests, we can try to compare Mozart and Picasso on creativity. Initially, we may say that Mozart and Picasso are both creative geniuses, but in different ways, so they are incomparable to each other. If, however, we create a spectrum of people with different amounts of creativity, say take Picasso and decrease his creative talent until we have a person who is just starting to learn how to paint and can imitate Picasso's style poorly. Call this poor painter P-. Then we compare P- with Mozart, and it seems quite acceptable to say that P- has less creativity than Mozart instead of being incomparable to him. The question now is: where are the borders of comparability between Mozart and Picasso? At the point where P- is compared with Mozart, we can say they are comparable; at the point where

Picasso is compared to Mozart, they are incomparable. But if Picasso and Mozart are truly incomparable, then a small impoverishment of Picasso's creativity should not make any difference in terms of their comparability. And by successive uses of *modus ponens* (i.e. 'the rule of logic which states that if a conditional statement "*if p then q*" is accepted, and the antecedent *p* holds, then the consequent *q* may be inferred'),[31] no amount of small impoverishments will ever make Picasso and Mozart comparable. But this seems simply implausible, because it is hard to believe that the greatly impoverished version of Picasso, P-, is not less creative than Mozart. Here the question about vague boundaries emerges: at what point do Mozart and P- become comparable? What kind of border exists between their comparability and incomparability?

The crux of the problem here, I believe, is that both *comparanda* (Picasso and Mozart) and the covering value (creativity) in this comparison are indeterminate and not precisely measurable. This indeterminacy goes beyond that of Eubulides's puzzle, for the latter is only indeterminate in terms of the *semantic* scope of the terms 'heap' and 'non-heap'; namely, this is a problem of the vagueness of language describing a reality, but not a problem of the reality *itself* — for at any moment the number of grains of sand can be measured precisely and we can know for certain how many more grains of sand heap no. 1 has than heap no. 2.[32] But comparing Mozart and Picasso is different, because it is not the terms we use to describe their relation that are vague, but the very reality we are trying to describe that is indeterminate, for we are comparing items of *qualitative* difference, not simply *quantitative* difference, in regard to a cover value that is highly contentious. (What constitutes creativity? What standards should we use to measure it?) This means that, with qualitatively different *comparanda* and non-objective cover values for comparison, we need a vague zone that allows for non-linear and ambiguous positioning of differences. In this case, the boundary between comparability and incomparability of such indeterminate *comparanda* is vague because it neither has a precise cut-off point nor is necessarily singular.[33]

If we return to comparative literature with this view of vague comparability, we can easily recognize that the *comparanda* of comparative literature — different literatures and cultural forms — are polyvalent, resist precise measurement, and therefore require vagueness in comparison. Nor can an accurately quantifiable or objective 'covering value' — in comparative literature's case, the respect to which two or more texts are compared and connected (*tertium comparationis*) — exist for such vague *comparanda*. The qualitative differences of different literatures make it impossible to position them linearly on a graded spectrum denoting a single value scale. Consequently, comparability is a flexible relation that depends on the interpretative context and is always open to contention. In fact, this problem of the indeterminacy of comparing literatures has been remarked upon by a writer and critic as ancient as Horace.[34] In his letter 'To Augustus' (*Epistles* 2.1), Horace asks: when it comes to evaluating Latin writers in comparison to Greek ones, how old does a writer need to be in order to be old enough to be considered an ancient classic? Horace criticizes the tendency of his contemporaries to set antiquity and

Greekness as the standards of literary excellence, then raises his question in a Sorites form:

> Just because we know that of the Greeks
> The earliest writers are best, we therefore use
> The same set of scales to compare them with our writers
> [...]
> If poetry, like wine, improves with age,
> Then tell me, I'd like to know, how do you know
> Exactly in what year a particular poem
> Turns into a good one?[35]

Horace goes on to assert that it is impossible and absurd to fix a precise time limit when a poem 'matures' into excellence, because it is the text's qualitative aspects — its grace, polish, and didactic value, for example — that matter, not its quantitative historical age. Comparisons between Greek and Latin writers should therefore be made with regard to their literary quality, regardless of their antiquity or contemporaneity. It is worth noting that firstly, Horace denies that a precisely quantifiable *tertium* (temporal duration) can meaningfully compare Greek and Latin literatures; and secondly, he asserts that these literatures are comparable when the *tertium* becomes 'literary quality' instead. This implies that the same texts can be made incomparable or comparable depending on what *tertium* or relation the comparatist wants to construct them with. Although Horace, having clear ideas about the standards of literary merit, does not problematize the *tertium* of literary quality as critics now would do, he does not say whether one can decide *exactly* how much better one text is than another. Given his expressed disapproval of the mathematical way of evaluating literature ('He's bound to be baffled [... he] who counts by annals, grain by grain'),[36] very possibly he would agree that though a text can be superior in quality to another, its superiority cannot be stated as an exactly measurable amount. This example supports my argument that when it comes to comparing literatures, we need a vague comparability.

In what specific aspects does the notion of vague comparability transform our understanding and construction of comparisons between literatures? The first obvious conclusion is that ranking i.e. evaluative comparison is unsuitable for comparative literature, because literatures are complex bundles of qualitative differences and are vague *comparanda* (even in the case when the comparatist wants to rank literatures, as Horace did, the ranking can only be a fuzzy one). That ranking should not be the concern of comparative literature is significant, since many problems in the field are caused by consciously or unconsciously smuggling into the comparison a ranking evaluation (e.g. pre-modern Chinese narratives about the super-natural seen (erroneously) as a prototype of modern fiction; and the Arab novel judged as less advanced in literary realism than nineteenth-century French novels). I will come back to this point later. The second conclusion is that comparability and incomparability in comparative literature are not on a linear spectrum and the boundary between them is neither singular nor definite. The 'covering' topics and perspectives through which literary texts can be compared are numerous. Depending on what perspective they are considered under, the same texts can be both comparable and incomparable. Therefore, to answer the question 'when do literatures become comparable?' (or incomparable), it can be said that depending on the particular construction of comparability, the borders between comparability and incomparability can be *anywhere*. For instance, it makes sense to compare nineteenth-century Romantic poetry with medieval Chinese poetry on their depictions of the human-nature relation, but it does not make sense to compare them on the use of idiomatic expressions in classical Chinese — this aspect being non-existent in Romantic poetry, which was not written in Chinese. Or one could compare Greek Surrealist writings by Nikos Engonopoulos and Andreas Embirikos with psychedelic writings of Aldous Huxley, Henri Michaux or William Burroughs on the use of incongruous imagery and exploration of madness; but it would be out-of-place to compare them in regard to how historicist these writers were in their literary creations, because historicism was not an issue which they engaged with. These examples show that comparability and incomparability in literature are not absolute: not only can the comparability of the same *comparanda* change depending on the viewpoint they are examined from, but also that the relation between the comparable and incomparable is a matter of vague extents of 'more and less comparable' rather than two mutually exclusive categories (the very notion of vagueness already pre-empts such mutual distinction). The 'incomparable' does not mean 'not comparable at all', but rather, 'a degree of comparability so low that it makes the comparison not worth making'. For we must realize that the fact that texts can be compared on a certain point does not necessarily mean that the comparison is important or insightful. The crucial task for the comparatist is therefore to find a stronger and more significant comparability, so better instead of worse comparisons can be made.

The third conclusion following upon the second is that, since comparability and incomparability between literatures can be potentially constructed from any pertinent viewpoint, comparability and incomparability are decided not by *what* one compares, but by *how* one compares. From this we understand that the comparability or incomparability of the literatures that are compared does not exist *a priori* in the literatures themselves, but is invented by the particular comparison and comparatist in question (in the case of incomparability, it stems from the comparatist putting the *comparanda* in an unsuitable or insignificant comparison). Views that declare some texts and cultures to be incomparable or comparable are constructed discourses that reflect two fundamentally different worldviews: one that sacralizes an irreducible alterity that refuses comparison because it cannot enter into any exchange system where it can be 'translated' into a 'common currency' — be it the *lingua franca* of English, or the canon of world literature that has global circulation (Apter, Young, and Levinas as discussed above fall into this category);[37] and another worldview that recognizes alterity only in so much as it is always already the result of comparison, whereby asserting a fundamental communicability and openness between different things and phenomena in the world, and not least its languages, literatures, and cultures (Susan Friedman,[38] Zhang Longxi, Lloyd fall into this category).

Contrastive Comparability and the Question of the *tertium comparationis*

The above examination of ranking comparability in philosophy gives new salience to the nature of comparison in comparative literature by highlighting how the latter is ill-fitted for evaluative judgement. Now we can turn to consider if Weber's contrastive comparability can better address comparisons between qualitatively different *comparanda* such as thought systems and literatures. As cited earlier, contrastive comparability is not about ranking, but considers similarities and differences between the *comparanda* in order to illuminate them and/or the covering topic of their comparison. This covering topic is the much-debated *tertium comparationis*, which exists for comparative philosophy as well as comparative literature. In Weber's view, the *tertium* is 'a point of commonality' with 'minimal and maximal conceptions': 'minimally, the expression refers to a "common" respect (equally relatable to both *comparata*) and, maximally, the expression refers to something like a "common" property (shared by both *comparata*).'[39] Now, in Weber's view, the problematic overlap between ranking and contrastive comparabilities, as mentioned in his discussion with Chang, is that there is a 'pre-comparative tertium' that preliminarily determines the *comparanda*. For instance, if I decide to compare the works of Aristotle and Xunzi on human nature, I have already assumed that Xunzi is at least a philosophical thinker if not a 'philosopher' in the Greek sense, that there is a notion of 'human nature' that Xunzi can relate to, even though there was no theoretical formulation of the concept at Xunzi's time (third century BCE).[40] But these assumptions are inevitably based on the biased view that it makes sense to talk about a 'human' nature that is presumably different from 'non-human' or 'animal' nature, on views about what philosophy is like and what concepts are. In this sense, the comparatist is already judging and categorizing Xunzi by certain criteria that do not necessarily apply to him. This pre-comparative determination of the *comparanda* therefore inevitably introduces inherent biases and imposed frameworks into the comparison.

This problem finds its parallel in comparative literature, which is why conflicts and debates arise between what I call 'evaluative' and 'dialogical' comparison. Indeed, in the early years of comparative literature, evaluation was crucial, for comparison aimed at drawing conclusions about cultural superiority and progress. For example, during the first few decades of the twentieth century, when China was looking eagerly towards European modernity in the hope of re-invigorating a Chinese culture that was seen to be weak and decaying, the critic Hu Shi compared Mohist (a school of rhetoricians in early China) argumentation with ancient Greek reasoning in his *Outlines of the History of Chinese Philosophy* (1919). His chosen *tertium* was, however, logicality in the syllogistic, namely, Aristotelian sense; and his aim was to prove that the ancient Chinese could think as logically as the Greeks, in short, that ancient Chinese culture was not inferior to the Greek. This is obviously a ranking comparison where the *tertium* imposes a culturally biased framework on one *comparandum*, for Hu Shi's conclusion does nothing other than reinforce the Eurocentric view that ancient Greek literature and culture are the standards for cultural greatness. Or, in *fin-de-siècle* France, when translations of Far-Eastern and

South-Asian literatures gradually increased against the background of Goethe's vision of *Weltliteratur*, the French school of *littérature comparée* still tended to compare French literature with foreign literatures to re-affirm the centrality and superiority of the former, and the exotic 'strangeness' of the latter.[41] This is evaluative comparison at its worst. Now, however, comparative literature has moved towards the dialogical, having gone beyond this simplistic, un-self-critical Eurocentric criticism, with comparatists being increasingly more aware of issues of cultural bias, power hierarchy, and the imposition of European ideas about literature on non-European texts. Nevertheless, the problem of evaluation and a neutral comparability has not disappeared and remains central. The pivot of this problem, just as in comparative philosophy, is still the *tertium*. I will now turn to discuss the *tertium* in more detail, referring to Weber's arguments for clarification at relevant points.

To begin with, the *tertium* has been one of the thorniest problems in comparative literature; as Haun Saussy has remarked, the history of comparative literature is nothing more than 'a series of attempts to discover or name the *tertium comparationis*.'[42] Whether a suitable *tertium* can be found is crucial to deciding the comparability of the texts in question. Nevertheless, it is important to first recognize that the *tertium* needs some vagueness in its definition. As I have argued, literatures are vague *comparanda*, therefore the *tertium* that connects them in comparison cannot be a measurable objective denominator like 'sugar content in grams' or a simple attribute like 'redness'. That Weber has denoted minimal and maximal conceptions of the *tertium* shows the *tertium* has a relatively flexible semantic scope. In comparative literature, we could broadly define it as the respect in terms of which literatures are compared, denoting a common ground such as a broad theme with which different texts can engage rather than a precise literary attribute that is a single aspect or quality shared between the compared literatures. For instance, the *tertium* can be a semantic field such as 'the grotesque' or 'humour' that includes a cluster of notions and themes that share family resemblances, but cannot be pinpointed to one definition. There is no need, therefore, to understand the *tertium* in too restricted a sense such as an invariant that levels the *comparanda* onto one scale. Secondly, the biggest problem with the *tertium* is that it seems impossible to find a neutral *tertium* for any comparison in literature. Since the *tertium* shapes the differences and relations between the compared texts, its bias is then extremely infelicitous, because the comparative framework becomes pre-disposed to weight one *comparandum* over the other, or reflects some broad ethnocentric prejudices of the comparatist. With regard to this, comparatists are generally divided between two attitudes: one denying that *tertia* can be found at all because of the incompatibility of differences between literatures; another asserting that *tertia* can be found, but that there never exists a completely neutral, non-culturally-centric *tertium*.[43] The first view asserts the impossibility of comparison, and is only endorsed by very few, mostly in the early phases of comparative literature, such as the Romanian critic Lovinescu, who believed that unless works 'are among the same content [...] and the same aesthetic formula', they are unintelligible and incomparable to each other.[44] This view carries to the extreme the particularity and singularity of each text, to the extent that one can say that not even two contemporaneous texts written in the same language and cultural background can be compared. Being unpalatable and easily refutable, this view is not my focus here.[45] The second view, however, is the prevalent view among comparatists now, and can be further divided into two sides: one side concluding that because the *tertium* is always biased, comparison is a deeply problematic method and should be used with extreme caution and only in limited contexts (e.g. Radhakrishnan, Bruce Lincoln, Melas); another side arguing that despite the biased *tertium*, comparison not only needs to go on but also should be increasingly applied to more texts and topics (e.g. Alexander Beecroft, Wiebke Denecke, Lloyd). While I agree that comparison should be used carefully and as self-critically as possible, I am on the second side that advocates comparison despite its biases. This is because the *tertium*, I argue as follows, does not pose as many difficulties as it seems to.

What I find interesting is not the question of whether the *tertium* is neutral or biased, but that this question should arise at all. If one is enclosed within one's own biased conceptual frameworks, how could one even become aware that the *tertium* is biased? This is like the case of fish that do not know what water is. The very recognition of the prejudicial character of the *tertium* is already the result of an initial comparison. Without taking into account the foreign, marginalized Other, there would be no self-critical gaze. This confirms that comparison is not only an activity crucial to discovering one's own biases and trying to overcome them, but also a process of inquiry that, instead of starting from a perfect, unbiased and finalized *tertium*, progressively reveals more about it. Presumably, besides better understanding the texts that are compared, an important aim of comparison is to better articulate the *tertium* that connects the texts in comparison. This means that at the beginning of comparison, the *tertium* is incomplete, open to change and not an invariant. As Weber comments thoughtfully, after the comparison, both the *comparanda* and *tertium* are different from what they were at the start of comparison, for 'my understanding or knowledge of that which [...] I set out to compare is different from that which my comparison ends up having compared.'[46] This transformation of the *tertium* is the process of a certain topic being gradually fleshed out as comparison goes on. In this way, the *tertium* not only does not need to be completely justified right from the start, but also is the site where its inherent biases can be exposed through comparison. It is inevitable that we start with a *tertium* that depends on certain preconceptions and prejudices (because complete neutrality is impossible), but the strength of comparison is that it can help us discover these preconceptions and be more critical of them.

This processual idea of the *tertium* would require a processual notion of comparability, for the *tertium* is key to constructing comparability. As the *tertium* and the *comparanda* are transformed through comparative examination, comparability emerges as the process of developing and establishing comparability. Starting from a more biased and less self-critical point and moving to a more critical point where certain biases will have been deconstructed, comparability increasingly shifts from the ranking to the contrastive, the evaluative to the dialogical. The borders between evaluative and dialogical comparabilities are therefore constantly changing. If we are committed to the view that the ethics of comparative literature should be dialogical instead of evaluative, then the expansion of comparative methods and studies should of course be commended, since one of the significant consequences of comparison is to increase our awareness of other literary traditions, linguistic and cultural particularities, and better resist ethnocentric presumptions and parochialism. As Geoffrey Lloyd argues in his most recent *Analogical Investigations* (2015), although comparatism (i.e. comparative method) has been used for various oppressive purposes, it can also be used as 'a stimulus to revision, to criticism and to dissent, [...] allowing for differences but not in a bid to determine hierarchies of superiority or inferiority, nor yet to proclaim mutual unintelligibilities, but rather to make the most of the opportunities for broadening our horizons that those differences present.'[47] The understanding of comparability as processual, flexible, and multiple, which I have argued for, supports this positive use of comparison and envisages comparison as a dynamic act of inquiry rather than a category of reason's 'logical operation' (as Kant saw it).[48]

Conclusion

By way of conclusion, through relating the philosophy of comparison to comparative literature, I have argued that the notions of comparability and incomparability in comparative literature are relative, vague, and can be constructed in many different ways. Consequently, comparison in literary criticism is also a multiplicity of processes, concepts, and methods. By comparing comparison in philosophy and comparison in comparative literature, we can better clarify the particular uses and methods of the latter, thus showing that dialogues between philosophy and literary criticism can be fruitful. More specifically, in this essay I have also proposed the following points.

Firstly, comparison in comparative literature is not concerned with ranking measurable *comparanda*, and comparability and incomparability are not mutually exclusive but co-exist in a vague zone of 'more or less comparable'. Moreover, depending on the viewpoint of comparison, the borders between comparability and incomparability can be anywhere. Thus, comparability and incomparability are dynamic processes emerging from the activity of comparison rather than conceptual structures that require determination before comparison begins.

Secondly, the flexibility of borders between the comparable and incomparable means that they are constructed through discourses that are, just like the much-criticized *tertium*, never neutral. Every comparative discourse tends to favour either incomparability or comparability depending on who is wielding the view to what purpose. The aporias of incommensurability and untranslatability, as well as the possibilities for comparability and translatability, do not exist *a priori* in the literatures that are compared or translated but are created through discussions that aim to make them so.

Thirdly, similar to ranking and contrastive comparisons in philosophy, a distinction between evaluative and dialogical comparisons exists in comparative literature. I believe that the ethical imperative is that comparative literature *should not* be evaluative, but aim to show insight into the heterogeneity of literatures and languages, and break down cultural centrisms. Although the *tertium comparationis* always poses problems of bias, it can transform during the comparison as a process of revealing and deconstructing some (if not all) of its own biases, and enable comparatists to be more self-critical of their presumptions and conceptual limitations.

The vagueness and multiplicity of comparability and the *tertium* explain largely, in my view, why there is still much uncertainty about the status of comparative literature, to the extent that René Wellek's remark that comparative literature 'has not been able to establish a distinct subject matter and a specific methodology' still stands.[49] But this disciplinary fluidity is not necessarily bad. Indeed it can even be a strength that distinctly established disciplines do not have, for constant self-reflexive questioning avoids entrenching comparative literature into petrified positions and allows open-mindedness towards new and disparate ways of comparing texts, revealing numerous possibilities for interpretation, as well as new attempts to rethink the notions of literature and text. We do not, therefore, need to dismiss the 'comparative' from the discipline of comparative literature as a misnomer. If comparison is expanded so that it is increasingly protean and processual as a concept and constructed in increasingly diverse ways as a method, there is no reason why the comparative cannot accommodate and guide what critics in comparative literature are exploring. The transformation of the ideas of comparability, the *tertium*, and comparison would then be an interactive process that continues simultaneously as comparative literature shapes itself.

Notes to Chapter 13

1. Gayatri Spivak, 'Rethinking Comparativism', *New Literary History*, 40.3 (2009), 609–26 (p. 611).
2. Thomas Claviez, 'Done and Over With — Finally? Otherness, Metonymy, and the Ethics of Comparison', *PMLA*, 128.3 (2013), 608–14 (p. 613).
3. Robert Young, 'The Postcolonial Comparative', *PMLA*, 128.3 (2013), 683–89 (p. 684).
4. David Ferris, 'Indiscipline', in *Ten Year Report on the Discipline, Comparative Literature in the Age of Globalization*, ACLA Report, 2006, pp. 78–99.
5. Andrei Terian, 'The Incomparable as Uninterpretable', *World Literature Studies*, 2 (2013), 52–63 (p. 53).
6. See Longxi Zhang, *Mighty Opposites: From Dichotomies to Differences in the Comparative Study of China* (Stanford, CA: Stanford University Press, 1998); and Geoffrey E. R. Lloyd, *Analogical Investigations* (Cambridge: Cambridge University Press, 2015).
7. Gayatri Spivak, *Death of a Discipline* (New York: Columbia University Press, 2003), p. 406.
8. Levinas quoted in Thomas Claviez, 'Done and Over With — Finally?', p. 609.
9. Emily Apter, *Against World Literature* (New York: Verso, 2013), p. 587.
10. Terian, 'The Incomparable as Uninterpretable', p. 54.
11. Apter, *Against World Literature*, p. 590.
12. The possibility to translate/compare and whether they directly influence each other is an issue different from Apter's arguments. A comparatist who has a good grasp of the different languages of her compared texts may think that these texts are nevertheless untranslatable; vice versa, a critic who thinks certain texts are translatable may not think that they are comparable.

13. David Damrosch, 'Comparing the Incomparable: World Literature from Du Fu to Mishima', *Renìxa*, 3 (2012), 133–55 (p. 147).
14. *Les Nouvelles Voies du comparatisme*, ed. by Hubert Roland and Stéphanie Vanasten (Gent: Academia Press, 2010).
15. See articles in *PMLA*, 128.3 (2013), published by the Modern Language Association (US).
16. Ralph Weber, 'Comparative Philosophy and the Tertium: Comparing What with What, and in What Respect?', *Dao*, 13 (2014), 151–71.
17. See Ralph Weber, '"How to Compare?" On the Methodological State of Comparative Philosophy', *Philosophy Compass*, 8.7 (2013), 593–603; and Brook Ziporyn, *Beyond Oneness and Difference: Li and Coherence in Chinese Buddhist Thought and its Antecedents* (Albany: SUNY Press, 2013).
18. Ruth Chang, in Dao Article Discussion — Ralph Weber on Comparison in Comparative Philosophy, on website: <http://warpweftandway.com/discussion-comparative-philosophy/> [accessed 20 Dec. 2015]
19. Ralph Weber, in Dao Article Discussion — Ralph Weber on Comparison in Comparative Philosophy, on website as previous [accessed 20 Dec. 2015]
20. Ibid.
21. Ibid.
22. Ibid.
23. Ibid.
24. Natalie Melas, 'Versions of Incommensurability', *World Literature Today*, 69.2 (1995), 275–80.
25. Dominic Hyde, 'Sorites Paradox', <http://plato.stanford.edu/entries/sorites-paradox/> [accessed Sept. 2014].
26. Aristotle, *Physics* VI: 9, 239b10, trans. by R. P. Hardie and R. K. Gaye, The Internet Classics Archive: <http://classics.mit.edu/Aristotle/physics.6.vi.html> [accessed 29 Dec. 2015].
27. See the summary of different responses to the Sorites paradox in <http://plato.stanford.edu/entries/sorites-paradox/> [accessed Sept. 2014].
28. Ruth Chang, *Making Comparisons Count* (New York and London: Routledge, 2002), p. 3.
29. Ibid., p. 4.
30. Ibid., p. 123.
31. See *OED* definition: <http://www.oed.com/view/Entry/238362?redirectedFrom=modus+ponens#eid> [accessed 28 Dec. 2015].
32. I thank Derek Parfit for clarifying this point in his talk on 9 Feb. 2015 about avoiding the Repugnant conclusion.
33. For more analysis of vagueness in philosophical comparison, see John Broome, 'Is Incommensurability Vagueness?', in *Incommensurability, Incomparability, and Practical Reason*, ed. by Ruth Chang (Cambridge, MA: Harvard University Press, 1997).
34. I am grateful to Sebastian Matzner for pointing out Horace's example to me.
35. Horace, *Epistles 2.1*, trans. by David Ferry, *Arion*, 3rd ser., 8.2 (2000), 63–73 (p. 63).
36. Ibid.
37. As Durkheim observed in his 'Les Formes élémentaires de la vie religieuse' (1912), to be sacred is to be valued incommensurably.
38. See Susan Stanford Friedman, 'Why Not Compare?', *PMLA*, 128.3 (2013), 753–62.
39. Ralph Weber, 'Comparative Philosophy and the Tertium', p. 153.
40. See Weber, 'Comparative Philosophy and the Tertium', and discussion with Chang on website <http://warpweftandway.com/discussion-comparative-philosophy/> [accessed 20 Dec. 2015].
41. See Siraj Ahmed on how colonial rule demanded that disparate literatures and cultures should be unified under one universal history of literature and civilization, 'Notes from Babel: Towards a Colonial History of Comparative Literature', *Critical Inquiry*, 39 (Winter 2014), 296–326.
42. Haun Saussy, 'Comparison, World Literature and the Common Denominator', in *A Companion to Comparative Literature*, ed. by Ali Behdad and Dominic Thomas (Chichester: Wiley-Blackwell, 2011), pp. 60–64 (p. 62).
43. Arguably, there is a third attitude, the view that the *tertium* is not necessary for comparison. I believe that advocates of this view in fact mean that a single universally shared *tertium* that can be

pinpointed in the *comparanda* does not exist. So this view objects to the strictly logical definition of the *tertium* which I already criticized, but does not mean that comparative criticism needs no points of contact to proceed. I will not examine this view here.

44. Cited in Andrei Terian, 'The Incomparable as Uninterpretable', p. 56.
45. Minimally, there are at least two *tertia* that can connect whatever *comparanda*: one is the fact that the *comparanda* all exist in the universe, existence being a universally shared aspect between any two or more things (as Moore observed); another is the comparatist who takes an interest in comparing these *comparanda*. So it is wrong to say that no *tertia* exist for literary comparison. Also, comparison cannot be between identical *comparanda* (which do not exist anyway).
46. Ralph Weber, in Dao Article Discussion — Ralph Weber on Comparison in Comparative Philosophy.
47. Geoffrey E. R. Lloyd, *Analogical Investigations* (Cambridge: Cambridge University Press, 2015), p. 40.
48. Kant included comparison as one of the three most fundamental logical operations: i.e., comparison, reflection, and abstraction, see Immanuel Kant, *Lectures on Logic*, trans. and ed. by J. Michael Young (Cambridge: Cambridge University Press, 1992), p. 592.
49. René Wellek, 'The Crisis of Comparative Literature' (1959), in *The Princeton Sourcebook in Comparative Literature: From the European Enlightenment to the Global Present*, ed. by David Damrosch, Natalie Melas and Mbongiseni Buthelezi (Princeton, NJ: Princeton University Press, 2009), pp. 161–72 (p. 162).

INDEX

Abbasid period 86
Abrahams, Mike 99
Adriatic 60
Aeneas 7
Aeschylus:
    Agamemnon 13, 101
Africa:
    North Africa 41, 57, 63
Agrippa 47
Aleppo 6, 87
Alexakis, Vassilis 127
    La Langue maternelle 117, 126–27
    Paris-Athènes 126–27
Alexandrowicz, Conrad:
    Mother Tongue 117
Algeria 7, 55–56, 58–60, 62–63
Algiers 57, 58, 60
Alighieri, Dante 117
Amoore, Louise 21
Anderson, James 84
Anderson, Miranda 163
Anglo-Irish Treaty (1921) 97
Antigua 124
Antonine dynasty 41
Apple 1
Apter, Emily 202–03, 210
Arabian Nights [*Alf layla wa layla*] 6, 9, 76–77, 81–88, 90, 92–93
Arctic University of Norway 22
Aretxaga, Begoña 103
Aristotle 211
    Physics 206
Asiatic Society of Bengal 81
Association for Borderlands Studies (ABS) 22
Association of European Border Regions 22
Atacama desert 72
Atlantic 45, 60, 169–70
    Atlantic coast 3, 41
Attlee, Clement 98
Audisio, Gabriel 7, 54–58, 63–64
    L'Algérie littéraire 56
    Amour d'Alger 55
    Sel de la mer 56–57, 59
Augustus 47
Austin, J. L. 102
Australia 122
Austria 118–19

Aviv, Nurith:
    Perte, Vaters Land 117
    D'une langue à l'autre: Misafa Lesafa 117

Bach-y-Rita, Paul 140
Baja California 26–27
Balkans 22
Balzac, Honoré de 172, 184
    Clotilde de Lusignan, ou le beau Juif [*Clotilde de Lusignan or the Handsome Jew*] 173
Bandini, Juan 34–35
Bandini-Couts family 28
Bandini-Couts, Isabella 30
Bangladesh-India border 1
Barad, Karen 150, 158–62
    Meeting the Universe Halfway: Quantum Physics and the Entanglement of Matter and Meaning 151
Barber, Fionna 103–04, 112
Barrault, Emile 53
Barrera, Mario 26, 37
Barrett Browning, Elizabeth 172
Battersby, Christine 145–46
BBC 97, 105
Beckford, William 79, 90
    Vathek 79
Bédollières, Gigault de la 179
Beecroft, Alexander 213
Belfast 103, 105–06, 111
Belfast Agreement, *see* Good Friday Agreement
Belgium 14
Bell, Anthea 14
Belloc, Marie A. 170
Bendib, El Yamine 58–59
Bengal 87–88
Benjamin, Walter 3
Bennet, Jane 158–59, 161–62
Bergson, Henri 161
Bergvall, Caroline 2, 6, 9–11
    Alyson Singes 73
    Drift 9, 67–68, 74
Berlin 17, 63, 129
Berlin Wall 1, 17, 128
Bernhard, Thomas 121
Bertrand, Louis 56
Bhabha, Homi 15
Biondi, Franco 128
Bodleian Library 77, 79, 81, 90

Bohemia 118–19
Bohr, Niels 158
Bolton, Herbert Eugene 26
Bonito, Vito M. 21
Bonnici, Ġużè:
    Lejn ix-Xemx 7, 53–55, 60, 62–63
Border Crossing Network 22
Border Poetics/Border Culture Research Group 22
Borutta, Manuel 57
Bouraoui, Hédi 122
    'Letter to the French Language' 122
Bourbon dynasty 172
Bradley, R. N. 55
Braudel, Fernand 57
Brexit 97
Britannia 41
British Army 99, 103
British Museum 87
Browning, Robert:
    Agamemnon 13–14
Burke, Edmund 177
Burroughs, William 210
Bussoletti, Gianfranco 18
Butler, Judith 158
Buzzetti, Luciano 19
Byron, Lord (George Gordon) 172

Caesar 47
Cairo 6, 82, 92
California 25, 26–27, 30, 32, 34–35
California State Parks 28, 32
Callard, Felicity 163–64
Calypso 61
Cambridge University 174
Cameron, James 140
Camus, Albert 7, 55–56
Canada-United States border 5, 19
Canetti, Elias:
    Die gerettete Zunge 117
    Mutterzunge 125
Cape Town 111
Capitol (temple of Jupiter) 4
Caracalla 41
Caraher, Peter 99
Carinthia (Kärnten) 118
Carlotto, Massimo:
    Cristiani di Allah 7, 53, 61
Carthage 7
Cassandra 101
Cassin, Barbara 202
Castoriadis, Cornelius 54–55
Catholicism 182
Celan, Paul 116–17
Cella, Gian Primo 21
Certeau, Michel de 73
Ceuta border fence 58

Chaillot, Amédée 179
Chalmers, David 12, 138–40, 143
    'The Extended Mind' 155–56
Chang, Ruth 204, 206–07, 211
Chevalier, Michel 53
China 211
Christ Church's library 88
Christov-Bakargiev, Carolyn 101, 111
Circe 61
City Factory Gallery, Derry 100, 112
Clark, Andy 12, 138–40, 150–51, 153–58, 162
    Being There: Putting Brain, Body and World Together 156
    'The Extended Mind' 155–56
    Natural Born Cyborgs 157
    Supersizing the Mind 157
Classicism 183
Claviez, Thomas 201, 202
CNN 26
Cohen, Margaret 170
Colebrook, Claire 156–58
Connelly, William 150
Corn Law 179
Couts, Cave Johnson 30–31
Croatia 22
Crossmaglen 102

Damrosch, David 201, 203
Dana, Richard Henry 28, 34–35
    Two Years before The Mast 26, 33–36
Danube 41
Darbo-Peschanski, Catherine 3, 7
Darwin, Charles:
    On the Origin of Species 152
Davis, William Heath:
    Seventy Five Years in California 33
Davison, Nathaniel 82
Defauconpret, Auguste Jean-Baptiste 14, 178–84
Defauconpret, Charles-Auguste 178
Dekkan 81
Delacroix, Eugène 173
Delaroche, Paul 173
De Luca, Erri:
    Solo andata 58
Democratic Unionist Party 100
Denecke, Wiebke 213
Derrida, Jacques 27, 151
    'Des tours de Babel' 13
Derry/Londonderry:
    city 97, 100, 102, 105–07, 111–12
    county, *see* Ireland: County Derry
Descartes, René 143
deSouza, Allan 99
Detienne, Marcel 203
Dickens, Charles 178
Dido 6–7

Diodorus Siculus 4
Doherty, Willie 10, 97, 100–04, 106, 111–12
   'At the Border' 107, 110–12
   'The Blue Skies of Ulster' 100
   'Border Incident' 104, 107
   'Border Road' 107
   'Buried' 100
   'Ghost Story' 107
   'God Has Not Failed Us' 100
   'The Only Good One is a Dead One' 101
   'The Other Side' 105–06
   'The Outskirts' 107
   'Remains' 100
   'They're All the Same' 101
Dolben, John 81
Douglas, clan 169
Downing Street Declaration 105
Dryden, John 13
Duchamp, Marcel 74
Dumas, Alexandre 184

East, W. Gordon 17, 18
East India College 81
East India Company 81
École d'Alger 54–56, 59, 64
Edinburgh 179
Egypt 41, 81–83, 90, 92
Egypt-Libya border 19
Eliot, George 165
   Felix Holt, the Radical 174
Embirikos, Andreas 210
England 14, 76, 81, 169–70, 172–75, 180, 183
English Channel 170–73, 175, 178–80, 183
English Constitution 175
Engonopoulos, Nikos 210
Engstrand, Iris 29
Enlightenment 63
Eratosthenes 45–46
Estonia 196–97
Eubulides of Miletus 206, 208
Euclid:
   Elements 43–44
Europe 1, 3, 6, 7, 22, 76, 84, 171, 178
   Eastern Europe 63
European Union 1, 22, 97
Evans, Arthur B. 169

Farina, Mirko 142
FBI 1
Fénelon, François:
   Les Aventures de Télémaque 6
Fenimore Cooper, James 178
Ferishta (Muhammad Qasim Hindu Shah) 81
Ferris, David 201
Fisher, Jean 111
Fitzgerald, Des 163–64

Flack, Roberta 135
Ford, John:
   Stagecoach 26
Fortune 46
Foster, Roy 98
Foucault, Michel:
   Archaeology of Knowledge 41
France 3, 7, 58, 62, 120, 122, 170–75, 178–79, 183, 211
François, Anne Isabelle 10
Franke, Anselm 70
French Republic, *see* France
French Revolution 171–72, 174
Friedman, Susan 210

Galen 7, 41–44, 47–49
Gall, Franz Joseph 154
Gallagher, Shaun 157
Galland, Antoine 9, 76–77, 79, 81, 83–88, 92
Gallien, Claire 6, 9, 11
Gardini, Nicola 2
Garratt, Peter 12
Gee, Gabriel 102, 112
Gekas, Sakis 57
Gelder, Geert Jan van 86
Genet, Jean 121
Genette, Gérard:
   Paratextuality 82
Genlis, Madame de (Stéphanie Félicité du Crest de Saint-Aubin, Comtesse de Genlis) 173
Germany 128
Gibraltar, Straits of 61
Gilroy, Paul 82
Glorious Revolution 174
Goethe, Johann Wolfgang von 116, 178, 212
Goldhill, Simon 162
Goldsmiths University 70
Goncourt Prize 120
Good Friday Agreement 98–99, 104–05, 110
Google 1, 106
Gosselin, Charles 179
Gothic 183
Government of Ireland Act (1920) 97
Graham, Colin 100, 105–06, 111
Great Britain 41, 101, 170, 174
Greece 57, 62
Grima, Adrian 6–7
Grub-Street translations 76
Guadalupe Hidalgo, Treaty of 26, 28
Guizot, François 174
Gülsüm, Baydar 27
Guzmán, Patricio:
   Nostalgia for the Light 72

Hadrian 41
Hadrian's Wall 49

Haileybury 81
Hall, Alexandra 21
Hannibal 7
Haraway, Donna 150
Harman, Graham 159–62
Harrison, Nate 37
Hartshorne, Richard 20
Hastings, Warren 81
Hathaway, Donny 135
Heaney, Seamus 98
   'Mycenae Lookout' 101
   'The Other Side' 105
   'Whatever You Say Say Nothing' 102–03
Heidegger, Martin 137, 144–46, 156
   Being and Time 11–12
Heidelberg 137
Helsinki 13
Herder, Johann Gottfried 178
Hergé (Georges Prosper Remi):
   L'Île noire 184
Hermes 127
Herzfeld, Michael 54
Highland Boundary Fault 170
Highland Line 170, 177
Highlands, *see* Scotland
Hindustan 81
Honorius, Julius:
   Cosmographia 47
Horace:
   Epistles 208–09
Hornsby, Jennifer 143
Horovitz, Josef 86
Houle, France 22
Howe, Susan:
   The Europe of Trusts 74
Hugo, Victor 172, 184
Hungary 22
Hunt, Ian 110
Hunt Jackson, Helen 28
   Ramona 30, 33
Husserl, Edmund 160
Huxley, Aldous 210

Ibn 'Abd Rabbih 86
Ibn Khaldûn:
   The Muqaddimah 53
Inayat-Allah Kamboh:
   Bahar-Danush (Bahar-i-danish) 81
Inderscience 22
India 81, 169
Indiveri, Magda 21
Inland Sea, *see* Mediterranean
Institute for British-Irish Studies 99
IRA 98, 105
Iran 41
Iraq 41

Ireland 63, 97–99, 170
   Celtic Tiger 98
   Counties: Cavan 98; Donegal 98, 106, 111;
      Monaghan 98, 99
   Republic of 99, 105
Irish border, *see* Northern Ireland border
Irish Civil War 97
Irish War of Independence 97
Islam 77
Israel 62
Israeli West Bank barrier 1
Italy 10, 57
Izzo, Jean-Claude:
   Les Marins perdus [*The Lost Sailors*] 7, 53, 60–62

Jackson Turner, Frederick 3
Jacobite Rebellions 173
Jacobs, Adriana X. 2
James I: 106
James V: 169
James, Henry 165
Jones, Terry 37
Joyce, David 43
Joyce, James 121, 165
July Monarchy 174
Jupiter 4–5

Ka'abah (Kaaba) 86
Kafka, Franz 118
Kaminer, Wladimir:
   Es liegt mir auf der Zunge 117
Kant, Immanuel 214
Karelian Institute 22
Kelly, Aaron 110
Khan, Eradut 81
Kilito, Abdelfattah 85
Kincaid, Jamaica:
   Lucy 124
Kirkland, Richard 103–05
Kiverstein, Julian 142
Klar, Kathryn 37
Klepfisz, Irena:
   A Few Words in the Mother Tongue 117
Knights of St John 60, 62
Kristeva, Julia:
   Étrangers à nous-mêmes [*Strangers to Ourselves*] 123–24
Kütt, Madli 14
Kuwait 41

Labour 98
Lackner, Ruth 116
Lahiri, Jhumpa:
   The Namesake 120
Lake Poets 172
Lampedusa 1
Latour, Bruno 152, 159

Lattre, Alain de 189
Lavan, Rosie 10
Lazarova, Rouja:
   Sur le bout de langue 117
Lebanon 62
'Left-to-Die' Boat Case 67, 70, 74
Leigh and Sotheby 81
Leuvrey, Elisabeth:
   La Traversée 54, 58–59
Levinas, Emmanuel 202, 210
Li, Xiaofan Amy 15
Liauzu, Claude 56, 60
Libya 10
Lifford 111
Lincoln, Bruce 213
Livy 4
Lloyd, David 99
Lloyd, Geoffrey E. R. 202, 210, 213–14
Loch Katrine 169
Loh, Vyvyane:
   Breaking the Tongue 117
London 76, 112, 178–79
Longman and Co. 81
Longxi, Zhang 202, 210
Louis Philippe I 174
Lovinescu, Eugen 212
Lowlands, *see* Scotland
Lumsden, Alison 176
Lyons, Martyn 179

Macnaghten edition 86
Maggin, William 174
Maghreb 59
Mahler, Gustav 152
Mahmoud-Moussa, Fatma 79, 81
Malafouris, Lambros:
   How Things Shape the Mind 163
Malta 7, 60
Mamo, Juann 57
Maraise, Sophie de 179
Marin, Cheech:
   Born in East LA 26
Mars 4
Marseilles 58
Martin, Joseph 179
Martin, Tom 10–11, 71
Martínez, Demetria:
   Mother Tongue 117, 120
al-Masadi, Mahmud 8
Matt's Gallery, London 112
Maturana, Humberto 154
Matvejević, Predrag 54
Mauthner, Fritz 119
   Memoirs 118
   'Muttersprache und Vaterland' [Mother Tongue and Fatherland] 118

Mavors, *see* Mars
May, Cliff 37
May, Karl:
   Durchs wilde Kurdistan [*Across Wild Kurdistan*] 118
Maze/Long Kesh prison 100
Mazure, François A. J. 174
McCann, Eamonn 101
McCarthy, Cormac:
   Blood Meridian 25
   The Crossing 5
   Western Trilogy 25
McEwan, Ian:
   'Mother Tongue' 117
Médicis Prize 126
Mediterranean 1, 6–8, 10, 21, 53–64
Melas, Natalie 205, 213
Melilla border fence 58
Mellah, Fawzi 7
   Clandestin en Méditerranée 8
Merleau-Ponty, Maurice 156
Mesopotamia 41
Messina 8
Mexican Revolution 32
Mexico 27, 30–31, 34
Mexico-United States border 1, 5, 21, 25–26, 28, 36
Michaux, Henri 210
Middle Ages 174
Middle East 21
Middle Sea, *see* Mediterranean
Minh-Ha, Trinh T. 130
Mirabeau, Compte de (Honoré Gabriel Riqueti) 175
Mitchell, Timothy 82, 90, 92
Mokeddem, Malika:
   N'zid 7, 53–55, 58–59, 62, 64
Montague manuscript 9, 11, 76–77, 79, 81–85, 88, 92
Montague Oriental library 82
Montesquieu (Charles-Louis de Secondat, Baron de La Brède et de Montesquieu) 175
Morgan, Ben 2
Morgan, Sydney (Lady Morgan) 180
   Florence MacCarthy 179–80
Moroccan Western Sahara Wall 1
Morton, Timothy 156, 159–62
   Hyperobjects 151–55, 160–61
   Realist Magic 162
Moscow 13
Mozart, Wolfgang Amadeus 207–08
Mughal dynasty 81
Müller, Herta 128
Mury, Cécile 59
Museum of Modern Art 156
al-Mutanabbi, Abu al-Tayyib 86

Napoleon 172
Napoleonic Empire 171, 174
Narcissus 170

New Mexico 5, 120
New York 124, 156
Niagara River 5
Nicolle & Ladvocat 179
Nodier, Charles:
   Trilby ou le Lutin d'Argail [*Trilby or the Fairy of Argail*] 173
Noë, Alva 142, 156
   Action in Perception 155
North and South Korea border 1, 19
Northern Ireland 97–105, 110–12
   border 10, 97–99, 111
   counties: Antrim 97; Armagh 97, 99, 102; Derry/Londonderry 97, 105–06; Down 97; Fermanagh 97; Tyrone 97
   Troubles: 99, 100, 102, 105–06, 110
Northern Ireland Civil Rights Association 98
Nourbese Philip, Marlene:
   She Tries Her Tongue, Her Silence Softly Breaks 117, 122–23
Novello, Neil 21

O'Brien, Paul 104
Oceanside 28
O'Driscoll, Dennis 106
Odysseus, *see* Ulysses
Ó Gráda, Cormac 98
Old Spanish Lighthouse 27–28
Old Testament 119
Omri, Mohamed-Salah 2
Õnnepalu, Tõnu (Emil Tode) 14, 187, 194–96, 198
   Piiririik [*Border State*] 196–98
Orchard Gallery, Derry 102, 112
Orientalism 92–93
O'Shea, Tony 111
Ouseley, William 76, 81, 84–85
Ovid:
   Fasti 3–4
Oxford University 174
Özdamar, Emine Sevgi 128, 130
   Mutterzunge 117, 128–30

Pacific 60
Paisley, Ian 100
Pales festival 4
Palestine 62
Papotti, Davide 2
Paris 62, 127, 179, 197
Parmenides 206
Partridge, Eric 172
Paternoster-Row 76
Peloponnesus 45
Penelope 61
Perthshire 177
Philadelphia 5
Philostratus 44

Picasso, Pablo 207–08
Pichot, Amédée 179
Pico, Pío 32
Pinochet, Augusto 73
Plato 44
Polybius 45–46
Pommier, Jean 56
Prague 118
Presbyterianism 173
Prévost, Antoine François (Abbé Prévost) 175
Proclus 43
Protestant Reformation 182
Proust, Marcel 187–89, 191, 194, 198
   À la recherche du temps perdu 187, 193–96
   Le Temps retrouvé 14, 187, 190–91, 198
Ptolemy, Claudius:
   Geography 44–46
Puhvel, Madli 196

Quan, Betty:
   Mother Tongue 117
Québec 122
Qu'ran 82, 86

Radhakrishnan, Rajagopalan 201, 213
Rahimi, Atiq 120–21
   Syngué sabour, Pierre de patience 120
Rancho Guajome 27–32, 34, 37
Rea, Stephen 107
Reformed Kirk of Scotland 182
Reign of Terror 171
Renaissance 163
Restoration 174
Revolution of 1688, *see* Glorious Revolution
Reynolds, Matthew 2, 102
Rich, Adrienne 121
Rilke, Rainer Maria 116
Rodriguez, Robert:
   Mariachi Trilogy 26
Rolston, Bill 104
Roman Empire 3, 41, 47, 49, 56
Romanticism 183
Rome 4, 7, 45
Romulus and Remus 4
Rosetta 81
Rousseau, Jean-Jacques 175
Rowlands, Mark 150
Royal Library (France) 87
Royal Society 82–83
Royal Ulster Constabulary 103
Russell, Alexander 87–88
Russell, James 84

Sabiron, Céline 14
al-Safti, Umar 79
Said, Edward 56, 58, 84, 90, 92–93

Sainte-Beuve, Charles Augustin 173
Salomon, Dale 32
Salvatici, Silvia 23
Salzmann, Marianna:
   Muttersprache Mameloschn 117
Sand, George 172
San Diego 25, 26–28, 31–33, 35–36
San Diego County 27
Sands, Bobby 104
San Francisco Symphony Orchestra 152
San Ysidro 27
Saussy, Haun 212
Sayeh, Samira 56
Schami, Rafik 128
Scharf, Thomas 29
Scheffer, Ary 173
Schengen:
   Agreement 1, 17
   area 22
Schwab, Gabriele 55, 58
Schwarzenegger, Arnold 140
Science Wars 151
Scotland 122, 169–70, 173, 177–78, 181, 183
   Highlands 169, 173, 176–77, 182
   Lowlands 169, 176
Scott, Jonathan 6, 9, 76–77, 79, 81–88, 90, 92–93
Scott, Walter 169–70, 172–75, 177–83
   The Antiquary 171, 179
   Black Dwarf 173
   Guy Mannering 172, 175, 179
   The Heart of Mid-Lothian 180
   Ivanhoe 172, 173, 174, 184
   The Lady of the Lake 169
   Life of Napoleon Bonaparte 175
   Old Mortality 172. 180
   Quentin Durward 172, 174
   Rob Roy 14, 169, 172, 180, 182
   Waverley 14, 169, 174, 176–77, 180
   'Waverley novels' series 180, 182, 183
'The Seafarer' 69
Sebald, W. G.:
   Austerlitz 14
Sedira, Zineb:
   Mother Tongue 117
Seguret, Olivier 59
Sénac, Jean 60
Sergi, Giuseppe 55
Sétif 60
Severan dynasty 41, 49
Shakespeare, William 172
Shi, Hu 211
Shockley, Evie 123
Sicily 8, 45
Sidon 7
Simon, Anne 188
Sinn Féin 102

Sismondi, Jean Charles Léonard Simonde de 174
Skerrett, D. M. 197
Skinner, John 122
Sletto, Bjorn 21
Slovakia 22
Slovenia 22
Smythe, William 28
   History of San Diego 32
Sontag, Susan 97, 111
Sorites paradox 206–07, 209
Sotheby's, *see* Leigh and Sotheby
South Africa 111, 122
Spain 3, 45, 57
Spanish Mission San Diego de Alcala 27–28
Spinoza, Baruch 161
Spitzer, Leo 117
Spivak, Gayatri Chakravorty 14, 201–02
Spurzheim, Johann 154
Staël, Madame de (Anne-Louise Germaine Necker, Baronne de Staël) 172
Starkie, Enid 172
Stegner, Wallace:
   Wolf Willow 5
Steiner, George 178
Stormont government 98
St Paul's Cathedral 76
Strabo 45–46
Suchet, Myriam 35
Sue, Eugene 172
Sutton, John 146
Swartwood, Jeffrey 3, 13
Switzerland 22
Syria 22, 41

Tafolia, Carmen 26
al-Tahtawi, Rifa'a 6, 8
Tallis, Raymond 154
Tamalet, Edwige 59
Tansonville 191
Terian, Andrei 202
Terminalia 3
Terminus 3–4
Thatcher, Margaret 101
Thierry, Augustin 174
Thousand and One Nights, see *Arabian Nights*
Tijuana 26
Tilson Thomas, Michael 152
Tóibín, Colm 102, 111
   Walking along the Border, later *Bad Blood: A Walk along the Irish Border* 111
Toschi, Umberto 19
Tribble, Evelyn 163
Tsvetaeva, Marina 116
Tunis 6
Tunisia 8, 63, 122
Tunisia-Libya border 1

Turkey 1, 41, 62
Turner Prize 97

Ulster 98
Ulster Museum 100
Ulysses 7, 54, 61, 62, 64
United Kingdom 1, 97–98, 106, 170
United States 2, 25, 28, 31, 35–36, 124, 169
Université de Montréal 22
University College Dublin 99
University of Eastern Finland 22
University of Paris 178
US-Mexican border, *see* Mexico-United States border
US-Mexican War 30

Varela, Francisco 154
Vatican Library 87
Venice 190
Verger, Mathias 121
Verne, Jules 170, 184
    Les Indes noires [*The Underground City or The Black Indies*] 169–70
Vertot, René-Aubert 174
Vesta 4
Vichy regime 60
Vidal, Fernando 154
Vigny, Alfred de 184
Villemain, Henri 179
Viney, Will 163
Virgil 7
    Aeneid 14
Vitrac, Bernard 43
Voltaire (François-Marie Arouet) 63, 175
    Philosophical Dictionary 175
    Philosophical Letters 175
Vygotsky, Lev 154

Walsh, Brendan 98
Waugh, Patricia 152
Wayne, John 25
Weber, Ralph 204–05, 211–13
Wellek, René 215
Welles, Orson:
    Touch of Evil 26

West, Richard 111
Westminster government 98
Wheeler, Michael 12, 150, 156
    Reconstructing the Cognitive World 156
White, Joseph 81
Whiteread, Rachel 74
Whittaker, C. W. 47
Williams, Roger:
    Mother Tongue 117
Winkler, Josef 118
    Der Ackermann aus Kärnten [*The Ploughman from Carinthia*] 118
    Menschenkind [*Son of Man*] 118
    Muttersprache [*Mother Tongue*] 117–18, 125
    Das wilde Kärnten [*Wild Carinthia*] 118, 125
Wolf, Christa:
    Medea 73
Wolff, Larry 63
Woods, Angela 163
Woolf, Virginia 165
Wordsworth, William 172
World Exhibition 90
World War I: 63
World War II: 54, 60, 63, 102, 178
Wortley Montague, Edward 76, 81–83, 87–88
Wortley Montague, Fortunatus (Mas'oud) 81
Wortley Montague, Mary 81
Wylie, Charles 107
Wylie, Donovan 99
    British Watchtowers 99–100
    The Maze 100

Xunzi (Xun Kuang) 211

Yacine, Kateb:
    Le polygone étoilé [*The Star-Shaped Polygon*] 124–25
Young, Robert 201, 210

Zeno of Elea 206
Ziff, Trisha 99, 110
Ziporyn, Brook 204
Zuhayr, Bahâ' al-Dîn 86

www.ingramcontent.com/pod-product-compliance
Lightning Source LLC
LaVergne TN
LVHW061250060426
835507LV00017B/1995